The Story of Swahili

Africa in World History

The Story of Swahili

John M. Mugane

OHIO UNIVERSITY PRESS   ATHENS, OHIO

in association with the

OHIO UNIVERSITY CENTER FOR INTERNATIONAL STUDIES

Athens

Ohio University Press, Athens, Ohio 45701
ohioswallow.com
© 2015 by Ohio University Press

To obtain permission to quote, reprint, or otherwise reproduce or distribute material from
Ohio University Press publications, please contact our rights and permissions department
at (740) 593-1154 or (740) 593-4536 (fax).

Cover photograph of Pumulani dhow from AfricaboundAdventures.com
Cover design by Beth Pratt

Printed in the United States of America
Ohio University Press books are printed on acid-free paper ⊗ ™

25 24 23 22 21 20 19 18 17 16 15   5 4 3 2 1

Library of Congress Cataloging-in-Publication Data
Mugane, John M., author.
The story of Swahili / John M. Mugane.
    pages cm. — (Africa in world history)
Includes bibliographical references and index.
ISBN 978-0-89680-292-6 (hc : alk. paper) — ISBN 978-0-89680-293-3 (pb : alk. paper) —
ISBN 978-0-89680-489-0 (pdf)
1. Swahili language—History. 2. Swahili language—Social aspects. 3. Swahili-speaking
peoples—History. I. Title. II. Series: Africa in world history.
PL8701.M77 2015
496'.392—dc23

                    2015014795

brought to contrast with a grant from

Figure Foundation

in language do all the times daydream

To our sons Amani wa Muratha and Daudi wa Muratha
and Judith aka ma'Gane
my bountiful blessing!

CONTENTS

ILLUSTRATIONS

Figures

Maps

Table

ACKNOWLEDGMENTS

An old Gĩkũyũ saying has it that *Andũ nĩo indo,* "People are the wealth," and boy am I ever rich! I am the beneficiary of the kindness of many, and to thank them is important, bragging though it be. My colleagues, associates, students, friends, and family cut across many intellectual traditions, cultures, languages, and religious persuasions. I want to mention a few who came through for me in important ways as I worked to complete this book.

First and foremost, I owe a great debt of gratitude to Joseph Miller and David Robinson, the editors of the Africa in World History series who got me fascinated by the idea that I, a linguist, might use my knowledge of Swahili to tell the history of the African–Indian Ocean world to a general audience. Joe and Dave have been phenomenally generous with their time and resources of the mind, and I have learned a great deal in the process and developed a love of history. They are inspired and inspiring scholars. I am far more grateful to them than the spoken word can say. I am also very grateful to Emmanuel Akyeampong, my friend and colleague, for his encouragement to persevere and for reading the manuscript at a critical stage of the writing process and providing me with vital advice. I extend my thanks, as well, to my colleague Jacob Olupona for his interest in and mindful awareness of the progress of this book. And to the wonderful Africanist colleagues at Harvard who are rather too many to list.

I acknowledge the input of my teachers Issa Haji Zidi and Ali Mwalimu Rashidi and their students at the State University of Zanzibar and also Mzee Gora of Zanzibar for his manuscripts of Swahili written in Arabic letters. Their knowledge of the island's multilingual and multiracial ethnic mix displayed in Swahili and their hospitality have been extremely helpful to me. I would like to thank my colleagues at Nairobi University and the University of Dar es Salaam for affording me time to articulate and explain my "heresies" in the great enterprise of the language question in Africa having to do with language study and linguistic description. I thank Mahmood Mamdani for inviting me to Columbia University to tell the story, Fallou Ngom for sharing his unparalleled knowledge of the Pan-African Ajami writings, and John Thornton for his wonderful insights into Congo and his experience with its languages on the ground.

I also acknowledge the input given by the many present and former graduate and undergraduate students who have read various versions of this book in my courses or in graduate seminars where I have presented it in the past. Among the students are Nkatha Kabira, Ayodeji Ogunnaike, Lowell Brower, Stephanie Bosch, Chambi Chachage, and Oludamini Ogunnaike. Former students (now colleagues) include Laura Murphy, Carla Martin, and Cherie Rivers. I am also grateful to Laurie Carafone, Katherine Petti, and G. Robert Mmari (University of Massachusetts–Amherst) and Jonathan Kimani (Bunker Hill) for their editorial work. And my appreciation goes to Ayodeji Ogunnaike for all the help with Arabic in understanding Swahili Ajami and to Mohamed Khalifa for lessons on the Arabic script. I thank my undergraduate and graduate students in the Introduction to Africans course for responding to earlier versions of this book and helping me make it an appealing read.

Then there is family in Kenya, Tanzania, and abroad; they are my secret. Luckily there is a rule against counting family members so I cannot mention names except the one Gathoni, my mother. It is through her that I thank my families. Saying thank you to family is seldom, if ever, enough even though it means so much. I feel woefully inadequate saying *Asanteni!* but I hope the simplicity of this expression will suffice for all of my family. Still, to my wife, Judy, and our sons, Amani and Daudi, I dedicate this book saying in vernacular: *Thengiū!* (modest though it be) for your unqualified enthusiasm and support. The writing is done, so let the reading commence. I can hear my friends saying *tosha!* "enough already!"

CHAPTER ONE

Swahili, a Language Alive

ONCE JUST an obscure island dialect of an African Bantu tongue, Swahili has evolved into Africa's most internationally recognized language. In terms of speakers, it is peer to the dozen or so languages of the world that boast close to 100 million users.[1] Over the two millennia of Swahili's growth and adaptation, the molders of this story whom we will meet—immigrants from inland Africa, traders from Asia, Arab and European occupiers, European and Indian settlers, colonial rulers, and individuals from various postcolonial nations—have used Swahili and adapted it to their own purposes. They have taken it wherever they have gone to the west, to the extent that Africa's Swahili-speaking zone now extends across a full third of the continent from south to north and touches on the opposite coast, encompassing the heart of Africa.

The historical lands of the Swahili are on East Africa's Indian Ocean littoral, a 2,500-kilometer chain of coastal towns from Mogadishu, Somalia, to Sofala, Mozambique, as well as offshore islands as far away as the Comoros and Seychelles. This coastal region has long served as an international crossroads of trade and human movement, where people from all walks of life and from regions as scattered as Indonesia, Persia, the African Great Lakes, the United States, and four or five countries in Europe all encountered one another. Hunter-gatherers, pastoralists, and farmers mingled with traders and city-dwellers. Africans devoted to ancestors and the spirits of their lands met Muslims, Hindus, Portuguese Catholics, and British Anglicans. Workers (among them slaves, porters, and laborers), soldiers, rulers, and diplomats were mixed together from ancient days. Anyone who went to the East African littoral could choose to become Swahili, and many did.

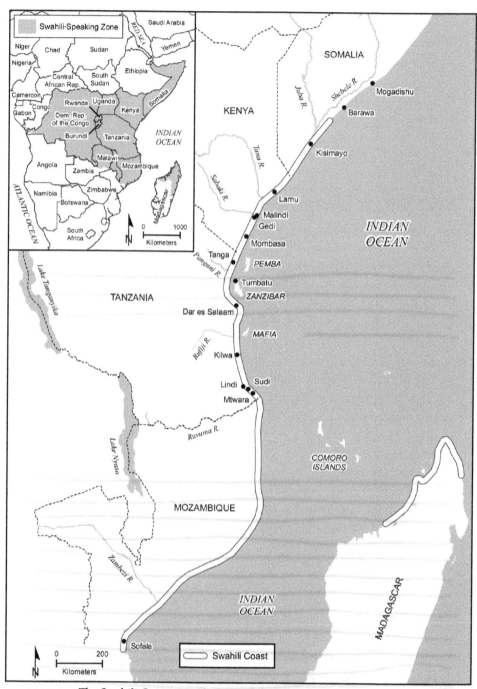

MAP 1.1 The Swahili Coast. *Map by Brian Edward Balsley, GISP*

The Vitality of Modern Swahili

Today, the roll of Swahili enthusiasts and advocates includes notable intellectuals, freedom fighters, civil rights activists, political leaders, at least a dozen scholarly professional societies created to promote the language, entertainers, and health workers, not to mention the usual professional writers, poets, and artists. Foremost among intellectuals advocating for Swahili has been Nobel Laureate Wole Soyinka, a Nigerian writer, poet, and playwright who since the 1960s has repeatedly called for use of Swahili as the transcontinental language for Africa.[2] The African Union (AU), the "united states of Africa," nurtured the same sentiment of continental unity in July 2004 and adopted Swahili as its official language. As Joachim Chissano (then the president of Mozambique) put this motion on the table, he addressed the AU in the flawless Swahili he had learned in Tanzania, where he was educated while in exile from the Portuguese colony.[3]

A song in Swahili that I learned in my childhood in Nairobi spoke for all Africans about the need for a common bond, a common purpose, and a common ideal:

SWAHILI LYRIC	ENGLISH TRANSLATION
O Afrika nchi yetu	Oh Africa, our country
tunataka tuungane	we want to unite
tujenge taifa letu	to build our nation
lenye nguvu na umoja	having strength and unity
Na lakini ni lazima	But it is a must
tusahau ulegevu	we forget sluggishness
unyang'anyi na uchoyo	plundering and stinginess
hizo zote zinadhuru	all those are harmful

The song spoke of Africa as *nchi yetu*, "our country," and it implored Africans to unite (*tuungane*) in building (*tujenge*) a strong and unified nation (*taifa*). The song told Africans to shun sluggishness (*ulegevu*), plunder (*unyang'anyi*), and stinginess (*uchoyo*). The song had a great impact on my ambition and morale and in fact still does. It taps into the optimism of the 1950s and 1960s when Kwame Nkrumah, the first president of an independent African nation in Ghana, called for a united states of Africa. Nkrumah had been educated at Lincoln University in Pennsylvania and was also heir to the Back to Africa movement of the nineteenth-century United States. The African Union did not adopt Swahili as Africa's international language by happenstance. Swahili has a much longer history of building bridges among peoples across the continent of Africa and into the diaspora.

"Oh Africa, our country" no longer resonates in the current challenging economic and political realities of the continent, but its promise is maintained in the idea of a common language. The feeling of unity, the insistence that all of Africa is one, just will not disappear. Languages are elemental to everyone's sense of belonging, of expressing what's in one's heart. Chissano's historic address in Swahili marked the first time the AU had ever permitted use of a sub-Saharan language at its meetings. The organization's intention is to hold the nations of Africa together using the language as the continent's lingual glue and to express its innermost character; its distinctiveness among the world's peoples; and its place in globalized modernity conducted in English, Arabic, Chinese, Russian, and other international languages. The AU's decision to bless Swahili as an official language is particularly striking given that the populations of its member states speak an estimated two thousand languages (roughly one-third of all human languages), several dozen of them with more than a million speakers.[4]

How did Swahili come to hold so prominent a position among so many groups with their own diverse linguistic histories and traditions? Swahili is the eastern African language most associated with the struggle for independence from European colonialists in the 1940s and 1950s. During the decades leading up to the independence of Kenya, Uganda, and Tanzania in the early 1960s, Swahili functioned as an international means of political collaboration, enabling freedom fighters throughout the region to communicate their common aspirations even though their native languages varied widely. The rise of Swahili, for some Africans, was a mark of true cultural and personal independence from the colonizing Europeans and their languages of control and command. Tanzania is the linguistic standard-bearer of autonomy and respect because, uniquely among Africa's independent nations, its government uses Swahili for all official business and, most impressively, in basic education for the nation's youth. Swahili has engendered both national and continental pride—with charity beginning at home (in Tanzania and Kenya).[5] Indeed, the Swahili word *uhuru* (freedom), which emerged from this independence struggle, became part of the global lexicon of political empowerment.[6] The highest political offices in East Africa began using and promoting Swahili soon after independence. Presidents

Julius Nyerere of Tanzania (1962–85) and Jomo Kenyatta of Kenya (1964–78) promoted the use of Swahili as integral to the region's political and economic interests, security, and liberation. The political power of language was demonstrated, less happily, by Ugandan dictator Idi Amin (1971–79), who used Swahili for his army and secret police operations during his reign of terror.

Tanzanian president Mwalimu Julius Kambarage Nyerere was foremost among these African leaders in promoting Swahili as a language of African liberation and pride. Under Nyerere, Tanzania became one of only two African nations ever to declare a native African language as the country's official mode of communication (the other is Ethiopia, with Amharic). Nyerere personally translated two of William Shakespeare's plays, *Julius Caesar* and *Merchant of Venice,* into Swahili (as *Juliasi Kaisari* and *Mabepari wa Venisi*), in order to demonstrate the capacity of Swahili to bear the expressive weight of great literary works. Nyerere is an icon of the dignity that Swahili has enjoyed in Africa, especially in its spillover into the African diaspora of North America. He even made the term *Swahili* a referent to Tanzanian citizenship. Later, this label acquired socialist overtones in praising the common men and women of the nation, standing in stark contrast to Europeans and Western-oriented elite Africans with quickly—and by implication dubiously—amassed wealth.

Ultimately, the term grew even further to encompass the poor of all races, of both African and non-African descent. In my own experience as a lecturer at Stanford University in the 1990s, for instance, several of the students from Kenya and Tanzania referred to the poor white neighborhood of East Palo Alto, California, as *Uswahilini,* "Swahili land," as opposed to *Uzunguni,* "land of the *mzungu* [white person]," which was the word we used to refer to the affluent (and incidentally also white-dominated) Palo Alto on the other side of Highway 101. Nyerere considered it prestigious to be called Swahili, and with his influence, the term became imbued with sociopolitical connotations of the poor but worthy and even noble; this in turn helped construct a Pan-African popular identity independent of the elite-dominated national governments of Africa's fifty-some nation-states. Little did I realize then that the Swahili label had been used as a conceptual rallying point for solidarity across the lines of community, competitive towns, and residents of many backgrounds, ranging from the inland hills to the Indian Ocean coast to the Persian Gulf, for over a millennium. The language was not only an outcome of a thousand years of dynamic history on Africa's eastern coast but also a means of forging a sense of collectivity for all the diverse people who settled there.

Indeed, growing out of Nyerere's efforts, many African Americans used Swahili during the culture wars of the 1960s in the United States to underscore the acceptance that they sought on terms independent of the racialist culture that had long excluded them. Unlike some of their predecessors, they did not wish to "assimilate" and adopt values that they did not feel were theirs, and they found an inspiring alternative in the Pan-Africanism and political independence that Nyerere—and Swahili—seemed to symbolize. In 1966, Maulana Ron Karenga associated the black freedom movement with Swahili, choosing Swahili as its official language and creating the Kwanzaa celebration.[7] The term *Kwanzaa* is derived from the Swahili word *ku-anza*, meaning "to begin" or "first," and the holiday was intended to celebrate the *matunda ya kwanza*, "first fruits" in Swahili; thus, according to Karenga, Kwanzaa symbolizes the festivities of ancient African harvests. Karenga's singular achievement was his coinage of the word *kwanzaa* (*kwanza* plus *a*)—a smart neologism that permitted a new word very closely resembling the familiar one, *kwanza*, to enter into the Swahili lexicon, bearing his name and his brand of ideas.

Celebrants were encouraged to adopt Swahili names and to address one another by Swahili titles of respect. Based on Nyerere's principle of *ujamaa* (unity in mutual contributions), Kwanzaa celebrates seven principles or pillars (*nguzo saba*, translated literally as *nguzo* [pillars] and *saba* [seven]): unity (*umoja*), self-determination (*kujichagulia*), collective work and responsibility (*ujima*), cooperative economics (*ujamaa*), shared purpose (*nia*), individual creativity (*kuumba*), and faith (*imani*). Internationally, Nyerere also became the icon of "community brotherhood and sisterhood," which distinguished the United Republic of Tanzania during his leadership, under the slogan of the Swahili word *ujamaa*. That word has gained such strong appeal that it has been used as far afield as among Australian Aborigines and African Americans and across the globe from London to Papua New Guinea[8]—not to mention its ongoing celebration on many US college campuses in the form of dormitories named ujamaa houses.

Today, Swahili is the African language most widely recognized outside the continent. The global presence of Swahili in radio broadcasting and on the Internet has no equal among sub-Saharan African languages—with Arabic (which is arguably African due to the extent of its currency from Egypt to Morocco in North Africa) constituting the only competition. Swahili is broadcast regularly in Burundi, the Democratic Republic of the Congo (DRC), Kenya, Liberia, Nigeria, Rwanda, South Africa, Sudan,

Swaziland, and Tanzania. In Kenya and Tanzania especially, the undisputed language of radio and television is Swahili. On the international scene, no other African language can be heard from world news stations as often or as extensively as Swahili. Swahili-language radio broadcasts outside Africa include programs on Radio Peking, Voice of America (VOA), the British Broadcasting Corporation (BBC), Radio Germany (Deutsch Welle), Radio Japan International, and Radio Moscow International. In terms of print media, Swahili has been on the scene since the nineteenth century. *Msimu-lizi* (Narrator), the first Swahili newspaper, initially appeared in 1888 in Zanzibar, and it was followed by *Habari za Mwezi* (Monthly News) in 1894, also in Zanzibar; both were published by the Universities Missionary to Central Africa (UMCA)[9] to further the goals of spreading Christianity and ending slavery.[10]

In recent years, television and film have likewise kept Swahili in the limelight, though Hollywood's long tradition of featuring Swahili-speaking African characters on the big screen has contributed to the misimpression that Swahili is "the language of Africa." At least as far back as *Trader Horn,* a 1931 film depicting an ivory trader in central Africa, Swahili words and speech have been heard in hundreds of movies and television series, such as *Star Trek* (1966–2009), *Out of Africa* (1985), Disney's *The Lion King* (1994), *Lara Croft Tomb Raider: The Cradle of Life* (2003), and *The Last King of Scotland* (2006), to name only a few of the most popular. *The Lion King* featured several Swahili words, the most familiar being the names of characters, including *Simba* (lion), *Rafiki* (friend), and *Pumbaa* (be dazed). Swahili phrases in the animated film included *asante sana* (thank you very much) and, of course, that no-problem philosophy known as *hakuna matata* (no troubles/no problems) repeated throughout the movie. Paramount's *Lara Croft Tomb Raider,* starring Angelina Jolie, had black tribesmen characters speaking Swahili.

Since the beginning of the twentieth century, tourism has also increased the name recognition that Swahili enjoys around the world. Luminaries visiting Africa's Swahili-speaking regions have included Theodore Roosevelt, Sir Winston Churchill, and Queen Elizabeth II. Among Swahili's most famous music are the songs "Jambo Bwana" (Hello Sir), the quintessential tourist song, and "Malaika" (Angel), introduced in 1960 and first sung by Kenya's Fadhili Williams, then popularized by world-famous musicians Miriam Makeba, Harry Belafonte, and Angelique Kidjo. "Malaika" was for a time a popular song at weddings throughout East Africa. To the delight of many Swahili speakers, African American musicians also have sprinkled Swahili into their lyrics. Michael Jackson's song "Liberian Girl," for example, includes the Swahili sentences *"Nakupenda pia"* and *"Nakutaka pia, mpenzi!"*—"I love you too" and "I want you too, my love!"—despite the fact that Liberia is in far-off West Africa where Swahili is not spoken. The "Hakuna Matata" song was originally titled "Jambo Bwana" (1982).

Although Swahili lacks the numbers of speakers, the wealth, and the political power associated with other global languages such as Mandarin, English, or Spanish,[11] it is distinctive in being primarily a second language for close to 100 million speakers. Its popularity is growing tremendously, and it has rapidly spread throughout eastern and central Africa in particular as a lingua franca—that is, a second language that speakers of any number of home languages use to communicate with one another informally, particularly in public settings. Swahili appears to be the only language boasting more than 100 million speakers that has more *second*-language speakers than native ones: indeed, for every native speaker of Swahili, there are about one hundred nonnative speakers! By comparison, English and French both have approximately one native speaker for each nonnative speaker, and Spanish has about five native speakers for every person who speaks it as a second language.

By immersing themselves in the affairs of a maritime culture at a key commercial gateway, the people who were eventually designated *Waswahili* (Swahili people) created a niche for themselves. They were important enough in the trade that newcomers had little choice but to speak Swahili as the language of trade and diplomacy. And the Swahili population became more entrenched as successive generations of second-language speakers of Swahili lost their ancestral languages and became bona fide Swahili—much as Spanish-speaking Mexican families take three generations on average to fully assimilate into American culture (including losing their Spanish).[12] Nearly all of the people from overseas arrived with greater wealth than the people of eastern Africa possessed, and they had military strength that was superior to that of the indigenous population. Furthermore, these migrants came from linguistic backgrounds in some of the world's most widely spoken languages: Arabic for over a millennium; Portuguese since the sixteenth century; and German, English, and Hindi since the end of the nineteenth century. Yet Swahili speakers took in these newcomers, borrowing strategic parts of their vocabularies and integrating them into their own evolving language.

The key to understanding this story is to look deeply at the Swahili people's response to challenges; at the ways in which they made their fortunes and dealt with misfortunes; and, most important, at how they honed their skills in balancing confrontation and resistance with adaptation and innovation as they interacted with arrivals from other language backgrounds. These adaptations produced steady developments in the language itself long before the label "Swahili" came about in the fourteenth century. Consequently, a full historical account must go back more than a millennium before that point. Despite high traffic from every corner of the world, the people of the coast managed to maintain a Bantu tongue.

The Story to Follow

The story of Swahili is a narrative about the human condition in a maritime world at the confluence of the Indian Ocean, the Mediterranean Sea, the Red Sea, and the Atlantic Ocean, told from the perspective of the dynamism of language. Swahili resilience rests on three core factors: cosmopolitanism (the willingness to navigate differences), geography (the setting, in terms of both times and places), and Islam (the capaciousness of a monotheism with universalist ambitions). Swahili scholars hold the last factor as the most pivotal. Chapter 2 uses the Swahili language as a means by which to explore the history of Swahili society. It introduces the peoples who developed the language, the individuals who had a deep and dynamic history through a cosmopolitan ethos at the crossroads of social and trading networks traversed by Africans from the interior of the continent and transients and settlers from overseas.

Chapter 3 examines the lexicon—the vocabulary—of Swahili as the cultural DNA, the genetic heritage, of the modern language. Swahili words and phrases today mark the encounters between the residents of the coast and diverse other visitors. Speakers of Swahili borrowed words from other languages, and those words reveal the nature of their contacts, much as a visitors' book at a wedding contains the names, signatures, and dates of all who were there. To cite one example, the names of the wares in a simple rural shop, or *duka,* are a veritable archive of the trade and social contacts among a wide variety of peoples speaking different languages who brought the wares to the shelves. The people of Africa's eastern coastal bays and islands have been in contact with persons from all corners of the Indian Ocean and Mediterranean worlds for two thousand years: Greeks of the Ptolemaic era, Arabs, Persians, Indians, Malaysians, Portuguese, Turks, French, Germans, and the British. The coastal people traded with and learned from all of them, building up an ever more complex and nuanced lexicon from historical ties among the peoples and cultures of the vast Indian Ocean region.

Chapter 4 draws on the vistas of the past in the language of today to look at the Swahili-speaking region from 1000 to 1500 CE. During these years, the cities of the coast enjoyed their greatest commercial prosperity and political autonomy, with their heyday in the twelfth and thirteenth centuries. Using the image of the *mnazi* (coconut tree) and the *sambo* (*chombo*) (ship/ vessel) as the icons of Swahili cosmopolitanism, the chapter details the core values of the Swahili culture and the ways that East Africa's independent city-states negotiated foreign trade and diplomacy, both separately and as confederations. Swahili patricians grew wealthy during this time of relative peace and considerable prosperity, increased their knowledge and observance of Islam, and built cities of coral stone that were filled with mosques and elaborate tombs. They patronized artists and architects who, together with traders in the markets and along the shore, worked creatively in the idioms of the imported traditions. The chapter reveals the Swahili language and culture as cosmopolitan, infused with the Islamic enlightenment of the era, urbane, and possessing a rich material culture drawn from numerous places near and far. During this period, Pan-Swahili culture came to dominate East Africa's Indian Ocean littoral, from modern Mogadishu in Somalia to what is today northern Mozambique. It is noteworthy that the earliest known use of the word *Swahili* comes from the fourteenth-century zenith of coastal prosperity, in a report from the famous Moroccan Berber Muslim traveler and writer Ibn Battuta. At that time, an integrated Swahili commercial society was going about the business of conducting East Africa's Indian Ocean trade. The ways in which that society used the mnazi and the sambo reflect the development of indigenous knowledge at its best, showing how the people employed local initiatives to solve problems and to adapt to changing circumstances. A close look at the Bantu etymology of words describing various parts and uses of the mnazi and the sambo leaves little doubt that the Swahili culture has always been a vibrant system of give-and-take whose whole has always been greater than the sum of its parts. The concepts the words represent show a full elaboration of marine technology and nautical know-how, with the terms in the lexicon being mixed between Bantu and visiting languages, especially Arabic.

Chapter 5 looks at the unexpected arrival of the Portuguese and their military occupation of the east coast of Africa beginning around 1500, followed by the Omani Arab occupation of the coast from around 1700 to the 1850s. Diverse Swahili religious, political, and social networks literally exhausted the Portuguese in their attempts to dominate the coast militarily. The coastal residents finally forced the Portuguese into a compromise, by which they submitted to the continuing role of the Swahili as middlemen in eastern Africa's Indian Ocean trade. The Swahili-Portuguese toleration nonetheless led to an eventual economic downturn that prompted the departure of the Portuguese around 1700. The ruling house of the sultanate of Muscat, at the mouth of the Persian Gulf, took advantage of the vacuum of external power to settle on the island of Zanzibar and establish a plantation economy growing cloves. The Swahili towns of the coast slowly shifted from their reliance on trade to grain agriculture from the 1840s and to sugarcane along the northern coast of Tanzania from the 1860s. This new plantation economy resulted in thousands of slaves being forcibly transported from inner Africa in order to provide free labor to the sultanate, with Swahili patricians, inland warlords, and Indian financiers all profiting at the slaves' expense. Many other captives were sold abroad, especially in the Arab world and in India. By 1700 CE, the Zanzibar dialect of Swahili was already a trade language spoken on the lengthening caravan routes between the coast and the far interior. Swahili also became the language of diplomacy among various slave-raiding warlords there. Many of the individuals who were enslaved and taken to the coast subsequently converted to Islam and pragmatically adopted Swahili as their primary language over time.

There is a reason why native languages are called mother tongues, as mothers or nursemaids or other females everywhere—at least until recent years—have been the primary residents of the households or villages where children are born and learn to speak. This was certainly the case for Swahili, where Bantu-speaking women conducted daily life within the compounds in which city residents lived. Meanwhile, foreign men—Arab or Persian, Indian, and Portuguese traders; colonial officials; and the officials of Islamic sects—brought foreign vocabulary to discussions of business, politics, and other public affairs. Chapter 6 follows the distinctive roles Swahili women have played in maintaining the Bantu heritage of the language in domestic and family spheres, whatever the Muslim veneer of public religion. I will look at their contributions to teaching the language to men in the interior of the continent, for they often served as companions in the coastal trading caravans moving there. I will discuss their literal wearing of the words in the colorful *kanga* cloths that bear Swahili proverbs. And I will explore their roles as protagonists in Swahili literature. The men wrote down modern standardized languages for public affairs, but it was the women of the coast who were pivotal in preserving the vital qualities of Swahili.

There is a canon of verbal aesthetics that exists without writing. Although we cannot call it a literary canon, given the absense of writing, it offers a panoramic view of Swahili poetry, illustrating how oral compositions were remembered verbatim for centuries until they were finally written down in the 1800s. Thus, we recognize as false the divide between the oral and written works of Swahili—and elsewhere by extension. Swahili traditions of oral composition and performance were blossoming long before the Kenyan cities of Lamu and Mombasa became centers of scholarship and authorship in the nineteenth century, writing Swahili poetry in Arabic script. Chapter 7 follows the extension of a Swahili oral canon of proverbs and poetry into written prose, chronicles, and epic narratives, with the literary character of this verbal art deeply embedded in the Arabic Ajami script in which it is written. The corpus of thought, indeed wisdom, and the intricate, condensed, and allusive style of this verbal aesthetic come from the deep and intimate traditions of oral performance and listener collaboration along the coast, and these elements of shared familiarity have been adapted in the written style that developed more recently, perhaps over the last four centuries. Swahili is thus at the same stage of expressing orality in writing—a world very different from the literate world of anyone reading this page. It has paralleled and crossed the points and periods where the poetry of Homer became the theater of ancient Greek writing, en route to the fully prose-styled works of Aristotle and Plato; where the poetry of medieval English moved through Shakespeare's plays toward the modern novel; and where Dante's *Inferno* defined modern Italian or Cervantes's *Don Quixote* became the paradigm of modern Spanish. The chapter uses classic Swahili motifs, stories, and writers to contrast the world of orality and the literate world through performance, visually and audibly, as well as the ideas expressed.

Chapter 8 studies Swahili documents written in Arabic script, often referred to as Ajami. The Ajamization of Arabic script so that it could be used to write Swahili reveals that the Swahili people went beyond adaptation to innovation and ultimately ownership of a syncretic writing system as they built a most important archive of memory unique to Swahili. The value of the written documents is revealed by the content of what has been authored and bequeathed to future generations. Much of the poetry mentioned in chapter 7 as well as Swahili chronicles on various city-states, correspondence between rulers and traders, records of deeds, and a host of other things are all written in modified Arabic script. Such writing still persists in many Swahili households in places such as Zanzibar and Pemba, recording the various issues and concerns of the authors.

Chapter 9 explores the colonial century from the 1850s to 1960, the year of African independence. The abolition of slavery in Europe in the 1840s prompted European missionaries, naval commanders, and diplomats to demand and enforce an end to slaving in the Indian Ocean world. Abolition brought the plantation economy of the Swahili sultans tumbling down. During this period, the British and Germans weakened the Arabo-Swahili sultanates, and the Germans occupied the Swahili country militarily, used Swahili as their language of command, and established a language standardization regime that demanded official Swahili be written and spoken only in the manner approved by the colonizers. In this period, the multidialectal literary tradition fell into the hands of that standardization regime. From then on, the Swahili used in published literary products had to be approved by a board known as the Inter-territorial Language Committee (ILC), and Shaaban Robert emerged as the undisputed Shakespeare or the poet laureate of Standard Swahili. Those who used this new Swahili effectively were promoted, whereas those who maintained the integrity of their own dialects were marginalized. Indeed, the twentieth century saw repeated colonial and national efforts to "purify" the Swahili language based on the Zanzibar dialect and rid it of its Arabic vocabulary. After World War II, Swahili nationalists sought to create Kiswahili Mwafaka, "Swahili agreed upon by consensus," by substituting Bantu or Afrocentric bases for all the many foreign words borrowed into the language. But could Swahili, a language that had resulted from change and open engagements with outsiders, really be stabilized and controlled by anyone? Based on the discussions in the final three chapters, the answer would be no.

Chapter 10 tells the story of how people of diverse cultures and languages in Kenya make themselves comfortable using Swahili by infusing it with their own vernacular influences. This situation has historical roots further back into the colonial era of KiSetla (Swahili as spoken by settlers), KiHindi (Swahili as spoken by Indians), and KiKAR (Swahili as spoken in the colonial military). This chapter recounts the consistent failure of various attempts to control Swahili. Members of today's young generation in Kenya and to a certain extent Tanzania use some form of nonstandard Swahili, in which they inflect the language with new words and expressions to distinguish themselves from their elders and from the guardians of the official form of the language. Perhaps the best example is the modern urban form of Swahili known as Sheng. City life and its attendant freedoms gave birth to this creative Swahili pidgin. The chapter sees mobile texting in Kenya and Tanzania as heralding the ultimate nightmare to the users of the standard form, especially the school system, as pidgins go literate (become written) in digital spaces through computers and mobile devices (in Twitter, e-mail, and the blogosphere), the most vibrant of all communication modes.

Chapter 11 describes the ways in which African Americans used Swahili in the culture wars of the United States. In making Swahili their own by slanting the meanings of words or embellishing them, African Americans joined the historical tradition of personalizing Swahili and suiting it to individual circumstances. Thus, we observe in the diaspora a versatile adaptation of Swahili not unlike that in its East African homeland. Swahili has appealed to African Americans in particular, and it has become the most widely taught sub-Saharan language in US institutions of higher education. The language was central in the US black liberation struggles of the 1960s, as well as in subsequent community-building efforts among African Americans. Swahili's cultural appeal for this community is reflected in the celebration of Kwanzaa. It is also expressed in the taking of Swahili personal names, as when Ron Karenga adopted the name Maulana (Swahili for "Master" but used to refer to "God" in ordinary Swahili); when his wife adopted the name Tiamoyo Swahili (for "encourage" but literally meaning "put heart" or "add courage"); and when the name Amiri Baraka was taken (*amira* meaning "commander" and *baraka* meaning "blessing"). The fact that Swahili was the language used in the independence struggle in Tanzania and Kenya had symbolic cachet as an identity-rallying concept in the formation of the kind of black community Karenga had in mind. The chapter views Nyerere's efforts in Tanzania as part of the historical conditions that led African Americans to become adapters and learners of Swahili in the 1960s, even as other equally expressive and widely spoken African languages—such as Hausa in modern northern Nigeria or Zulu in South Africa—have not experienced the same rise in popularity.

In closing, chapter 12 speaks of Swahili as a language for the living. Although it is a modest language compared to its extrovert peers in the top dozen international languages of the world, it will be supremely well placed in the future if it continues to be guided by its centuries-old cosmopolitan dispensation.

CHAPTER TWO

Swahili, the Complex Language of a Cosmopolitan People

A black "boy" ... comes up to ask for employment. "What is your tribe?" you ask. He answers, "Swahili." "What was your mother?" "A Makoa (Makua)" (A tribe in Portuguese East Africa). "And your father?" "Oh, he was killed long ago in a war at home, and then my mother was brought to Mombasa while I was still a child." He does not mention that she was a slave. "Well then, if both your father and mother were Makoa, you are a Makoa." "Yes, that was my origin. We Swahilis are all like that; each one is Swahili, but he has his own tribe as well. I have been a Swahili as long as I can remember." "What is your name?" "Jamezi (James). I was educated in the mission."

Now let us tackle a reverent-looking old gentleman, dressed in a long flowing joho and turban, as his antecedents. He has a grey beard of straight hair and the light complexion of an Arab. Under his arm is a Koran, as he is making his way to the mosque to read and pray. "Good evening, Sheikh." "Good evening, master." "What is your name?" "Ali bin Fullani bin Fullani" (Ali, son of So-and-so, son of So-and-so). "Oh, you are an Arab?" "No, I am a Swahili," he says with some pride. "What is your descent?" "I am sprung from the Nabahans: my grandfather was Bwana Mkuu of Pate. See, here is my descent from the time that the

Nabahans left Arabia," and he produces a slip of paper from his
Koran, showing a line of ancestors reaching back to a date about
level with Magna Charta.

Now ask him if Jamezi is a Swahili, and he says, "No, he is a
slave. . . ." Ask Jamezi if this man is Swahili, and he says, "No, he
is an Arab." (Stigand 1913, 115–16)

WHO ARE the Swahili? Are they a race, a tribe, a mixture, or what? This is
the question that Captain C. H. Stigand, British adventurer, colonial military
officer, and writer, was addressing when he wrote this vignette indicating
that he was accustomed to thinking of Africans in only the most simplistic
terms of "tribes." For Europeans and Americans in Africa, who often think
about Africans as marked indelibly by so-called tribal origins, guessing what
homogeneously and utterly unambiguously labeled group an individual
might come from is a common practice. But it is a losing effort, since African
people form affiliations and display them to others for many different purposes and then move among them as appropriate to the situations they encounter throughout their lives. Far from being confined to any single group
identity, Africans find that the many social and cultural affiliations available
along the coasts of eastern Africa offer them a smorgasbord of opportunities.
Employing the conventional notion of a tribe or ethnic background is
thus not a useful way to understand who might be Swahili in a given context. Bantu languages, including Swahili, initially recognize the relevant
distinctions by embedding the root concept "Swahili" in a grammatical system, marked in the first instance by prefixes, that speaks, for example, of the
language as Kiswahili and the people as Waswahili. Could it really be that
an individual (*Mswahili*) who, like Jamezi and Ali, speaks Kiswahili is Swahili? That standard would make me a Mswahili myself, but nothing about
Swahili, whether the people or the language, is really that simple. Rather
than trying to answer the riddle of the chicken and the egg—which came
first, the language or the people?—the Swahili reorient the question from
"either/or" (not one or the other) to "both/and"—and more. The social context of living together, or geography—location, location, location!—begins
to get at the historical process of Swahili.
Jamezi and Ali bin Fullani had at least two things Swahili in common:
their shared location along the Indian Ocean coast, which was their adopted home, and the African women there with whom they lived. I will

return to the African women, but for now, I would suggest that Stigand's paradoxical vignette implies the existence of some core group of Swahili people to which neither Jamezi nor Ali bin Fullani really belonged, owing to their claims to ancestries elsewhere—for Jamezi, the far southern regions of what it now northern Mozambique, and for Ali, the legendary remote land of the Prophet himself. How could both claim to be Swahili if neither recognized the other as belonging? Jamezi was nonchalant about how his having immediate Makua descent factored into his Swahiliness. Similarly, Ali was proud of his Omani Arab lineage, but he would not admit that he was thereby Arab and not Swahili. Why, then, would neither man—one of humble station and the other heir to the elite religious tradition of the area—assert a hyphenated category, such as Makua-Swahili for Jamezi or Arab-Swahili for Ali, and thus open the possibility of an additional nonhyphenated "true" Mswahili identity? Jamezi realized what Stigand was up to and added matter-of-factly, "We Swahilis are all like that; each one is Swahili, but he has his own tribe as well." He was simply saying, "Look around! We are all compound, we are all mixtures of many pasts, and the present moment also." What about Kiswahili, the language—is there any hope of understanding the language if we cannot find a Mswahili?

A Maritime Crossroads

It is impossible to say when the mixture that became a Swahili language (much less the Swahili people) began to form, but we know something about the setting in which the language developed. The word for the language, *Kiswahili,* is derived from the Arabic *sahil,* meaning "coast," "edge," or "border"—a place—and *sawahil,* meaning "Swahili country."[1] Swahili is thus the language of the prime Indian Ocean coastal strip stretching from Mogadishu in Somalia to Sofala in Mozambique and reaching out to all the adjoining islands (Pemba, Zanzibar, Lamu near the coast, and the Seychelles and Comoros farther offshore) as far as northern Madagascar—a distance of about 2,000 miles from the mainland.[2] This area of the western Indian Ocean has long been a crossroads traversed by people bearing numerous cultures and languages from at least three different worlds—mainland Africa itself, the maritime world of the Indian Ocean including India and Indonesia, and the Mediterranean world. It was in this crucible of commercial contacts that traders from overseas and local producers of the African commodities they sought elaborated Swahili from an obscure dialect of an African Bantu language to one of the world's leading international languages.

Africa's Indian Ocean littoral and its offshore islands have regular seasonal rainfall that supports a rich ecological system, with vast stretches of the equatorial grasslands (*nyika*) known in English as savanna. The nyika supports enormous herds of grass-eating hooved animals, classically antelopes of all sizes, and it is also suitable for domestic livestock, primarily cattle. For millennia, these rich pastures have drawn African herders, or pastoralists, into the region.

The coast itself is replete with tidal swamps overgrown with mangrove forests, which may have drawn the attention of the first seaborne traders from the wood-short deserts of southwestern Asia. There, they found a good trade in taking mangrove poles (*mikoko*) back to the Red Sea and Persian Gulf areas for construction; the poles were also sewn together to build boats. In addition, the traders bartered the products of the nyika's large game animals—elephant ivory, rhinocerous horns—and of the coast itself, including the tortoise shells that since antiquity had been highly sought after by wealthy householders in the cities of the Persian Gulf and the Mediterranean. Perfumes extracted from a variety of aromatic tropical plants found in the region were also profitable.

The major rivers of modern-day Somalia, Kenya, Tanzania, and Mozambique have long provided access to interior regions from the Swahili coastline, making them fertile hinterlands for agriculture. In fact, the area has been fertile enough to feed significant numbers of people in a string of Swahili cities that have flourished, one after another, on the sandy coral reefs of the coast for more than a millennium. As we shall see, the local linkages of towns looking outward toward the water and inward-looking supply lines for food and people, all of which are basic to Swahili life and language, reflect this segmented ecology. The chain of riverine systems going south along the coast from Mogadishu, the first habitable locale beyond the barren sands of Somalia, and Sofala, the southernmost point accessible on the dependable winds from the north, include the Juba River in Somalia; the Tana River and the Athi River (also known as Sabaki and Galana along its course) in Kenya; the Rufiji River in Tanzania; the Ruvuma, which forms part of the border between Tanzania and Mozambique; and the Zambezi. These major rivers, as well as innumerable smaller creeks, were the channels of communication between the coast and the interior (Pouwels 1987, 7). The enslaved Waswahili such as Jamezi (and his many predecessors) were carried to the coast along these waterways.

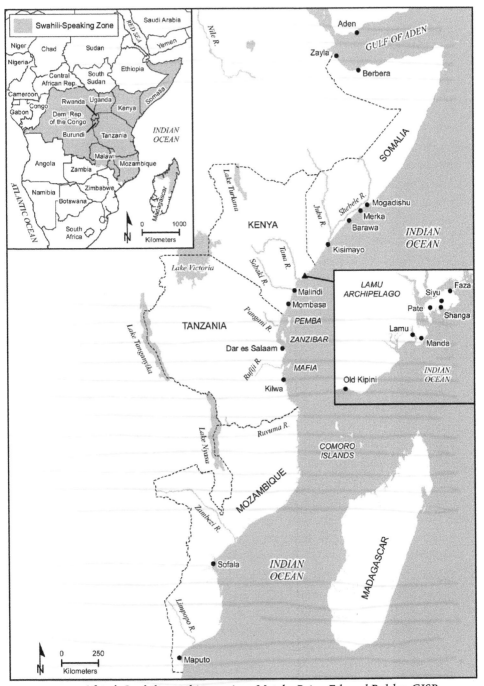

MAP 2.1 Africa's Swahili-speaking region. *Map by Brian Edward Balsley, GISP*

Besides Africans from the hinterland, the most frequent early visitors to Swahili country were Arabs from the Persian Gulf, many Persians, Indians, some Chinese, and Malaysians. They utilized a seasonal reversal in the prevailing winds (the monsoons) of the western Indian Ocean to travel to the east coast of Africa. As reported by Randall Lee Pouwels (1987, 6), the southeasterly monsoons called *kusi* (short for *pepo za kusi,* meaning "southerly winds") last from May through September. They usher in the major wet season, *mwaka* (also known as *mvua ya masika,* "the heavy rain"), from July to September or October, the ideal time for planting. The *vuli* (meaning "lesser rains") come between October and November. In October, the monsoon winds, then called *kaskazi* (short for *pepo za kaskazi,* or "northerly winds"), shift toward the northeast, bringing in the dry season, which lasts from December to May. The dry season is hot and cloudless, baking the soil and blowing away the topsoil. The mwaka/masika rains mark the season for cultivation; in the dry season, cultivators turn to fishing to supplement their diet of cereal grains, fruits, and vegetables. Business thrived with the kusi monsoon from the north, which brought dhows arriving from the Persian Gulf and the Red Sea and from the eastern Indian Ocean as far away as India and China.[3] The dhows left the region on the kaskazi monsoon, blowing back toward the north. Ali bin Fullani's claimed forebears from Arabia routinely traveled to and from East Africa on these alternating seasonal winds.

Swahili has been the language of everybody we will meet in this story: slaves from the nyika, the locally born, traders, porters, laborers, soldiers, and rulers, as well as diplomats, colonizers, and missionaries from far away and—in modern times—freedom fighters, politicians, poets, and intellectuals. By speaking Swahili, everyone who went to the East African littoral could choose to become Swahili, and many decided to do just that.

What was it about the east coast of Africa that drew so much attention from so far away? The Swahili have a saying that applies here: *Mkono mtupu haulambwi,* "An empty hand is not licked." From the point of view of the visitors, the Swahili region was a hand filled with prospective wealth, which had attracted traders from the Mediterranean to the South China Sea since a thousand years before 1000 CE.

The earliest Mediterranean written reference to the east coast of Africa was in connection to trade in the area, and it appeared in a document known as *The Periplus of the Erythrean Sea.* This guide to navigating the waters of the coast was written by an anonymous Greek traveler around 100 CE. According to this source,

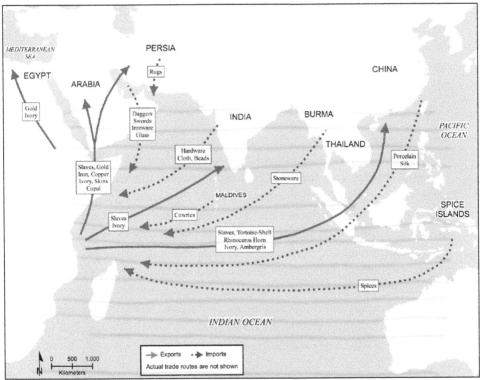

MAP 2.2 East Africa trade, 1000–1500 CE. *Map by Brian Edward Balsley, GISP*

men of the greatest stature who are pirates inhabit the whole coast and at each place have set up chiefs. The chief of the Ma'afir is the suzerain, according to an ancient right which subordinates it to the kingdom which has become the first in Arabia. The people of Mouza hold it in tribute under his sovereignty and send there small ships, mostly with Arab captains and crews who trade and intermarry with the mainlanders of all the places and know their language. . . . Two days' sail beyond the island lies the last mainland market town of Azania, which is called Rhapta, a name derived from the small sewn boats the people use. Here there is much ivory and tortoiseshell.[4]

The *Periplus* also refers to trade among a diverse array of Africans, Arabs, and Persians who intermarried and spoke a local language. Presumably, the influx of indigenous Africans to the coast was based on (among other factors) the need to trade their goods; archaeological data suggest that the

Bantu-speaking farmers had arrived at the littoral in the last centuries BCE, had mastered sailing techniques, and had founded the coastal settlements.[5] The idea of "mastering" is more of an adaptation that must have come as people of diverse hinterland origins intermarried with the overseas traders and as their offspring became bicultural.

The farmers along the bays of the East African Indian Ocean littoral gradually distinguished themselves from their rural neighbors by assembling in towns that serviced the maritime activities of the traders who rode the monsoon each year and then lay by to await the returning winds. They exploited their seaside locations by fishing and became expert builders of seafaring vessels. Eventually, with ventures of their own, they built up sufficient navigational knowledge to find their way to the Persian Gulf, to India, and on to China.[6] Everything Swahili is a fusion of influences stemming from these contacts, compounded over time in a stimulating cultural potpourri. The architecture of *Uswahilini*—or *U-swahili-ni,* where the initial *U-* indicates an abstraction and the concluding *-ni* marks a place—reflects a similar blending of multiple influences—African, Arab, Indian, and Persian—before the modern overlaid the colonial infrastructure. The local dialectical variations of Swahili are no less diverse.

Enslaved human beings were an important component of the Swahili trade with the Indian Ocean, a trade going back to the first millennium of the Common Era. A slave trade of significant proportions seems to have taken the people visitors knew as the Zanj overseas to the lands of the merchants who came to the East African coast. By the eighth and ninth centuries, black (*zanj*) slaves were present in Arabia, Iraq, and Persia in significant numbers (the word *zanj* was a medieval Arabic collective reference to blacks).[7] Zanj had been taken to Mesopotamia to reclaim the Tigris-Euphrates delta from the waters of the Persian Gulf, in order to prevent the salty marshland from flooding and keep it arable. The number of enslaved Zanj assembled was large, as was evident in the famous Zanj revolt involving more than half a million slaves from all over the Muslim empire of the time. The revolt resulted in a successful seizure of the city of Basra, now in southern Iraq, for fifteen years (869–883 CE) before the Abbasid caliphate was able to regain control.[8]

A Bantu Synthesis

The earliest recorded direct reference to Swahili was made by the Moroccan Berber Ibn Battuta, an Islamic scholar and world traveler who visited the east coast of Africa in 1331. He reported:

> I embarked at Maqdashaw [Mogadishu] for the Sawahil [Swa-
> hili] country, with the object of visiting the town of Kulwa
> [Kilwa, Quiloa] in the land of the Zanj. We came to Mambasa
> [Mombasa], a large island two days' journey by sea from the
> Sawahil country. It possesses no territory on the mainland. They
> have fruit trees on the island, but no cereals, which have to be
> brought to them from the Sawahil.[9]

At that time, the country of the "shore people" known as Swahili was south of Mogadishu and north of Mombasa Island in modern Kenya. Kilwa, much farther south in what is now southern Tanzania, was not in Swahili country but in the land of the Zanj, and Ibn Battuta left no doubt about how striking he found the appearance of these people: they were "jet black in color and with tattoo marks on their faces."[10] *Swahili* at that time was an Arab description, none too complimentary, of a specific group of non-Muslim Africans on the mainland, probably in the area of the Lamu archipelago (now in northeastern Kenya). Like *Zanj,* it was more of an epithet than an ethnonym, with overtones similar to *hillbillies* or *bumpkins* in American English. Only many centuries later did the term *Swahili* come to be applied more generally (encompassing even the sophisticated Muslim merchants of Mombasa Island), though again, it was an outsiders' stereotype—this time from the European colonial powers of the late 1800s. No references to the Swahili have been found in records from the two centuries of Portuguese military presence on the east coast of Africa (1500–1700), though the component local coastal communities—the Segeju, Zimba, Makua, Samia, and others—are prominent in the documentation (Whiteley 1969, 35–36). The Portuguese did talk of coast-dwellers whom they called Moors, a name much used throughout the Iberian Peninsula for Muslims. *Swahili* as an ethnic term was—again with some prejudice—given a broader meaning by the Omani who established the sultanate on Zanzibar in the early eighteenth century: they used the word *Sawahil* to designate the mainland adjacent to the island and the word *Swahili* for the people who lived there and the language that they spoke.[11]

Although Zanj and Sawahil were names of Arabic origin and obviously designations given by outsiders, historical techniques of language reconstruction, as we shall see, leave no doubt that that languages spoken on the coast were of the Bantu family. Some of the early Arab travelers provided confirming snippets of recognizably Bantu vocabulary. Writing in the tenth century, Abu al-Hasan Ali ibn al-Husayn ibn Ali al-Masudi noted that the people of the coast spoke an "elegant language" and had a capital city ruled by a king titled *mfalme*. He added, very improbably, that this mfalme commanded an army of three hundred thousand horsemen. As horses do not thrive on the coast of eastern Africa and as a cavalry of that size would have exceeded the scale of the Chinese cavalry at the time, al-Masudi was clearly taken in by his informants' hyperbole, meant to create an awesome impression of a person he never met. However, his terminology was more reliable, since *mfalme* actually is, to this date, the Swahili word for "king"; this suggests that al-Masudi's informants were ancestors of the Swahili somewhere north of Mombasa, of whom Ibn Battuta heard three centuries later.

Al-Masudi mentioned other vocabulary thought by some modern linguists to be Swahili words—*waklimi, maklandjalou,* and *kalari*—but it has also been noted that the etymologies of these and other words are controversial. Considerations of etymology, the study of the origins and permutations of words, are notoriously tricky. Take, for instance, the twelfth-century geography of al-Idrisi (who lived from 1100 to 1166). Written in Arabic, it is known as the *Kitab Rujar* (Book of Roger), for it was dedicated to his scholarly patron, King Roger II of Sicily. In it, he made the first mention we have of Unguja, the ancient name of one of the islands of the Zanzibar archipelago (cf. Ugunja, Pemba, and several other small islands). He seems to have been impressed by the bananas he ate there, and he recorded the names of several of them—*fiilii, kundu, kikonde, mkono wa tembo, muriani, omani,* and *sukari.*[12] Although al-Idrisi made no mention of Swahili by name, these words are very much in use in present-day Swahili.

What may well be the first word list of the Swahili language was collected by William Payton in 1613 on a visit to the Comoros Islands. The list includes *Gumbey* (*ng'ombe* in current Swahili), meaning "a bullock"; *buze* (*mbuzi*), "a goat"; *coquo* (*kuku*), "a hen"; *tundah* (*tunda*), "fruit"; *demon* (*ndimu*), "lemons"; *mage* (*maji*), "water"; *cartassa* (*karatasi*), "paper"; *sinzano* (*sindano*), "needle"; *arembo* (*urembo*), "beauty" (in this case referring to things used to beautify, such as bracelets); and *soutane* (*sultani,* the Swahilized pronunciation of the Arabic word *sultan*), "king" (Whiteley 1969, 37). But can we find Swahili in vocabulary alone? According to linguists, what defines a language is the way the words work together, that is, the grammar of the language. Looking at words listed in old records in order to identify Swahili is much ado about nothing.

What linguists say about Swahili is that it is a Bantu language, one among four hundred or so spoken everywhere in Africa, from the fringes of the great equatorial forests in modern Cameroon east to Swahili and south to the edges of the Kalahari Desert in southern Africa.

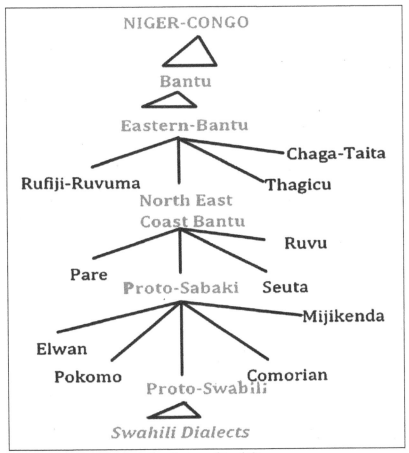

FIGURE 2.1 The linguistic family tree of Swahili

The Bantu languages as a group, however numerous and geographically dispersed, form one sub-sub-subgroup in the world's largest family of related language, Niger-Congo. Within Bantu, the languages diverged over the last five thousand years as their speakers gradually moved into the diverse environments where their descendants now live, in discernible phases enabled by changing historical challenges and opportunities. Swahili is part of what is called the northeast coastal Bantu language cluster, spoken today by the heirs of cultivators of sorghum and millet who gradually settled in the wetter altitudes and on the coast of the area east of the Great Lakes region—Victoria, Albert, Tanganyika, and others—in what is today Uganda. It shares many features—much vocabulary—with the Mijikenda and Pokomo languages spoken in the immediate coastal hinterland, from the Tana River near Lamu south to what is now northern Tanzania. The

Swahili of the coastal towns have always been connected to the cultivating communities of the immediate hinterland and beyond. Indeed, the Swahili to this day refer fondly to the Mijikenda as *Wajomba,* that is, "maternal uncle's people."[13] As "mothers' brothers," they were in-laws, the people who provided wives—and allies or political and economic connections—for the male traders who came to the coast.

Swahili and its sister languages, along with Pare, Seuta, and Ruvu, have in turn been elaborated from a hypothesized mother language that linguists label, somewhat arbitrarily, Proto-Sabaki. Its speakers, who lived somewhere in the hills inland from the coast, would not have known themselves or been known by anyone else in the region—some of them mobile bands who supported themselves by hunting and gathering, others pastoralists moving through the region with their herds of cattle—by this modern analytical label. The notion of a protolanguage or ur-language is the linguist's best approximation of a language that must have existed but disappeared as the descendants of its speakers elaborated it toward its modern manifestations. The only direct evidence for the protolanguage lies in words and other features of the modern languages that they could share today only through quite regular sequences of changes in pronunciations of the same root words in the past.

Linguists' best guesses at these sequences produce genealogical "trees" such as the one shown in figure 2.1. Swahili shares the greatest number of basic features with its sister languages—Elwana, Mijikenda, Comorian, and Pokomo. The geography of these languages confirms the impression of close connections, even including Comorian, which is spoken on islands midway between the mainland and the northern tip of Madagascar, obviously a direct extension of the language of commerce of the coast. At the next level of linguistic reconstruction, less closely related "cousins"—Pare, Ruvu, and Seuta—are similarly more dispersed geographically, in the hills just inland from Mombasa and the hills and river valley immediately to the south. Presumably, these descend from southward-trending settlers roughly contemporaneous with the northward-trending group that has retrospectively been reconstructed as "Proto-Swahili," perhaps some time in the first half millennium of the Common Era (100–500 CE). These two groups share still less with the other (hypothetical) "Eastern Bantu" languages—Thagicu, Rufiji-Ruvuma, and Chagga-Taita—that are spoken today in an outer ring of locations as far south as southern Tanzania and as far inland as Mount Kenya; thus, they are more widely separated both in distance and in time and subsequently interact less intensively, if at all.

Very approximate dates may be estimated for the waves of settlement that separated communities in the differing environments where they continued to elaborate the distinguishing features of the languages spoken today, through a method called lexicostatistics. This method counts the words in a vocabulary referring to things every linguistic community must talk about—"father," "mother," "water," "tree," "dog"—that the languages in question have in common. If, as the method assumes, languages develop their distinguishing features at broadly constant rates, then the percentages of shared modern vocabulary correspond to the length of time that has passed since their speakers began to talk among themselves, independent of their shared ancestors.

Swahili is thoroughly Bantu, like its neighbors, in grammar and vocabulary. Malcolm Guthrie's (1967–71) classic survey of the entire set of four hundred Bantu languages defined a standard common Bantu vocabulary and calculated that Swahili includes over 44 percent of these words; this percentage is about the same as the so-called purely Bantu languages spoken among people with no histories of interaction with non–Bantu speakers, such as Bemba (spoken in Zambia) and Luba and Kikongo (spoken in the Democratic Republic of the Congo as far west as the Atlantic coastal plain). But typical as it is of Bantu languages in these basic respects, Swahili is unique among them in being the one that lacks semantic tones. "Tone" in linguistics refers to vocal inflections that are highly communicative in face-to-face oral engagements; an example would be the way in which an English speaker raises the pitch at the end of a sentence when posing a question or drops off to convey disappointment at whatever the semantic content of a sentence may be. Everyone recognizes the contrasting implications of a mother's voice as it rises with interest in asking, "What are you doing?" or falls with concern when she has caught her child involved with something that disappoints her, "Look what you have done."

Intonations in English work at the level of sentences (or other utterances) and convey the attitude of the speaker about the meanings of the words. But in Bantu languages, as with many other languages around the world, the syllables of the words themselves bear modulations in voicing that convey meanings, similar to a line of song. Tones in Bantu languages are a big deal. They are an aspect of speaking that is as discriminating as vowels and consonants in meaning. Tones usually mark high, middle, and low pitches, with rising and falling permutations between syllables, words, and phrases. As a result, words that have identical combinations of vowels and consonants mean quite different things when intoned differently, depending on where the tone is positioned. Since Latin, which provides the alphabet we use in English, did not feature semantic tones, we have no letters for the tonal aspects of Bantu languages. For example, the word *iria* in Gĩkũyũ (a Thagicu Bantu language spoken in central Kenya), transcribed in terms of its three syllables is *i.ri.a.* When each vowel in the word is pronounced with a "low" tone the meaning of the word is "ocean," but when the syllables are pronounced with "low-high-low" respectively, the meaning of the word is "milk."

Tone represents an aspect of communicating by speaking with creative possibilities where voice modulation of syllables has the final say on what a word means and not the spelling of the word—something that makes linguists consider tone-marking an essential part of the spelling of Bantu words. And that's not all. The tone of a word also depends on the tones of the words next to it in a given utterance. You cannot learn a tonal language merely by memorizing the set pronounciations of a list of isolated consonant-vowel clusters. These have meaning only in the contexts in which they are used as (tonally inflected) words.

If you are reading about linguistic tones for the first time, they may sound brutally difficult to comprehend or master. But you are merely in the position of an Arabic or Persian trader trying to do business with members of communities that spoke tonal Bantu, like the Pokomo or Mijikenda of today, in eastern Africa. You could blunder through, using a lot of gesturing and embarrassing yourself in the process, but only at the cost of making a tremendous effort to understand what is being said. You could not begin to capture the intonations with Arabic script. Linguists think that Swahili and all its dialects had cohered in the places where they are now spoken, without tones, before 800 CE, with northern and southern groups. The northern dialects centered on the Lamu archipelago and Lower Tana valley, that is, the southern Somalia coast to an area just south of Mombasa. Southern dialects were those from Chivumba southward, as shown in map 2.3.

If tones had not been lost by then, some of today's dialects would be tonal and others would not. It is the absence of tone, as much as any other feature, that identifies this dispersed grouping as part of the same language. This linguistic background frames the Sawahil that Ibn Battuta reported in the fourteenth century as the language of trading along the coast at the time; it was transmitted through trade and, perhaps more important, through marriages, since the mothers taught their children to speak. This evolution gradually reduced the reliance on tone and eventually led to the integration

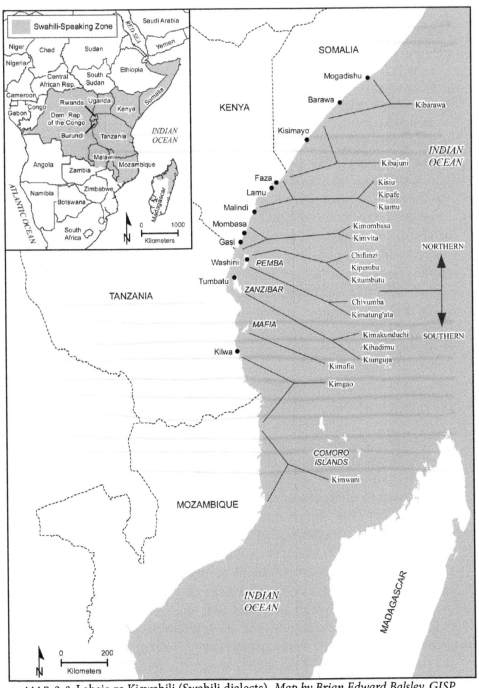

MAP 2.3 Lahaja za Kiswahili (Swahili dialects). *Map by Brian Edward Balsley, GISP*

of new ways of speaking, distinctive for Swahili, that did not depend on tone at all. All of the many Bantu languages spoken near the coast—Mijikenda with its nine dialects (Chonyi, Digo, Duruma, Giryama, Jiβana [Dzihana, Jibana], Kambe, Kauma, Raβai [Rabai, Rahai), and Riβe [Ribe, Rihe]) as well as Zigua, Doë, Kwere, Zaramo, Makonde, Luguru, Kami, Makonde, Mwera, Makua, and Mabia—are tonal. Only Swahili is not.

Swahili turns out to be measurably easier to learn and more easily adaptable than other languages because it shed its Bantu tonology. Some of the evidence supporting this openness comes from the US Department of State. The State Department (which includes the Foreign Service Institute, a professional training school for the personnel the department sends to every language area of the world) groups global languages according to how difficult they are to learn. The easiest languages for speakers of English are the Romance and Germanic languages of Europe, which are both ancestral to modern English, followed immediately by Swahili. Other Bantu languages are not included among these favorite few.[14] On top of that, in terms of accessibility Swahili is more cosmopolitan than most other Bantu languages (other than in African terms) because it has many borrowings from Arabic, Persian, and Indic languages from before the turn of the second millennium—from Portuguese in the sixteenth and seventeenth centuries, from German for a few decades in the nineteenth century to the end of World War I, and from English from the nineteenth century to the present. Speakers of languages from all these backgrounds thus find at least isolated outcroppings of familiarity to which they can cling as they struggle to stay afloat in the swirling currents of learning to speak an otherwise largely foreign tongue.

Swahili's role as a version of a broad language family "dumbed down" for foreigners to speak parallels that of English among the Indo-European languages of Western Europe. Like Swahili, modern English was elaborated under predisposing historical circumstances from earlier languages spoken elsewhere, by others. Seafaring immigrants to the North Sea coasts of England in the fifth and sixth centuries CE from Denmark and the northwestern coasts of present-day Germany and the Netherlands brought a cluster of related dialects. These dialects fell within the Germanic branch of the Indo-European language family, with its quite elaborate categorization of nouns into "cases" marked with complex sets of endings to confirm their positions—as subjects, objects, and so on—in utterances of length and intricacy that modern speakers of English find challenging to follow. Isolated from their Continental Germanic ancestors and cousins, the immigrants in northeastern England began to develop their own distinctive ways of speaking and by 600 CE had settled into what we call Old English, or Anglo-Saxon, spoken at least as a second language throughout most of modern England.

However, the defining moment in the history of English—and the one that left it with the openness and grammatical simplicity that surely contributed to its eventual standing as the second language that everyone can learn and thus as the international language of today—followed the invasion of southern England in the eleventh century by the French-speaking Normans. Significant vocabulary used in contemporary English for the finer points of life comes from French, brought by Norman aristocrats. The more homely elements of the language are derived from the Germanic Anglo-Saxon. So too is the grammar of the language, though it has been shorn of the syntactic complexities of Germanic noun classes that must have baffled the Normans, for Romance languages do not feature such refinements. The Romance languages—Romanian, Portuguese, Spanish, and Italian, in addition to French—exhibit other grammatical simplicities that are themselves products of a parallel process of vulgarization. They all derive from classical Latin, which also featured intricate declensions of nouns according to their positions in sentences. But the Roman (and other) soldiers, settlers, and traders who deposited the Latin overlay in northern and western Europe used a simplified Vulgar Latin, or Gallo-Roman, to engage the local Gaulish-speaking populations among whom they lived, minus the grammatical nuances found in the refined and literate expression of the upper classes in Rome.

Toneless Swahili coalesced along the east coast of Africa because people from tonal language backgrounds within the Proto-Sabaki subbranch of Eastern Bantu began to engage uncomprehending foreign traders along the Indian Ocean coast. Initially, the languages used to communicate must have taken many rudimentary forms. But by around the ninth century, business must have been good enough in the vicinity of the modern Lamu archipelago and the lower Tana River valley for children to grow up speaking without tones and for a community to form communicating in dialectal varieties that would eventually be called Swahili. The people of the Lamu archipelago speak Tikuu, Siu, Pate, and Amu, and their communities have been more isolated geographically on islands than the settlements on the mainland farther south; the latter have been in constant contact with the adjacent language communities in the last millennium (Nurse and Hinnebusch 1993, 267). Linguistically coherent communities define themselves and identify themselves to others by elaborating their distinctive ways of speaking. Migrations to Barawa and Muqdisho around 1100 CE and the Bajuni Islands by about 1300 CE led to the northern dialects. With each movement, the emigrants came into contact with different neighbors. ChiMwiini speakers were influenced by the Mijikenda-Pokomo speakers with whom they were neighbors. Mombasa became a regional power by the fifteenth century and influenced adjacent dialects of Swahili (Nurse and Spear 1985, 61). By the nineteenth century, Lamu had become influential in the archipelago, and the island's Kiamu dialect influenced the other dialects there as well as dialects on the adjacent mainland to the mouth of the Tana.

Presumably, the initial ninth- or tenth-century traders then moved south along the coast with the renewed wave of Arab and Persian interest in eastern Africa in that era, introducing Proto-Swahili as the language of trade at the settlements where they established themselves to do business. Thus, they seeded the local language communities that have since developed the dialectical variants of the modern language, all without tones.

Complexities of Swahili

Who are the *Waswahili wa asili* (the original Swahili)? Given the complexities of the coast, with its diverse resident families of many heritages from all over the world, this is a trick question at best, though for outsiders who still think in simplistic terms of one-dimensional tribes where every person is just like everyone else, it might have overtones of seriousness. For Swahili speakers, the question excites great debate nonetheless, since they simultaneously emphasize the subtle distinctions of accent and locality that divide them and compete to claim authenticity as bearers of the common heritage. An Anglophone wit once remarked, "England and America are two countries separated by a common language."[15] The Swahili are not divided by an ocean but rather by dialects, geography, and claims to ancient and honorable ancestry—not unlike the people of the United States.

Swahili speakers identify themselves by the locations of the various dialects of the language, centered on the towns and islands where they have clustered through the years (Chiraghdin and Mnyampala 1977; Mbaabu 1985). The small groups of people scattered through Kenya, Tanzania, Burundi, Rwanda, and Uganda inland from the coast, who claim to be Swahili, as well as in the Comoros Islands in Mozambique and South Africa are relatively recent settlers in these areas, going back only a century or two. Many other inland speakers of Swahili use it as a second language, including those speaking pidgins such as Sheng, and have never claimed nor been said to be Swahili.[16]

Accordingly, by location, the core Swahili include: the Wabarawa, the Swahili of the city of Barawa off the Somali coast; the Waamu, the Swahili of the island of Lamu; the Wapate, the Swahili of Pate; the Wamvita, the Swahili of Mombasa; the Wasiu, the Swahili of Siyu; and so on for the Washela, the Wamalindi, the Wakilifi, the Wamtang'ata, the Wakilindini, the Wajomvu, and the Wavanga, all in present-day Kenya; and the Wamafia, the Wamrima, and the Watumbatu in Tanzania. Most of these groups' locations go back several centuries, and a few of them—such as Mombasa, Lamu, Malindi, Kilwa, and Sofala—are over a thousand years old. Swahili dialects are also known by the names of cities, towns, and islands. Thus, for instance, Kibarawa is Barawa Swahili; Kisiu is the Swahili of the island of Siu; Kiamu is Lamu Swahili; Kimvita (Kimombasa) is Mombasa Swahili; and Kiunguja is Unguja (Zanzibar) Swahili.

But not all Swahili have urban identities. Beside every town or city were scores of fishing and farming villages (far more numerous than towns) all along the coast, most of them in shanty condition, where the farmers, fishermen, masons, carpenters, leatherworkers, and boatbuilders lived.[17] All of these were considered the *wenyeji* (native peoples) and the *wananchi* (the owners of the land). Here as elsewhere, those who came earlier were considered by those who came later as the native, or "true," Swahili. There is a tendency to think of the Swahili as only those who dwelled in stone-built town centers or figured their ancestry by paternal descent. This is not the case. There were many people of the coast who were not traders and businessmen, and they did not necessarily calculate their descent through paternal lineage alone. The Watumbatu, Wapemba, and Wahadimu did not own slaves or acquire much political or economic power, and they counted their kin inclusively (and still do), through both paternal and maternal links rather than by the patrilineal descent used by most other Swahili. Swahili life was dynamic and far more than a simple gathering of traders. Those who came into a community and were an underclass found ways to move up the social ladder to more amenable standings. It is said, for instance, that the Wahadimu were once relegated to ritual duties such as blowing the *siwa* (a great brass and ivory horn) at patrician weddings, and they were also given "polluting occupations" such as the washing of corpses. They eventually abandoned the latter role in true Swahili style, by changing their names to those of patrician Swahili society.[18] This move would have required adopting the language of the patrician Swahili, which perhaps explains why the Wahadimu are said to have spoken Swahili with a peculiar accent marked by a noticeable singsong intonation in their greetings.[19] Although the wenyeji were demographic majorities, they have been given short shrift in the conventional story of Swahili, which is centered on the mercantile elites in the trading towns.

The local dialects are distinguished from one another by variations in their sounds, or what linguists call their phonologies. A Mswahili of Mombasa says *ndoo* when he wants you to "come here," but a counterpart in Zanzibar (speaking Kiunguja) says *njoo*. The sound shift for the consonant—*d/j*—in this initial nasalized position is consistent throughout the two dialects. The Mswahili in the Lamu archipelago and speakers of Kisiu, Kiamu, or Kipate say *nchu* for "person," but in Kiunguja (and in modern Standard Swahili), the word is *mtu*. Other consonants that shift among the dialects of Swahili, as distinguished in English spellings (orthography), include *l* and *r*, the most unstable; both are sliding constrictions of the throat or tongue particularly characteristic of the differing rhythms of languages, as is known by any English speaker who has struggled with *r* sounds in Romance languages, and the orthographically similar sounds that are spelled *rr* but are radically distinct to speakers of Portuguese or French. The gutteralness of *r* varies noticeably—even stereotypically—among the dialects of English, from the light touch of an upper-class accent in Britain to the nasalized sharpness of the working-class neighborhoods of Boston to the throaty midwestern sound of standard media American English. In Swahili, the distinction emerges in northern dialects to distinguish the two components of a lengthened, or double, vowel. One scholar put it this way: "Take the dialects down the coast in order: Amu, Kimvita (Mombasa), Kimrima (German East Africa), and Kimngao (Kilwa). The following words with two consecutive vowels occur in Amu: Mtee, kae, guu, pua, chooko, mbaazi, lia, kwea. When you reach the Mrima you hear 'guru,' 'pura,' 'choroko,' 'mbarazi,' but the last two remain the same; while in Kingao you even hear 'lira' and 'kwera'" (Stigand 1913, 118–19).

Hard consonants such as *ch* and *t* and *n* and *m* vary as well, as we have seen in *nchu/mtu*. Other slippages occur between *f* and *s*, *g* and *j*, *g* and *k*, *j* and *d*, *l* and *y*, *s* and *sh*, *sh* and *ch*, *t* and *ch*, *v* and *f*, *v* and *z*, *z* and *d*, and *z* and *th*. To an English speaker's ear, the sound changes among dialects increase as one moves south. Another difference among dialects due to the differing historical experiences of the diverse localities along the coast is the varying degrees to which they include sounds from the quite distinct phonetic range of Arabic. Such accents often signal pretensions to high social status. The farther south one gets, the less they are used. The dialects of the Lamu archipelago in the far north (see map 2.1) and of Mombasa have more Arabic sounds than dialects farther to the south.

The technical distinction between different languages and different dialects of the same language is that dialects are mutually intelligible to their speakers whereas languages are not. Dialectical variations notwithstanding, speakers of Swahili understand one another without effort. Some of the closely related neighboring Bantu languages are partially intelligible as well, much like Spanish and Portuguese. The word *kulola* (seeing/to see) in old Kimvita was identical to the corresponding words in two neighboring languages, Kingoni and Kigiriama. In Kitaita, it is *kuwona*, which is very similar to *kuona* in today's Kiunguja and Kimvita Swahili. This example introduces another detail of Bantu grammar (including that of Swahili), which is that the standard way of referring to verbs, the action words in sentences, uses the prefix *ku-*, so that "to see" (the infinitive form) is *ku* + *ona/wona*.

The language of Swahili has never been circumscribed by family descent, or genealogy. Genealogies "are not always statements of actual ancestry but are validations of present authority and position: descent and kinship are socially defined and measured for validation of status and may not be biologically or historically true."[20] Also counted as core Swahili are some families who claim to have lineages going back to Arabia and who view "being civilized" (*uungwana*) as urbanity. Among these *waungwana* (members of the Swahili aristocratic class), who are credited with being the architects of the Swahili mercantile economy and "claim themselves to be the most orthodox in Islam," are the Sharifian groups, which trace their lineage back to the Prophet's house in the Arabian Peninsula.[21] Their forebears are said to have arrived in the eastern shores of Africa in about the sixteenth century, and they distinguish themselves from other Sharifian groups that came three centuries later from the Hadramaut, the southwestern corner of the peninsula in modern-day Yemen. Shirazi families, who claim to have originated from Persia, are also part of the aristocracy. They are found mainly in the Mrima region and on the islands of Zanzibar and Pemba, in the Comoros, and in Kilwa in the far southern mainland.

Length of residence along the coast seems to matter in distinguishing between the core Swahili with Arab descent and others deemed "Arabs." The Manga, who arrived from Oman in the eighteenth century and formed the core of the sultanate of Zanzibar, and the Shihiri, who came from the Arabian port of el-Shihr in the Hadramaut and settled in towns along the coast during the final years of the nineteenth century, are considered "New Arabs," despite their adopting the Swahili language. In the twentieth century, a wave of immigrants from the Hadramaut, most of them laborers from the lowest ranking social groups in that region, arrived and worked as assistants to the higher-ranking Hadrami retailers and did other menial jobs, such as selling coffee.[22] Evidently, every century witnessed Arab migration into Swahililand.

Returning to the vignette with which this chapter opened, Ali bin Fullani could fit any of the descriptions of the Swahili of Arab descent. The elite Arab-descended families have been at the top of the social hierarchy along the coast since the eighteenth century. In social rankings by descent, the outright Arabs came after any Swahili who could trace or claim Arab descent; then followed the Zanj population, from which slaves were drawn. However, records of genealogy such as that claimed by Ali bin Fullani were often fabricated in order to validate social standing achieved in other ways.[23]

One thing that the Swahili appear to have in common is African maternity. Though Ali bin Fullani did not mention his mother, grandmother, or indeed any woman in his ancestry, in all likelihood they were Africans, as only a very few, if any, Arab women went to the Swahili coast. Additionally, the women in his adult life—his wife or his concubine—would also have been African, just as in Jamezi's maternal line. The African woman was not only mother to Jamezi and wife to the inlander but also slave, concubine, and wife to the city-dweller and the immigrant from overseas. Ali's list of female ancestors, if available, would lead straight into the hinterland of Africa, perhaps dating even to the time of the Magna Carta and beyond. Such women are not accounted for in patrilineal descent narratives. Since motherhood is a fact and fatherhood is an opinion (especially at a busy crossroad), then it is in regard to their mothers that we find common ground among those who profess to be Swahili. By the mid-nineteenth century, at least half of the inhabitants of the towns were slaves, meaning that the descendants of slaves subsequently constituted a substantial portion of the general Swahili population.[24]

Beyond fabricated genealogies, the term *Arab* means many things in any practical sense. A racial definition of an Arab, Erskine Childers (1960, 70) tells us, disappears "hopelessly in waves of several thousand years of migration, invasion and intermarriage." Similarly, when the peoples, cultures, and languages that make up Swahili are combined, they make nonsense of the notion of origins. In addition to all the diverse communities who claim Arabness on Africa's eastern coast and who are without doubt also Swahili, the "Africanness" of the Swahili is equally stereotyped, with literally hundreds of ethnicities behind the people who claim that identity. This diversity is evident in purely linguistic terms. All four major language families of Africa—Afro-Asiatic, Khoisan, Niger-Congo, and Nilo-Saharan—converge in the Swahili hinterland and thus contribute to the maternity of most of the people of the coast. Tanzania bears the distinction of having languages of all of these four families spoken within a single country,[25] even within a single district (Kondoa District) of central Tanzania—the only place in the continent with such richness.[26] The diversity of genetic backgrounds in eastern Africa is stupendous, and the fact that the Swahili population has been replenished from these inland peoples for over a millennium at least means that the Swahili culture is inflected at every level with a hodgepodge of influences from far and wide. It would miss the point of the catalytic power of the mixture to attempt to determine which elements might be more important than others, in spite of common claims to the contrary by Ali, by other "Arabs," by Swahili aristocrats, or by any other claimants—until, that is, one meets the *mzungu,* or the "white person."

The Mzungu Factor

Jamezi, Ali, and the Swahili all confronted the violence that was spawned by European ideas of one-dimensional homogeneity, as opposed to tolerance of multiplicity and complexity. Many readers of this book in the West are heirs to this kind of stereotyping. Jamezi told Stigand, a mzungu, that to ask "Who is Swahili?" was to miss the point entirely about the complexity and cosmopolitanism of Swahili society. That there was no such person as a pure Swahili was an open-and-shut case to both Jamezi and Ali, even though neither of them could admit that the other was the real thing. Ali invoked a class distinction, with himself as an implicit standard, in which patricians were the Swahili and slaves and their descendants were not; Jamezi invoked a racialized, similarly self-referential criterion by which Arabs such as Ali did not qualify.

Thus, because Stigand offered a rigid set of mutually exclusive categories from which he expected an unambiguous choice—racial, tribal, or some mixture thereof—he found it difficult to tell who the Swahili were, even though they were in plain sight all around him. But the irrelevance of his expectations did not stop him. He believed that Ali bin Fullani met both the "descent" and the proficiency in Swahili qualifications but that Jamezi met only the latter. Stigand (1913, 121–22) concluded that "a disinterested observer"—presumably one like himself—had to "decide which of the two is correct," and so he did. He judged that "if being a Swahili is a matter of descent, Ali is correct, but if the term includes all who speak a common language, Swahili, whether of a pure or corrupt form, both these people should be considered Swahilis." Accordingly, Ali, the Arab, was Swahili in both descent and language, but Jamezi, the Makua, was Swahili only on a linguistic technicality—his "corrupt" Swahili. The mzungu invoked the idea of pure and corrupt Swahili to signal the weakness of Jamezi's claim to being Swahili, and this kind of view held sway for decades before and after the 1960s, as will be addressed in chapter 9.

So we have an intruder in the story, the mzungu acting as the decider. Stigand was not particularly qualified in any of the possible aspects of what he was trying to define—not culture, not language, and certainly not biology. He was something of a freelance adventurer, a sometime soldier and administrator, a traveler and hunter of big game, and an explorer and amateur ethnologist. The story of Swahili, inclusive as it is, encompasses the intrusions of the *mzungu* (white person) because, in due course, the mzungu took charge as a kind of big brother, in the Orwellian sense of being the one who set the terms by which people ended up thinking about the concept "Swahili." The mzungu was not a remote, "disinterested observer" in the story of Swahili but an imposer of ill-informed stereotyping. In this book, I will return repeatedly to the mzungu's wiles, but let me start here by pointing to one of the white person's most enduring fallacies: the idea that Arab descent was a necessary attribute of being Swahili. The moneyed descendants of the generation of Arabs who settled and ruled much of the littoral in the eighteenth century and the early part of the nineteenth (such as the Nabahanis of Pate and the Mazrui of Mombasa) regarded themselves as Waswahili (Swahili), not Omani Arabs, and that fact gave rise to the impression among the Europeans with whom they consorted that the Swahili were Arabs.[27]

Prior to the arrival of Europeans in the 1800s, the question of Swahili identity, though present, was not the obsession that colonial authorities made it out to be. But in their turn, the Europeans actually made it matter because they politicized the question. The Europeans arrived after their presumably homogenous nation-states developed in the nineteenth century. This period was one of relative internal unity and equality for them—a time of citizenship in a political sense, marked by strong and dangerous tendencies toward racialized superiority. Further, a significant component of their sense of national unity was defined through contrast with others, whether within Europe (which fought two world wars fueled by competing senses of national destiny) or at the cost of denigrating peoples in Africa and Asia as culturally and racially inferior. The twin developments of nation-states and imperial conquests confirmed the Europeans' notion of single-dimensioned political unity: one nation with one language and one flag and a single normative standard to which everyone should conform, exemplified by propertied "white men," whatever one's sex or wealth or skin tone. The European fallacy was that every such imaginary people had its place on the globe and a singular origin. But of course, this illusion was as patently false in Europe as it was in East Africa. When the British and Germans began to impose their way of thinking in the region, they projected their obsessive idea of a coherent people onto the Swahili and all other groupings in the area, at whatever limited level they perceived them, as stable and homogenous tribes. Such is the genesis of Stigand's impossible choice.

Why, despite the complex cosmopolitanism among Swahili, did Stigand pick Ali as the core Swahili person and dismiss Jamezi as the Swahili wannabe? Part of his reasoning surely was related to the fact that the Mzungu did not consider the dark-skinned African as capable of producing a civilization with the sophistication, urbanity, and refined standards of Swahili society. To the European colonizer, inlanders such as Jamezi were ahistorical—imagined as endlessly warring tribes until the Europeans arrived to pacify them. Surely they could not have contributed to the cosmopolitanism of Swahili culture, which—by default—could only have had a foreign source. Richard Burton (1821–1890), a British explorer sent by the Royal Geographical Society in London to explore the east coast of Africa in the 1850s, described the Swahili as "mulattos, descended from Asiatic settlers and colonists, Arabs and Persians of the Days of Ignorance, who intermarried with the Wakafiri or infidels" (Burton 1872, 408). As late as the 1960s, a founder of British archaeological investigations of the Swahili stone towns, James S. Kirkman (1906–1999), still put it plainly in his book titled *Men and Monuments of the East African Coast*: "The historical monuments of East Africa belong, not to the Africans but to the Arabs and Arabised Persians, mixed in blood with the African but in culture utterly apart from the Africans that surround them" (Kirkman 1964, 313). And one of his illustrious colonial compatriots, Neville Chittick (1924–1984), wrote: "We should picture this civilization as a remote outpost of Islam."[28] Others, not always Africans, have followed these Mzungu in seeing the African experience as marginal to the human experience of progress. A distinguished South Asian historian, Kirti Chaudhuri (1990, 36), went on record as claiming that "African communities appear to have been structured by a historical logic separate and independent from the rest of the Indian Ocean." Despite the apparent, deep-running African current in south Asian historiography, Sugata Bose's *A Hundred Horizons: The Indian Ocean in the Age of Global Empire* (2006) attributed no horizon to the people of the east coast of Africa.

Jan Knappert, a foremost scholar of Swahili history and literary tradition, said that "Swahili culture is essentially Oriental, not African, in its material as well as in its spiritual aspects,"[29] and he romanticized the Swahili, saying that they were "neither African nor Asian, but *sui generis,* an open society tolerant and free,"[30] the large number of them who arrived as slaves notwithstanding. Another scholarly definition centered on religion, such that anyone even nominally Muslim at the coast in the nineteenth century was called Swahili. This definition surely favored the Ali type of Mswahili. Frederick Johnson (1939, 442) made his definition even more flexible when his dictionary identified a Mswahili by dress alone—"anyone who wears a kanzu" (a man's full-length, long-sleeved calico gown); he clearly missed the women behind the men, even though he recognized that he himself, a European, could pass as Mswahili with the proper attire. The clothes apparently made the man, and even Jamezi could pass. A. H. J. Prins (1961, 11) saw exactly the same complexity as Jamezi did, observing: "It is always true that a man is never a Swahili and nothing else."

Mzungu saw the Swahili in terms of opposing absolutes—those with inland lineages versus those with overseas ones, those who were slaves and descendants of slaves versus the freeborn, laborers versus the patricians. False dichotomies such as these have made many writers see the story of Swahili as a series of geographically demarcated oppositions—the Zanj versus the coast; *mashenzini (ma + shenzi + ni)* the infidel inland versus the *ustaarabuni (u + sta + arabu + ni),* or "civilized" Swahili coast; *desturi,* or "customs" (with overtones of quaintness or worse) of the hinterland, versus *utamaduni,* or "culture" (i.e., class) of the coast; the encroaching "infidel" inland Zanj population versus the devoutly Muslim Swahili coast. These politicized "culture wars," no less agitated on Africa's Indian Ocean coast than in the equally multiple and complex culture of the United States, underlie much of the story of the Swahili language that follows.

The narrative arc in this story is that the development of a language—its constitution pertaining to grammar and vocabulary, its geographic spread and increase in the volume and composition of the population that speaks it—feeds from or is simultaneous with people's life experiences in facing and surmounting challenges, achieving, creating, innovating, and adapting to a variety of situations. Michael Halliday (1992, 66) put it rather well, observing that "the history of language is part of human history, it is not some mysterious surrogate process that goes bubbling along on its own." The emergence and development of the Swahili language is in lockstep motion with the Swahili experience. Through a variety of networks, many of them social and mercantile, Swahili has passed through numerous stages of change, adaptation, and expansion, and it is still on a roll.

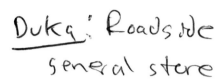

CHAPTER THREE

Duka: Roadside
general store

A Grand Smorgasbord of
Borrowings and Adaptation

MODERN SWAHILI is an archive of the history of East Africa's littoral people encountering the world, shaping and being shaped by it. The region was a mercantile crossroads, attracting a host of other peoples who interacted with the coastal population and left indelible imprints on the Swahili language and the Swahili people. Something of the diversity that resulted from these commercial and cultural encounters is evident in an anecdote about the wares included in a Chagga-owned roadside stall or *duka*. The Chagga live on the slopes of Mount Kilimanjaro in northeastern Tanzania—a rural area that Swahili and other cosmopolites might consider "hill country." The commercial advertisement announces what is up for sale in the *duka*.

TUNAUZA:

> sukari, mayai, baiskeli, kanga, pilau, walikuku, sambusa, tairi za trekta
>
> madaftari, bia aina zote, petroli, terafini, nywele za kusukia, nazi,
>
> vitumbua, mitumba, supu ya utumbo, maziwa, mabati, vocha, mtego wa panya,
>
> makabati ya nguo, kompyuta, juisi, mboga, mahindi ya kuchoma, pilipili,

sabuni, kufuli, bajaji, dawa, sementi, leso, vitanda, gondoro, bangili, na kadhalika. *Aisee, huyu mangi anawaza nini kwa biashara
hii?*

We sell:

sugar, eggs, bicycles, kanga, pilaf, chicken-(cooked)rice, samosas, tractor tires, notebooks, all kinds of beer, petroleum, turpentine, hair for weaving, coconut,

fried dough, second hand clothes, soup made of goat/cow intestines, milk,

iron sheets, vouchers (phone cards), mouse traps, wardrobe
cabinets, computers, juice, vegetables, roasted corn, hot peppers,
soap, padlocks, three wheeled scooters, medicine, cement, leso,
beds, mattresses, bangles, etcetera.

"I say, what is this mangi thinking about this business?"

This ad was intended to caricature a Chagga person's business for its lack of
specialization or, oddly, its specialization of everything. It plays on the stereotype that the Chagga people of Tanzania have a very entrepreneurial style. Yet
if one were to write an ad for a typical general merchandise duka anywhere
in eastern and central Africa, the seemingly endless mixture of wares for sale
would not raise an eyebrow. What these dukas lack in size—and many are
markets in miniature—they make up for in inventory. Most dukas stock anything and everything, and prices are often negotiable. As mentioned in the
introductory chapter, the sources of the duka's inventory are the hinterland
and the ports of the Swahili coast, and they are as varied and widespread as
the sources that have contributed to the Swahili language itself.

If you walk into any duka in Africa's Swahili-speaking region and reach
for an item for sale there, you will be holding a historical relic. Basic items
such as tea leaves, sugar, milk, notebooks, soap, pencils, corn, medicine,
juice, rice, coconut, phone cards, bangles, pepper, and padlocks all reflect
the Swahili's long tradition of borrowing and adapting goods. When you
eat *samosas, chapatis,* and *bhajias,* drink *chai* (tea) with *maziwa* (milk) and
add *sukari* (sugar), roast *mahindi* (maize), sleep on a *godoro* (mattress),
cover yourself with a *blanketi* (blanket), buy *vocha* (a phone card), wear
bangili (bangles), buy *dawa* (medicine), or secure your box of valuables

with a *kufuli* (padlock), you are the beneficiary of a long history of contact between the Swahili and peoples, cultures, and languages both from Africa's hinterland and from overseas.

In the Swahili text of the advertisement for the Chagga shop, all the underlined words are the names of goods that came from somewhere else. Each item's name hints at its source and, for the discerning linguist, recalls when and where the particular item first arrived in the region, always by way of trade. Some wares first arrived more than a millennium ago, some came more recently, and others are arriving even now. In explaining why East Africa's duka wares bear the names they do, one would have to subpoena many nations, peoples, and languages for evidence. For instance, the underlined words in the ad are from a vast range of languages, including Malay, Arabic, Persian, Hindi-Urdu, English, and German, together with a number of Southern Cushitic and Bantu languages. Such loanwords, retaining their usage over time, have become permanent signatures in the Swahili "visitor's book." They testify to the vast array of cultures and languages that Swahililand has brought under its fold over the centuries. The lexicon of the duka is from diverse sources: From Bantu, there is *kanga* (piece of cloth used to wrap oneself), *mabati* (iron sheets), *mayai* (eggs), *mboga* (vegetables), *mitumba* (used clothing), *mtego wa panya* (mouse trap), *nazi* (coconut), *vitanda* (beds), *vitumbua* (fried dough), and *walikuku* (rice with chicken); from Cushitic, *nywele za kusukia* (hair for braiding) and *maziwa* (milk); from French, *petroli* (petroleum); from Arabic, *biashara* (business), *madaftari* (notebooks), *dawa* (medicine), and *kadhalika* (etcetera); from Portuguese, *terafini* (turpentine), *pilipili* (pepper), *bajaji* (three wheeled scooter), and *leso* (piece of cloth used to wrap oneself); from Hindi, *kufuli* (padlock), *pilau* (pilaf), *sambusa* (samosa), *mahindi ya kuchoma* (roasted corn), and *gondoro* (matress); and from English, *baiskeli* (bicycle), *bangili* (bangles), *bia* (beer), *juisi* (juice), *kompiuta* (computer), *makabati ya nguo* (wardrobes), *sementi* (cement), *sukari* (sugar), *supu ya utumbo* (soup made of animal intestines), *tairi za trekta* (tractor tires), and *vocha* (voucher).

The duka is much more than just a place to buy things. It is a point of convergence where people talk about a variety of matters and form friendships, business partnerships, and even new families through marriages. Almost everywhere in eastern and central Africa, a duka starts out as a makeshift stall in a *soko* (market), a large open-air space where people gather once or twice a week to buy and sell and talk. Over time, as business increases and the trade wares become cumbersome to carry back and forth from home on soko days, some duka stalls are transitioned into semipermanent structures and then permanent buildings. The dukas are viewed as landmarks that herald the beginnings of a town. The more that are built, the faster the town will grow into a city.

The dukas and the soko imitate, on a smaller scale, the structure of the much grander Swahili emporium. They were—and are—the setting in which the Swahili lexicon has borrowed and adapted the names of goods, the ideas behind them, and the means to talk about both. As dukas became permanent buildings, owners added rooms to serve as their residential quarters, and before long, a bustling town emerged with its own native-born, permanent residents. These residents developed codes of conduct that were enforced by recognized authorities, finally culminating in the historical Swahili city-state. The parallels between the imports in the duka and the story of Swahili and its own borrowings show the impossibility of understanding even the most local centers of human interaction without taking much wider connections into account—and Swahili towns had connections to distant lands. Even the most localized soko, in fact, represented an aspiration for the global and the cosmopolitan

Let me step back and stock the duka with the vocabulary of modern Swahili. I will begin by offering a rough historical chronology. Starting as far back as possible, we discern a lot from the purely linguistic evidence of words. We have seen the limited supplies that we can gather from the early written documents. As I have already noted, Ibn Battuta wrote down the word *Swahili* for the first time in the 1300s, and the earliest list of words found in modern Swahili is from the seventeenth century.

African Lexical Diversity

East Africans, as we have seen, speak languages from all four of the major African language families: Niger-Congo, Nilo-Saharan, Afro-Asiatic, and Khoisan. And, as noted earlier, they added words from Arabic, Persian, and such Indic languages as Hindi and Gujarati for a very long time before they also incorporated words from European languages, beginning in the sixteenth century: Portuguese in the sixteenth and seventeenth centuries, French in the seventeenth century, and English and German from the middle of the nineteenth century.

The earliest human speech communities of eastern Africa were hunter-gatherer bands speaking the so-called click languages that were ancestral to the Khoisan spoken today only in parts of southern Africa; their roots may go as far back as fifty or seventy thousand years. Much later, perhaps five thousand years ago, pastoralists from the highland regions of modern Ethiopia drove their growing herds of cattle south into the drier parts of the region; they spoke languages of the Cushitic branch of the Afro-Asiatic languages now spoken from northern Kenya throughout much of the Sahara Desert, including Arabic and Hebrew in southwestern Asia. These two groups then intermarried and lived as neighbors. More recently still, by the middle of the first millennium CE, speakers of Bantu languages—the linguistic group that includes the Swahili—arrived on the scene from the west, as we saw in chapter 2. Given this belated arrival, how did the modern demographic majorities of the entire region inherit the Bantu languages that included the language of commerce and diplomacy along the Indian Ocean coast?

As Bantu-speaking communities gradually moved out through the southern half of the continent in a series of migrations, they seem to have incorporated the populations they met through intermarriage. Many Swahili words have cognates in Proto-Bantu, the hypothesized language of the original groups who left what is now southeastern Nigeria some five thousand years ago. These remote ancestors, according to Nurse and Spear (1985), were specialists in moving through the great equatorial forests to their east, and modern Swahili still uses the words they employed to talk about the opportunities they found there, including hunting with bows and arrows and traps, collecting honey and wax, fishing with hooks and lines, weaving nets and baskets, paddling canoes, raising goats, molding pottery, collecting water, cultivating root crops and palms, and grinding and pounding these vegetable foods. This heritage from the formative forest generations of Bantu-speaking communities—perhaps two millennia of them—explains Swahili words and phrases that are also found in Ur-Bantu (the original, or proto, language) having to do with aquatic technologies, such as "boat," "paddle," "to float," "to fish with a line," "net," and "hook." Because the dense tree cover of the forests kept sunlight from reaching the ground to support the growth of grass, they (presumably) had no need for ideas or words for cultivating or cooking grains.

The forest Bantu emerged in the open, sunny, grassy savannas of eastern Africa in the vicinity of the Lakes Region, centered on modern Uganda. There, further settlement necessitated a shift from forest hunting and riverine fishing to cultivating grain and herding cattle. The Bantu-speaking communities learned pastoralism from the Southern Cushitic–speaking herders, who had been the first food producers on the scene some four to five thousand years ago (Sutton 1968, 86–88). These Cushitic pastoralists, who had driven their herds south from what is now the highlands area of Ethiopia, maintained their linguistic heritage in groups identified today as Oromo (or Galla) and Somali, and they also established the first permanent settlements in the drier regions along the east coast (Middleton 1992, 12). Their expertise in grazing their herds to live in the lower, drier regions of the topographically quite varied interior of eastern Africa complemented the skills of the Bantu-speaking arrivals in the moister, often more forested higher elevations. The Bantu speakers specialized in adding sorghum and millet—both grains they encountered around the Lakes Region—to their agricultural systems, and they used these cereals to occupy arable terrain all the way to the coast.

The complementary environmental skills of the Bantu- and Cushitic-speaking communities rewarded those groups that found ways to collaborate; this included exchanges of personnel with the respective skill sets, among them women entrusted to their counterparts as wives. As these distinct linguistic communities intermarried, they shared far more than DNA. The Cushitic speakers engaged in these relationships tended to settle into the larger, more permanent Bantu communities and to create new local dialects and then languages derived from their shared Eastern Bantu backgrounds. But as the Bantu adopted their ways suited to the savanna, including grain cultivation and maintaining new types of livestock, they adopted Southern Cushitic words for the animals—"sheep," "donkeys," "chickens," and cattle" (Nurse and Spear 1985, 37–39). The Bantu also learned goat herding and millet farming from Cushitic speakers, incorporating the relevant vocabularies as they did so. The Southern Cushitic word /*tama/ (grain, specifically sorghum, or millet) was imported into Proto-Swahili (the hypothesized language, around 100 to 500 CE, from which Swahili has descended); the word is still found in most Swahili dialects today.[1] Similarly, ng'ondi (sheep) in the Kiamu (Lamu) dialect of Swahili is taken from the Cushitic root /gwand/,[2] and maziwa (milk) in Kiunguja (modern Standard Swahili) is derived from the South Cushitic root /ʔiliba/.[3] The modern words in Swahili show that the Bantu were impressed with the farming techniques of the Southern Cushitic people. Moreover, the Bantu apparently admired the way they wove, plaited, and braided their hair—or perhaps it was that the Cushitic-speaking women whom Bantu-speaking communities took in as wives brought their own words for the personal stylings that made them attractive. The Cushitic people used the root /suk/ to describe that aspect of personal grooming, and the Swahili adapted the word *suka* for "braiding."

Now let us take a closer look at three ancient words that the ancestral Bantu speakers borrowed from the Cushitics to create the specific version of that linguistic heritage that became Proto-Swahili: /*tama/ (sorghum, millet), /gwand/ (goat), and /ʔiliba/ (milk). First, note that the -t- sound in /*tama/ was changed to fit the sound patterns of the later Swahili dialects. In Comorian, for example, the Proto-Swahili -t- regularly became -r-, so the Comorians now refer to grains as *rama*. In other Swahili dialects (Kitikuu, Kisiu, and Kipate), -t- became -ch-, so that they say *chama*.[4] Second, the Cushitic word /ngwand/ survives as *ngondzi* in Kingazija, another modern Swahlili dialect; as -*ngʼonzi* in the Chivumba and Kiunguja dialects; and as -*ngʼondi* in the Kiamu dialect, as indicated previously.[5]

These modifications in pronunciation are typical of Bantu languages. For example, an initial *n-* was added in each case to make the new words conform to Bantu rules for noun classification. These rules class nouns that are borrowed words in a group defined by an initial nasalization—here, *n-* (or before other consonants, *m-*). A further general modification is the addition of a vowel at the end of each root, which makes the word comply with the strict Bantu prohibition against words ending in consonants. Why did each Swahili dialect add one particular vowel and not another? That is a question involving the regularity of sound changes from earlier to later languages, a topic that interests linguists but does not illustrate history in the way that word borrowings do, so this question will not detain us here. Similarly, the root /ʔiliba/ (milk) was adapted in different ways to elaborate the modern Swahili dialects. In Chimwini, the root survives as *iziwa*; in Kitikuu and Kisiu, it is *ithiwa*; and in Kipemba, it is *thiwa*. And finally, in Kingazija, it has become *dziwa,* a form that resembles both Mombasa Swahili and modern Standard Swahili.

Linguists use the term *sound changes* to describe the general process of how languages incorporate sounds foreign to native speakers. Sound changes thus also provide markers for the historical circumstances that led people to import specific words. With regard to Proto-Swahili and its later dialects, the patterns of sound changes from Southern Cushitic roots indicate that Bantu speakers made these changes *after* their ancestors had borrowed the roots. Had it been the other way around—that is, had Cushitic speakers made these sound changes among themselves—the modern Bantu words would be pronounced just as they are pronounced in Cushitic, which is not the case.[6] As speakers of the Bantu languages put their tongues to work pronouncing the Cushitic borrowings, what comes out of their mouths are modified or tweaked versions of particular sounds, recognizable as regional accents. We call this process "adaptation." The words taken in went through several sound adjustments to suit the pronunciation habits of the borrower. Settled adjacent communities influenced each other through verbal interactions, and as a result, sound changes made by one community spread to neighbors even as "other changes started at other points and spread, so that after some time the whole area was crisscrossed by lines of pronunciation (and other) differences."[7] A language's sounds, words, and grammatical elements come from inheritance, from convergence with or divergence from a common mother language, as well as from borrowing.

Borrowings from the Indian Ocean World

To envision a timeline for the arrival of Arabs and Persians along the east coast of Africa, we need to remember that the *Periplus of the Erythrean Sea*, written around 100 CE, stated explicitly that these groups had already established trade and family ties with residents of the coast region by that time. The *Periplus* document also revealed that the Arabs knew the language(s) that the mainlanders spoke.

Today, much as in the past, you will miss the liveliest aspects of the modern duka if you do not join in the verbal exchanges and drama that take place there as the shopkeeper and customers interact. Indeed, those who simply buy and pay without pausing to talk to the shopkeeper are considered eccentric or worse. As a result of over two millennia of warm business encounters of this type, as much about people as about products, numerous words and concepts entered the Swahili vocabulary. Though we cannot hear specific voices in the many dukas from centuries past, repeated conversations have left the words that now serve as mileposts marking the Swahili experience through the years.

Imagine a likely recent scenario in which an Indian set up a duka at the coast and was observed to lock up his valuables using an object whose name to Swahili ears sounded like *kufuli*. The Indian sensed that there was a market for padlocks and soon stocked them. To someone stopping by the ancient duka who was unfamiliar with padlocks, the Indian shopkeeper had to answer one question: what was this object for—that is, what was the problem for which the kufuli was a solution? The Indian demonstrated how the trade wares he brought along—including *bangili* (bangles), *godoro* (mattresses), spices that were rare at the coast such as *bizari* (curry), the much-needed *kaniki* (calico cloth), and other treasured possessions—were all kept securely locked up in a room or a cabinet by using the kufuli, thereby protecting them from thieves. Thus, the practice of keeping things under lock and key was adapted from India at the coast and moved into the hinterland, where the kufuli became a regular feature on the front doors of most dukas and homes; it was even known by essentially the same name—*kiful* (in Dholuo, a language spoken in Kenya near Lake Victoria) or *kufuri/kuburi* (in Gĩkũyũ, spoken from Nairobi to the Mount Kenya region).

Meanwhile, the Arabs arrived at the duka of the first-millennium Indian Ocean coast of Africa with all sorts of trade goods that local people had not seen before and for which they had no names, including *madaftari* (notebooks) to keep records and *dawa* (medicine) to treat various illnesses. People saw these things as desirable, and they quickly learned to ask for them by the names their suppliers gave them. Because their emporium was cosmopolitan and embraced diversity, the Swahili adopted a number of Arabic words to facilitate acquisition of these prestigious and useful imports. These words came from such Arabic terms as *souq* (market); *bai'a(t) wa-širā'* (trade [lit. "buy-sell"]); *bid'a* (goods/commodities); *fā'da* (profit); *khasara* (loss); *ghālī* (expensive); *rakhīs* (cheap/inexpensive); *mukātaba* (contract); and *rahn* (mortgage). Obviously, exchanges required some common vocabulary between buyers and sellers, and so the people of the coast took from Arabic what they needed to buy what they wanted—but not verbatim. Instead, they adapted and changed the words. Swahili today elide the glottal stop (') and foreign consonants in Arabic and pronounce the words *bai'a(t) wa-širā'* as *biashara*, *bid'a* as *bidhaa*, *fā'da* as *faida*, *khasara* as *hasara*, *mukātaba* as *mkataba*, and *rahn* as *rehani*. They left *ghali* as it was and rendered *rakhīs* as *rahisi*.

As these examples show, the Swahili adjusted almost every foreign word to suit their own Bantu patterns of pronunciation, or phonology. None of these borrowings took place through written communication; in the oral exchanges, pronunciation and accent constituted the words themselves. As noted earlier, the Bantu cannot help but add vowels to all borrowed words that end with consonants, and the Swahili derivatives from Arabic words exhibit this pattern: thus, the Arabic *sukar* became *sukari* in Swahili, and *sabun* was pronounced *sabuni*. Nor can Swahili borrow a noun without adding a class prefix to it: so, for instance, *daftar* (notebook) became *madaftari*, adding the collective plural prefix *ma-* to accent the plurality of a stockpile of notebooks. In fact, every borrowed word was naturalized phonologically as it was being adopted by word of mouth.

Furthermore, the residents of the coast adopted foreign words only as they needed them to refer to novelties. For example, they borrowed the word *sabuni* (soap) from the Portuguese *sabão*, but they did not borrow the word *maji* (water) because they had plenty of water of their own. From Arabic, they borrowed *kahawa* (coffee), the imported caffeinated refreshment, but not the word *uji* (porridge). They took in monotheistic religious terminology from Islam, including *malaika* (angel), *sala* (prayer), *dini* (religion), *waumini* (adherents), *msharika* (participants), *shetani* (satan),[8] *dhambi* (sin), and *Mola* (Lord God) (this could be from *mu* + Allah). However, they did not borrow Allah, keeping the word *Mungu* instead. Here is a list of some of these words and the host languages that bequeathed them to Swahili (Swahili words are underlined, source words are italicized):

bandari (Persian), harbor/port, *bandar*; bamia (Persian), okra, *ba:mia*; bangi (Persian), hemp, *banqu*; busu (Persian), kiss, *ba:s(a)*; bustani (Persian), garden, *busta:n*; chai (Persian, Hindi), tea, *sha:I*; laki (Persian, Hindi), one hundred thousand, *la:qa*; johari (Persian), gem, *jawhar*; karabai (Persian), acetylene lamp, *ka:rhabaa*; nanasi (Persian), pineapple, *anana:s*; sabuni (Persian), soap, *sa:bu:n*; sanamu (Persian), statue, *sanam*; saluji (Persian), cement, *sa:ru:j*; siti (Persian), lady, *sitt*; sukari (Sanskrit, Persian), sugar, *sukkar*; kababu (Persian), kebab, *kabāb*; daftari (Greek, Persian, Arabic), ledger, *daftar*; dinari (Latin dinarius), gold coin, *di:na:r*; kafuri (Sanskrit), camphor tree, *ka:fu:r*; karafuu (Greek), cloves, *qaranful*; karatasi (Greek), paper, *qirta:s*; kanisa (Aramaic via Greek), church, *kani:sa(t)*; kima (Persian, Hindi), minced meat, *keema*; dibaji (Persian), preface, *di:ba:ja*; dirisha (Persian), window, *di:ri:sha(t)*; duka (Persian), shop/stall, *dukka:n*; and paradiso (Persian), paradise, *firdaus*.

Broadly speaking, loanwords from the world of the Indian Ocean into Swahili abound. One scholar (Lodhi 2000) lists at least 726 loanwords from the Arabic, Persian, Gujarati, and Hindi into Swahili, consisting mainly of mercantile vocabulary involving the exchange of money and such imported goods as cloths and hardware. Further, Indians have been prominent in East Africa for a very long time. Records of trade between areas in the Gulf of Cambay (Cutch, Kathiawar, and Gujarat) and the East African coast date as far back as 60 CE. At that early date, Indian traders sold wheat, rice, butter, sesame oil, cotton cloth, girdles, and "honey" (a juice from a reed called *sacchari*). Indians and Persians appear to have been present in the mercantile sector of Swahili society throughout its history. The Portuguese found Indians alongside the Arabs when they arrived at the east coast in the sixteenth century, and Muslim and Hindu Indians still preside in the duka of eastern Africa today.

The long coexistence of Persians, Indians, and the Swahili has led each of these people to absorb much from the others. The Hindi word *rang* (color), borrowed into Swahili as *rangi*, must have been important in discussing the finer points of the textiles that were traded. Such words as *pipa* (barrel) from Portuguese and *gunia* (sack) from English (as in gunnysack) must have been no less important for packaging, storage, and measuring quantities bought and sold. The Swahili word *cheti*, from British English *chit*, refers to a passport, note, or certificate necessary for authenticating or transferring ownership of goods; it was borrowed from English presumably through Hindi. It is not surprising that the movements of goods resulted in the infusion of the word *gari*—any transportation device on wheels—into Swahili, from French through Hindi. Also borrowed through Hindi is *tumbaku* (tobacco) from Arabic *tabbaq*,[9] and *chai* (tea) is taken from Arabic or Hindi, as is the word *dhobi* (laundromat), which has been absorbed by Swahili as *dobi*. Foodstuff names borrowed from Hindi include *embe* (mango), *fenesi* (jackfruit), *kosha* (sweet palm wine), and *papai* (paw paw) (Mbaabu 1985, 40). Words for weights and measures borrowed from Hindi into Swahili include *tola*, meaning "half an ounce for weighing gold, silver, oil, perfume"; *jora*, or "thirty-yard piece of calico textile material"; *laki*, "a hundred thousand"; and, from English through Hindi, *korija*, a "score (or twenty) used in sale of beads, usually sold in lots of twenty" (Mbaabu 1985, 40).

Much of the basic seafaring vocabulary in Swahili comes from Persian, or Farsi (as it is known in modern Iran). Navigation and sea trade word borrowings include *mnara* (lighthouse), *Kiwida* (a hole in the beam of a dhow in which the mast is fixed), *nanga* (anchor) (Lodhi 2000, 39), and *bandar* (port, *bandari* in Swahili). Other words include *darbyn* (telescope, *darubini* in Swahili), *kwurdum* (wheel, *gurudumu* in Swahili), *karani* (clerk, *karani* in Swahili), *pilao* (pilaf, *pilau* in Swahili), and *diricha* (window, *diri-sha* in Swahili). Many words for food crops and plants also have come into Swahili from Persian.

Given this broad range of source languages for words in Swahili, it is surprising that Zawawi (1979, 73) found that "a collection and collation of loanwords in Johnson's *Standard English-Swahili Dictionary* yielded a total of 3,006 words of foreign sources out of which 2,354 (80%) were of Arabic origin." Such calculations do not seem to account for the borrowings from Persian, Hindi, and other sources that we have articulated here. But what does it really mean to say that given words came from Arabic, which itself includes words from a variety of other languages? Words from Persian, Hindi, Greek, Aramaic, and even long-dead Latin and Sanskrit abound in modern Arabic. Swahili has borrowed from other languages through Arabic as a conduit. These languages also have their own sources of further borrowing. Therefore, it is very difficult to determine whether words of Persian, Greek, and Hindi origin were in fact borrowed directly into Swahili or whether they arrived via Arabic, which would explain Zawawi's statistic. Moreover, Swahili may have acquired some words via more than one other language.

A number of words have come to Swahili by contiguous transfers through two or three languages. The word *chai* (tea), for instance, could have come from Persian, Hindi, or Arabic. *Sukari* (sugar) originated from Sanskrit but reached Swahili through the Arabic *sukkar*. *Kanisa* (church) came from Aramaic through Greek and then moved into Swahili also through Arabic. Older Persian words appearing in Swahili have been replaced by Arabic loanwords in contemporary Persian. Other words in Arabic, Persian, and Indian languages are so similar that it is difficult to distinguish a single contributing language.[10] Like the Swahili people themselves, then, many words in the language are thoroughly blended products of two millennia of cosmopolitan contacts throughout the western Indian Ocean.

The relationships between Swahili traders resident on the coast and their immigrant partners were personal as well as market oriented. Exchanges took place in terms of individual relationships, not abstract and anonymous markets. These relationships were often confirmed when merchants and sailors married daughters of the Swahili families with whom they traded.[11] We know that the such families had become devoted to Islam by the beginning of the second millennium. Around 1331 CE, Ibn Battuta described Mogadishu as a Swahili town whose inhabitants had personal ties with Asian merchants and shared residences and the Islamic faith with Arabs. These ties became the foundations for the deep friendships, mutual trust, and hospitality that were benchmarks of the trade along the coast.[12]

Swahili Borrowings from European Languages

Portuguese, German, and English are the primary European languages from which Swahili speakers have developed the lexicon of their modern language: Portuguese first, then German, and finally English. The Portuguese asserted their naval superiority along the coast of eastern Africa during the two centuries from 1500 to 1700 CE. Residents in the region adopted—and their descendants have continued to use—at least 120 Portuguese words, about a quarter of which are maritime related. In addition, the Swahili adopted Portuguese words relating to flora as they indigenized new plants that the Portuguese brought with them. These include *caraco*, from which Swahili made the word *korosho* (cashew nuts); *limão*, which became *limao* (lime); and *ananas* (pineapple), which became *nanasi* in Swahili.[13] *Pera* (guava) remained the same; *pistol* (pistol) became *bastola* in Swahili (nowadays *pisto*); *copo* (bowl) is *kopo*; *vinho* (wine) was taken in as *mvinyo* and extended to include distilled spirits; *trombeta* (trumpet) is *tarumbeta*; *boleo* (droppings) became *mbolea* in Swahili, meaning "manure"; *bandeira* (flag or pennant) is *bendera*; and (from Latin) *avia*, through the Portuguese and/or Hindi *ayag*, is *yaya* (nanny). The word *gereza*, meaning "prison" in Swahili, comes from *igreja*, the Portuguese word for "church." Perhaps this creative semantic comment reveals the attitudes of Muslim Swahili, who reacted with hostility to Portuguese Christian pressures and wryly observed that the Portuguese built churches in their many fortresses, including Fort Jesus in Mombasa, to shelter their houses of worship from contamination by Islam.

The first German travelers and missionaries arrived in the middle of the nineteenth century, and by the 1880s, Otto von Bismarck's growing political and industrial strength in Europe led to German military forces establishing their charge over several large territories in Africa, including what they referred to as German East Africa. This area encompassed present-day Rwanda, Burundi, and Tanganyika (the mainland part of modern Tanzania). The Germans established plantations, producing the industrial raw materials of the era—sisal, cotton, rubber, sesame, peanuts, copra—as well as coffee and other crops, and they built a basic infrastructure of roads, a railway line, hospitals, and schools. However, what they regarded as improvements were made at the significant expense of Swahili people and their resources. To control the local populations, on whom they in fact depended, the Germans set up a system of governance known as indirect rule, in which they enlisted local chiefs as proxies. They adopted Swahili as the official language of this colonial network because they opposed teaching German to their African subjects. Nonetheless, the Swahili took in a number of German words to talk about their experiences with these intruders. They adopted the word *Heller,* from a Schwabian coin (and also meaning "bright"), for "money," and its Swahili form, *hela,* has persisted. So too has the word *shule,* from the German word *Schule,* referring to the basic educational system established in the colony. As well, *barawani,* for "bathtub," was an adoption of the German *Badewanne.*

The English-speaking British claimed military and political control over Zanzibar Island and the coastal (and inland) regions north of German East Africa in the same decades at the end of the nineteenth century. The line separating the two colonies (and still today the modern countries of Tanzania and Kenya) runs straight southeast from Lake Victoria, which both colonial powers wanted to access, toward the Swahili coast; there is one deviation to the south, leaving the dramatic Mount Kilimanjaro in German Tanganyika, said to be a dramatic gift from Queen Victoria in England to her distant German cousin, Kaiser Wilhelm.[14] English words started appearing in Swahili en masse during British colonial rule, and by the time the British colony was dismantled in the late 1950s (with independence following in 1963), such words were too basic to modern life in eastern Africa to disappear.

Borrowings from English are too numerous to list or even categorize here, but they range through calendar months, academic subjects, weights and measures, and technical terminologies. The numerous Swahili dictionaries produced by the Institute of Swahili Research at the University of Dar es Salaam detail the profound influence of English over the Swahili language since the mid-1800s. The Swahili spellings of these imported words are determined by the Swahili perception of the English pronunciation, not by English orthography, with extensions to accommodate the Swahili rule of ending all words with vowels; thus, *molecule* is pronounced as "molekiuli," *oxygen* as "oksejeni" or "okisijeni," and *virus* as "virusi." Though there is a certain deference to perceived English sounds in these spellings, they assume the consonant-vowel order expected of Swahili words. This "Swahilization" embeds the English words solidly within the language. The English-derived Swahili words for units of distance and time include *futi* (foot), *inchi* (inch), *kilometa* (kilometer), *maili* (mile), *yadi* (yard), and *sekunde* (second), all spelled according to their Bantu adaptations. Names of weights such as *aunsi* (ounce), *lita* (liter), and *paundi* (pound) are all borrowed from English, too. English terms for currencies, though appearing late in East African trading circles, now dominate in Swahili. These include *pauni* (pound) and *shilingi* (shilling, in the colonial currency), *peni* (coin), and more recently still *dola* (dollar).[15] Such English-influenced words of the modern global economy have replaced earlier words that came from the Indian Ocean realm, for example, *rupia* (rupee) from Hindi and *dinari* (gold coin) from Latin. These shifts reflect the use throughout the region of currencies introduced by British colonial administrations in order to pay wages and collect the currency back as taxes.

Swahili Loans to Other African Languages

When Swahili borrows words from overseas languages, eastern and central African languages in turn borrow some of their words from Swahili. Beyond being two-way streets, multilingual contacts are crossroads and conduits. Swahili borrowings from Arabic, Hindi, Portuguese, English, and so on have been passed on to the languages of eastern Africa.[16] For instance, in Gĩkũyũ, Kalenjin, and Luo, the word *bicycle* is likely borrowed from English via the Swahili form, *baiskeli*. In effect, neighboring languages have borrowed from languages of other worlds by way of Swahili.

As traders, the Swahili bequeathed their own words for most of the items in the *duka* to the inland languages that its customers used as they gossiped among themselves when they gathered there to stock up on necessities. The languages of the hinterland have borrowed tremendously from Swahili, both as a direct source and as a conduit of its own lingual influences. The Swahili words *kikombe* (cup), *mchele* (uncooked rice), *ndoo* (bucket), *sabuni* (soap), and *sahani* (plate) all have been passed from Swahili into Kinyarwanda (spoken in Rwanda) through the sort of Bantu phonetic filter that we have seen—thus, they became *igikombe* (*igikoom*), *umuceri*, *indobo*, *isabune*, and *isahani*, respectively. In Luo (or Dholuo, a non-Bantu language spoken in western Kenya and Tanzania and therefore with a different phonetic filter), the same words are borrowed as *okombe*, *ochele*, *ndoo/pind*, *sabun*, and *san*. *Mũthũagĩ* (toothbrush) in Gĩkũyũ (a Bantu language of Kenya) is taken from Swahili *mswaki*. *Mbeca* (money) is taken from Swahili *pesa*, which was initially taken from Persian *paisa*. And *kĩbiriti* (matchbox) is from Swahili *kiberiti*; *gĩciko* (spoon) is from Swahili *kijiko*; *thani* (plate) is from Swahili *sahani*; and *mũiko* (ladle) is from Swahili *mwiko*. Similarly, *sufuria* (metal cooking pot) is borrowed as *sugria* in Dholuo and as *thaburia* in Gĩkũyũ, whereas *suruali* (pants) became *sirwaru* in Luo, *surualiit* in Kalenjin, and *thuruarĩ* in Kikuyu. Such examples abound in the commercial vocabularies of the languages of eastern Africa, Bantu and non-Bantu alike.

The Duka Is an Archive

The humble duka is an archive of history—a living archive of the Swahili trading past. The name of every item on the duka's shelves provides a glimpse into the region's history of contact with other peoples. Even more fascinating, however, are the processes by which Swahili speakers added these words to their vocabulary and transformed them to make them their own. Through examining the names of particular wares, we have developed some understanding of the foreign historical roots of things people from eastern Africa now view as familiar and, indeed, unquestionably African. But this influence has gone both ways. Swahili is part of the story of many other major languages, including Arabic, Hindi, Persian, Portuguese, German, and English. Many books that tell the stories of these better-known languages neglect the part played by the Swahili in the world of the Indian Ocean.

The borrowings discussed in this chapter reveal that the exchange of goods and services, diplomacy, administration, religion, and maritime activity all constituted living spaces for the borrowing and adaption of words into Swahili. Since the early decades of the twentieth century, scientific terminology, including that used in academic disciplines, has increasingly moved from English to Swahili, as well. Yet again, these words borrowed from English are themselves often borrowings from yet other languages. In turn, Swahili has served as a conduit of loanwords, which has led to the enrichment of the vocabularies of surrounding African languages.

Extensive as the presence of foreign loanwords in Swahili may seem, these words are concentrated in very specific spheres of life, such as Muslim religion, governance, science (including flora and fauna), rites of passage, and agriculture. These strategic patterns of lingual borrowings reveal the cosmopolitanism, resilience, and resourcefulness of the speakers of Swahili who borrowed them. If these outside influences are exaggerated, they make Swahili history seem only the story of foreign sailors fathering children by local women, willy-nilly, and giving them new vocabularies to talk about lives more exciting than those of the largely passive Africans in the hinterland. But nothing could be further from the Swahili experience. Borrowing was not a copy-and-paste, unilateral adoption of foreign words but rather a pragmatically creative process. Nurse and Spear (1985, 15) point out that even borrowings from Arabic were limited to specific cultural areas—primarily jurisprudence, trade, religion, and maritime affairs—added on to the basic Bantu elements of early Swahili. In fact, impressive as the occurence of Arabic words is in Swahili, there is a caveat, "Arabic material" in Swahili are "a recent graft onto an old Bantu tree" (Nurse and Spear 1985, 6). Borrowing continues unabated today, and the vocabulary of Swahili is still growing, allowing us to carry on to discuss current changes in real time.

CHAPTER FOUR

A Classical Era

The Peak of Swahili Prosperity, 1000–1500 CE

The coconut palm is the Swiss Army knife of the plant kingdom; in one neat package it provides a high-calorie food, potable water, fiber that can be spun into rope, and a hard shell that can be turned into charcoal. What's more, until it is needed for some other purpose it serves as a handy flotation device.[1]

The ship is of all things the most cosmopolitan.[2]

Sambo ni chombo yuwani	The sambo you must know
kilichoundwa zamani	is a vessel built long ago
na mtume fahamuni	you must understand by a prophet
nae ni Nuhu sikiya	and he was Noah

(Ahmed Sheikh Nabhany 1979)

THE SWAHILI vocabulary borrowings described in chapter 3 were the products of a dynamic coastal culture with surplus food; specialized occupations; tolerance of immigrants; monumental buildings; lavish tombs and burial grounds for rulers and elites; representational art; a great literary tradition; and, centrally, Islam as a way of life. Elite families formed a ruling oligarchy that coerced tribute, waged warfare, and relied heavily on slavery and the slave trade to support their lavish lifestyle. A robust economy teemed with consumers, producers, and distributors of local and imported goods. The much more numerous townspeople and rural dwellers inland from the coast followed these prestigious examples in their habits of speaking, even if

58

they could not also attain the elites' wealth and comforts. The cosmopolitan details of this civilization are revealed in the vocabulary of modern Swahili, elaborated here in a linguistic microcosm of two words—one a natural resource, the *mnazi* (coconut palm), and the other a complex technological instrument, the *sambo* (sea vessel), referred to as originating from Noah's Ark in the poem quoted at the outset of this chapter from Nabhany (1979, 9). Both the mnazi and the sambo were foundational in the material, spiritual, and linguistic prosperity of the Swahili in their classical era, the five centuries between 1000 and 1500 CE.

The Mnazi and the Sambo

The mnazi and the sambo were at the heart of the Swahili civilization, including the Swahili language—the former for the raw materials of daily life and the latter for the trade that enriched the coastal culture. A recent National Science Foundation study concluded that "coconuts may hold clues to ancient civilization."[3] Map 4.1 shows how the history of the coconut is interwoven with the history of traveling peoples. Two clearly differentiated types of coconuts were brought under cultivation in two separate locations, one in the Pacific basin and the other in the Indian Ocean basin and therefore right in Swahili country.[4] Indeed, "coconut genetics preserve a record of prehistoric trade routes and of the colonization of the Americas."[5]

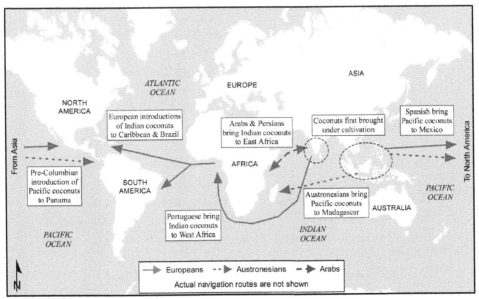

MAP 4.1 Coconut migration. *Map by Brian Edward Balsley, GISP*

The description of the mnazi as the "Swiss Army knife of the plant kingdom" in the quotation at the top of this chapter is accurate, considering the fundamentals of the Swahili society. The reliance on the mnazi for all manner of convenience by the people of the Swahili coast is expressed in Swahili verbal arts and attested in the words used to discuss cuisine, construction, and trade. In fact, it is difficult to conceive of the Swahili civilization without the mnazi. Over a hundred years ago, a poem titled "Utumbuizo wa mnazi" (The song of the palm) extolled the ubiquity of the mnazi in Swahili life.[6] The poem, which had existed for centuries in the oral tradition, is thought to belong to the Liyongo tradition, which means it might have been composed in the time of Fumo Liyongo, "one of the most impressive personalities in the oral and literary tradition of the Swahili Coast."[7] Liyongo may have lived as long ago as the eighth century[8]— well before the heyday of the Swahili civilization. The high quality of his poems indicates that Liyongo built upon a well-established literary tradition. The poem says:

Pani kiti nikaye kitako	Give me a seat to sit down,
iwambiye sifa za mnazi	that I may relate the attributes of
	the coconut tree
Mti huu wenzapo kumeya	when this tree starts to grow,
makutiye yangapanga wazi	its fronds spread out widely,
Baadaye hushsusha kigogo	later on a strong stem grows
hutoleza mapanda na mizi	with the mapanda and roots;
Hatimaye hutenda matunda	finally, it bears fruits
matundaye ina hwitwa nazi	which are called coconuts;
Huyanguwa hwambuwa	I pick the coconut, remove the husks and
makumbi hapikiya wali na mtuzi	(with its milk) I cook rice and curry;
Kifuvuche hatonga upawa	its shell is made into a ladle
k'apikiya Sada muwandazi	which Sada, the maid, uses to prepare food,
Na t'akize hamwaya yaani	and I throw away its chaff on the dump
kat'akuwa jimbi mt'akuzi	where the cock scratches for it,
Makumbiye hasokota k'amba	and twist the fibers of the husks into ropes
haundiya sambo na jahazi	which I use in building sea-going vessels
Makutiye hazambiya nyumba	Its thatch I use for thatching the roof
hazuiya p'epo na fusizi	to ward off winds and breezes
Kigogoche hafanya mlango	With its stem I make a door
hazuiya harubu na mwizi.	to protect myself from invaders and thieves.[9]

This poem of praise celebrates the mnazi as the source of many things that are prized by the Swahili. It is basic to Swahili cuisine—providing the *tui la nazi* (coconut milk made from ripe coconut) in which one steeps rice and meat (poultry, goat, sheep, or fish), the staple food on the east coast of Africa. Without tui la nazi, the premier dishes of Swahili fame—*wali* (cooked rice) and *samaki* (fish)—would hardly be the sensation they are, in the rituals of both preparation and consumption. Green coconuts called *madafu* are full of the thirst-quenching *maji ya dafu* (juice of unripe coconut). They are portable sources of the liquid necessary to sustain crews and passengers on long ocean voyages and thus vital in the cargoes of ships at sea. The sap of a standing mnazi tree is tapped, and in about a day, it becomes palm wine, also known as *mnazi,* and a few days later palm wine vinegar, or *siki.*

The mnazi appears to have been tailor-made for the daily convenience of the Swahili. Its *makuti* (branches) are just right for thatching houses in the warm, moist climate along the Swahili coast. Its *kigogo* (stem) is strong enough for use as *milango* (doors) (or, as the poem describes the purpose, to keep out invaders and thieves), yet it is light enough to float (*kuelea*), fitting usefully in the seafaring life of the Swahili. Beyond its importance as a source of materials for building shelters, boats, homes, and cities, mnazi has also been an income generator: its plaited palm fronds were exported overseas to Arab lands and to the Persian Gulf. Whatever remains from the coconuts themselves, in the form of husks, makes an excellent fuel for cooking fires. It should therefore not come as a surprise that some Swahilis say, "If people own a certain number of coconut palms, they can retire happy."[10] The mnazi has been the subject of poetry, proverbs, and stories in Swahili folklore.

In the "Utumbuizo wa mwana nazi" (The song of lady coconut), Liyongo finds *mwana nazi* (the lady coconut) is the ideal metaphor to express the benevolence of his love. The word *utumbuizo* means "to soothe musically," hence the first stanza of the song says:

Pani kiti nikaye kitako	Give me a chair so that I may sit down
t'umbuize wangu mwana mnazi	And soothe my Mwana Nazi
T'umbuize wangu mwanamke	That I may soothe my lady
mpanguwa hamu na simanzi	Who takes away my longing and sorrow[11]

To hear the song performed takes one back to what the recitations must have been like during ancient Swahili evenings. The words *pani kiti nikaye kitako* indicate that the narrator is in no hurry to run through the praises of his beloved. As we will see in chapter 6, the word *mwana* meant "female king," making the poem a lavish praise song offered by the narrator for his lady, reminiscing about her love and dedication to his welfare[12]—a metaphorical allusion to what the mnazi means to the Swahili. The *Utumbuizo* stands in Swahili literary tradition as a poem with few equivalents in imagery and symbolism. More recently, Ahmed Sheikh Nabhany, the stalwart Swahili poet and *mwanachuoni* (independent scholar), wrote *Umbuji wa mnazi* (The constitution of the coconut palm), telling of the usefulness of the tree in Swahili society. Its importance is recorded in very similar terms in the faraway archipelago of San Lazaro in the modern-day Philippines, where a different subspecies of the plant was originally bred by Antonio Pigafetta, traveling in one of Ferdinand Magellan's ships in the year 1521:

Cochi are the fruit borne by the palm trees. And just as we have bread, wine, oil, and vinegar in their several kinds, these people have the aforesaid things which come only from the palm trees. And know that wine is obtained from the said palm trees in the following manner. They make an aperture into the heart of the tree at its top which is called *palmetto*, from which is distilled along the tree a liquor like white must which is sweet with a touch of greenness. . . . The palm tree bears a fruit, named *cocho* [coconut], which is as large as the head or thereabouts, and its first husk is green and two fingers thick, in which are found certain fibers of which those people make the ropes by which they bind their boats. Under their husk is another, very hard and thicker than that of a nut. This second husk they burn and make of it a powder that is useful to them. And under the said husk there is a white marrow of a finger's thickness which they eat fresh with meat and fish, as we do bread, and it has the flavor of an almond. From the center of this marrow there flows water which is clear and sweet and very refreshing, and when it stands and settles it congeals like an apple. And when they wish to make oil they take this fruit called *cocho* and put it in the sun and let the said marrow putrefy and ferment in the water, then they boil it, and it becomes oil like butter. When they wish to make vinegar, they let the water of the said *cocho* ferment and put it in the sun, which turns it into vinegar like white wine. From the said fruit milk can also be made, as we proved by experience. For we scraped that marrow, then mixed it with its own water, and being passed through a cloth it became like goat's milk . . . two of these trees will sustain a family of ten persons. But they do not draw the aforementioned wine always from one tree, but take it for a week from one, and so with the other, for otherwise the trees would dry up. And in this way they last one hundred years.[13]

The parallels with Swahili uses of the nazi are a spot-on match. The Swahili fascination with the coconut once more illustrates the cosmopolitanism of the culture, as mariners must have carried the local subspecies to eastern Africa from western India.[14]

Understandably, the mnazi is the tree of life for the Swahili, as summarized in this South Seas (Polynesia) saying: "He who plants a coconut tree plants food and drink, vessels and clothing, a home for himself and a heritage for his children." One could also add that the coconut palm as a raw material for boat construction made sea travel possible, providing portable drink, food, and fuel for fire. The palm tree has great significance in Islam as well.

The sambo, like the mnazi, is indelible in Swahili culture and history. One poem on the sambo indicates that the ship dates back to *Safina*, the "ark" of the prophet Noah (of the Old Testament) in Swahili imaginary:

Sambo ni chombo yuwani	The sambo you must know,
kilichoundwa zamani	is a vessel built long ago,
na mtume fahamuni	you must understand by a prophet,
nae ni Nuhu sikiya	and he was Noah
walioleza wa p'wani	The people of the coast
kuunda maundiyoni	imitated this in their yards,
mitepe yenye thamani	building the useful mitepe
bidhaa kupakiliya	to carry the cargo.[15]

The understanding is that Noah was a prophet guided by divine instruction, so ultimately, the boat has deep religious significance as a providential innovation, a notion that is steeped in the Islamic spirituality of the Swahili. The vocabulary of shipping technology presents a compelling illustration of the Swahili's knowledge about seafaring vessels. Many kinds of vessels are familiar to the Swahili, and they are expert builders of some of them. The range of these vessels shows once again the wide geographic range and heterogeneity of Swahili culture on the western end of a single vast basin dominated by a huge regional wind system.[16] This maritime integration permitted a great deal of exchange of ideas about shipbuilding as well as a lot of borrowing from the common technological pool. Quite often, virtually the same type of ship can be found in different regions, bearing different names.

Seafaring vessels known by the Swahili include the *bedeni, sambuk, dau, mtepe, mtumbwi, ngalawa, mashua, jahazi, jalbut,* and *mashua.* A brief introduction to each follows. The bedeni is a small dau (dhow) whose front and back are identical in shape. It carries cargo of about 15 to 20 tons. This type of vessel was sailed to the Swahili coast from Oman and the Persian Gulf, where it was widely used. The Swahili employed the bedeni for fishing and short trips along the coast. The sambuk (named from the Chinese word *sampan*) is a larger vessel, originating in Southeast Asia. Ibn Battuta traveled on one in the Red Sea in the fourteenth century. At the Beit Al Ajaib museum (which seems to favor imports), the dau is described as a wooden sailing vessel used extensively in the western Indian Ocean. The word *dau* was popularized by the British navy during the nineteenth century as a general term for sailing vessels in the region. The mtepe is a sailing vessel with a long projecting prow, an upright mast, and a square matting sail.[17] The mtepe, like many of the boats in the Indian Ocean, was sewn together with coconut fibers rather than nailed together. The choice of rope over nails was based on a fear that the sea contained magnetic rocks that could pull nails out, causing damage and possible destruction of the mtepe. Of course, the saltwater of the sea would have corroded iron nails, and copper—generally Africa's "prestige metal"—was far too valuable in creating and confirming political relationships to be diverted into shipbuilding uses. The Swahili, sensibly enough, therefore stitched their vessels together and found them to be more versatile and less likely to break up on the coral-laden shores of the Indian Ocean.

The most rudimentary and smallest type of boat used on the Swahili coast is the mtumbwi, a dugout canoe made by hollowing out the trunk of a large tree—the mango tree is favored today—and used for fishing in mangrove creeks and other still water estuaries. The mtumbwi is certainly the oldest type of boat used in East Africa, and its basic design probably replicates that of the very first boats crafted by humans. A more elaborate and distinctive variation on the mtumbwi is the ngalawa, which also links distant Malaysia, Philippines, and Indonesia to the Swahili experience. The

Swahili word *ngalawa* is thought to have come from a Malay word, *gadawa*. In eastern Africa, it refers to a type of canoe about 5 to 6 meters long and supported by a narrow outrigger on each side, making it sufficiently stable to be propelled by a sail. The ngalawa is generally used for fishing close to shore, as well as for transporting passengers across protected channels such as the one between Mafia and Chole Islands in the Mafia archipelago.

The largest traditional sailing vessel in wide use off the coast of East Africa is the jahazi, which measures up to 20 meters long; its large, billowing sails are a characteristic sight off Zanzibar and other traditional ports. With a capacity of about a hundred passengers, the jahazi is mainly used for transporting cargo and passengers over relatively long distances or in open water, as, for instance, between Dar es Salaam and Zanzibar. Minor modifications in the Portuguese and Omani eras notwithstanding, the design of the modern jahazi is roughly identical to that of similar seafaring vessels used in medieval times and before. The name *jahazi* is generally applied to boats with cutaway bows and square sterns, built on Zanzibar and in nearby parts of the mainland. Similar boats built in Lamu and ports in Kenya are called *jalbut* (possibly derived from the English *jolly boat* or the Hindi *gallevat*);[18] these vessels have a vertical bow and wineglass-shaped stern. Smaller but essentially similar in design, the mashua measures up to 10 meters in length, has a capacity of about twenty-five passengers, and is mostly used for fishing close to the shore or as local transport.

The Swahili's intricate knowledge of boat construction is demonstrated by the almost equal use of Bantu-derived vocabulary and other terms from overseas in naming the generic component parts of a large vessel (see figure 4.1).

The vocabulary used in assembling the sambo components is drawn primarily from Bantu and Arabic. There are many Bantu words: *mli* (stem), *tundu* (whole), *choo* (convenience [toilet']), *kiungo cha mbee* (main yard [the front spar supporting the sail]), *kiungo cha kati* (main yard [the middle spar supporting the sail]), and *kiungo cha nyuma* (main yard [the back spar supporting the sail]). *Mbee, kati,* and *nyuma* are all standard Swahili indicators of location, meaning "front," "middle," and "back." *Tunda* refers to the "ring fixing boom to mast," *mpira* to the "fender–protective cushion," and *fundo la muongote* to the "mast beam or thwart–crosswise seat in boat." Some words used to describe the human or animal body are also employed to personalize the boat, as is done in English: *tumbo* is its "belly" or its protruding underbelly and visible space, *tavu* is its "cheek," and *uti* is

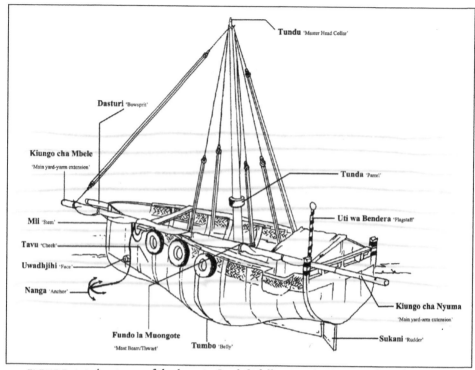

FIGURE 4.1 Anatomy of the boat in Swahili following A. H. J. Prins's *Sailing from Lamu: A Study of Maritime Culture in Islamic East Africa* (1965)

its "backbone" as used in *uti wa bendera* to mean "flagstaff" (the "spine of the flag or pennant"). All these terms show that the boat was native to the region or was very well domesticated. There are also many words from Arabic: *dasturi*, "spar projecting from front of ship"; *uwadhjihi*, "face"; *sukani*, "rudder"; *falka*, "hold—ship's cargo space" (inside the belly); and *dhufanyi*, "wales—wood forming sides of ship." The actual story behind each word may elude us today, but the nativization of the seafaring vessel into Swahili culture is evident in the boat language, which incorporates, in great detail, words that are hybrids between form and function—that is, between the architecture of the boat and the practical utility of the component parts.

The metaphor of the ship is pervasive in Swahili culture.[19] The hybridity of everything Swahili was constantly shaken, stirred, and revitalized around arriving and departing ships. In Swahili, the image of the ship is a microcosm, often used to symbolize families, societies, countries, and communities: each is a *sambo* that has *wenyeji* (citizens) who are *abiria* (passengers) or *wasafiri* (travelers) and a *kiongozi* (leader) who is the *nahodha* (captain) of that ship. In writing *The Black Atlantic,* Paul Gilroy similarly found that the ship in motion on that sea was a "chronotope" in the ocean on the other side of Africa:

> I have settled on the image of ships in motion across the spaces between Europe, America, Africa, and the Caribbean as a central organising symbol for this enterprise and as my starting point. The image of the ship—a living, microcultural, micro-political system in motion—is especially important for historical and theoretical reasons.... Ships immediately focus attention on the middle passage, on the various projects for redemptive return to an African homeland, on the circulation of ideas and activists as well as the movement of key cultural and political artefacts: tracts, books, gramophone records, and choirs. (Gilroy 1993, 4)

The Swahili ship was a micro-Swahili civilization afloat. The fact that original boats in the Indian Ocean were sewn together with coconut fibers is of inescapable symbolism: the mnazi held the ship together, it provided the water to drink in a sea of brine, and it also provided a means of flotation whenever the ship was in trouble at sea. That the mnazi and the sambo pervade the Swahili lexicon is not surprising—they were bedrocks of Swahili mobility and cosmopolitanism. The Swahili proverb *Mwenda tezi na omo marejeo ni ngamani* is steeped in the topography of the ship, translating as "Whether one goes to the quarterdeck or to the forecastle one will eventually return to the hold." This proverb magnifies the ship to represent the universe of interaction. It also says that—whether one goes to either end of the boat, be it the forecastle in the bow or the quarterdeck aft—the balance remains in the center. The ups and downs of life are then expressed with maritime language: hard times threatening the boat are the *mawimbi,* or "waves"; the threat to the vessel is the *dhoruba,* "the tempest"; and the sea of life is construed as harboring many mysteries, not a few of which are ominous, with *papa,* "sharks," and *nyangumi,* "whales," among the most frequently mentioned.

Material Culture and Language

Increasing trade supported the Swahili language in the cosmopolitan environment of the coastal towns. New vocabularies were constantly being absorbed into Swahili in the course of people merchandizing, intermarrying,

littoral: of or relating to or situated on the shore of the coast or lake

and practicing Islam while coming into contact with all manner of visitors to East Africa's littoral. The elite classes of these towns had a cosmopolitan identity as "the Swahili." Towns made it possible to store and protect wealth in commercial goods, to impose tariffs, and thus to pay for the public services necessary in these emporia. With increasing wealth, towns became larger, and growing demands for security of merchandise led to the construction of more complex buildings and a political system in which the financiers and borrowers recognized Islamic political authorities, known as sultans. These Swahili townspeople came to think of their urban lifestyle as *ustaarabu*—a word built with Bantu extensions on *Arab*—with overtones of "civilized" as opposed to "traditional and rural." In these towns, local communities remained devoted to hunting, agriculture, and pastoralism. Swahili leaders became deal makers, rulers, princes, and part of the elite of the transoceanic trade. And their language became the language of commerce and diplomacy among the numerous city-states of the coast.

The trade goods that passed through Swahili hands between the tenth and fifteenth centuries CE were generating big fortunes. In the first half of the second millennium, the East African coast had trading relations with China, the islands of Malaysia, Indonesia, Ceylon, India, Persia, the ports of the Arabian Peninsula, and Egypt. From the Chinese empire came silk and porcelain bowls, swords, daggers, tools, and pots and pans of iron. India also sent metal implements, as well as brightly colored cloth *kaniki* and beads. From Burma and Thailand came stone jars and pots of excellent quality. With each transaction, Swahili life continued to be more globalized, and Swahili became more of a player in the Indian Ocean world.

There are a couple of vantage points from which to view the Swahili society in this era—that of members of the patrician ruling class, who were always the minority with real (and also fabricated) roots in Asia, and that of the laborers, who primarily hailed from the *nyika* (hinterland) and were the demographic majority.

The *waungwana* (patricians) formed the core of every village and governed their inhabitants according to a number of matrilineal and patrilineal family lines, all of which were socially ranked.[20] Women and their daughters owned the land, and political power, wealth, and status went from father to son. Landownership was of great importance because the Swahili were primarily cultivators, growing sorghum, millet, rice, coconuts, and various fruits and vegetables for their own consumption and for trade. Lands close to the villages were the most valuable, as cash crops were grown there. The waungwana owned many of these plots and supervised the production of cash crops, bringing in newcomers as clients—and later as slaves—to expand the size of their followings and thus to maintain political power. It was these waungwana who married off their daughters to wealthy traders from Arabia.

Swahili villages and towns were divided into wards, each consisting of one or more matrilineal groups of sisters and their husbands; married Swahili men tended to live with their wives' families. Swahili waungwana jealously guarded against diffusion of their wealth and protected their high status by intermarrying with prominent families of equal social standing. Wards were ranked by wealth in landholdings, prestigious occupations, and Muslim piety as demonstrated in charitable works, often the building of mosques. Each ward was known by the name of its leading families, who interacted daily, pursued similar vocations, and worshipped at the same mosque. Each village or town had a northern half and a southern half. One half usually included the waungwana, the oldest and most prestigious families, whereas subsistence farmers and fishermen lived in the other.

The perspective of the *sheikh* (ruler) and the rich waungwana has generally held sway in narratives concerning the Swahili civilization, as evident in the following description of Swahili towns:

> Perched on the foreshore or on small offshore islands, their whitewashed houses of coral rag masonry crowd around a harbor where a few seagoing dhows are tied. Along the coral houses are a number of small mosques where men from the immediate neighborhood gather in their white gowns and small embroidered caps for prayers and outside of which they gather afterward to discuss town affairs in measured tones. Their wives and daughters are not seen until evening [when] . . . in flowing dark robes, they visit discreetly with their female relatives and friends. (Nurse and Spear 1985, 1)

There were professionals, too. As Jan Knappert, a foremost scholar of the Swahili cultural traditions, put it in the mid-twentieth century, "In the towns craftsmen can be seen working in wood or leather, in silver and gold. . . . Dhows and other ships of Arabic and Indian make, sailing by means of large triangular sails, call in ports of Swahililand, coming in from Hadramaut [modern Yemen] and the Persian Gulf, from Oman and Bombay."[21] The patrician perspective saw the Swahili living in comfortable homes on the very edge of Africa's Indian Ocean coastline, looking outward to the sea and ready to sail with the next monsoon. The waungwana dressed and lived in the manner of Muslims and had enough material wealth to allow women a secluded lifestyle. So irrelevant was the hinterland in this view and in the prosperity of the Swahili that Knappert concluded, "The Swahili coast belongs to the orient and not to Africa."[22] This elite orientation beyond the horizon of the Indian Ocean would hardly be surprising to Westerners. Let me explain using a few of the city-states along the coast as examples.

Mogadishu, the northernmost city of the Swahili, is on the Benadir coast—the largely desert region between the Gulf of Aden and the Juba River in present-day Somalia or the Lamu archipelago in far northeastern Kenya. The Benadir coast has projections of land and sandspits that form at the mouths of seasonal rivers, creating hospitable maritime anchorages.[23] From at least the tenth century, Muslim traders from the Persian Gulf and the Hadramaut had settled on these shores. The merchant families descended from settlers provided the sheikhs,[24] or headmen, and the waungwana oligarchies that ruled the Swahili towns. Some of these clans claimed to be of Shirazi (that is, Persian) origin. Indeed, the name Mogadishu is thought by some to be derived from the Persian word *Maq'ad-i-Shah,* meaning "the seat of the Shah" or political authority.[25] A perspective from the south holds that the name for Mogadishu, as the northernmost Swahili city in the chain of trading towns to the south, is a Somali mispronunciation of the Swahili phrase *Muyi (mji) wa mwisho* (the last city), implying Somali (Cushitic) engagement with Swahili (Bantu) as the historical process behind the rise of Mogadishu. The two etymologies could not capture the inward and outward perspectives of the Swahili more clearly.

As products of the two communities, Mogadishu merchants were ethnically and racially mixed and were joined in their shared pride of place through social networks built with patronage by the wealthy. The Syrian traveler Yaqut al-Hamawi, visiting Mogadishu in the twelfth century, described the residents of the town as dark-skinned Berbers[26]—a Mediterranean word derived from the Greek *barbaros* (English term "barbarians") and applied to nomadic desert-dwellers, such as the Somali, in the Sahara. In the thirteenth century, Mogadishu was reported to have been the most important town on the coast, with nomadic neighbors in the backlands and foreign Muslims in the town.[27] In the fourteenth century, the famous Moroccan traveler Ibn Battuta described "Maqdashu" as "an exceedingly large city" with a community of cotton producers and wealthy merchants supplying the people of the interior with cloth and also exporting it to Egypt.

According to Ibn Battuta, the town had a wise and pious sheikh who ruled flanked by authorities in Islamic law and *sharifs,* or aristocratic descendants of the Prophet, as well as a chief judge, or *qadi,* who was knowledgeable and articulate in points of Islamic religious law. At the height of Mogadishu's prosperity in the fourteenth century, local merchants appear to have monopolized the buying and selling of goods. Foreign merchants visiting Mogadishu in those days had to lodge with one of the leading local traders, and sell their goods through him.[28] Much of this commercial prosperity came from the town's position as the northern gateway to the trade in gold from the Sofala coast—modern Mozambique in southern Africa. Mogadishu also supplied local ivory, gum, honey, and wax and was noted for breeding and selling horses. It had supplied ivory to China, as well as rhino horn, turtle shell, ambergris (a fragrant marine fixative), and live wild animals, a commerce that went back to at least the ninth century and was of such importance that Chinese ships visited the Benadir coast in the fifteenth century. Mogadishu imported cloth from India and ceramics, porcelain, and silver from Persia. Gold, silver, ivory, and cloth were among the rich booty that the Portuguese took in 1506 when they raided Barawa, another town on the Benadir coast, indicating the commercial wealth of the region. At the close of the fifteenth century, in 1499 CE, explorer Vasco da Gama observed that Mogadishu was a "large town, with houses several stories, big palaces in its center and four towers around it."[29]

Malindi, the next large trading town to the south, was ruled by a sultan at its height, also in the fifteenth century; the Portuguese described him as a "Moorish" king. The town featured many "fair stone and mortar houses of many floors, with great plenty of windows and flat roofs," in arrangements that struck the Portuguese as quite well planned. The town was famed for its "great barterers in cloth, gold, [and] ivory."[30] Malindi had plenty of food—*mpunga* (paddy rice), *mtama* (millet), *ngano* (wheat), and many fruits from numerous gardens and orchards. The city owned a good deal of livestock—round-tailed sheep, cows, and hens. A day's sail from Malindi to the south is Mombasa, which also struck visitors as a beautiful city. It was said to be "a fair place, with lofty stone and mortar houses, well aligned in streets after the fashion of Kilwa. The wood is well-fitted with excellent joiner's work. It has its own king, himself a Moor. The men are in colour either tawny, black, or white."[31] Mombasans wore fine garments of silk, and gold was in abundance. The harbor of the city was filled with vessels great and small. There was plenty of water in Mombasa, and nourishment was not lacking:

millet, rice, oranges of various kinds, lemons, pomegranates, Indian figs, many kinds of vegetables, and fine sheep could all be found in abundance. In addition, there were plenty of cows and other cattle and chickens, all of them fat. Elite Mombasans, who followed the Shafi'i rite known as *madhab*, or "school of jurisprudence," were rich, and the urban infrastructure seemed impressive even by the sophisticated standards of visitors.

The largest city to the south—the last in the chain of Swahili towns and the market where traders from the north bought gold from the region of Great Zimbabwe—was Kilwa. In 1331, the great Muslim traveler Ibn Battuta said that Kilwa was located in the land of Zanj and was "one of the most beautiful and well-constructed towns in the world."[32] In the fifteenth century, Kilwa issued its own coinage and was in control of Sofala, the source of the gold from the interior (Oliver and Mathew 1963, 131). In 1505 CE, Hans Mayr described Kilwa at its height, right before its destruction by the Portuguese:

> In Kilwa there are [multi]storied houses very stoutly built of masonry and covered with a plaster that has a thousand paintings. . . . This city lies upon an island that can be circled by ships of five hundred tons. The city and the island have four thousand souls. It grows quantities of fruits, and has a great deal of guinea corn, butter, honey, and wax . . . here grows very sweet oranges, lemons, radishes, and tiny onions, marjoram and basil which they water from wells. (Newitt 2002, 12–13)

Even after enduring destruction from the Portuguese, Kilwa was rebuilt and restored to a level that led to Duarte Barbosa's admiring description:

> Going [north] along the coast from this town of Moçambique, there is an island hard by the mainland which is called Quiloa, in which is a Moorish town with many fair houses of stone and mortar, with many windows after our fashion, very well arranged in streets, with many flat roofs. The doors are of wood, well carved, with excellent joinery. Around it are streams and orchards with many channels of sweet water. . . . And in this town was plenty of gold, as no ships [from the north] passed [south] towards Çofala without first coming to the island. Of the Moors there are some fair and some black, they are finely clad in many rich garments of gold and silver, and cotton, and the women as

well; also with much gold and silver chains and bracelets, which they wear on their legs and arms, and many jeweled earrings in their ears.[33]

Sofala, far to the south, sat on the banks of the Sofala River (now the Buzi), reaching the sea with the Pungwe River in a bay, now the site of Beira in present-day Mozambique. Sofala was a popular trading city, regularly visited by vessels from Kilwa, Mombasa, and Malindi. It was the marketplace for gold, which was brought in from Zimbabwe and elsewhere in southern Africa. In exchange for the gold, the Africans took cotton cloths, silk cloths, and beads and brought in ivory. The people of Sofala were described as Moors. Black and tawny, some spoke Arabic, but most spoke Swahili, the language of trade. Sofala also developed a weaving industry. It had millet, rice, meat, and fish as the main nourishments.

The Swahili towns are evident today in the *magofu* (ruins) scattered along the coast from Mogadishu to Kilwa. The most famous magofu are at Gedi, a Swahili town of which there is no record save the archaeological information gleaned from monumental ruins left behind. According to Kirkman, the name Gedi (or Gede) is from the Oromo (formerly Galla, pastoralists from southern Ethiopia); it means "precious" and may well have been the name of the last ruler of the town, the name of a conqueror, or simply the Galla name of the town before it was destroyed. Kirkman and others also raise the possibility that Gedi may have been known as Kilimani, from the name Quelman, indicated in the region on a 1639 map by Petrus Bertholet (Vincent 1800, 140). The ruins are located 10 miles south of Malindi and 65 miles north of Mombasa.[34] The obscurity of Gedi in the historical records of the coast was not singular among the region's many prosperous sites. Indeed, anonymous ruins of long-forgotten cities are strewn along the entire Indian Ocean littoral of East Africa, and their obscurity has actually preserved their remains for archaeological study. Excavations at Gedi revealed that the town occupied about 54 acres, only part of which were built up with permanent structures using coral, red earth, and coral lime. A good number of other dwellings were poorer structures made of mud with wattle walls and roofs thatched with palm leaves and grass.

The population of the city, protected by a 9-foot wall with at least three gates, is estimated to have exceeded twenty-five hundred people. A newer wall enclosing a much smaller area was built as a barricade and incorporated the walls of existing houses in its line, apparently a last-ditch retreat for residents under siege, presumably by Oromo raiders. Among its land-marks is a large oval tombstone that has an epitaph incised in plaster, with a date in the Muslim calendar equivalent to 1399 CE inscribed on it. The tombstone thus provides a place in time to which everything else at Gedi can be related and thereby dated. It is estimated that Gedi was founded in the thirteenth or early fourteenth century, reached its height in the fifteenth century, and was abandoned early in the seventeenth century. A tomb of fluted pillars present at Gedi resembles the monolithic pillars of Madagas-car and an architectural motif typical of Ethiopia and Somalia.

Gedi had one great mosque and seven smaller ones, a palace, and large stone residences with plastered walls. One building with four apartments, each with an outer and an inner room, a lavatory, and four open courts, gives us a sense of the luxurious standard of living enjoyed by Gedi patri-cians. The houses had bathrooms with plumbing—drains and flush toilets. Lavatories were small cubicles with low partition walls between them and had one square hole and a urinal channel. Wells supplied water to the gen-eral Gedi population. Some of the findings included beads from Venice, coins and a Ming vase from China, an iron lamp from China, and scissors from Spain.

The privileged classes of Swahili society have endowed the Swahili lan-guage with a lexicon of luxury. The written Swahili history of Pate (in the Lamu archipelago south of Mogadishu and Kismayu) illustrates the point. Pate once had a prince named Bwana Mkuu (meaning "Great Lord" in Swa-hili) who discovered silver in an unnamed offshore island that made Pate very wealthy during his reign. We are told the Pate people were so rich that they "made large houses and put in them brass lamps, with chimneys, and they made ladders of silver to climb up into bed with, and silver neck chains. Into pillars of houses they beat silver studs and nails of gold on top of them."[35] Another version of this chronicle has it that the residents of Pate lived in elegant multistory houses with glass and porcelain, their beds inlaid with silver and ivory and their women offering a "foretaste of Islamic para-dise."[36] We learn something about what life there may well have been from none other than Fumo Liyongo, a hero of Swahili song and poetry (whom we shall meet again in chapter 7) who is said to have lived in the Pate region sometime between the ninth and thirteenth centuries. Liyongo composed a wedding song, "Utumbuizo wa Liyongo Harusini," that praises the good life of Pate's patricians.[37] In the song, aristocrats of high rank wear fine *hariri* "silk" clothes and well-made *zisutu,* or "clothes of dark red color worn by

women." They are scented with expensive perfumes available in great variety—*pacholi* (patchouli), which is an herb of the mint family; *zafarani*
(saffron); and *zabadi* (a perfume similar to that from ambergris). And their
halls are filled with sweet aromas from incense of *ambari* (ambergris) and
udi (aloe wood), pure musk of the civet, *zito za karafuu* (clove-buds), *itiri*
(good body oils), and *kafuri* (perfume from fine camphor). The wedding
gifts as related in the poem are *tumbitumbi miyongo miyongo*, that is, "numerous presents all arranged in tens," including *fedhati* (silver coins), *k'owa
za Hindi* (Indian armlets), *mikufu* (necklaces) that could "richly cover the
chest," and *makapu makapu ya nguo* (several baskets of garments).

Save for the names of perfumes and the nautical terminology, there is
almost a total absence of Arabic or Persian words in Liyongo's songs. Instead, the material world depicted in the elaborate descriptions of the Swahili city-states is expressed in the Bantu vocabulary of Swahili. If there is any
truth to the "golden rule of language"—whoever has the gold imparts their
language to those without—then the virtual absence of Arabic loanwords in
the Liyongo tradition and the presence of Bantu words termed Old Swahili
may be due to the rules of the genre of the poems.[38] But it also means that
the sheikhs and waungwana (of whom Liyongo was one) celebrated their
imported wealth in the local culture.

These infusions from overseas in the lives of waungwana people paralleled what happened in Anglo-Saxon England after the Norman invasion of
1066. The Norman Conquest introduced French customs and words into an
exclusively Anglo-Saxon culture. This influx led to the era when Norman
French became, for a time, the language of the English court. From then on,
the Anglo-Saxons built cathedrals in the French style, thereby imbuing the
Anglo-Saxon landscape itself with Norman culture. However, the blending
and mixing did not reproduce a French civilization but instead produced an
English cultural idiom. In like manner, the East African seaboard civilization remained Bantu, with an Islamic elite class claiming Arabic and Persian roots, even though we know that rulers with Arabic names were sons of
local people and that others with very Bantu-sounding names were in fact
Arabs, as we shall see in the Swahili chronicles.

Obviously, many other people in the towns were working to support the
high standard of living that the patrician sector of the Swahili society enjoyed. In 1505, the explorer Francisco d'Almeida said of Kilwa: "In this land
there are more negro slaves than white Moors. They work in the garden
tilling the maize."[39] Many accounts of the classic age of Swahili leave out

the other side of its grandeur, namely, "the vastly larger number of mud and wattle houses surrounding the coral houses at the Swahili town center, and the farmers, fishermen, masons, carpenters, leather workers, and boat builders who live there" (Nurse and Spear 1985, 22). In this less genteel side of all the towns mentioned previously, few people claimed aristocratic lineage or attended the Koranic madrassas or performed their prayers as required by Islamic law; instead, they clustered around rituals and practices to commune with ancestral spirits, engaging in what devout Muslims condemned as witchcraft and magic to protect themselves and whatever they owned. These were the demographic majorities of the Swahili, the founders of the villages that immigrant merchants later built into large towns. The less genteel Swahili women could ill afford to stay secluded indoors but had to work cultivating the crops, gathering firewood, and drawing water. Their men had to rise before dawn to go to their fishing grounds and work throughout the daylight hours. The written records of the classic era refer to the people in the less respectable parts of towns and villages as Zanj.

The vocabulary of the languages heard in these modest quarters, in the streets, and on the fishing shores shifted from the cosmopolitan speech of the patricians to the more local, more nyika, more agricultural inflections inherited from forebears on the African side of Swahili. Al Idrisi—the Arab traveler, geographer, and cartographer who had lived at the court of King Roger II in Sicily—thought that Malindi was a town of Zanj, primarily hunters and fishermen.[40] These Swahili populations on the fringes of the cities have kept Swahili a Bantu language at its core.

Mombasa was intimately connected with the nyika mainland at its height of prosperity. To build its mercantile interests in the Indian Ocean emporium, its merchants maintained ties with mainland populations, their sources for the commodities they sold (such as ivory, honey, and wax). Diplomacy was needed to keep in check the tensions inherent in financing this trade with the inlanders on credit. One famous characteristic of Mombasa is that it was "oft-times at war and but seldom at peace with people of the mainland, and they carry trade with them" (Barbosa 1866, 12). Nor was Kilwa in control of the Zanj: Ibn Battuta mentioned that the authorities there were constantly raiding the Zanj in a Muslim holy war waged against them as infidels. Immigrant Arabs thus did not dominate the Swahili coast in its classic period of prosperity. Rather, patrician families of local descent in prosperous towns affected the manners of their Islamic suppliers in their buildings, in their grooming and dress, and in their religion, surrounded by a diversity of local people. As a consequence, the Muslim religion gradually became prevalent along the littoral, but it had little appeal for the inland cultivators of the nyika, on whom the wealthy depended for the regional commodities they added to the gold of Sofala at the core of their Indian Ocean commerce.

The Linguistics of Archaeological Excavations

The finds in archaeological excavations tell us something about the people who lived in the time period revealed by carbon dating. A study of the names of things discovered at Kilwa and Shanga does tell us certain things about the Swahili language and culture. These farming communities are evident in archaeological excavations outside the walls of the towns. Research has indicated that the cultivators who settled on the coast in the last centuries BCE first adopted maritime knowledge and skills and founded the coastal settlements. Excavations at Kilwa show that inlanders and outsiders were partners in the growth and establishment of the city-state. According to Nurse and Spear (1985, 17–20), the earliest inhabitants of the city between 800 and 1000 CE ate fish, worked iron with local technologies, made pottery in local styles, and traded.[41] Without fussing too much about the words *fish, iron,* and *pottery,* it is worth mentioning the information we glean from their equivalents in Swahili. In Old Swahili, fish was called *swi,* a Bantu word present as *nswi* in Pokomo.[42] The Arabic word *samaki,* in current use for fish, was adopted later. As described in chapter 6, pots belong to the Swahili woman's world. The *chungu* is now used for cooking rice and the *kaango* for cooking fish, meat, and vegetables (Donley-Reid 1990). Potters (*wafinyanzi*) make all kinds of pots bearing Bantu names, including the ubiquitous *mtungi* (plural *mitungi*), an earthenware container for storing and cooling water, juice (such *togwa* juice made of sorghum), milk, and locally brewed beer. Even pieces of earthenware pots are called by the Bantu word *vigae.*

Postholes, red earth, and sorghum seeds dug up at Kilwa, dated to 1000–1200 CE, reveal that these farmers lived in rectangular mud and wattle (*msonge*) houses (*nyumba*). The first masons used squared coral blocks set in mud mortar as foundations for these structures of mud and wattle (Nurse and Spear 1985). The lexicon of the dig signals that the people of Kilwa at the turn of the millennium were indigenous: *udongo* (red earth/soil), *mtama* (sorghum), *kibanda cha udongo* (mud hut), and *fito* (shelter of clay and wattle); this last is currently also known as *nyumba ya mbavu za mbwa* (house [built] with ribs of dogs"), referring to the woven lattice of wooden strips on which daub (plaster made of mud) is applied to make the wall of a mud hut. The lexicon of the dig is all Bantu, indicating the foundations of Swahili language. The 1000–1200 period also witnessed an increase in the importation of sgraffito wares—ceramics with engraved slip from the eastern Mediterranean, dating to the ninth and tenth centuries and common by the classic Swahili era—and steatite stone bowls from Madagascar. The word for porcelain in Swahili is *kauri,* which is borrowed from the Hindi *kauri,* showing that Indians were early visitors.

After about 1200, Kilwa grew in size and acquired masonry houses and mosques (*misikiti*) made of coral blocks and lime mortar; there was a general expansion of trade, bringing the imported glass beads that replaced local shell ones. Though pottery making and ironworking continued in local styles, spindle whorls for spinning and copper coins were added, and Chinese porcelain appeared in increasing quantities. In the two following centuries (1300–1505 CE), elaborate and extensive building of stone structures marked Kilwa's high point, including domed extensions of the mosques. Chinese porcelain also became increasingly common, and local pottery, which continued its dominance, changed markedly in style. Local spinning and ironwork disappeared, though mud and wattle building persisted.

Excavations at Shanga—a town in the Lamu archipelago—reveal parallel innovations and growth, which archaeologists have categorized in five periods between 850 and 1440 CE.[43] In the initial period, 850–920 CE, Sassanian (Persia/Iran) Islamic, tin-glazed, and early sgraffito pottery wares were added to local ironworking, pottery, agriculture, and cattle herding. No clear indications of house structure have survived. The second period, 920–1020 CE, featured continuing styles of local ironworking, pottery, agriculture, and herding. Circular patterns of postholes overlaid by rectangular patterns indicate a change of building design from earlier—presumably local—circular layouts to rectangular patterns that were presumably introduced from elsewhere. Kilwa did not provide evidence of much imported pottery. The third period, 1020–1250 CE, saw further changes in architectural styles, as the residents at Shanga drove poles into square coral blocks and mud mortar foundations to support more durable wattle and daub walls. The first mosque at Shanga appears to have been built around 1120 CE, with the initial construction using coral rag (rough-shaped blocks of coral) and mud mortar for walls.[44] Islamic trade—and evidently resident merchants—seem to have inspired considerable local prosperity and with it (as mentioned in chapter 3) the "grafting" of

"Arabic words into an old bantu (the Swahili variety) tree,"[45] with even more coming in during the fourth period.

In the fourth period, 1250–1320 CE, resident patrician families apparently sponsored building with lime mortar and plaster to construct larger and more elaborate mosques with vaulted timber roofs. Ordinary dwellings, however, continued to be made of wattle and daub. The fifth period, 1320–1440 CE, exhibited an extensive use of coral rag and lime mortar in housing construction. One hundred and thirty-nine houses, two mosques, and a number of elaborate pillar tombs have been counted within walls that had recently been built around the town for protection. Evidently, local wealth was provoking someone's jealousy—among merchants of other towns, perhaps, or farmers of the nyika. The vaulted roof of the mosque was replaced with a flat coral one supported with heavy cross timbers. This classic period of prosperity exhibits larger amounts of imported potteries—celadons (a pale gray-green glazed ware from China), Chinese porcelains, and Islamic monochromes. The glazed and unglazed imported wares, glass, and beads from the Middle East, China, and India testify to the cosmopolitan nature of the Swahili coast in its commercial heyday. For the first time, we find, in the coral house floors and lime concrete, evidence of considerable technical sophistication in home construction—and no doubt an expansion of Swahili vocabulary and cultural influence from overseas. Thereafter, as archaeological evidence shows, the fall of Shanga came quickly, and the settlement was abandoned in 1440 CE.

Swahili Prosperity and Its Lexicon

Every prosperous moment in the history of a regional population gathers people of diverse origins together and elaborates its linguistic heritage. I have discussed how the mnazi and the sambo—the imported, indigenized, and later exported coconut and the ships that brought it to eastern Africa and then carried away its commercial products—were vital to Swahili life. And they have left an array of words, concepts, and allegorical meanings, all of which are highly specific and detailed as they relate to professional work. The mnazi represents the agricultural preoccupations of the Swahili, and it also was the bridge to the maritime components of Swahili society. That one can talk in Swahili about the intricate details of shipbuilding and find navigators skilled in using the compass is a modern reality rooted in the classic era of Swahili towns that saw the building of Swahili settlements such as Gedi, Mombasa, Malindi, Kilwa, and Sofala.

The classic Swahili civilization was not the result of some copy-and-paste approach, as was insinuated by certain colonial era proponents of its exotic origins; Chittick, you will recall, called it "a shipwreck" of another civilization on the coasts of eastern Africa. Rather, it was the product of knowledge acquisition, preservation, use, and dissemination by and among the coast's Bantu-speaking residents. Archaeology reveals a set of robust city-states with lifestyles that were impressive to visitors from the wealthiest centers of the Mediterranean Sea region and of southwestern Asia—prompting Ibn Battuta in 1331 CE to describe Kilwa as one of the world's best cities. Among the aspects of Swahili towns and local populations that were praised by cosmopolitan visitors were mastery of the ocean, including building and piloting ships using the compass; ample food supplies in most cities most of the time; textile manufacturing, especially at Mogadishu; and elite echelons of society living in luxury and guided in righteousness by Islamic law. In the background, of course, slave trading and slavery, skirmishes with neighbors in the nyika, and rampant wars and coerced tribute from other cities also supported the lifestyles of the rulers.

It is significant that the first mention of the word *Swahili* was made in the fourteenth century, right at the zenith of the classic era of Swahili commercial prosperity as the people were going about the business of conducting East Africa's Indian Ocean trade. The urban civilization on the east coast of Africa from around 1000 to 1500 CE was an amalgamation of contributions by the many peoples who congregated there, a cosmopolitan ethos of eager engagement with every kindred tongue and nation they encountered, and an embrace of anything they found enriching to their own lives. The first half of the second millennium CE was a time of relative peace, during which Swahili patricians grew wealthy, increased their knowledge and observance of Islam, and built stone cities with mosques and elaborate tombs. Then came the *mzungu* (the white man). The encounters that followed, the subject of the next chapter, were less productive.

CHAPTER 5

Consolidation of a Popular Language, 1500–1850s

Mreno hatamsahau Mswahili hadi kesho.
"The Portuguese will not forget the Swahili until tomorrow."
—Swahili saying

Kilichoniuma jana, uchunguwe nikauona, kamwe hakinitambai tena.
"That which caused me pain and agony yesterday shall not as much as crawl on me again."
—Swahili saying

THE SWAHILI encounter with the Portuguese is memorialized in these two proverbs. Proverbs arise from experience and often constitute a summary of knowledge about the world, as we will see in chapter 7. Here, for the Swahili to say that "the Portuguese will not forget the Swahili until tomorrow" tells us something about the troubling aspects of the Luso-Swahili experience. But as we know full well, "tomorrow never comes"—an English adage that is applicable in this context, for the Swahili see themselves as more than a vanishing memory from the Portuguese tenure in the Indian Ocean. It is significant that even though Arabs, Indians, Persians, and many other non-Swahili peoples also will not vanish from memory, it is to the Portuguese that the first proverb was directed. The second proverb, "That which caused me pain and agony yesterday shall not as much as crawl on me again," is a Swahili affirmation or at least evidence of a determination to learn from history, that is, not to forget the circumstances that are memorialized in the first proverb.

The Luso-Swahili encounter was dramatic and stormy, much like the maelstrom that erupts when the currents of two oceans converge. At their meeting point, the Atlantic and Indian Oceans collide, punch, and wrestle each other to exhaustion. Theirs is not a placid encounter but rather a very spirited struggle and intermixing in which there is no obvious winner or loser. The Mozambique-Agulhas current flowing south and west from the Indian Ocean meets up with (better still, crashes over) the Benguela current flowing north from Antarctica in the Atlantic and produces stormy weather and seas so rough that Bartholomew Dias, the first European on record to see this clash of currents, named the rocky promontory where they collide the Cape of Storms. Those storms are the dynamic products of the merger of the Indian and Atlantic Oceans.

This is an apt metaphor for the relations between the Swahili and the Portuguese successors of Dias in the years between 1500 and 1700 CE along the eastern coast of Africa. As we will see, the Portuguese planned to deliver a knockout punch to would-be opponents of their mission to establish control over the maritime trade of the western Indian Ocean and beyond to the Spice Islands of southeastern Asia. The Portuguese were mobile and seaborne and relied on bombarding the trading entrepôts of the region's merchants. In a manner of speaking, the Swahili transformed the takeover moves made by the Portuguese into a kind of dance in which they could, on occasion, steal or take on the leading role. In some instances, they feigned an embrace, befriended the Portuguese, and appeared to cooperate; in others, they rejected, rebelled, antagonized, and destabilized the Portuguese, often successfully frustrating the monarchy seated in faraway Portugal. This often tumultuous meeting up of a centralized superpower with a loose network of city-states is captured metaphorically in the clash of two contrasting currents intermixing in rough seas and producing storms that exhausted themselves, only to repeat the struggle with the next wave arriving on eastern Africa's Indian Ocean shores.

The prelude to these struggles dates to 1488 CE, when Bartholomew Dias, the Portuguese navigator, became the first European on record to sail around southernmost Africa's Cape Peninsula. As a consequence, Dias discovered that a sea route from Europe to India existed, even though he himself did not continue on to reach India. His discovery interested the Portuguese Crown a great deal. Dias named this southern tip the Cape of

Storms, but upon his return home, the Portuguese king, John II, changed the name to Cape of Good Hope—the name it bears to this date (with a Swahili translation as *Rasi Ya Tumaini Jema*)—because its discovery opened the rich promise of the Indian Ocean to Europe.[1]

The Portuguese combination of challenge and promise, struggling to turn "storms" into "hopes," persisted as Dias's successors continued north to Kilwa, Malindi, and Mogadishu and beyond to India and the archipelagos farther to the east. They challenged the Swahili to be at the top of their game to maintain their niche as Africa's agents in the trade of the western Indian Ocean. Like the meeting of the oceans, the Swahili-Portuguese encounters were often turbulent. The monsoons from the north brought in Muslim traders who were willing to work with and sometimes to become part of the Swahili cosmopolitan elite. However, the Europeans from the Atlantic side were Catholics with a pronounced hostility to Islam and a winner-take-all belligerency in trade, politics, and religion.

The two antithetical approaches, one Portuguese and the other Swahili, played themselves out at the Pan-Swahili coast for two centuries (1500 to 1700 CE). The situation culminated in a recession that left the area open to the establishment of a plantation economy introduced by Arabs from Oman, the sultanate at Muscat on the Arabian side of the straits leading to the Persian Gulf. The next century and a half (1700 to 1850 CE) was the era of heightened slaving, to provide workers for island plantations producing cloves and mainland estates producing foods for the slaves and the residents of growing cities. Because "the history of language is part of human history . . . not some mysterious surrogate process that goes bubbling along on its own," Swahili thrived as the new arrivals—Portuguese and later the enslaved people from the interior of Africa in the plantation economy—struggled to communicate with one another.[2]

Portuguese vocabulary entered the Swahili language, leaving tracks showing the extent and nature of Swahili involvement with the newcomers from the Atlantic. The evolving Swahili language spread inland along the trade routes, and many people—much like Jamezi, whom we met in chapter 2—were taken to the Swahili coast as slaves from as far inland as the Congo. Meanwhile, the wealthy Swahili of the towns were also using the Arabic script to write on topics and issues both old and new—a significant move toward standardizing the modern language, as will be described in chapter 9. The present chapter, then, is about the consolidation of Swahili as the coastal language, propelled by trade to become a lingua franca in the adjoining hinterland to the Great Lakes—a language with a landmark space we now term Africa's Swahili-speaking region, from the area's encounter with the Portuguese and the Omani to the arrival of the modern cohort of British and German colonizers.

The Swahili Lexicon Marking the Engagement with the Portuguese

The meeting between the Swahili and the Portuguese was a sea change for both. Dias's return to Portugal was followed by the dispatch of a fleet of ships around the cape to India. Vasco da Gama succeeded in reaching western India in 1500 CE by enlisting the services of pilots knowledgeable about the course from the Swahili maritime community. From the Swahili perspective, this initial encounter seemed potentially promising, bringing new cargoes and contacts. These imports came with new words from a strange language known as Kireno (from *reino,* or "kingdom," the word used by the Portuguese to refer to the sovereign and homeland in whose service they were sailing), and a new religion known as *Kikristo* (Christianity, with the *ki-* prefix classifying it along with other languages, such as Kiswahili). But the Portuguese insistence on exclusive control of the trade of the region tested the sovereignty that most Swahili cities had enjoyed and the cosmopolitanism that typified the lifestyle of the *wenyeji,* or "natives"—the exact attractions that had brought people together along the coast in the dynamic social engagements that had produced the diverse vocabulary of the language and the cultural openness of the coast.

The Portuguese asserted naval superiority with their mobile and heavily armed ships along the coast of eastern Africa during the two centuries from 1500 to 1700 CE. The beleaguered residents took in—and their descendants have continued to use—at least 120 Portuguese words, about a quarter of which are maritime related. Accordingly, the *barquinha,* from the diminutive for *barque* ("bark" is the cognate in English) is the word from which Swahili made the word *barakinya,* referring to a type of sailboat—the overtones here with *baraka,* "blessing," not escaping the Swahili—and also the *batela* (from *bateira*), another type of sailboat. Nautical vocabulary includes *boriti* (from *barrote*) for "beam," the transverse member of a ship's frame used to support the deck and to brace the sides against stress; *roda* (also *roda* in Portuguese, meaning "wheel" or anything that revolves) for "winch," a mechanical device used to pull in (wind up) or let out (wind out) and otherwise adjust the tension of a line on a ship; and the word *boya* (from *boia,* or "float"), which is used for "buoy."

The Portuguese must have come with decks of playing cards, obviously useful for passing time during their long voyages at sea. The basic lexicon of card games in Swahili is derived from Portuguese. The word *karata*, "game of cards," is from Portuguese *carta*, "card," and *pao* (from *pau*, or "stick," usually wood) is the suit of "clubs." "Club" is called *karanga*, "peanuts" or *mavi ya mbuzi*, "excreta of goats," because goat droppings come in peanut-sized pellets; *shupaza* (from *espadas*, "spades") is currently also called *jembe*, "spade"; the "ace of spades" is called *dume la shupaza/jembe*; *kopa* (from *copa*, "top" or "crown") is "hearts," which is also called *moyo*, the Swahili for "heart"; *uru* (from *ouro*, "gold") is "diamonds" in English; and *turufu* (from *trunfo*) is a "trump"—the card chosen out of a pack that is in the suit that "triumphs" over the other cards in play. The fact that we also have the word *dadu* (from *dado*, a "die" or "datum"), meaning a "game especially of dice," and *dama* (from *damas*, the "queens") or "checkers"[3] shows that the Portuguese are also memorialized in the Swahili lexicon in association with games of dice and checkers. Playing cards may well have been one way of passing time for the Portuguese who were locked up at Fort Jesus in Mombasa for long periods at the end of the seventeenth century, after relations between them and the Mombasans went sour.

In addition, the Swahili adopted Portuguese words relating to the flora that the Portuguese brought with them as they indigenized these plants. These include *caraco*, for "cashew nuts", from which Swahili made the word *korosho*; *limao*, from *limão*, for "lemon"; *ananas*, "pineapple," which became *nanasi* in Swahili; *pera* (Portuguese for "pear"), which remained the same word but was used for a different fruit, the local guava; and *zambarau* (from *jambulão*[4]), "java plum fruit." Once a Bantu language takes in the name of a fruit, the name of the plant that produces it is formed by adding *m-* (for the singular) and *mi-* (for the plural) as prefixes to the names of the fruit—*mkorosho*, "cashew plant"; *mlimao*, "lime tree"; *mnanasi*, "pineapple plant"; *mpera*, "guava tree"; and *mzambarau*, "java fruit tree." By this regular Bantu process of creating words by extending roots, adaptation of such terms into Swahili was complete. And by giving plants bona fide names in their language, the Swahili signaled that they not only consumed them as foreign exotica but also grew them.

The martial aspect of the Portuguese presence in Swahili territory is reflected in the word *bastola*, "pistol" (from *pistola*). The pistol was one of the earliest small firearms the Swahili had seen, and thus, they had to borrow its name from the foreigners who arrived armed with it and prepared to use it.

Similarly, the word *bendera* (from *bandeira*), meaning "flag" or "pennant," speaks to the arrival of new symbols of military power and the notion of political allegiance to an abstract authority (the *reino,* or "kingdom") rather than to known persons, patrons, and families. Other cultural markers from the Portuguese world are the *chapeo* (from *chapeu*), for "hat with brim," and the unmistakable *shumburere* (from Spanish *sombreiro*), "hat," which the sailors from Portugal must have brought along on their voyages. The *leso* (from *lenço*), at first denoting "handkerchief" or "scarf," has evolved to denote a piece of cloth decorated with words, patterns, and objects; it was initially used by dignified ladies in Mombasa and then became synonymous with the kanga cloth that Swahili women wrap around themselves in many fashionable ways.

Other words that testify to the engagement of the Swahili with the Portuguese include: *foronya,* "pillow" (from *fronha*); *bomba,* "pillowcase" (from *bomba,* "pump"); *batata,* "a type of potato" (from *batata*); *pipa,* "barrel" (from *pipa*); *kopo,* "can/tin" (from *copo*); *vinho,* "wine," (taken in as *mvinyo* and extended to include distilled spirits); *tarumbeta,* "trumpet" (from *trombeta*); and *mbolea,* "manure" (from *boleo,* "droppings," though not in modern Portuguese).

Though we may not know the precise circumstances under which particular words entered into Swahili usage, the semantic fields provide us with some idea of the general nature of the conversations between local residents and the Portuguese. The Swahili were evidently not tempted to become Lusophone, as they adjusted the Portuguese words that they found useful to adhere to Bantu pronunciation. Swahili and Bantu languages more generally do not allow certain sequences of consonants. The consonant cluster /fr/, common in Romance and Germanic languages, is not found in Bantu; hence, the Portuguese word *fronha* was taken in as *foronya* by inserting /o/ between /f/ and /r/. Likewise the /rt/ in *carta* became *karata* and much the same happened with the vowels inserted in *trunfo* → *turufu*, *trombeta* → *tarumbeta, espadas* → *shupaza*, and *sombreiro* → *shumburere.*

Similarly, since Swahili words never end in consonants, the Portuguese plural that ends in /s/ disappeared, so *ouros* became *uru, damas* came in as *dama*, and so forth. Alternatively, Swahili added the required concluding vowel: consequently, *ananas* became *nanasi*. Some Bantu-sounding Portuguese words remained unchanged—for example, *pipa, batata, kopo, and pera.* Swahili does make the contrast between /l/ and /r/, so the shift from /l/ to /r/ in the borrowing appears unwarranted until one recognizes that the speakers of Swahili originally spoke Bantu languages where either the /l/ and /r/ difference was not made or the /l/ did not exist. For speakers of a good number of Bantu languages, it is a challenge to make the distinction effortlessly.

The Luso-Swahili Encounter

The Swahili-Luso engagement that generated the lexical adaptations that are important parts of the Swahili language today began in 1498. Bartholomew Dias's report of a possible opening to the Indian Ocean was heartily received upon his return to Portugal, and further voyages were planned. To fulfill the hope, the Portuguese Crown appointed explorer Vasco da Gama to lead an expedition of four ships. They left Lisbon on July 8, 1497, destined for India via Africa. Sailing around the southern tip of Africa, da Gama reached the Cape of Good Hope on November 22, 1497, and continued on to the Swahili city of Sofala (in modern Mozambique), where he arrived on May 2, 1498. Da Gama wrote in his ship's log that he found "infinite gold" there. He also called in at other towns along the coast and discovered what he reported as their treasures. The authorities in some towns, such as Malindi, received him well; others, among them the leaders in Mombasa, did not welcome him.

At all points along East Africa's Indian Ocean littoral, da Gama encountered people whom he termed "idolaters," as well as Muslims, whom he referred to as "Moors." *Moor* was a word used throughout Spain and Portugal for Muslims, reflecting an ethnocentricity that designated non-Christians—particularly those perceived as darker in complexion—as different and unequal. For da Gama, Andalusians, Moroccans, and the Swahili were all Moors. In addition, he and other Portuguese who traveled to East Africa tended to equate the Muslim religion with Arab ethnicity, and that did not comport with the many ethnically African Muslims of the Swahili cities. The Portuguese thus introduced polarized distinctions of hierarchy based on a combination of race and religion—idolaters (black and uncivilized) and moors (dark-skinned Muslims) were contrasted with the Portuguese, who considered themselves superior in being both Christian and white. It is no surprise that the Swahili never adopted the *moor* into their language, even though the Portuguese presumably used it there among themselves and publicly.

The sultan of Mozambique Island, well to the north of Sofala, provided da Gama with an Indian pilot, Ibn Majid, who guided the explorer to Calicut,

India, where the expedition arrived on May 20, 1498. After loading his ships with spices, da Gama returned home and reported to his king about the immense wealth, including much gold, that he had seen on the Swahili coast. He also noted the prevalence of Islam and the independent cities that were immediately seen as sitting ducks, ready for the taking by the powerful Portuguese Crown.

The renaming of the Cape of Storms as the Cape of Good Hope turned a mariner's encounter with the challenge of the seas into a symbol of optimism for the Portuguese—the calm after the storm. But for the Swahili, the introduction of another entire ocean (the Atlantic) into the logic of the Indian Ocean was no small matter. In fact, it marked an end to the Swahili heyday that had extended for roughly three centuries. If the Portuguese saw calm after the storm, the Swahili experienced a storm after centuries of calm, due to the bellicose manner in which the Portuguese arrived at the Swahili coast and sought to overturn everything. For their part, the Swahili were prepared to domesticate the Portuguese, something they had done with Arabs and Indians for centuries.

The Portuguese hoped to take control of East Africa's portion of the Indian emporium, but the Swahili were not prepared to give in or let go. The Portuguese believed that their large cannonaded ships would terrify the Swahili into relinquishing their role as successful trade middlemen and become God-fearing servants of their king. The problem was that this expectation required the Swahili to change their orientation from the holy lands of Islam to face west, where a faraway European monarch who was a sworn enemy of Islam demanded subservience.

The Portuguese had sharpened their skills as brutal conquerors during the vicious Reconquista wars of the Iberian Peninsula (710–1492 CE), from which they emerged as victors. Over these eight centuries, the Portuguese, among other Christian populations in the peninsula, had developed a militant hostility toward Islam. The expulsion of Moors from the Iberian Peninsula at the final Castilian conquest of Granada in 1491 CE, almost simultaneously with Dias's turning of the Cape of Storms, was viewed as a religious victory of Christianity over Islam, and this crusade mentality against Islam was still vibrant by the time of the Portuguese arrival on Africa's eastern coast less than a decade later. As G. S. P. Freeman-Grenville puts it, in going to eastern Africa the Portuguese were driven by a "desire to increase geographical knowledge; to expand Portuguese trade, to discover the real strength of the enemy Moors, to find Christian princes whose aid might be enlisted against them (Moors), and finally to make increase in the faith of our Lord Jesus Christ and to bring him all the souls that should be saved."[5]

The Portuguese were inspired to relentless religious conquest especially by the legend of one Prester John, a rumored Christian king who had been besieged by Muslims and nonbelievers somewhere to the east, beyond the Islamic Mediterranean. Reaching the land of this legendary king captured the imagination of all of Christian Europe from the twelfth to the seventeenth centuries, and the Portuguese in the Indian Ocean found themselves in the lead. Ethiopia, situated in the horn of northeastern Africa, fit the bill. It was a Christian kingdom that was experiencing threats from neighboring Muslim sultans, especially Harar, as well as the Galla (Oromo), pastoralists who qualified as nonbelievers. The existing conflicts made the region ripe for the Portuguese to insert themselves. In 1490, Pero da Covilhã arrived in Ethiopia by land, believed the monarch who welcomed him there to be Prester John, and presented him with a letter from the king of Portugal. The letter, which was addressed to Prester John, was the beginning of the Portuguese attempt to establish influence over the Indian Ocean and to convert Ethiopia from its Coptic style of Christianity to Catholicism. Not surprisingly, the religious zealotry of the Portuguese resulted in bitter religious conflicts, which culminated a century later in the expulsion of all foreign missionaries during the 1630s and an Ethiopian hostility toward the Portuguese that was to last until the mid-nineteenth century.[6]

Pope Nicholas V charged the Portuguese with a crusading mission in an officially sealed bull to Afonso, king of Portugal, authorizing him "to conquer, to besiege, to fight, and to submit all the Saracens, Pagans, and other enemies of Christ, wherever they may be; and to seize the kingdoms, the dukedoms, the princedoms, the lordships, personal properties, landed properties . . . to submit these persons to a perpetual slavery; to appropriate . . . and make use of them personally and with their offspring."[7] Consequently, the Portuguese arrived on the east coast of Africa intent not only upon controlling the trade of the western Indian Ocean but also upon converting the Swahili to Catholicism, by force if necessary. Having been schooled in the caustic rivalries of Europe, the Portuguese fell upon the tolerant and cosmopolitan Swahili with a ferociousness unlike anything the local population had ever encountered. The independent Swahili city-states looked like easy prey: as separate entities, they could not quickly assemble a united front, and each seemed to be pursuing its own agenda with regard to government and trade. The Portuguese could move swiftly by sea to bombard them, one by one. Many city-states had only fragile diplomatic alliances with inland Africans, perhaps deliberately in order to be free to deal with as many trading partners as possible, and the Portuguese also took full advantage of this apparent vulnerability. They imposed tributes and loyalties on the city-states with considerable ease, and they plundered and burned cities each time the Swahili resisted, faltered, or failed to pay tribute.

But the Swahili never gave in. The more the Portuguese tried to overwhelm them, the more the Swahili proved resilient. They became more and more dispersed, even to the extent of evacuating a city and disappearing into the hinterland among their relatives and allies when the Portuguese arrived in full force by sea. The goal of converting the Swahili, cosmopolitan and Muslim as they were, to a docile and subservient people remained elusive for two centuries, and in the end, the Portuguese found they had incurred enormous costs trying to tame the Swahili, with little success. Prior to the Portuguese, no military power had attempted to conquer the independent cities. The Swahili elite enjoyed prosperous, even extravagant lifestyles, and it is not surprising that they fought hard to keep their independence. Indeed, these people knew what it was like to live as masters attended by servants and slaves, and they had no intention of relinquishing their privileges. They lived in secure city houses filled with the luxuries of their overseas trade, but they also observed on a daily basis the difficult lives of village laborers, who lived in mud huts. The threat of being forced into slavery by the Portuguese sustained a vigilant defiance. The Swahili were also fiercely protective of their religion, and they did not readily accept outside faiths—recall that they had taken several hundred years to embrace Islam fully. Thus, the Portuguese invaders' insistence that they convert immediately to Catholicism was viewed as a declaration of cultural and religious war. The Swahili reacted with fierce and creative resistance on all fronts, succeeding in their goal of making the Swahili coast a costly and ungovernable region for the Portuguese.

Among the cities that the Portuguese destroyed was Kilwa, the city that Ibn Battuta in the fourteenth century called "one of the most beautiful and well-constructed towns in the world." Kilwa had controlled the gold trade from Sofala in the south, and by the fifteenth century, it had its own coinage, which was used from Sofala to areas as far north as Mafia (Oliver and Mathew 1963, 131). The Portuguese razed Kilwa and deposed its sultan. Hans Mayr, a German merchant aboard one of the ships of the Portuguese viceroy of India, Francisco d'Almeida, recorded the massacre of Kilwa and observed that "in this land there are more negro slaves than white Moors who work in the gardens tilling the maize"[8]—and the slave population drawn mainly from the hinterland had a significant influence on the Swahili language.

The Portuguese also repeatedly ransacked the city of Mombasa until it was utterly destroyed. They "cut down all the trees and shrubs in the island, destroyed all boats in the creeks," and murdered many residents, leaving "no living thing in it, neither man nor woman, young or old, nor child, however little: all who failed to make their escape had been killed or burnt" (Knappert 1979, 9–10). Taking away booty always accompanied the destruction.

During this time, the Muslim Ottomans were steadily gathering imperial strength throughout the eastern Mediterranean, conquering the eastern orthodox Christian capital at Constantinople in 1453 CE. They too eyed the wealth in trade in the western Indian Ocean, including in the Swahili country, and launched fleets against Portuguese positions from the 1550s onward. One Mir Ali Bey, thought to have been either a commander of a Turkish fleet or an unscrupulous adventurer, made overtures in the cities of the Swahili that ended in riots against the Portuguese invaders. On his first visit to the Swahili coast in 1585 CE, Ali Bey managed to convince Mombasa, Mogadishu, Barawa, Pate-Yunga, Lamu, and Faza to submit to the Ottoman sultan, who also claimed the mantle of the caliph—worldly commander of the faithful and heir to the Prophet—of Islam. That a mere promise of support from someone who arrived in a single Turkish ship and whose credentials were unclear could instigate a revolt in a string of Swahili city-states is testament to the determination of the Swahili to seek alternatives to the Portuguese. The Portuguese were so violently hated that Ali Bey was received everywhere with open arms.[9]

For their part, the Portuguese already had defeated the Ottomans in the eastern Mediterranean, so they saw Ali Bey's campaign as an unjustified attack on their power and position in the region, as well as an Islamic affront to Christianity. For the Portuguese, the cooperation of the Swahili with Muslims was unforgiveable, and they punished offenders thoroughly for it. In 1587, a Portuguese fleet violently quashed the rebellion and simultaneously dismantled a number of Swahili town dynasties. The king of Lamu was deposed and fled, and the king of Pate claimed pardon on the pretext that he had been forced to join the Turks. The king of Mombasa fled to safety as the Portuguese began to burn his city's houses and cut down coconut palms, although he subsequently negotiated forgiveness in return for paying a substantial fine (Knappert 1979, 11). The citizens of Faza and their king—known by the rebel name Sitambuli, meaning "I don't recognize" in Swahili[10]—were massacred by the Portuguese. The victors reportedly sent Sitambuli's head to Goa as a trophy, and the city's fishing boats and ten thousand coconut trees all were destroyed.

In 1588 CE, following the brutal Portuguese punishment of the Swahili rebellion, Mir Ali Bey returned again, this time with five ships instead of one. On this second occasion, he was welcomed in Mogadishu, rejected by Malindi, and finally defeated by the Portuguese in Mombasa. He went into hiding in the city of Mombasa, where the Portuguese eventually found him and arrested him. Ever the adventurer, Ali Bey is said to have converted to Christianity then (Strandes 1968, 134–39), though we may assume that his conversion was a strategic one designed to save his life more than his soul. Following the mass rebellions Ali Bey prompted, he became "something of a myth among the East African Muslims" (Knappert 1979, 12).

Amir Ali Bey's adventures at the Swahili coast were by no means the only Ottoman overtures to their coreligionists in the Swahili cities. Though the Turks did not impinge on Swahili lands, the presence of Turkish words in Swahili vocabulary indicates their felt presence there. It is difficult to say precisely how Swahili speakers took these in, since Amir Ali Bey's escapades in the region were brief. However, his jailing of dissenters, his use of ambassadors to ensure allegiance to the Ottoman sultan, and above all the Swahili hope of Muslim deliverance from the Portuguese Catholics were the sorts of conditions that often led to the adoption of new borrowings into the Swahili language. Of course, it may be that these words did not come into Swahili from direct contacts with Turkish but rather through such other languages as Arabic and Persian (although this narrative goes well beyond the focus of this book). Some examples of the Turkish influence on the Swahili language are the words *balyus*, "ambassador" (in Swahili *balozi*); *bughsha*, "envelope" (*bahasha*); and *caixa*, "wooden box" (*kasha*). Turkish loanwords are especially prevalent in military and police matters, as reflected in such terms as *efendy*, "sir" (police/military) (in Swahili *afendi/afande*); *tapo*, "troop, regiment"; *baioneti*, "bayonet" (*bayoneti* in Swahili); *baruti*, "gunpowder/ explosives"; and *kohkoni*, "jail" (Swahili *korokoroni*) (Knappert 1979, 40).

Swahili Domestication of the Portuguese

As soon as da Gama arrived in Mombasa, the Swahili attempted to cut the anchors of his ships so that they could destroy the vessels when they drifted ashore. Da Gama then fled to Malindi, but he never forgave Mombasans for their hostility. Force superseded diplomacy and led to a series of clashes during the two hundred years of Portuguese aggression. But the greatest form of resistance that the Swahili marshaled against the Portuguese was their resilience and willingness to fight and rebuild their lives and their cities, time and again.

Since the gold of East Africa was of extreme importance in the Indian Ocean trade, the Portuguese had to fight not only the Africans but also the Arabs and others. The Swahili of Mombasa were so unrelenting in their resolve that the Portuguese could live there securely only by building a fort, the famous Fort Jesus. Built in 1593 CE, Fort Jesus was strategically placed to fight off hostile incoming ships. It also served as a Portuguese refuge from the Swahili townspeople and mainland Africans. It is likely that the words *Kristo*, "Christ" (from Portuguese *Cristo*), and *Yesu* (from *Jesus*) were heard in Swahili during the Portuguese presence and then became part of the Swahili lexicon through the work of missionaries in the late nineteenth century. The name Fort Jesus was clearly not intended to appeal to Muslims but rather to mock and even undermine their deity. And try they did. The word *gereza,* meaning "prison" in Swahili, comes from *igreja,* the Portuguese word for "church." Perhaps this creative semantic shift reveals the attitudes of Muslim Swahili, who reacted with hostility to Portuguese Christian pressures and wryly observed that the Portuguese built churches in their fortresses, including Fort Jesus in Mombasa, to shield their houses of worship from the contamination of Islam.

Swahili resistance is best illustrated by a succession story about a "tyrant" king of Mombasa. The story has it that when the Shirazi ruler of Mombasa died with no apparent heir, the Portuguese captain of Mombasa placed al-Hasan ibn Ahmad, king of Malindi, as ruler of Mombasa because of the latter's loyalty. Upon experiencing political tensions, King Ahmad went to Goa, the Portuguese administrative headquarters in the western Indian Ocean, to ask for assistance but was given only verbal assurances, which he found unconvincing. This prompted him to flee inland to live with the *nyika,* the inland Africans who, instigated by the Portuguese, proceeded to murder him. Since Ahmad's son Yusuf was too young to succeed him, the Portuguese sent the boy to Goa to receive a Christian education. Yusuf returned to Mombasa in 1630 CE as an adult with a new name, Dom Hieronimo Chingulia, and with a Portuguese wife. As Muslims, the people of Mombasa understandably would not accept a Christian as sultan. Yusuf thus converted back to Islam, much to the dismay of the Portuguese. On the Feast of the Assumption on August 15, 1631, as the apostate Portuguese puppet on the Mombasa throne, Dom Hieronimo Chingulia (also known as Yusuf Chingulia) initiated an attack on the Portuguese who had gathered for the festival. He killed a majority of the residents who refused to disavow their Christian faith and all of the Portuguese, save four priests and one layman, and sent at least four hundred Christians as slaves to Mecca (Oliver and Mathew 1963, 140). Yusuf then called for other city-states to revolt. With that prompt, the kings of Utondwe, Manda, Luziwa, Chwaka, Pate, Siu, Pemba, Tanga, and Mtang'ata, all of whom had refused to pay tribute to the Portuguese, rose up in defiance. At the end of 1631, the Portuguese in Goa sent a fleet to punish the rebels. At Mombasa, the residents used Fort Jesus against its own architects when they starved out the occupants, in collaboration with Arabs in the region. After another attempt in 1632 CE, the city of Mombasa was found in ruins and the fort abandoned. Yusuf led his followers to stir this series of revolts from 1631 to 1637 CE before he died at Jiddah, the Red Sea port serving Mecca. He is remembered as "the tyrant king" in the Portuguese record (Oliver and Mathew 1963, 141).

Through this crisis, we learn something about the very human inroads that the Swahili and the Portuguese had made with each other—there were converts to Catholicism, and there were personal relationships, friendships, and other connections that produced conflicting reactions in moments of heightened crisis where loyalties were at stake. From this turmoil came one of Swahili literature's most significant bonuses—a poem, one of the oldest extant pieces in fact, composed by a woman during the Portuguese evacuation of Fort Jesus in Mombasa when the townspeople rose against the Europeans' coercive mistreatment of the Mombasans. According to William E. Taylor (1891, 95), "an old gentle woman" learned of the planned massacre and hastily composed a song to warn Miguel, a Portuguese friend who was a padre, about the impending calamity. Evidently, the Swahili knew Miguel had made friends among the townspeople. The words to the song are:[11]

Mzungu Migeli, u muongo	Miguel the European, you are a liar
Mato yako yana t'ongo!	Your eyes have tongo[12]
Kwani kuata mpango	Why leave the troop
Kwenda kibanga uani?	To go to a hut in the courtyard?

The old lady instructed her maidservant to sing the song outside Miguel's window until he asked her to stop. Miguel understood the message sent to him through the song and was able to escape to the safety of a boat waiting in the port on the day of the massacre.[13] A treasure in Swahili, the song speaks to the complex relationships that had evolved between the Swahili and the Portuguese—to the point that, apart from martial conflict or defeat, hearts and minds were also at play in the various encounters. And why should that not be the case? We do not know the nature of relationship between the old gentle woman and Miguel other than that it was a caring one. But for the community more broadly, cohabitation was obviously one avenue through which children grew up hearing Portuguese and at the same time developed affinities to multiple identities.

With regard to language, the ode introduces us to an early example of the Swahili dialect of Mombasa known as Kimvita. In the poem to Miguel, the words *mato* (eyes) and *kuata* (to leave) in Kimvita are, respectively, *macho* and *kuacha* in Kiunguja—the dialect from which the standard variety of Swahili is drawn. Examples of the Kimvita sound /t/ occurring as /ch/ in Kiunguja are numerous, as the following Kimvita/Kiunguja pairs indicate: *mtawi* (witch) is *mchawi*, *mtuzi* (gravy) is *mchuzi*, *tui* (leopard) is *chui*, *mtele* ([uncooked] rice) is *mchele*, and *kitwa* (head) is *kichwa*.[14] The /t/ and /ch/ difference in Kimvita cannot be considered stereotypical, as there are many instances in which the sound variation does not happen. Words in which *ki* is a prefix use the *ch*, so that *ki-akula* is rendered *chakula* (food), *ki-angu* is *changu* (mine), *ki-umba* is *chumba* (room), *ki-ura* is *chura* (frog), and *ki-uo* is *chuo* (book) (or *kitabu* in Kiunguja, taken from Arabic), just to mention a few examples. These and borrowed words such as *chai, chaki,* and many other words that begin with *ch* whose plural forms begin with *ma* (such as *chungwa/machungwa,* or "orange/oranges," and *chenza/machenza,* or "tangerine/tangerines") do not change the /ch/ into /t/ in Kimvita.[15] Mombasa Swahili (that is, Kimvita) actually belongs to an older civilization than Kiunguja, so it is more appropriate to view Kiunguja as the dialect in which Swahili became altered in transit.[16]

The ode also provides information about the Swahili word *mzungu* (white person). It is clearly not a derogatory word, since we see the beloved Miguel is addressed by that term. The word was in use during the reign of the Portuguese. The Bantu root form is *zungu*, which has a range of meanings—strange, surprising, startling, clever, a feat, a trick, instinct, or any device or expedient for getting out of a difficulty. The personalized form of the word is a rich one in Swahili. In addition to being adapted to refer to Palo Alto as *uzunguni* (white country), as opposed to the *uswahilini* (poor neighborhood) of East Palo Alto, as mentioned in chapter 1, the word is used to describe picture cards in a deck of playing cards. The queen is *mzungu wa pili* (the second white person, with a score of two); the jack is *mzungu wa tatu* (the third white person, with a score of three); and the king is *mzungu wa nne* (the fourth white person, which means the king scores four). Clearly, cards was a mzungu game at that time.

Swahili resistance, embodied by Yusuf, and the affectionate embrace, signified by the ode to Miguel, combine to explicate the adage headlining this chapter: *Mreno hatamsahau Mswahili hadi kesho*—The Portuguese will not forget the Swahili until tomorrow." This saying reveals a conflict between two frames, the elite authoritarian and the intimate. The authoritarian frame was solely about having the upper hand in ruling the cities; the intimate from was about interpersonal relations (friendships, cohabitation, and the like). On rulership, the Arabic history of Kilwa records this observation: "Those who knew the truth confirmed that they [the Portuguese] were corrupt and dishonest persons who had only come to spy out the land in order to seize it."[17] But on the interpersonal, we have Miguel's case, portraying a Luso-Swahili social scene that contradicts the political image. At Malindi, where the Portuguese were well received, the angst about control was very much in the townspeople's minds. At first blush, Malindians saw the Portuguese as "bringers of war and corruption, and were troubled with very great fear" that made them cooperate in giving the foreigners "all they asked, water, food, firewood, and everything else" (Freeman-Grenville 1962, 140–41). Meanwhile, as the years wore on, the social networks between people were developing. This partially explains why the vocabulary borrowed from Portuguese into Swahili (discussed earlier) involves much more than war and uprisings: we get terminology for foods, wine, nautical items, card games, utensils and containers, and fruits and fruit trees—something more than just control-oriented words such as *bastola*, "pistol" (*pistola* in Portuguese), or *bendera*, "flag" or "pennant" (from the Portuguese *bandeira*). This resulted in the intake of *igreja*, Portuguese for "church," as *gereza*, or "prison," in Swahili, clearly a subversive switch. With the famous siege of 1632 during which the Portuguese remained locked up in Fort Jesus, one can relate to just how useful *karata* (playing cards) must have been to the besieged—an interesting merging of the martial with the social and a situation in which the volatile outside world had a calm, albeit ominous, inside dimension.

Eventually, the Portuguese reduced the armed confrontations with the rulers of coastal towns and began establishing alliances and collaborations with them. The commercial agents in the cities depended on the goods and services of the region for their own prosperity, and wars made it impossible to conduct business (Newitt 2002, xvii). Because of the independent city-state model, the Swahili were able to respond to Portuguese incursions in many creative albeit small ways, which ultimately led the frustrated and exhausted Portuguese to accept the established framework of the Swahili emporium. The city-states forced the Portuguese to concentrate on rewarding friendly cities and punishing those that resisted, instead of treating them all as a single entity. In addition, the Swahili often escaped inland when they were overwhelmed, leading the Portuguese to the realization that they could never take over the Swahili city-states without also defeating inland Africans. Interestingly, the word *mvita* (which is another name for Mombasa) is said to be derived from two sources, *vita* (war) and *ficha* (hide). The more popular term is *mvita,* for it underscores the warlike stance that the ruling elites of Mombasa took against invaders. The less well known term is *mfita* (one who hides), for Mombasans were known to flee to the hinterland when necessary to escape war, as when the Wapate (Pate people) swept down the coast or whenever the Portuguese attacked.[18] Thus, the very source of the word *mvita* tells us something about the ruling elite politics of war and also about a place where the Mombasans mingled with the people of the hinterland in an effort to save their lives.

By the early 1700s, the Swahili and the Omani Arabs made a concerted effort to expel the Portuguese from the entire Swahili coast, and save for the far southern portion beyond Mozambique Island, they succeeded. The constant uprisings staged by the Swahili and decreasing profits from the Indian Ocean trade, combined with the unwelcome intrusions of the Omani Arab, Dutch, and British interests in the region, made control of the East African littoral a very costly venture for the Portuguese.

Slavery and the Spread of Swahili Inland

In 1698, after a long siege of Fort Jesus in Mombasa, the Arabs from Oman finally defeated the Portuguese and kicked them away from the East African coast for good. Attempts by the Portuguese to take over Mombasa in 1728 and again in 1769 failed. The Portuguese exited at a time when the Swahili economy was in recession. The sultans of Oman, led by Sayyid Said, resorted to a plantation economy in order to foster recovery. The sultanates invested heavily in growing crops for export, using slave labor. The Swahili economy continued to depend on material resources inland, and African inlanders continued to serve as porters of cargoes; they were also considered commodities to be bargained for, used, and sold. Over time, the linguistically and ethnically diverse population of slaves from the hinterland not only contributed their DNA to the Swahili makeup but also left a legacy of lexical and cultural practices in Swahili life.

Slave trading grew markedly in the 1730s, and within a very short time, large plantations developed (Harris 1971). This demand for labor increased the numbers of traders, trade routes, and slave caravans. Absent modern mechanized farming, importing slaves as laborers was the only way to boost production. Most slaves were captured far inland, as far as central Africa. Slaves "were made to carry ivory with them from the interior, and on their arrival at the coast they and their ivory were sold," according to Joseph E. Harris (1971, 6–7). Some slaves were kept to work the plantations on the coast and islands; others were shipped to various locations, including Muscat (Oman), India, the Mascarene Islands (then French Bourbon and Île de France, east of Madagascar), the Seychelles, and Zanzibar and Pemba just offshore, among many other destinations. The Mascarene Islands and the Seychelles were French sugar plantation colonies that depended on slave labor from the mid-1730s to 1810. Also absorbing large numbers of slaves were coastal towns and adjacent islands, led by Zanzibar, where rice and clove plantations became legendary. There were reports at the time of Hindu merchants (*banyans*) in Zanzibar buying and selling slaves and becoming wealthy, though they themselves did not travel inland to search for slaves. The Arabs of the sultanates who owned plantations were the main slave buyers, and the slave dealers were usually Swahili; the Swahili also served as armed guards and porters in the caravans sent into the interior, carrying textiles and other imports to offer in exchange for slaves.

The more northerly trade routes, starting from Mombasa and Tanga and extending into present-day Kenya, involved little slave traffic. Instead, most of the slave trade routes began on the coast opposite Zanzibar at Bagamoyo and Pangani, thereby avoiding the pastoralist Maasai, who are recorded as having denied the rights of passage through their territory. The Maasai exclusion of slave traders diverted the route from Tanga through the region of the Chagga on the southern slopes of Mount Kilimanjaro, as can be seen on map 5.1. These trade routes were instrumental in spreading Kiunguja (Zanzibar) Swahili to the far reaches of the interior, wherever the trade caravans went.

When the Portuguese pulled out of the Swahili coast, the Ya'ruba dynasty (1624–1744 CE), led by Yarubi Arabs, ruled Oman. The sultan of Oman (at

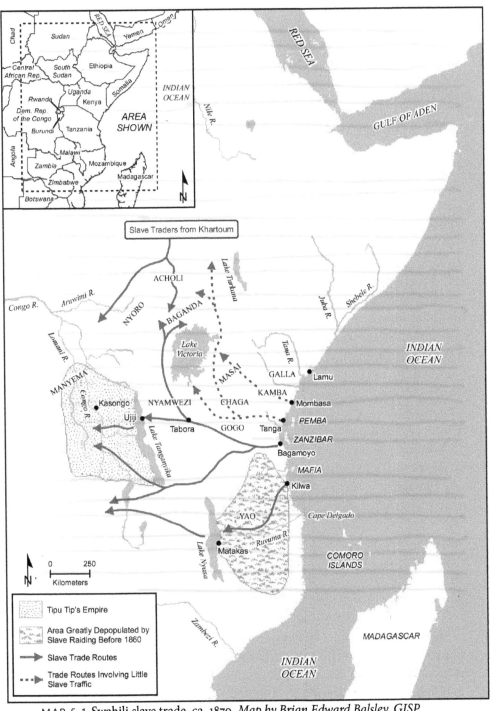

MAP 5.1 Swahili slave trade, ca. 1870. *Map by Brian Edward Balsley, GISP*

the time going by the title imam) appointed a governor, or *liwali,* to oversee Zanzibar, Lamu, and Mombasa, which were distant Omani possessions. When the Yarubi were replaced by the Busaidi dynasty after a long civil war, the new ruler, Ahmad bin Said al Busaidi, installed governors from the Busaidi family in Zanzibar, Pemba, Lamu, and Kilwa, but Mombasa remained under the rulership of the Mazruis, a rival Omani family. What followed were high-stakes intrigues involving murder, betrayal, and exile, played out between the Mazruis and the Busaidi Omanis. The latter prevailed.[19]

In 1804, Ahmad bin Said died in battle, and his two sons, Salim (aged fifteen) and Said (aged thirteen), jointly inherited his kingdom. In 1806, Said was crowned sultan of Oman and the East African coast. At that time, the Omani economy had been compromised greatly by wars and drought, making Zanzibar attractive for its trade at the coast and caravans to the interior. During this period, about eight thousand slaves were transported to Zanzibar every year, many carrying ivory. In 1812, Saleh bin Haramil al Abray, an Arab from Muscat, introduced clove trees into Zanzibar from the island of Bourbon (present-day Réunion). The resulting clove plantations used up any surplus of slaves available and created an even greater demand for slave labor, so that Arab traders pushed farther and farther inland. By 1820, they had established a trading center in Kazeh, near Tabora in Tanzania, five hundred miles from the coast.[20] In 1840, Sayyid Said, the sultan of Muscat and Oman (1804–56), moved his capital from Muscat to Zanzibar and began to reorient Swahili trade toward exports. Between 1840 and 1870, Said established clove plantations in Zanzibar and Pemba, displacing food crops.

By the 1860s, Zanzibar had become the world's top producer of cloves. Plantations gave rise to slavery in the islands. To infuse capital into the emporium, Said encouraged western (Hindu) Indians to settle in the area, and they bankrolled the new interior trade. In seeking new markets for his economy, Said was eager to establish trade relations with the United States, culminating in a formal treaty granting American citizens full liberty to buy and sell within the sultan's dominions (Gray 1962, 196–99). In the early nineteenth century, Americans also went to Swahili country to sell New England textiles in the lucrative Africa–Indian Ocean market. Representatives of the thirteen British colonies had signed the Declaration of Independence, which stated that "as free and independent states, they shall have full power to levy war, conclude peace, contract alliances, establish commerce and do all other acts and things which independent states may of right do." Accordingly, trade with the Indian Ocean world could be carried out without restrictions

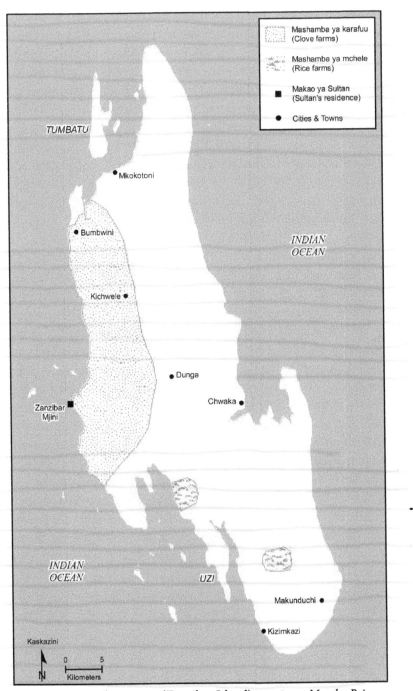

TUMBATU

INDIAN
OCEAN

Mkokotoni

Bumbwini

Kichwele

Dunga

Chwaka

Zanzibar
Mjini

INDIAN
OCEAN

UZI

Makunduchi

Kizimkazi

Kaskazini

0   5
Kilometers

N

MAP 5.2 Kisiwa cha Unguja (Zanzibar Island), ca. 1870s. *Map by Brian Edward Balsley, GISP*

from Great Britain. The new markets there, supported by cloves sold for silver Maria Theresa dollars, attracted the attention of merchants of the new nation in North America. In 1799, the Marine Society was formed in Salem, Massachusetts, and twelve American ships reportedly visited East African ports five years later. Ships sailed to Zanzibar from the Massachusetts cities of Salem, Lawrence, and Lowell and from Manchester in New Hampshire, taking dollars and cotton goods to Africa and returning with ivory, tortoise shell, gum copal, and hides (Gray 1962, 194). Between 1828 and 1861, gum copal was shipped from Zanzibar to Salem as the principal source of one factory's cleaning gum. The factory ceased to exist when a 10 percent duty was imposed upon unclean gum, causing the cleaning to be done in Zanzibar by Germans before being shipped to America (Gray 1962, 196).

On March 18, 1837, Richard Palmer Waters arrived in Zanzibar as the first US consul. In 1839, Said sent his ship *El-Sultan* to the United States, bearing a cargo of assorted products from Zanzibar, East Africa, Arabia, and the Persian Gulf. The *El-Sultan* returned home with firearms, ammunition, china, beads, and bales of *amerikani* cloth (Gray 1962, 213). This unbleached cotton sheeting, produced in the mills of Massachusetts and New Hampshire, replaced a Swahili coarse calico known as *kaniki,* which for centuries had been imported from India. By 1848, amerikani had "come into universal use in Arabia and on the coast of Africa and was threatening the markets of British and Indian textiles from Abyssinia to Mozambique" (Gray 1962, 196). Zanzibar increased its stature as a commercial spot on the Africa–Indian Ocean trade. It was in the sultanate (post-Portuguese) era that most of the Arabic borrowings mentioned in chapter 3 were "grafted into an old Bantu tree," as Nurse and Spear (1985, 6) phrased it. Swahili was the language of diplomacy and trade, even with foreign powers. Swahili interpreters used the middleman language in transactions within the emporium among the diverse peoples who congregated in the slave markets. By the 1860s, the loss in human life was huge, with thousands dying from wounds or from starvation (Livingstone and Waller 1875, 59; Harris 1971, 20). Omani Arab slavery conducted through the Swahili commercial agents was a truly ugly enterprise. Frederic Elton, the British vice-consul in Zanzibar, wrote:

> [Slaves] are mere skeletons of skin and bones, festering with sores and loathsome skin-diseases, and looking as if they were on the very threshold of death. . . . The mouth is opened, the teeth examined, the eyes carefully looked at, the hands and nails passed

muster; the limbs handled, and the condition felt in exactly the same manner in which a horse would be looked over at a fair; and when the competition is eager, and the lot is passed over from one intending buyer to another, each one stepping aside to put one or two questions and endeavoring to ascertain temper—an important qualification—and finally, in the case of women, retiring with the chattel under the cover of an adjacent shed, the more minutely to estimate the value of her attractions. . . . My picture is far from being overdrawn. (Elton and Cotterill 1879, 43)

David Livingstone, who saw the captured slaves, wrote that the main disease afflicting them was the brokenheartedness that resulted from free men and women being reduced to slavery. Field labor was arduous, and the days were long (Cooper 1977, 170–71). The intensification of slavery, both in capture and in practice, on clove, copal, and other plantations rivaled the American model in its brutality.

The caravans heading for the interior hired huge numbers of personnel from the coastal cities. Tippu Tip, a nineteenth-century renowned Swahili slave trader, assembled caravans that had more than four thousand people. These caravans acted as mobile Swahili colonies in Africa's heartland. Members of the party spoke Swahili and remained for many months far in the interior of Africa looking for slaves and ivory. By 1870, there were numerous caravans journeying from the eastern coast of Africa to central and southeast Africa.

Describing the conditions under which it was advantageous for a trader to know Swahili, Harris (1971, 13) wrote:

On arriving at a village or market place, the Arab or Swahili head of the party would contact the local African ruler and promise him muskets, gunpowder, and other goods for slaves; sometimes the slavers encouraged war with a neighboring people for the purpose of capturing slaves. In the course of such wars, men, women, and children were carried away as villages burned. After a raid, other Africans were rounded up and organized in gangs for the march. Frequently, those captured were not taken directly to the coast but were marched to other areas until a caravan large enough to send back was assembled.

In such situations, hearing the Swahili language must have brought terror to the victims of slavery. The Swahili language was the language of negotiations in the acquisition of slaves, and it was the language spoken to the enslaved as they were marched to the coast. An account of a slave market in Tanzania shows how the Swahili served as middlemen in the Arab collection and purchase of slaves:

> The Swahili or Arab traders would send a message to Mfumwa Kengia informing him when they intended to arrive at his court. Then Kengia would make this news known to as large an area of North Pare as possible. On the appointed day, people who had slaves to dispose of brought them to Kiriche and tied them to a tree at the slave market. The traders came to the market and bargained for the prices. (Kimambo and Temu 1969, 128)

Between 1870 and 1880, the powerful African chiefs who controlled the entire slave trade conducted all their business in Swahili. The most famous of these were Tippu Tip, Chief Kivoi of Kibwezi, King Mirambo of the Nyamwezi, and Chief Mlozi in Malawi. The Kamba (especially Chief Kivoi), from the area that is now Kenya, were also major suppliers of slaves. The warlords sent merchants to travel up the Tana River to Mount Kenya collecting slaves from various designated points inland (Harris 1971, 12). King Mirambo dominated slavery to the west in the area between Tabora and Lake Tanganyika and the caravan routes to Karagwe and Buganda; Tippu Tip, the ruthless Swahili trader, controlled the slave and ivory trade in the Congo region beyond Lake Tanganyika; and Chief Mlozi controlled the trade in the Lake Nyasa region. All three men were well equipped with Arab-supplied firearms to overrun competitors in the interior. The Baganda, north of Lake Victoria, also colluded with Arab and Swahili traders in the acquisition of slaves, in hopes of acquiring political power and accompanying wealth. These overlords recruited their own people to work in the caravans, primarily on the basis of their ability to speak Swahili. Thus, inland people, especially those near the Great Lakes—such as the Bisa living west of Lake Tanganyika, the Yao residing east of Lake Nyasa, and the Nyamwezi living north of Lake Nyasa—were also employed in the slave caravans. Africa's Great Lakes region and the Congo were, however, the sources of the vast majority of slaves in the eighteenth and nineteenth centuries. As was mentioned in chapter 3, more than 44 percent of Swahili vocabulary is of Common Bantu stock (Guthrie 1970, 50), a quality that it shares with central African languages such as Bemba (spoken in Zambia) and Luba (spoken in the Democratic Republic of the Congo). We now understand why. Swahili succeeded as a trade language because central Africans found they could learn it from the traders, and those who ended up as slaves on the coast were able to learn it there.

Slave markets flourished in Swahili towns along the East African littoral and on the islands of the Indian Ocean. From the north, these included the towns of Merca, Mogadishu, Brava, Lamu, Malindi, Mombasa, Pangani, Bagamoyo, Kilwa, and Sofala and the islands of Pemba, Zanzibar, and Madagascar. The center of trade in the entire area was Zanzibar, where the largest slave market in the region was located. The infusion of captives from the interior led to the rapid increase of the Swahili-speaking population at the coast, as well as in the Asian diaspora, while simultaneously fostering the rapid spread of the Swahili language inland. Zanzibari Swahili, the Swahili of the marketplace, flourished inland, more so than any other dialect of the language. This was not the dialect of the Swahili and Arab literate elite or the kind written in books; rather, it was the kind used for haggling and for speaking to people whose proficiency in Swahili was minimal. As we shall see in chapter 9, the choice to use the Kiunguja dialect as the basis for the standard was not exactly warmly received.

Slavery brought new lexica into the Swahili language, particularly terms used to describe various slave roles,[21] including *hamali* (*mahamali*), meaning "port worker" or "carrier"; *hawara,* meaning "concubine"; *huru* (*mahuru*), "manumitted slave"; *kibarua* (*vibarua*), "day laborer" (a lower status than *hamali*); *kijakazi* (*vijakazi*), "female slave"; *mkulia* (*wakulia*), referring to a person who was brought up locally in slavery or bought as a child; *mtoro* (*watoro*, "runaway slave"; *mtumwa* (*watumwa*), "slave" (the literal translation is "one who is ordered around"); *mwungwana* (*waungwana*), "free person without slave ancestry"; *mzalia* (*wazalia*), "locally born slave or a person of slave descent"; and *suria* (*masuria*), "slave made a secondary wife" (rather than a concubine). Slaves performed many different tasks. In addition to laborers, they were domestic servants, concubines, artisans, soldiers for local rulers, and ship captains for merchants. As a result, Swahili incorporates an extensive list of slave concepts and vocabulary.

The majority of slaveowners were Muslim, and some of them felt an obligation to convert their slaves to Islam. In line with Islamic practices, they had their slaves circumcised, and they taught them the devotions of the faith or sent them to Koranic schools. Though new slaves originally knew little about Islamic doctrines, the vast majority of successive generations of slaves were strict Muslims (Cooper 1977, 215). Still, as was the case with

Muslims elsewhere in Africa, they also continued many religious practices from their homelands.

Based on their heritage of generations of Islamic enlightenment, Arabs and the waungwana claimed a superior piety and status. The slaves were called the *washenzi*, a word derived from *Zanj/Zinj*, meaning "heathens and barbarians." Slaveowners gave them demeaning slave names such as Juma (a day of the week), Arobaini (forty dollars, the purchase price), and Faida (profit), reserving hallowed Muslim names such as Mohammed, Ali, and Aisha for the freeborn (Cooper 1977, 217). It is important to note that it was in the slave's best interest to become a Muslim because the Koran encouraged masters to free their Muslim slaves without payment and to permit converted slaves to marry. The immigration of captives to the coast had a profound impact on the resident Swahili population. Members of the Swahili aristocracy, particularly the Arabs, fathered many children with enslaved concubines, consorts, and wives. And slave wives and concubines were particularly influential in the consolidation of aristocratic families.

The most prominent example of the status afforded children born of slave mothers was in the household of Zanzibar's first sultan, Sayyid Said. All of his children, numbering over one hundred, were born of suria. Said's sons and daughters formed the core of Zanzibar's aristocracy, and it was they (and in turn their children) who inherited the sultan's throne (Fair 1996, 150).

Children of Arab fathers were regarded as equal in social status, regardless of the status of their mothers. As Laura Fair (1996, 150) explained, "The combination of Islamic law and east African customary law afforded these children status as the social equals of any children born by the father with a free woman." The child of a suria and a non-Arab free man was not accorded the same status. Mtoro bin Mwinyi Bakari noted, "If a freeman marries a slave woman, their child is a slave; but if a free woman marries a slave man, their child is free" (quoted in Worger, Clark, and Alpers 2001, 122).

Syncretic Expansion of the Swahili Language

Swahili words, like those of any other language, record the interactions between people of differing languages. It is easier to identify the words that got into Swahili from Portuguese than to identify words that Swahili has shared with its Bantu kin because Swahili is itself Bantu. Swahili speakers adopted words from Portuguese in precisely those areas in which they interacted. As we have seen, the Luso-Swahili relations were complex and nuanced, as the Portuguese and Africans were neither friends nor foes but something more syncretic in the social realm. A new social-cultural space emerged in which some Swahili as well as their Portuguese neighbors cultivated the cosmopolitan ethos of coexistence and cooperation despite differing worldviews, as when Swahili, being Muslims, and the Portuguese, being Catholics, lived alongside each other with civility. Following the Portuguese era, the Africa–Indian Ocean trade opened the interior of the continent in the eighteenth century and the first half of the nineteenth. The trickle of inlanders migrating to the coast and deciding to become Swahili then became a forced movement of massive proportions. Many of those sold into slavery in the coastal plantations and the islands never found their way back to their former communities and became Swahili. It is to the Omani period that we owe much of the Arabic vocabulary that is used in Swahili today. Of course, linguistic affinities do not always follow cultural ones (Myers-Scotton 1993, 24), and for the Swahili, that is all the more true, for the resident populations spoke numerous African and Asiatic languages and came from a diversity of cultures. The various populations moved to the Swahili coast at different times and under different circumstances; similarly, the structural changes that have affected Swahili "have taken place at different times, and are not the result of a single set of circumstances at a single time" (Nurse and Hinnebusch 1993, 331). Consequently, Swahili has always imbibed from the languages of Africa's eastern and central interior. And what led to its establishment as a lingua franca from the middle of the nineteenth century was in fact a process with deep roots in the history of the region. As we shall see in chapter 10, Swahili has never looked back. Many developments, some of them even more dramatic than those of the distant past, have since taken place in the language, most notably with regard to the evolution of a pidgin Swahili that is a far cry from that spoken in the cradle of the Swahili language. In the chapter that follows, I will discuss the women of Swahili as the advance guard in the spread of the Swahili language to the hinterland.

CHAPTER 6

The Women of Swahili

IN THE first record that we have about the East African coast, *The Periplus of the Erythrean Sea* mentioned in chapter 2, we are told of "Arab captains and crews who trade and intermarry with the mainlanders of all the places and know their language."[1] The women of the littoral are mentioned in the record and in connection with the language. This chapter brings the women of Swahili directly into our story. Where possible, I will mention specific names and accomplishments—to convey the audible voices and to recognize individuals such as Jamezi's mother (introduced in chapter 2), through whom we can trace the affinities between Swahili culture and language and the way peoples of the hinterland speak. Women were key players in the development and spread of Swahili thanks to their prodigious individual and collective memories and how they related them to their children. Their writings, adaptations, interpretations, productions, and performances of Swahili culture had a great influence on what Swahili is today. The women of Swahili were power brokers, trendsetters, and the ultimate connoisseurs of Swahili arts. Their cosmopolitan lives nurtured a small Bantu dialect into the international language that Swahili is today.

Who are the women of Swahili? Some people correct anyone who says, "I speak Swahili," insisting that the language is Kiswahili, not Swahili. They place a Swahili prefix on the word *Swahili* to mean the language or the Swahili manner of doing things. Two similar prefixes, *m-* and *wa-*, as in *Mswahili* or *Waswahili*, denote a person or persons who are Swahili. Another prefix, *u-*, makes *Uswahili* the abstract notion of what being Swahili means. Suffixes convey other meanings, such that *-ni* in the word

Uswahilini refers to the location or country of the Swahili. Asking the question "Who are the women of Swahili?" in Swahili yields *Wanawake wa Kiswahili ni kina nani?* This literally translates as "Women of Swahili who are they?" for the word *kina* denotes a group of similar people fitting a particular description. The term *wanawake wa Kiswahili* therefore refers to women in relation to the language while at the same time accenting the women as people (*wa-* in *wanawake*), women as fitting in the Swahili worldview (*Kiswahili*) to recognize themselves and be recognized as Swahili and to live among the Swahili in places such as Mombasa, Zanzibar, Pate, Lamu, and so on.

If our question concerns the women associated with Swahili history, culture, and language, why not just make their Swahiliness an aspect of them with an adjective *Swahili* modifying the women, as in *wanawake Waswahili*, "Swahili women"? Rather, it is "women who are Swahili." Sarah Mirza and Margaret Strobel identified the proper nuance when they translated the title of their book *Three Swahili Women* in English as *Wanawake watatu wa Kiswahili* (Three women of Swahili) instead of *Wanawake watatu waswahilii* (Three Swahili women).[2] The distinction between an essential quality, conveyed by the adjective, and an acquired quality—"women of Swahili"—means that those women of Swahili are not inherently different from the women of the adjoining hinterland, or *pwani* or *mwambao*, "coast," and on into the far interior beyond the Great Lakes of central Africa. The distinction underlines the specificity of the term *Swahili*, which, though it can be appropriated, cannot be owned.

Being Swahili is much more than an identity conferred by birth. The label "women of Swahili" carries with it the baggage of identity, which is a complicated matter, as we saw in chapter 2. Recall Jamezi's statement that "we Swahilis are all like that; each one is Swahili, but he has his own tribe as well,"[3] explaining why he was, as far as he could tell, as good a Swahili as any other even though his own father was of Makua background in Mozambique and had been brought to the coast as a child, probably as a slave. Both Jamezi's understanding of the situational mutability, or multiplicity, of who one is and the *Periplus* confirmation that Indian Ocean sailors intermarried with mainlanders "of all the places" imply that most women of Swahili came from the hinterland. Whoever they might have been where they were born, at the coast they also became "women of Swahili." The Swahili of Mombasa affirm this relationship when they call the Mijikenda—the "nine tribes" of the hills just inland, Digo, Giriama, Ribe, Rabai, Chonyi, Jibana,

Kambe, Kauma, and Duruma—*Wajomba,* which means "mother's brothers" or "maternal uncles." The bulk of the women of Mombasa (and also no doubt other Swahili towns) came from the hinterland peoples, including the Mijikenda of *mwambao wa pwani* (the coastal strip).

In this chapter, we will see how the women of Swahili have given Swahili a character and a voice of history. A study of the complex lives of women—their spiritual, material, and social situations—tells us much about developments in the Swahili language. The varied and vibrant nature of the Swahili language is illuminated as we pay attention to women's lives.

I will begin with a look at how women have been instrumental in the spread of Swahili in the post-Portuguese era, recognizing these women by name when I can and presenting them in roughly chronological order. I then will take a look at the lives of certain individual women to see what they tell us about the gender aspect of the growth and spread of Swahili. I will also consider the *kanga/leso*—"the cloth that speaks Swahili"—as a trend-setting innovation in the part of the Swahili economy that is managed by women. For centuries, women have draped their houses and themselves, their children, and their men in pieces of cloth with inscriptions in Swahili: in a palpable, visible sense, they wear their language from the cradle to the grave. The impact of the kanga in the spread of Swahili cultural literacy positions the contributions of women to the language in plain view. I will close the chapter with a look at women as the trustees of Swahili material culture.

The "Included"

The women of Swahili include Mbwasho, the mother of the folk hero of Swahili people, Fumo Liyongo, who is discussed in chapter 7. Mbwasho is a stoic figure whose odes represent a mother's angst about her son's destiny; the odes are at the foundation of the Swahili literary tradition, dating back perhaps earlier than the seventeenth century. The women of Swahili include town rulers such as Mwana Mkisi, the ancestral queen of Mombasa in the early 1500s, which was also known as Gongwa. They include, as well, that unnamed "old gentle woman" who appeared in chapter 5 when she sent a little poem to warn Miguel, her Portuguese friend (a padre and therefore a non-Muslim who was beloved by the townspeople), of the impending annihilation of the Portuguese missionaries in 1631.[4]

Another of the women of Swahili is Mwana Kupona, who wrote a poem—the only one she is known to have composed—around 1858 that is celebrated as a defining piece in the Swahili literary canon, enunciating what a "good" Swahili lady ought to be. The women of Swahili also include the three women presented by Mirza and Strobel (1989) in *Wanawake watatu wa Kiswahili*—Mishi wa Abdala, born between 1900 and 1905, probably of slave ancestry; Bi Kaje Mwenye Matano, a local woman who was born (free) around 1890; and Shamsa Muhashamy, an Arab born in 1919. Yet another woman of Swahili is Mwana Hidaya,[5] a Chagga originally enslaved in the foothills around Mount Kilimanjaro who went on to become a successful trader in Mombasa and was able to build a mosque—the only mosque in the city sponsored by a woman. Other women of Swahili include female slaveowners, such as Bi Kaje's grandmother, Bi Hindi, who lived during Mwana Kupona's lifetime and beyond and who owned Mwana Hidaya. Bi Hindi possessed two farms and more than thirty slaves, and she had relatives who worked for her.[6] She richly merited the respect shown her as indicated by the fact that her given name was prefaced with the honorific Bi, short for binti, or "daughter (of)" (Arabic), suggesting refinement and respectability.

Poets such as Zaharia binti Maimun and Siti binti Saad—perhaps the most renowned among all the female poets—are other prominent women of Swahili. Saad was named *mtumwa*, "slave," at birth (in the 1880s) and grew up as a slave but excelled to the point of being called *Siti*, "lady" in Arabic; she dined with sultans in their palaces and drew the attention of the entire Indian Ocean world with her music and songs, compelling many to sing along with her. Siti's fame and prominence were unmatched by anyone (male or female) before or during her time and have remained so ever since.

Among the anonymous women of Swahili are the *makungwi*, professionals who initated girls into womanhood; the seasoned travelers, guides, and scouts, who were problem solvers in their own right alongside the men; the harbingers of fashion; the numerous *hawara* (mistresses who were freeborn but usually unknown to the family); the *wazalia* (singular *mzalia*), the locally born slaves or women of slave parentage; the *masuria* (singular *suria*), slaves who were made secondary wives or concubines; and the *vijakazi* (singular *kijakazi*), female slaves who ran aristocratic households by providing child care and performing domestic chores.

These women of Swahili maintained the distinctive Bantu grammar of Kiswahili, despite constant exposure to the prestigious consonants and cadences of the Arabic that was spoken by men in public spaces and that conveyed the sacred truths of Islam. These women stamped African values and customs, derived from a vast hinterland, firmly onto the life and material cultures of Swahili families in coastal towns, while at the same time mixing their own heritages with the diverse resources—words and things—that came to them by way of the sea. Indeed, not unlike W. E. B. DuBois's great-grandmother in faraway America, they crooned "heathen" inland tunes to their babies in the middle of telling similarly heathen stories from the traditions of their kin in the hinterlands.

The Avant-Garde in the Spread of Swahili

The women of Swahili were vital in the conduct of the caravans that probed the far interior of Africa in the eighteenth and nineteenth centuries. Unknown numbers of women and children accompanied their husbands and fathers on these expeditions, and this nameless and faceless population was the key logistical support for the successes of Swahili inland trade. Women took care of the domestic chores of fetching water, setting up camps, gathering firewood, tending fires, and cooking. They were sent ahead of trade caravans to scout villages for supplies and information, to make contacts with and befriend local populations, and to prepare evening meals before the men arrived at designated stopping places (Fabian 1986, 27). Seldom perceived as threats, the women and children were sent in advance of the men to assure inlanders that the caravans' leaders had nothing but honorable intentions.

The women who went ahead of the caravans must have greatly facilitated the spread of Swahili inland because they were the ones who negotiated for supplies with the populations in the interior. They used Swahili as a trade language, since languages spoken by the inland people changed every few miles. Furthermore, the inlanders spoke Swahili in a great variety of ways, reflecting their vernacular tongues. They simplified the grammar and inflected vocabularies and pronunciations with the words and inflections of their mother tongues. Some of the Swahili women came from the areas the caravans passed through or had mothers who hailed from these areas. As a result, these women of Swahili were repositories of knowledge about local customs and spoke the local languages. Jerome Becker[7] wrote, "You can be certain that a traveler who returns with a rich harvest of information and of studies of customs owes most of them to the women of his escort."[8]

Since the women of Swahili had in fact been steadily drawn from inland populations from time immemorial (many coastal people had relatives inland), the women were also the avant-garde of cultural syncretism along the coast. Swahili women bore the memories of their own peoples' cultures. They passed these traditions down to successive generations in the Swahili language. They introduced multiculturalism from the African side into everything Swahili, complementing and enriching the Indian Ocean cosmopolitanism of the coast. As mothers, they passed on aspects of inland Africa's cultures and traditions in rites of passage from birth through burial, even among the aristocracy itself, since they gave birth to the children who inherited the wealth and position of their fathers.

As Edward Alpers has observed, the Swahili are "characterized by local variations on a general theme of Afro-Islamic culture, so that what one knows about Lamu or Bagamoyo may not hold true for Pemba at any point in time."[9] This diversity is particularly apparent among the women of Swahili. They have experienced life very differently from town to town and from one historical period to another. The extent of this diversity is illustrated by the contrast between the *watumwa*, "slaves," and the *waungwana*, "freeborn." The *mabibi*, "wives of Arabic descent," constituted the nobility, with freeborn women ranked after them, followed by the *mahuru*, "freed slaves." Among the enslaved women, the *suria*, or "slave wives," were at the top of the group because they were married to men of the elite class; they had a standing secondary to the mabibi. The *hawara* or *vinyumba*, recognized "concubines," occupied a middle rung among the enslaved women, above the *kijakazi*, "female slave," within the household. At the bottom of the hierarchy were the field slaves, used for all sorts of manual labor. The enslaved women of Swahili often moved up and down this ladder of respectability, or belonging, as happened with the slave wives whose children were welcomed in the Swahili aristocracy. In chapter 5, I remarked that the household of Zanzibar's first sultan, Sayyid Said, had over one hundred children born of concubines and slave women, progeny who became heirs to the sultan's throne (Fair 1996, 150). Children of slave women by Arab fathers were regarded as equal in social status to those born of free mothers.

The Words of the Women of Swahili

The women of Swahili have made seminal contributions to Swahili poetry, though they have not been fully appreciated. These women have always composed poetry, but traditional inhibitions against public expression have (in part) made them prefer anonymity.[10] J. W. T. Allen, a respected scholar of the language in the 1960s, recognized the key contribution women made to Swahili poetry. He said that women had a "profound influence" in Swahili verse, "a fact which is often overlooked and sometimes denied."[11] The ladies of the aristocratic houses are known to have custody of the best manuscripts in existence, and the oral tradition of the culture is in their heads. It is to them, therefore, that one turns for the best recitations of epic poetry known as Tenzi or Tendi.[12] According to Ali Jahadhmy, women of Lamu have been the "keepers of Swahili verse tradition."[13] Indeed, the words written by women provide an excellent venue through which to appreciate how the social history of the Swahili is both couched and exposed within the dialectal diversity of their language. Reading women's words is an actual encounter with the dialects of Swahili, something seldom seen in writing nowadays. Swahili women are also the keepers of Swahili enigma (riddling) verse, which delights and awes their listeners. And any man who attempts to understand Swahili poetry must of necessity have the assistance of a woman. Allen, himself a noted researcher of Swahili literature, repeatedly realized that without the constant help of his wife, he would never have made contact with most of the people in the community who had the manuscripts and tapes he was searching for.[14]

In what follows, we will hear Kipate, Kimanda, Kimvita, Kiamu, and Kiungunja—that is, Swahili as it is spoken in the islands of Pate, Manda, Mombasa, Lamu, and Zanzibar, respectively. Going chronologically, we will hear Kipate in an ancient ode attributed to Mbwasho (mother of the prime folk hero of the Swahili) addressing her son, Fumo Liyongo. We will then hear Kimanda (the Swahili of Manda) in a lament made by a woman in captivity, and after that, we will tune into Kimvita by revisiting the little song (introduced in chapter 4) composed by a woman to warn her Portuguese friend Miguel of a planned massacre. A song sung by a Pate woman in 1815 after her nephew was murdered in a succession skirmish at Lamu will bring us to focus on the Kipate flavor of Swahili, after which we will consider the harvest of words in Zaharia binti Maimuna's *Wimbo wa miti* (Song of trees), an enigma written in Kiamu (the dialect of Lamu). From the advice of a mother to her daughter on the ways of life, we are once again face to face with Kipate in the much celebrated poem *Mwana Kupona*. At the end of this section, we will meet Siti binti Saad, the crown jewel of the Swahili composition and performance tradition in Zanzibari Swahili (Kiunguja). We will hear Swahili in its dialectal grandeur as women communicated through song and recited poetry to describe, critique, and otherwise make sense of their experience.

One of the earliest cases of a woman of Swahili authoring a song for a particular task is found in the story of Fumo Liyongo, the folk hero of the

Swahili who is thought to have lived—or whose legend dates to—somewhere between 1230 and 1600 CE. Liyongo was a warrior famed for his prowess in battle and for his escapes from the many attempts on his life by thugs sent after him by his villainous cousin Daudi Mringwari, with whom he quarreled over the throne of Pate (an island in the Lamu archipelago off the coast of Kenya) throughout his lifetime. In the following song, Mbwasho, Liyongo's mother, pleads with him not to go to war:

> Fumo Liyongo, Sishike mata, wala matata
> Ukienda Gana, twaa nami, Fumo Liyongo
> Mwanangu, usifanye zita
> Mimi mamako mzazi, nakulilia

> Fumo Liyongo, leave weapons alone, and trouble-making
> When you go to Gana, take me along, Fumo Liyongo
> My son, do not engage in wars
> It is I, your mother (as a parent), crying up to you.

(Mbele 1996, 81)

Here, Liyongo's mother emphasizes the nonaggressive approach to problem solving over the path of warmongering, revenge, and killing that Mringwari and Liyongo were on.[15] The stanza has only one word borrowed from Arabic, *wala* (nor); the rest are Bantu. The poem is a gem that shows us the language of yesteryear. The word *mata* (weapons) may be derived from *uta* (the bow)—an old Bantu weapon. The presence of the word *matata* (trouble) in the poem indicates that it is an ancient word, though it has been popularized in modern times by the song "Hakuna Matata," arguably one of the best-known Swahili songs, recently featured in the film *The Lion King*. The word *zita* gives away the identity of the dialect used in the song as Kipate (also spoken in Lamu). The term would be *vita* in Kiunguja (or Ki-Standard, as I will refer to it in the rest of this section)—the standard dialect of Swahili, which is discussed in chapter 9. The change of *zi* in Kiamu/Kipate dialects to *vi* in Kiunguja is robust—*zijana* (youth) is *vijana*, *ziatu* (shoes) is *viatu*, and *ziazi* (potatoes) is *viazi*. Songs are the commentary through which we tune into the richness of the Swahili language from times past.

We encounter Kiamu in a narrative about a skirmish that arose as some Lamu people tried to groom a youth by the name of Fumoluti wa

Bayae for the Pate throne, on the basis that his mother was from Lamu even though his father was a Nabahan—a descendant of the Nabahan Arabs who had arrived from Muscat in 1815 CE.[16] The youth was murdered in the debacle that ensued, and his aunt, a Pate woman, lamented as follows:

OLD SWAHILI	STANDARD SWAHILI	ENGLISH TRANSLATION
Mwamu mwofu,	Mwamu mnyofu	A good Lamu man,
Thongo ni alifu.	Matata ni alifu	Has a thousand wiles.
Hoyo mpotofu	Mwamu mwovu	So a bad Lamu man,
Uya kaa iye?	Atakelije?	What will he be like.[17]

The animosity and stereotypes that Wapate (Pateans) had of the Waamu (Lamuans) is clear in the song, and it indicate the real or imagined historical tensions that existed between cities, perhaps in all of Swahili society. As the meanings of the words tell us about the perceptions of one city of another, they also present to us the geolinguistics of Swahili at the heart of the dialectal variance in the language. This song is a great addition to the previous one, enriching our grasp of how Kipate was spoken. Apart from the word *alifu*, meaning "thousand," which is borrowed from *alf* in Arabic, all other words are Bantu, just as was the case in the previous poem. The final line—*uya kaa iye*, "what will he be like"—is interesting for two reasons: first, it has three words where the Ki-Standard Swahili has only one—*ataketije*—and second, because of the sound changes that distinguish Kipate (and other dialects of the Lamu archipelago) from other dialects of Swahili. The sound *y* in Kipate is rendered *j* (like "j" in "judge") in Kiunguja and Kimvita. This means that *jambo* in the famous song "Jambo Bwana" is pronounced *yambo* and the word *umoja* ("unity") as *umoya*.

Turning to Kimanda (the Swahili of Manda), one account describes the 1339 CE overthrow and conquest of the town of Manda by the sultanate of Pate and how its people were made slaves.[18] Prior to the defeat, the people of Manda bore the nickname *weng'andu*, or "wearers of gold," due to the vast amounts of wealth they possessed. In slavery, the women were not spared from hard labor. According to the story, one Manda woman was weeping upon being beaten by a soldier because she refused to carry stones that were being used in building a wall to link Manda and Pate as a single city. Another woman close by uttered the following ode in lament:

Tuli kwetu Manda twali tukitenda,	When we were at our home in Manda it was we who were doing
Yeo tukitendwa twakataa kwani?	Today we are done so, why should we refuse?
Hutupa ukuta wathipetapeta,	They give us a wall to build winding hither and thither.
kutwa ni kuteta hatuna amani	All day is quarrelling—we get no respite.[19]

The woman's point is that they themselves were equally brutal to their slaves before they lost their autonomy. Given that Manda was a much older city whose aristocracy had governed Pate until the arrival of the Nabahans, the rulers of Manda had lorded over the Pateans. This is in fact recalled by a tale related in Stigand's work: "If a man was building a vessel in Pate harbor, when he hammered a nail to drive it into a plank, an order used to come from Manda.... The master is sleeping; do not make a noise,"[20]—despite the fact that Manda was too far away for anyone there to hear the sound. Here, we see the image of the women of Swahili as adapting to situations not of their own choosing, just as they had after arriving on the coast as slaves. The words of the poem have something to add to the earlier verses. The word *yeo,* "today," is pronounced *leo* in other dialects. The words *tuli* and *twali* indicate the Bantu aspects of Swahili grammar as spoken at Manda. Both words are conjugations of the Bantu verb *li,* "be," and *tu* indicates "we/us," such that *tuli* means "we are"; at the beginning of a sentence, this reads as "When we were." For that, Ki-Standard uses *tukiwa* (*tu-ki-wa* → *we-when-be* = *When we were*), another form altogether. Adding the past tense marker—*a* to *tu*—we get *tu-a-li* (*twali*), to mean "we were." Contradistinguished from the KiManda, it is *tulikuwa* (*tu-li-kuwa* → *we-PAST-be* = *We were*) in the Ki-Standard. The verb *li* is a relic in the Swahili of today, restricted to talking about locatives, as in *nilipo* (*ni-li-po* → *I-Past-at*), "where I am at," or in antiquated expressions such as *nili pweke* (*ni-li* → I am; *pweke,* lonely). In this poem as in the preceeding two, only one word, *amani,* meaning "peace," is borrowed from Arabic; all others are Bantu. I point this out to underscore the fact that Arabic words have historically been found in certain spheres of Swahili life but not much in others. The female-dominated social sphere of the nonaristocratic material world of the Swahili had fewer borrowed words than the religious, administrative, and ocean-faring spheres that sustained the Swahili aristocracy run by men. Recall the words of the little song (mentioned in chapter 5)[21] that "an old gentle woman" of Mombasa composed to pass a secret message to her friend Miguel, warning him of an impending massacre of the Portuguese by the Swahili, back in 1631:

Mzungu Migeli, u muongo	Miguel the European, thou art in the wrong
Mato yako yana t'ongo!	Thine eyes are blind on one side
Kwani kuata mpango	Why leave the troop
Kwenda kibanga uani?	To go (to) a hut in the courtyard?[22]

In this single stanza, we find one of the sounds that distinguish Swahili as spoken at Mombasa from other dialects. The words *mato*, "eyes," *t'ongo* (referring to the whitish or yellowish matter running from closed eyes usually during sleep), and *kuata*, "to leave" are *macho*, *chongo*, and *kuacha* in Ki-Standard, meaning that /t/ is used in Kimvita whereas /ch/ is deployed in Kiunguja.[23] Another sound difference salient in Mombasa Swahili is /nd/, which is rendered /nj/ in Zanzibar. Accordingly, *ndoo*, "come," is pronounced *njoo*; *ndia*. "road" or "path," is *njia*; *ndaa*, "hunger," is *njaa*; *vunda*, "to break," is *vunja*; and interestingly, *tinda*, "to kill," which combines both /t/ and /nd/, appears as *chinja*, "slaughter," in Zanzibar.

The Lamu dialect of Swahili is much celebrated as the language of classical Swahili literature. Zaharia binti Maimun, a Swahili woman poet, is one example of what Allen (1971, 112–13) and Mbele (1996) see as the ultimate patronesses and conservators of Swahili verse. Her "collection of manuscripts of Swahili poetry in the library of the University of Dar es Salaam" has proven invaluable to scholars.[24] "Wimbo wa miti" (Song of the trees) is one song whose authorship, preservation, and transmission are credited to women:

Yana niwene kisa adhimu	Yesterday I witnessed a notable episode
tena tafusirini walimu	And will you, the experts, explain it;
Miti yalikipijana mtendeti na mdimu	Trees were fighting, the date-palm and the lime tree
Hima ukaya mbiyo mpwera	Promptly the guava tree came running,
Nyuma muembe una hasira	And close behind it the furious mango tree,
Mzabibu akisema kunyamaa ni ujura	While the grapevine declared: "Passivity is stupidity."
Mara ukadhihiri mtesi sura zina ushiu na	Suddenly the mtesi appeared its face full of kasi impatience and intensity
Ukiwambiya mpwera kwetu hakuna rakhisi	And it told the guava tree, "With us there is no easy way."

Papo ukaya mpilipili	There and then came the pepper plant
Hapo kinena kwa ukali	And it was speaking angrily
Ukiapa kwa ziyapo miti pia siijali	And swearing with oaths: "I don't give a damn for trees!"
Punde wasiyesa kani zao	Before their fury was spent,
nde wawene mti uyao	They saw, outside, a tree coming,
Nao ni mberemende una panga na ngao	And it was the mberemende armed with sword and shield
Zita hatuchi twapo uwawa	"War we fear not, though we get killed,
Uta na zembe umetukuwa	For with bow and arrows we are armed."
Mbuyu ulipopita ukasimamakwa muwa	When the baobab tree passed by, it stopped to mediate:
Hela watani yenu mayowe	"Come, now, cease your noisy squabbling;
tela bure asiwazuzuwe	Let not Tela confound you
Kuna mti una hila humshinda kitunguwe	There is a tree more cunning than Hare
Shina la mambo haya nayuwa	The stem of these things I know;
Sawa nimeziye kutambuwa	Very well have I realized it.
Muyungu ndio fitina waloalisha mauwa	The pumpkin plant is the agitator that has called forth these blossoms."

This song is a treasure trove of information on history and language. The words of the song reveal the cosmopolitan nature of the Lamu dialect. In the song, all the underlined words are of Arabic extraction—*kisa*, "episode"; *adhimu*, "notable"; *tafusiri*, "translate"; *walimu*, "teacher/expert"; *ujura*, "stupidity"; *dhihiri*, "manifest/appear"; *rakhisi*, "easy"; *jali*, "care"; and *fitina*, "mischief made to cause emnity or rift between persons." The rest are of the Bantu mold with a flavor that is specific to Lamu Swahili, and its close resemblance to Kipate and Kimanda (mentioned previously) can be seen in the sound *y*, which is rendered *j* in Ki-Standard—the Kiamu words *yana*, "yesterday," *ukaya*, "(then) came," *uyao*, "coming," and *nayua*, "I know," are thus *jana*, *ukaja*, *ujao*, and *najua*, respectively in Ki-Standard. Each word in the song adds information about the social history of the singer and her audience. It is hard to fathom how else we can peer into the world of the Swahili without attending to its veritable enigmas that capture the many shades and strands of life in the history we seek.

According to Mbele, the woman who performed the song named it, *Wimbo wa miti* (Song of the trees) as a metaphor for a historical reference to a time long past when a huge misunderstanding arose among Lamu women. They spent their time backbiting and insinuating all manner of things against one another, and there was no peace. One woman then composed a song in which all characters were trees and other plants, leaving everyone guessing whether or when their parts in the distasteful affair had been revealed.[25]

Zaharia's poem presents us with a snapshot of life in Lamu in which female personalities are metaphorically presented as nine plants most of them trees—the *mtendeti*, "date tree"; the *mdimu*, "lime/lemon tree"; the *mpwera* (*mpera*), "guava tree"; the *muembe*, "mango tree"; the *mzabibu*, "grapevine'" the *mtesi*, "troublemaker tree";[26] the *mpilipili*, "pepper plant"; the *mberemende*, a tropical African shrub of the pea family; and the *muyungu*, the Lamu name for "pumpkin plant," popularly known as *boga* in current Ki-Standard. Notice how much the words for the plants mirror the Swahili in their makeup. All are prefixed with *m-*, placing them in a Bantu nominal class regardless of their place of origin. All the plants have Bantu roots except two—the *mzabibu*, which is derived from the Arabic *zabīb*, meaning "grapes," and the *mpwera*, which is from the Portuguese word *peras*, "pear," standing in for "guava" in Swahili. The two represent the overseas connections to Swahili. The other plants bear Bantu names no matter from whence they came. The mtendeti tree hails from the Middle East and is known as *daqal* in Arabic; the muembe and mdimu are from south Asia; the muyunga is from North America—all have been so long established in the region that their origins are buried in the shift of whatever names they carried to Bantu. Then there are the Bantu plants, the mpilipili, the mberemende, and the mtesi. The mpilipili is from the African hinterland, where it is known as *piri-piri*, a word from the Ronga languages of southern Mozambique that means "a very hot sauce made with red chilli peppers."[27] The mberemende, which is glossed as "a shrub in the African tropics," is of an indistinct, general description only, much like the unidentified populations of the hinterland that came to dwell at the Swahili coast. The mtesi name is even more mysterious and has a superstitious belief attached to it. Its root is *tesa*, which bears the meanings "contentious," "oppressive," "quarrelsome," and "troublesome" and refers to being shrouded in mystery. The mtesi is said not to be a specific tree but a branch or leaf that causes conflicts to arise if brought into a house.[28] We see in all the plants mentioned an allusion to the diverse places that those who are called Swahili came from: some are recent and known by a name that betrays where they came from, others are archaic and bear local names, and yet others are native but unspecific. It is not hard to see that the presentation of women as trees is an analogy whose explication is the story of Swahili.

Interestingly, the *mnazi*, or "coconut palm," does not show up in the song at all. Should we make anything of the fact that it is the *mbuyu*, or "baobab tree,"[29] that shows up and reveals the identity of the perpetrator? Absolutely we should, since many communities of eastern and central Africa go to the baobab tree to perform religious rituals. The mbuyu is a tree of tremendous religious and cultural significance in the societies of inner Africa, even greater for them than the coconut tree is for the Swahili, as described in chapter 4.[30]

Perhaps the most celebrated poetess is Mwana Kupona binti Mshamu (1810–60). *Utendi wa Mwana Kupona*—the poem that she composed in 1858 to instruct her seventeen-year-old daughter, Mwana Hashima binti Mataka, on a woman's place, roles, duties, and responsibilities with respect to her husband—remains a milestone in Swahili verse. Mwana Kupona's reason for producing the poem is given in verse 92, in which she disclaims any pretension to literary recognition by stating that she is just writing as a mother concerned with a daughter who is still naive in matters of marriage and the behaviors that become a Swahili lady. All underlined words, in what follows, exemplify the Patean Swahili, and the underlined and italicized ones are of Arabic origin):

Na *sababu* ya kutunga	My reason for composing
si *shairi* si malenga	It is not that I am a poet or an expert
nina kijana muinga	but I have a silly girl (lit. a foolish young person)
napenda kumuusia	whom I wish to instruct

In 72 out of the poem's 102 verses, she writes as a mother instructing her daughter;[31] the rest of the poem is a religious evocation addressed to women and Muslims everywhere. Mwana Kupona begins by laying out her philosophy of life:

Mwanadamu si kitu	The human being is nothing
Na ulimwengu si wetu	And the world does not belong to us
Walau hakuna mtu	There is none
Ambao atasalia	That shall endure

She tells her daughter, "If you heed what I tell you, you won't have trouble, my child, you will pass through this world and into *akhira* the next."[32] The word *akhira*, "paradise," is an Arabized pronunciation in Swahili, without which it is rendered *ahera*. Mwana Kupona then proceeds to tell her daughter what is required of her:

La kwanda kamata *dini*	the first thing is to hold fast to your religion
Pili uwe na *adabu*	the second is to behave properly
La tatu uwe *sadiqi*	the third is to be trustworthy

Mwana Kupona tells her daughter to hold on to religion by keeping the ordinances of God and to follow tradition when it is required.[33] She also counsels her to have a disciplined tongue, to see to it that she is loved wherever she goes,[34] to be trustworthy and meticulous, and to avoid the unjust.[35] She then goes on to advise her daughter on the proper relationships between people of different social classes. In verse 20, she writes:

Sitangane na watumwa	Do not consort with slaves
Ila mwida wa *khuduma*	Unless there is work to be done
wakuvutia tama	They will lead you astray
la buda nimekwambia	Perhaps I have told you before

This verse talks about the distance between the freeborn and the slaves, stressing that *mabibi* (the aristocratic women) are not to befriend them. Mwana Kupona is cautioning her daughter to present an image of piety and decorum because slave women were said to be fond of mischief and gossip, and they would habitually instruct brides on sexual matters and counsel them on how to take care of their husbands. Mwana Kupona states, "A woman requires five kinds of approval in order to have peace in this world and the next.—God, His Prophet; father, mother and husband."[36] The "decorum" Mwana Kupona suggests reeks of slavish obedience in advice such as *naawe radhi mumeo*, "please your husband," and *radhi yake izengee*, "seek his blessing." If nothing else, such behaviors would make the wife a slave even as, ironically, she herself is advised to keep away from the slaves who are doing the exact same things to her. The seriousness of the matter is called to the daughter's attention by reference to the day of reckoning: *Siku ufufuliwao nadhari ni ya mumeo*, "When you are resurrected, your husband's will will be sought," meaning that he will have the final say on whether the wife should enter ahera or go to hell.[37] Thus, the message here is that one should submit to slavery in life for fear of damnation in the hereafter.

If verses 35 and 36 are not the most memorable in the epic, they certainly are the most mysterious. They give advice on how a woman ought to treat her husband. Verse 35 counsels the wife to:

Mtunde kama kijana	Tend him like a child
asiyoyua kunena	that cannot yet speak;
kitu changalie sana	take great care of
kitokacho na kungia	the thing that goes out and comes in

Are the words *mtunde kama kijana asiyoyua kunena,* "tend him like a child that cannot yet speak," meant literally or figuratively? Are they intended to tell us something about men and the women they need to care for them? If the passage is more a commentary on men than on women, then the men of Swahili apparently are deemed to be hopelessly mired in immaturity, at least in matters domestic. If, however, the passage is directed to women, is Mwana Kupona telling the daughter that men are fragile and require adult female supervision? And if that is the case, then how does one understand the evidently amorous act implied in the rest of the stanza, *kitu changalie sana kitokacho na kungia,* "take great care of the thing that goes out and comes in." Is this that old adage suggesting the shortest distance to a man's heart is through satisfaction of his appetites and ego? The subsequent verse in the poem says:

Mpumbaze apumbae	Amuse him so that he may relax (lit. fool him until he is fooled)
amriye sikatae	do not oppose his command;
maovu kieta yeye	if it is ill-advised (lit. if he brings evil himself)
Mngu atakulipia	God will defend you (lit. God will repay you)

The word "amuse" does not do justice as a translation of *mpumbaze,* whose literal meaning is "stupefy." A more revealing paraphrase would be something like: "Stupefy him so that he is taken in by your wiles. Obey his command for if it is ill advised God will recompense you." Does this tell the woman that playing the fool is the only effective way of dealing with a fool? How about the idea that obeying a husband without a murmur absolves the wife from blame and bequeaths her recompense if the husband's orders are evil? Ibrahim Noor Shariff of Zanzibar, a Swahili scholar of note, thinks that "the poem is a masterpiece of allusions that play up the male ego in a society where men see themselves as masters over their womenfolk, while at the same time instructing the intelligent woman to treat the opposite sex as she would an infant."[38] Alamin Mazrui, commenting on the ideological orientation of the poem, remarks that to some, it "affirms and reinforces the patriarchal order in Swahili society, while others see in it a subversive, if disguised, antihegemonic discourse."[39] As with all great poetry, the epic still generates discussion and a lack of consensus on its true meaning, if there is one. In any event, the advice did apparently come in handy, as Mwana Kupona's daughter, Mwana Hashima binti Mataka, lived to the venerable age of ninety-two (1841–1933).

Mwana Kupona was explicit in verses 91 and 94 that by writing to her daughter, she was writing to Muslims in general and to Swahili Muslim women in particular:

Ntungile nili *saqimu*	I have composed it in illness
moyo usina *fahamu*	and without great understanding;
usomeni Islamu	but read it, Muslims,
mukiogozana ndia	when you help one another on the Way

Somani nyute *huramu*	Read it all women
maana muya*fahamu*	maybe you will understand
musitukue *laumu*	and be blameless
mbee za Mola *Jalia*	before Almighty God.

The conclusion, with its revelation of the author and an invocation of God as well as a prayer for the Prophet, his family, and his descendants, is typical of classical Swahili poetry. Once again, in the telling of the epic, we hear in the Kipate (Swahili as it is spoken in Pate Island) many Arabic words that would be expected of a lady in the highest echelons of Swahili society, where flaunting Arabic was an important marker of class. All the italicized words in the stanzas quoted here are derived from Arabic and made Bantu by adding ending vowels and disallowing consonant sequences by inserting a vowel after every consonant. They are: *sababu*, "reason"; *shairi*, "poem"; *walau*, "neither"; *dini*, "religion"; *adabu*, "character"; *sadiqi*, "trustworthy"; *illa*, "but"; *khuduma*, "service"; *labuda*, "maybe"; *radhi*, "blessing"; *nadhari*, "will"; *amri*, "command"; *huramu*, "Muslim women"; *fahamu*, "know"; and *laumu,* "blame." The word *mwanadamu,* "human," combines the Bantu word *mwana,* "child," with the Semitic word *Adamu,* "Adam," such that the word "human" means "child of Adam," echoing the coming together of hinterland and overseas peoples in the formation of the Swahili—but with a clear emphasis on Arabic, the language of their religion. The pronunciation of the word *Mungu* as *Mngu* is one way of rendering an Arabic-like pronunciation to the word *Murungu,* the Bantu word for "God," variations of which are heard across many Bantu languages. The underlined words in the quoted verse reveal more of what is typical of Pate Swahili, as I have described in table 6.1.[40]

TABLE 6.1 KIPATE DIALECT COMPARED TO KIUNGUJA

KIPATE	KIUNGUJA	ENGLISH GLOSS	CHANGES
muinga	mjinga	a foolish person	/j/ deletion
stangane	usichanganyike	do not mix yourself	/t/ and /ch/
mwida	mda	time/duration	Addition of vowels
khuduma	huduma	service	The /h/ sound arabized
kuyutia	kujutia	to suffer from	/y/ is /j/ in the std
la buda	labda	maybe	Vowel to break consonant cluster
mtunde	mtunze	take care of him	/nd/ is /nz/ in Kiunguja
asiyoyua	asiyejua	who does not know	/y/ is /j/
changalie	kiangalie	look after it	/ch/ is /ki/
kieta	kileta	When (he) brings	/l/ added in Kiunguja
Mngu	Mungu	God	pronunciation difference
ntungile	natunga	I am composing	Bantu type ending which indicates aspectual marking
nili	nikiwa	being	Bantu verb 'be' still in use in Standard Swahili
usina	usiokuwa na	without	Conjugation of the verb na 'to have' as kuwa na 'to be with'
ndia	njia	way/path	/nd/ is /nj/ in Zanzibari dialect of Swahili
mbee	mbele	infront of	/l/ removed between vowels

And here to represent the Kiunguja dialect is a person whose life exemplified the story of Swahili. Siti binti Saad started off as a slave and ended up dining with kings, though she never forgot her roots.[41] Siti's story is one of the most riveting accounts in Swahili history of an individual's triumph against great adversity. She was born into slavery in the village of Fumba, outside the town of Zanzibar, in 1880. Her father was Saadi, a person of the Nyamwezi tribe from Tabora, and her mother was of the Zigua tribe from Tanga; both were born in Zanzibar. In the course of her ascent to prominence, Siti became known by the Arabic name binti Saad, that is, "the daughter of Saad."[42] She moved into an area of Zanzibar town called Ng'ambo in 1911 in search of better economic opportunity and greater personal freedom. Ng'ambo is Swahili for "the other side/across," an area where former town slaves lived away from the affluent Arabs, Asians, and Europeans who occupied elaborate stone houses. Siti was a pioneering artist in the taarab genre of East African music. The word taarab (Swahili taarabu) is Arabic. It means "having joy with music" and refers to a popular type of music influenced by the cultures of the Indian Ocean world—eastern Africa, south Asia, and the Middle East. Siti was the first woman to sing in a band in public and also a pioneer in singing taarab in Swahili (previously, it had been sung in Arabic). Siti's compositions and performance appealed to many Swahili of humble means because they told about the joys and sorrows of daily life in Ng'ambo, often castigating the injustices with which she and her friends and neighbors were living.[43] Siti "depicted vividly and expressively, the real social life, the feelings and aspirations of the Zanzibari simple people and a lot of events of her time in her songs . . . she had a uniquely expressive tone which could make her listeners laugh or even bring them to tears."[44] She memorized words in languages as varied as Swahili (her own), Hindustani, and Arabic.

Siti binti Saad is one of the few singers or poets of Swahili who are celebrated as familiar household names. She rose to stardom in 1928 when the recording company His Master's Voice (RCA Victor) selected her to produce the first gramophone record in Swahili. The production took her to Bombay, India, where she and her band recorded many Swahili songs. Siti's coperformers included Subeit (Bash) Ambar; Buda Suwedi, a violinist of great fame; and Maalim Shaaban, a singer.

Siti was a star at home and abroad. She is remembered for taking taarab "out of the palaces and into the hearts of ordinary KiSwahili-speaking Zanzibaris" (Askew 2002, 110). Shaaban bin Robert, the famous Swahili writer, interviewed Siti shortly before her death, and went on to write *Wasifu wa Siti binti Saad*, a biography of Siti. The biography was published in 1967 (posthumously, for Shaaban died in 1962) and is thought to represent some of the best literature ever written in the Swahili language. In that book, we learn of Siti's various roles as a woman, wife, mother, musician, traveler, and staf. She kept company with the entire spectrum of Swahili society, from rags to riches. According to the biography:

> Mwanamke huyu hakuishi katika namna moja ya maisha kama wanawake wengi sana walivyokuwa. Aliishi katika maisha ya namna mbalimbali. Alikuwa msichana, mfinyanzi na mwuza vyungu katika kijiji, baadaye akawa mwanamke, mwimbaji, na mwigaji katika mji. Alikuwa mtu wa dunia na dini. Katika wakati huo huo alikuwa mke, mama na msafiri. Mwanamke huyu huyu aliyetetemeka; huyu huyu aliyepotelewa na sauti kwa haya siku chache tu zilizopita, alionekana amekaa imara sana akiimba kama mtu wa picha katika tarabu ya picha.[45]

> This woman did not live a singular lifestyle like many women did those days. She had a variety of lifestyles. When a girl, she was a potter and seller of clay pots in the village, later when a woman, she was a singer, an actor in the city. She fitted well in the secular world though yet religious. At the same time she was a wife, a mother, and a traveler. This woman who trembled, who had lost her voice not long before on account of being shy, was now seen confidently sitting as though in a picture depicting a seasoned tarab singer. (my translation)

Siti was the consummate cosmopolitan citizen of a world, well beyond Zanzibar and the Swahili coast. The most beautiful thing that I have heard said about her is that she made people of many worlds sing as her voice filled the airwaves. It is said that when Siti sang, "everyone started singing the songs, children, elders, women, and men, everyone started singing."[46] That includes the peoples of Tanganyika, Uganda, Kenya, Congo, Comoros, Somalia, southern Arabia, India, and wherever else her records were sold. Other men and women of Swahili had done many things that spread their language far and wide, but Siti surpassed them all in putting Swahili into people's mouths. The Mzungu, puzzled by the high culture among the Swahili that she represented, decided the secret of her success was that Swahili, with its borrowings from Arabic and other "civilized" languages, was more developed than the languages of inner Africa.

That patronizing view may have resonated with some Swahili who were apt to distinguish themselves in the eyes of the colonial authorities as non-African, but nothing could have been further from binti Saad, the lowly girl turned queen of taarab. In Siti, with her changing fortunes, we see a panoramic view or a composite of the women of Swahili. The poor slave girl became the Arab lady. But Siti was unequivocal about the triumph of brains over beauty, as it was said that she could not make the beauty pageant list in Zanzibar. A song composed by one of her jealous rivals to ridicule her asked, "What good was a voice if it did not have a face to match?" It also posed another question:

Siti binti Saadi kawa mtu lini,	When was Siti binti Saad someone,
Kaja mjini na kaniki chini,	She came to the city wearing kaniki,[47]
Kama si sauti angekula nini?	Were it not for her voice what would she eat?

In response to the challenge of that song, Siti composed the following ode (utilizing the High Swahili of Zanzibar, replete with infusions of Arabic words, underlined here). In it, she asserted there is not much real value in beauty, wealth, or good family roots; the real tragedy is a lack of brains:

Si *hoja* uzuri,	It matters little to be beautiful
Na *sura* jamali,	To have a pretty face;
Kuwa mtukufu,	To be well known ,
Na *jadi* kebeli,	And to have a fine lineage
Hasara ya mtu,	The real misfortune of a person
Kukosa *akili*.	Is to lack intelligence.

Like Swahili, which rose from obscurity to become a regional lingua franca, Mtumwa the slave became Siti the lady, the first voice from the eastern and central African region to carry Swahili across the airwaves, endearing both herself and the language to millions. According to her biography, she was called Mtumwa binti Saad, "the slave daughter of Saad," for thirty-one years but Siti binti Saad, "the lady daughter of Saad," for thirty-nine more.[48] When Siti's voice rang out singing songs about the travails of her day, she captured the attention of her listeners and entranced more than a few. With her words, Siti binti Saad put into her songs much of what I am trying to say in this volume—that Swahili has developed as part of people going about their lives, facing challenges, adapting, and innovating. Like Jamezi in chapter 2, Siti is someone whose roots are in the hinterland but whose identity is bona fide Swahili—someone whom every Swahili is proud of to this day. Siti's Swahili is Kiunguja, the language that, as we will see in chapter 9, spread into the hinterland and also became the standard form that is now considered the only grammatical Swahili by most publishers. In effect, the abandonment of the dialects of Swahili drew a curtain behind which women's artistic expression was hidden from view and, with it, the dynamism of Swahili at its cradle. It is sobering that the published poetry of today is predominantly in one dialect (the standard Zanzibar-based one) even as there are so many behind the veil. Here, we have sampled only a few.

Siti died in 1950 but not before she had inspired other women to unite and form taarab clubs that have continued to sing her songs and their own to this day.[49] A line from her eulogy—"*Kafa na urembowe kama kanga*" ("She died with her beauty like the kanga cloth")—expressed the allure she had in life as in death, for she was a presence in everyone's life just like the kanga, the cloth that speaks Swahili.

The Lives of Women of Swahili

Having men around and being associated with them was a long-standing moral obligation for women in a culture that integrated female, primarily African, domestic authority and responsibility with immigrant male commercial and political networks. It was an expression of *heshima* (respect) and *usalama* (safety and well-being) that the women of Swahili enjoyed. These women—some having the deepest family roots of the culture, some coming from contemporary Arab immigrant backgrounds, and some with the humblest of origins as slaves—opportunistically manipulated the infinitely diverse circumstances that these broad patterns of Swahili towns offered.

In their book *Wanawake watatu wa Kiswahili*, Mirza and Strobel (1989) provide perceptive views of the three main categories in which the women of Swahili lived—slave (or involuntary immigrant), freeborn (or local and of recognized parentage), and Arab (from families of aristocratic Omani descent). As mentioned earlier, the book is focused on three women: Mishi wa Abdala, born between 1900 and 1905 and probably of slave ancestry; Bi Kaje Mwenye Matano, a *muungwana* (freeborn) who was born around 1890; and Shamsa Muhashamy, an Arab lady born in 1919.

Throughout her life, Mishi wa Abdala was surrounded by the variety of religions, ethnicities, and languages found in the Swahili culture of the coast. Her mother and maternal grandparents were Muslims from the Makua area of Mozambique who migrated to Mombasa and converted to Christianity. Mishi's father was a Zanzibari Christian named Albert. Her mother had become pregnant with Mishi before marriage and was expelled from the church congregation. She went on to settle in Kisauni, where she and her husband converted to Islam and took up new names—Mishi's mother became Fatuma, and her father became Abdala. The shift from the hinterland to Christianity to Islam was a familiar pattern that enabled women to climb the vertical axis of Swahili society subject to the histori-cal time—converting to Christianity and then Islam while seeking *riziki*, "the provisions," needed to sustain them as they moved toward a better life. Mishi had several younger siblings, including Aisha, Tatu or Salma, Thula, Mbaya, Sudi, Buki, and Omari. The names of these siblings reflect the makeup of the Swahili people—Aisha, Salma, Sudi, and Omari are Arabic names, and Thula, Mbaya, and Buki are Bantu. Mishi was raised for three or four years by Bi Aziza Jeneby, a wealthy Arab lady. Mishi's *somo* (ini-tiator to adulthood) was named Thula and was described as "a person of Old Mombasa"—a description that translates as from among the *mijikenda* ("the Chonyi, Digo, Giriama") and underlines the inalienable posture be-tween the Swahili country and hinterland. Mishi married Mbaruk, a Mus-lim, who was a cook for the colonial military, and gave birth to Halima, her only child. The name Halima is Arabic and in keeping with the idea that children born of Arab fathers and local women (including slaves) joined the freeborn aristocratic class of their fathers. Mishi learned to sew, crochet, knit, darn socks, and perform other domestic tasks from the white woman at whose Nairobi house Mishi's husband worked for six years. Such oppor-tunities were secured by establishing connections, seeking patrons from an Arab family with deep connections in the Mombasa (Swahili) elite in order to attain some degree of personal autonomy via wages. By the time Mbaruk divorced her, Mishi was already in a position of considerable personal in-dependence, and the fact that, unlike her mother, she did not have multiple children made her desirable to an established Arab gentleman named Maz-rui Lamini of Takaungu, described as "a very good man." Mishi wa Abdala was representative of the vast population of women who went to Swahili towns from the interior regions of the continent and wound up becoming Swahili. It is not a surprise, then, that the Swahili language and traditions are imbued with a variety of words, habits, and practices from the peoples residing farther inland.

Bi Kaje Mwenye Matano was born around 1890 into the patrician class of Swahili families who are said to descend from the twelve indigenous tribes of the population in the Mombasa area. Bi Kaje's paternal grandfather—Mwenye Matano bin Msumbeni—arrived in Mombasa from Pemba and married her grandmother—Ndaasili—there. Together, they had four children, although two died during infancy and another passed away as a young adult. Bi Kaje did not go to school and was taught to pray but not to write for fear that she would correspond with men rather than be married through her parents' connections; in her own words, "They made us [women] idiots." During her youth, women were too secluded, in her opinion, and she was not allowed to dance. Later, as education was made available to women, they became independent and employable, and they could choose their own spouses.

Bi Kaje's grandmother, Bi Hindi, was the head of the household, and Bi Kaje's father worked for her—sewing and selling clothes. This woman owned a house with many slaves, and she was given two farms by her ex-husbands after divorcing them. As heir to the original twelve tribes native to Mombasa, Bi Kaje had social standing, and to her, all others (Arabs, Comorians, Indians) were immigrants. Her family did not want intermarriages with anyone whose freeborn status could not be established—even Arabs, since they could have been slaves back in their former homes. After Bi Hindi died, her heirs claimed their portions of her estate and left. Bi Kaje's father inherited a farm and two slaves—Faida (a slave name meaning "profit" in Swahili) and Takosani (meaning "what do I lack?"). Faida was a Luguru, from Morogoro in the hinterland of what is now western Tanzania, whom Bi Kaje's father treated as a concubine; they had a child who died. The second slave, Takosani, worked as she liked, and Bi Kaje didn't insist on greater service. Later, Takosani left to work for the Indians, and Bi Kaje lost contact with her. There were different shades of slavery among the Swahili. In many ways, the slaves in Bi Kaje's homestead were like other dependent members of the extended and fluid household. The personal autonomy and intimate presence of women such as Faida and Takosani could not help but contribute ideas and words from the mainland to the households in which children grew up on the Swahili coast. Consequently, Arabic prevails in the formal religion and in the aristocrat waungwana echelons of male public spaces (in the mosque, in trade records, among merchant and sailors), but

Swahili is dominant in the domestic arena and in the labor force—among farm laborers, fishermen, dockworkers, and porters—and it is infused with words from the hinterland from whence a majority of these people came.

Bi Kaje's parents married her to Mohamadi (a suitable relative) in 1907, but the marriage did not last, partly because Mohamadi did not work regularly and whenever he did his own mother took the money he earned. Bi Kaje gave birth to an infant who died. She sued her husband for not working, and one night, she ran away. She married again, this time to Ali Mohamad. She had two children with this second husband. Later, she married a third man, Athman wa Shemlandi, as a second wife and had three children by him. In Bi Kaje's life, we see what becoming Swahili meant to a woman. Marriages were strategic and serial because that is the way slave women such as Faida stepped into a better life as concubines. Other people, among them Bi Kaje's father, worked their way up, and women like Bi Kaje strove to stay up by marrying men with the right pedigree and, if circumstances demanded it, suing slothful husbands to force them to work.

Shamsa Muhashamy represented the Arab woman of Swahili. She was also called Mwana Kutani (meaning Princess Kutani), which suggests her pedigree. She was born in 1919 in old town Mombasa, at the end of World War I and as the British were establishing a significant colonial administrative presence in Kenya, transforming an earlier "protectorate" into a Crown Colony in 1920. Her father, a court clerk educated in Egypt who was part of this consolidation, provided for her a lifestyle that was the talk of the town. Though a conservative Muslim, he raised Shamsa in a European style very different from that of other Muslim girls of her time. She wore hats and pants and went out without a veil on some occasions. Her father allowed her and her mother to do the forbidden—ride bikes, drive an automobile, and shoot guns. Shamsa's mother did not remain secluded like other Muslim women in Mombasa, causing Shamsha's maternal grandparents to declare their disapproval: "*Huyu mtoto wetu anakwisha haribika*" ("Our child has been ruined" [lit. "This child of ours has already gone bad"]).

British colonial law notwithstanding, Muslim domestic law was respected, and husbands and fathers had the right to do what they wished with their wives and children.[50] Thus, when Shamsa was nine years old, she was enrolled in a Christian mission school because there was no school for Arab girls. In the 1930s, this decision provoked an uproar among Shamsa's many relatives, for they were opposed to a Muslim girl going to a mission school; they viewed this as eroding their Muslim way of life and a direct road to sin. Sheikh Al-Amin bin Aly protested in a booklet of entitled *Uwongozi* (Leadership) (1955, 1) under the heading *Wajibu wetu wetu kwa wanawake* (Our responsibilities to our women):

> Tazameni Tume wawata wamevaa nguo za kizungu hatuku-wambia neno, wameona ni jambo zuri walilotenda, wameingia kukata nyele Kizungu, na hili walipoona hawakuambiwa neno, wawavisha vijana vyepeu; na hao wengine sasa wenda misheni kusoma Kizungu, nasi tukimya twatofaraji. Na tukiendelea ka-tika mwendo huu si ajabu kesho watavua taji na kesho kutwa, hao wendao kwa Misheni, si ajabu kuingia kanisan! Basi hapo ndipo itakapotufunukia faida ya kupuzisha kwetu, na hapo ndipo tutakapo juta *na majuto ni mjukuu!*[51]

> Look, we have let them wear European clothes we didn't say a word to them, they have seen what they have done is a good thing. They resorted to cutting their hair like the Europeans and when they saw that we didn't tell them anything they dressed the youth in (European) hats; and the other ones are going to mission to study [and] get an English education. If we remain quiet we are comforting them. If we continue in this fashion it won't be a sur-prise tomorrow when they take off the crown and on the day after that to find those who go to mission also joining the church. That's when we will realize the returns of not acting [resting], and that's when we will regret, and *remorse is like a grandchild* [comes when it is too late to change anything]. (my translation)

Al-Amni bin Aly's book *Uwongozi* was a collection of lessons and advice on issues designed to lead Muslims along the right path in both religion and life, with a sense of urgency regarding the attractive distractions that were offered to Swahili youth by the British, potentially leading them away from their inherited Muslim Swahili respectability. Although Sheikh Al Amin, Islamic clerics and judges, and many parents of devout standing in the Muslim community saw these opportunities for the younger generation as detrimental to their own control of their children, a section of the women of Swahili were undeterred in embracing them—particularly those (slaves) who had no legacy to carry on. Trained in English ways, Shamsa became a woman's rights activist, following in the footsteps of her own mother, who had been an ardent organizer of Muslim women's groups raising funds for *arusi (harusi)* (weddings), *ngoma* (dances), and *mazishi* (funerals) within the Muslim community. Experiencing the difficulties of raising funds for public purposes, Shamsa spoke against the expensive family weddings that her mother had supported, arguing that being less extravagant did not undermine festivities involving family and community and had nothing to do with copying Europeans. Times had changed, she insisted, and funds had to be retained in order for women to help one another when the need arose in the expanding cash sector of the economy.[52]

Shamsa and her mother organized a kanga strike in 1942 to protest exploitation by the Indian traders who controlled the supplies of the imported cloths.[53] At the arusi, ngoma, and mazishi, women bought and wore *sare,* kanga that were identical for all female participants—a performance of shared support for the occasion that continues to this day. The kanga business was very good for Indian traders because they took cash deposits for the orders the women placed, having made their selections from a limited display of patterns in catalogs before the traders purchased the cloth specified. But then the traders employed the old bait-and-switch tactic that is universal in retailing and common in holiday sales in American supermarkets and department stores. They brought out other, better patterns, tempting the women to buy different materials and in the process forfeit their deposits on the less desirable cloths they had already committed to purchase. The magnitude of the racket was revealed when Shamsa and her mother went about collecting unclaimed receipts for deposits and came up with more than five hundred thousand shillings.[54]

Publicizing the magnitude of the practice united its victims to boycott the Indian traders and refuse to buy their kanga. Some women resorted to obtaining kanga from neighboring Tanganyika, but the demand was too great to satisfy the Swahili marriage market in that indirect way. As a result, after a year the Indians stopped collecting deposits, and the women of Mombasa returned to these traders. The boycott revealed that family and community celebrations held by women were a major factor in the Swahili economy and that women had the power to effect change in the cash economy of the colony.

The complementarity of this paring and the dignity accorded both sides is why Shamsa the activist said that "*Nataka niwe mtu kamili, nipate mume anioe*" ("I want to be a complete person, by getting a man to marry me"). Shamsa married, and in 1934, she and her husband went to Malindi to live, returning to Mombasa in 1942. Between 1946 and 1947, they separated, and

Shamsa went to Zanzibar and Dar es Salaam to visit (presumably) family or associates there. She forced her husband to divorce her by taking him to a *kadhi* (a judge who has jurisdiction over all legal matters involving Muslims), and they wound up splitting in 1949.[55] Four years later, she married Ali Salim Jeneby, a relative who was previously married (with children) and worked as a law clerk. Sequential marriages seem to have been a common strategy to gain autonomy for many women of Swahili. Young women's first husbands were often chosen by their male relatives. Because wealthier Muslim men could have as many as four wives each and because women in Islamic marriages had the legal right to leave their husbands if the latter failed to afford them a lifestyle that matched the conditions of their upbringing, there was a significant shortage of marriageable females. This situation encouraged the importation of slave women, and at the same time, it enhanced the ability of slave women to rise above the disgrace of their arrival, thereby reinvigorating the entire cycle.

Not all the women of Swahili succeeded. Many lost everything in pursuing strategies built around relationships with men. Zaru binti Abdala, for example, was a young Maasai woman who worked as a housegirl for an Indian and was kept as a suria by an Arab called Ali. In 1921, Ali took her to Muscat (in Oman), where they married and lived together for eight years. When Ali took Zaru back to Kenya, he abandoned her and took all her money and jewelry, as well as the personal documentation that British authorities required by that time. Destitute and with no colonial identity, Zaru vanished into the burgeoning colonial administrative and rail transportation center of Nairobi, in the high plains of the interior.

Some of the women of Swahili who were shortchanged by their entanglements with men fought for their rights. In 1902, Aisha binti Valli, Nyanya binti Hamisi, and Fatuma binti Shaabek confronted one another in court over disputed rights to property and to challenge the paternity of a child (Nyanya) borne by a concubine of Fatuma's late husband, Hamisi. The husband had had a slave suria named Aisha with whom he cohabited, but then, after a quarrel, he had married her off to a Mr. Mbaruku. Aisha had moved from Hamisi's house straight to Mbaruku's, where, eight months later, she gave birth to a child. Hamisi had died in the meanwhile before excluding Nyanya from his willed inheritance. Fatuma, the widow, went to court seeking to remove Nyanya from the estate, claiming that under Islamic law, Aisha was supposed to have observed *edat*—a three-month period of mourning before she could cohabit with the new husband. Fatuma won the case.

In December 1918, Korshen bin Zaid claimed in another Muslim court that he had given a house as *nathira* (an irrevocable gift) to his wife Mwanate binti Mzee. Later, he had divorced Mwanate and gone his way, only to return and ask his former wife to remarry him. She refused. Korshen alleged that there had been a verbal agreement for her to return the house should they divorce. Mwanate denied there had been such an agreement and won the case.

The marriages of the women of Swahili produced complicated family lives. But these women were not shy about fighting for the spoils of their strategies of dependency. Watching the experience of the women makes Mwana Kupona's advice to her daughter quite poignant; indeed, it was a treatise of immensely deep insights and understanding about the life of women in the rise of Swahili, the people, the language, and the culture.

Kangas/Leso—The Cloth That Speaks

Kangas are "two rectangles of cotton cloth, one worn as a dress fastened above the breasts, and the other as a headdress and shawl covering the shoulders," writes Sharifa Zawawi (2005, vii), noting that the kanga is "a centuries old communication device" because each has a *jina*, "name," that constitutes a message in Swahili. We know the kanga is centuries old, argues Zawawi, because some of the earliest mentions of "two pieces of cloth" worn by residents of East African littoral towns come from Arab traveler accounts, going back to Al Idrisi in the twelfth century and Ibn Battuta in the fourteenth and confirmed by the Portuguese Duarte Barbosa in the fifteenth and early sixteenth centuries.

The Indian Ocean coast of Africa has been a place of fashion for a very long time. One accounts notes, for instance, that in the sixteenth century the women of Mafia, Pemba, and Zanzibar "go bravely decked, they wear many jewels of fine Sofala gold, silver too in plenty, earrings, necklaces, bangles, and bracelets, and they go clad in good silk garment."[56] These articles of beauty and fashion were made of raw materials and technologies drawn from the African, Arab, and Asian worlds. Syncretism in fashion mirrors the diversity of sources that has been a defining characteristic of Swahili culture.

The kanga/leso is a piece of cloth that was originally Swahili and is now used widely by other communities of the East African region and beyond. The Swahili are wrapped in this cloth from birth to death. The kanga is worn by Swahili women and men, young and old, modern and traditional, rich and poor, educated and illiterate, in wakefulness and in sleep, from the Comoros Islands to Oman.[57] Babies are wrapped in kanga from the moment they are born. Women cover themselves in kanga when they perform their five daily prayers, read the Koran, and recite the Maulidi celebrating the Prophet Muhammad's birthday. The Swahili bride is presented with numerous pairs of kanga as her dowry. Women cover their heads in kanga during wakes and when attending a funeral, and kanga are among the pieces of cloth that are customarily used to cover a Swahili woman when she dies. Some men, too, wear kanga all the time, like a *shuka* or *kikoi*[58] from the waist down. Both Swahili men and women use kanga instead of bedsheets to cover themselves during sleep. Kanga make appropriate gifts to women and among women in all seasons and for all occasions. There are numerous ways in which the kanga is worn. Jeannette Hanby and David Bygott (1984) actually list 101 ways of tying the kanga for specific occasions. In Tanzania, kanga are used in most of the ways just outlined, even among the non-Swahili. Today, kanga are manufactured in China, Japan, India, and Holland, from whence they are imported into Swahili and Omani cities.

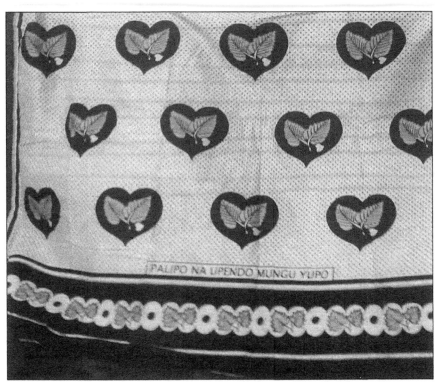

FIGURE 6.1 A kanga bearing the inscription *Palipo na Upendo Mungu Yupo,* "Wherever There Is Love God Is There"

Swahili sayings are printed on the kanga cloths, and the messages are part of the kangas' aesthetic (see figure 6.1). Beyond that, the words document historical moments, delineate social ethics, and speak to all sorts of personal issues—friendship, love, and marriage; hostility and resentment; family relationships; wealth and strength; patience, tolerance, and faith; kindness and generosity; Iddi greetings and festivity;[59] and politics and national identity. A kanga with no transcription is called *kanga bubu*, "unspeaking kanga." A kanga with inscriptions is *kanga jina*, "kanga with a name." The name of a kanga is its transcription. Accordingly the name of the kanga in figure 6 is *palipo na upendo Mungu yupo*, "wherever there is love, God is there."

The kanga bears a generic name and an inscription—a first name and a second name, both of which are laden with meanings. The generic name is the object represented in the design, and it may refer to things such as produce (for example, *embe*, "mango"; *chenza*, "tangerine"; *kungu*, "Indian almond"; *muhindi*, "maize/corn"; *korosho*, "cashew nut"; and *pilipili*, "hot pepper"), flowers (*yungi yungi*, "water lily"; *waridi*, "roses"; and *asumini*, "jasmine"), or household items (as with *msala*, "prayer mat"; *zulia*, "carpet"; and *mtungi*, "water pitcher").

The second name of the kanga is the message inscribed on it. Between 1984 and 2001, Sharifa Zawawi collected 750 kanga texts, of which 25.7 percent dealt with friendship, love, and marriage; 21.8 percent with hostility and resentment; 12.5 percent with family relationships; 9.2 percent with wealth, strength, cooperation, and competition; 8.3 percent with patience, tolerance, and faith; 8 percent with experience, knowledge, and action; 6 percent with kindness and generosity; 5.3 percent with Iddi greetings; and 3.2 percent with politics and national identity. A representative set of inscriptions appears at the end of this chapter.

Kanga inscriptions not only speak Swahili but also teach the culture. The inscriptions dealing with with friendship, love, and marriage narrate the Swahili space of social interaction, touching on various themes. The inscription *Dunia ina pepo wawili wapendanapo*, "There is heaven on earth when two people are in love," speaks to the rewards of avoiding self-centeredness, much as does *Tuishi kwa wema tupate neema*, "Let us live together amicably and we may be blessed." That moderation in the throes of such rapture is advised is captured in the admonition *Mahaba ni asali usiongeze sukari*, "Love is honey, don't add sugar."

Other kanga inscriptions convey hostility and resentment. The saying *Mbishi hakosi jibu*, "An argumentative person is never without an answer," tells of meaningless retorts from those who are dedicated to having the last word. The artificiality of the face value of things is compared to the more meaningful and enduring matters of the heart in *Shingo huvaa vyombo roho huvaa mambo,* "The neck wears jewelry; the soul wears issues." The inscription *Nimependwa na kaka yako wifi tulia,* "Sister-in-law cool down, your brother loves me," is sure to raise the uncomfortable aspects of the relations between women and their brothers' spouses, from the perspective of the wife spurned—in which the shared object of affection sparks conflict. Even the words of a popular song, *Wape wape vidonge vyao wakimeza wakitema shauri yao,* "Give them; give them their pills. It is up to them whether they swallow them or spit them out," are inscribed on the kanga to record times in which one is called upon to be forthright or tell off others, however they may take directness. The ambiguity of the kanga inscriptions creates a co-vert theater in which a drama between competing possible meanings takes place, without the wearer, or donor, saying a word. It is not unusual for kangas/lesos to be used to send subtle messages to friends, relatives, or adversaries (after all, they have deniability). Thus, the choice by a woman to wear a kanga that says *Nilidhani rafiki yangu kumbe mke mwenzangu,* "I thought you were my friend, but then I discovered you are my co-wife," may spark all manner of gossip and arguments.[60]

Examples of inscriptions relating to the other themes mentioned earlier include the saying *Undugu ni kufaana si kufanana,* "Family is taking care of one another, it is not resembling each other," which exploits the rhyming words *faana,* "to be good for each other," and *fanana,* "resemble each other," to say something about family relationships in a memorable way. The inscriptions *Vishindo vingi sio kutenda jambo,* "Too much fuss does not constitute doing something," *Kusema inshallah si kutekeleza,* "Saying God willing does not equal doing," and *Kuelekeza si kufuma,* "Aiming is not hitting," speak to the difference between preaching and practicing, planning and succeeding, and being belligerent and fighting. *Pesa fitina ya binadamu,* "Money is the instigator of discord among human beings," refers to greed for money as a malady; *Tulia kwanza,* "First, calm down," emphasizes patience and perspective; and *Mola ndiye mpaji sio mimi wala wewe,* "God is the provider, not you nor I," is an inscription that recognizes the omnipotence of the divine. Experience is inscribed in *Usipoziba ufa utajenga ukuta,* "If you do not fill the crack, you will [end up having to] rebuild the whole wall," explaining the need to take care of problems while they are still small and before they become overwhelming. Knowledge is inscribed using rice—the staple grain of the Swahili diet—in the words *Mchele moja mpishi mwingi,*[61] "There may be one kind of rice, but there are different ways of cooking it." Ostensibly, there are many ways of doing something and alas many ways of knowing.

Kindness and generosity without expecting anything in return is expressed in *Tenda wema wende zako usingoje shukrani,* "Do well and leave. Do not wait for gratitude." The inscription *Mpenzi wangu pokea mkono wa Iddi,* "My dear, accept my Idd greetings" (lit. "receive the hand of Idd"), is straightforward, as are the political statements *Wengi wape usipowapa watachukua kwa mikono yao,* "Give to the majority. If you don't give them, they will take with their own hands"; *Twalipenda azimio la Arusha,* "We like the Arusha Declaration";[62] and *Muokoa nchi ndio mwananchi,* "The citizen is the one who saves the country."

The kanga cloths carry the Swahili oral tradition from the distant past into the present and as such represent both antiquity and modernity as the successive generations read them and wear them. According to Rose Beck (2000), the kanga "became the means and visible sign of the integration of former slaves and immigrants from the African mainland into the Swahili-Muslim East African society." Zawawi tells us that "today *Kanga* texts in both Swahili and Arabic testify to this long cultural history of centuries of contact and change."[63] And now, they are more relevant than ever. They embody life, the drama, the social, the political, and the divine. The inscriptions, the textiles themselves, "regulate social behavior. *Kangas* use words to convey social values and issues and thus are capable of hurting as well as doing well. . . . They have served as a mirror of women's experiences, concern, participation and outlook on life over several centuries . . . they build cultural links anew."[64] The kanga is the ultimate ambassador of the Swahili language—as it is still the only textile that "speaks," making Swahili do more than T-shirts in that they have names that find a life of their own in social relations, including some that keep people guessing or excluded.

Spiritual and Material Culture

Like the members of recent generations whose personal stories we can know, women have hybridized the changing customs that have characterized Swahili life for centuries. Unlike the men, the enslaved women of Swahili brought with them the cultural practices of their inland origins. Among these, the puberty rites known as *unyago* are a case in point (Mirza and Strobel 1989, 59). In unyago, young women who have reached puberty are shown "the proper ways" by older women, *kungwi* (plural *makungwi*). The related ceremonies were introduced into Swahili culture by enslaved women from the Nyasa, Yao, and Ngindo areas in what is now Mozambique and Malawi (Mirza and Strobel 1989, 59). Ritual practice among the Swahili features traditional dances called *ngoma* (Swahili for "drum"). Kelly Askew describes a range of genres of ngoma and their functions in women's articulations and formations of Swahili society: *lelemama* (a dance of the freeborn Swahili women); *kunguiya, ndege,* and *ngoma ya unyago* ("initiation dances"); and *ngoma ya ndani* ("dances not performed in public but only privately in the company of other women") (Askew 2002; Fair 1996). As part of entertaining and educating, ngoma performances have been used to "exert pressure for the redistribution, or at least realignment, of power" (Askew 2002, 82). Even as some ngoma unified women on shared issues, other ngoma distinguished the slaves from the freeborn. Ngoma "involving arm and head movements were characteristic of elite, freeborn dance, while those involving hip and feet movements were far more common in dances performed among coastal slave populations. . . . Freeborn dance was performed in lines, while the dances of slaves were performed in circles."[65]

Material displays in Swahili have long been associated with women. Most archaeological finds in sites on the Swahili coast, including porcelain, beads, and dwellings, belonged to women. Often, these materials were given to women by fathers or husbands, and the recipients could not sell them (Donley-Reid 1990, 49). Porcelain plates are believed to provide protection against malevolent spirits, as they break when evil spirits are near. The use of these plates to warn of evil spirits of local origin again shows the syncretic nature of the Swahili culture, in this case led by women's mysticism, since the porcelain was imported from China. Swahili women also believe that glass beads prevent evil spirits from attacking them and their children. When a girl reaches the age of ten, her *kungwi,* or "adult female sponsor," ties a string of beads called *utunda* around her waist (Donley-Reid 1990, 51). Wearing beads is common among inland African women, and the practice on the coast is not surprising in view of the significant numbers of women calling themselves Swahili who came from inland areas.

The cooking pot is another meaningful focus in Swahili material culture—the *chungu* for cooking rice, or *ugali*; the *kaango* for cooking fish, meat, and vegetables; the *kidawa* for making medicines; the *jungu la mofa,* which is used as an oven and also as *dafina* (*jungu la mofa*) for keeping treasure; the *kia,* the lid used in the final stage of rice cooking; the *ziga,* which has been used since the fourteenth century as a portable stove (Chittick 1974, 331); and the *kijungu,* the toy pots made by girl children (Donley-Reid 1990, 53–55). The chungu, kaango, jungu la mofa, and kidawa are decorated with incisions that are "protective" in ways that their female makers and owners do not discuss: "If they were discussed, more power would be given to the women by the men, because the men would be admitting that the women could be a threat to them."[66]

Decorated pots (and other ornamented items) are associated with women. The incised lines have the mystical power of protecting the men (Donley-Reid 1990, 56). Food preparation is a cause of anxiety to a Swahili person unless it is done by a "well-trusted" person, and there are good reasons for this fear of food. Muslim masters worried about "being poisoned because their slaves and/or concubines were often freed after their deaths," [67] and the communities in the interior from which they had come were reputed to have strong magical powers. Once again, we see power available to slave women and concubines in the homes of Swahili society. An even more potent display of mystical power was the array of spirit possession cults rampant in nineteenth-century Zanzibar and elsewhere along the coast. They improved the circumstances of Swahili women by making them appear to men as being decidedly mysterious and beyond control. Invoking or entering paranormal states for women in a male-dominated society evidently has been an efficacious method of vocalizing protests against oppression, even leading to redress of deprivations (Alpers 1984; Lewis 1971; Rogers 1975).

Fumbo, the Riddle

Swahili males have always been under some form of influence exercised by the women in their lives, both in mundane things and in trade and other accomplishments, during their upbringing and in adulthood. I can imagine that the women of Swahili who had recently arrived from the hinterland would not have been too different from W. E. B. DuBois's great-great-grandmother who sang an African song to her children, who then passed it down to their children, until it reached him when he was a boy. In *The Souls of Black Folk,* DuBois wrote:

> My grandfather's grandmother was seized by an evil Dutch trader
> two centuries ago; and coming to the valleys of the Hudson and
> Housatonic, black, little, and lithe, she shivered and shrank in

the harsh north winds, looked longingly at the hills, and often crooned a heathen melody to the child between her knees, thus:

Do ba-na co-ba, ge-ne me, ge-ne me!
Do ba-na co-ba, ge-ne me, ge-ne me!
Ben d' nu-li, nu-li, nu-li, ben d' le.[68]

DuBois's family sang this tune right down to his own time in the wake of the American Civil War, "knowing," he said, "as little as our fathers what its words may mean, but knowing well the meaning of its music." DuBois continued: "The songs are indeed the siftings of centuries, the music is far more ancient than the words."[69] Melodies outlast words, and they convey the tone and meaning of the story, along with gestures and silences expressive of the cultures of the lost homelands. Stories of the myriad slave women from Africa's hinterland, such as DuBois's ancestors, who—despite being uprooted from the families that sang together—were still "crooning heathen melodies" to the Swahili children they were bringing up in the towns along the Indian Ocean provided a counterbalance to Arab tales of Sindbad the sailor; Abu Nuwas, the bad boy of the classical Arab caliphate; and the other transoceanic imports that Swahili children heard about from their fathers.

Though the story of the women of Swahili has often be truncated by neglect in male-dominated Western historiography, it has received attention in recent works by Askew (1999 and 2002), Fair (1996), and Donley-Reid (1990), among others. These authors have offered fresh insights into how the women of Swahili have been the creators of the entire story of language and culture told in this book. These women have strived to experience the fullness of life for themselves and their children under circumstances of enslavement and domestic seclusion. They have maintained and contributed to the rich Swahili literary tradition. They have been fashionable, not just the women of 1517 in Mafia, Pemba, and Zanzibar but continuously over the centuries, as evidenced by the robustness of the modern kanga/leso industry. They have emerged from being politically prudent, ruling when opportunities came to them. Through these and all the other ups and downs, African women have emerged as primary actors in the development, the spread, and the preservation of Swahili.

Languages reflect the activities, ambitions, and pleasures of their speakers. The poetry/song making, the taraab music performances, and the kanga cloth inscriptions are among the arenas of quotidian life in which women have composed and performed the development of Swahili. Songs and dances take us into women's daily communications, problem solving, relaxation, and enjoyment—*raha* (pleasure) time away from the watchful eyes of their male relatives and strangers around the towns. Songs and poetry, taarabu music, and kanga inscriptions provide a gendered view of the social interactions that produce Swahili culture and language.

Presenting women as rebels from the hinterland who refuse to work in farms, fetch water, cut firewood, and grind grain prompts a question that is heard from men at the coast: "What use is a woman of Mombasa [or some other coastal town]?" It is often answered in this manner: "She's a lazy woman who runs away and is taken in Mombasa, because she just wants to cool and eat, and she doesn't want lots of work . . . they get there, they have reached the land of luxury, they're lost."[70] In such words, we hear more than the lament of the ages as men lose their perceived control of women; we also perceive something of the contrast between the public display of power that men taunt versus the actual earth-shaping power of women in the private realm of life that, though inaudible in public, has formed the ethos of Swahili society. Women of Swahili are at once a proverb and a riddle. Like a proverb, they are "much matter decoded into few words,"[71] but like a riddle, they confound the public story of Swahili, compounding the plot when we pay attention to language. It is with language that we encounter women as the custodians of the spoken word—the key to understanding the hybrid (land and sea) nature of the Swahili language and culture. It is in their songs, their kanga world, their life stories, their spatial and spiritual migrations, their cultural practice, and their influence that we hear words that enhance our understanding of the world of the Indian Ocean. The women of Swahili have always been more than meets the eye, more than reaches the ear. This realization invites us to sharpen our focus and hearken to the sound of Swahili in order to improve our vision, to see history for what it is. We might, in fact, be well advised to listen more attentively to women's words.

Kanga Inscriptions (compiled and translated by the author)

1. *Akiba haiozi*, "Savings never go bad"

2. *Akufukuzae hwakwambii toka*, "One who wants you out does not have to tell you get out!"

3. *Asante ya punda ni mateke*, "A donkey shows its gratitude by kicking [its benefactor]"

4. *Asiyekujua hakudhamini,* "He who doesn't know you does not value you"

5. *Chako chetu,* "Yours is ours"

6. *Dua la kuku halimpati mwewe,* "A chicken's prayer does not affect a hawk"

7. *Eid Mubarak,* "Idd Blessing"

8. *Fikiri kabla hujasema,* "Think before you speak"

9. *Hakuna mlezi ashindaye mama,* "No foster parent takes the place of a mother"

10. *Halahala jirani japo ni baniyani,* "Take care of a neighbor even if he is a Hindu"

11. *Hisani haiozi,* "Kindness does not go bad"

12. *Hongera,* "Congratulations"

13. *Japo sipendezi kubembeleza siwezi,* "Though I may not be appealing, I can not sooth to be loved"

14. *Jaraha la moyoni haliponi,* "A wound/sore in the heart does not heal"

15. *Jungu kuu halikosi ukoko,* "A big pot is never without burnt bits sticking to it"

16. *Kanga fimbo ya mwanamke,* "Kanga is a woman's stick"

17. *Kanga nenda na urembo shani urembo na shani,* "Kanga go as an adornment, an ornament fine and delicate"

18. *Karibu sana,* "You are very welcome"

19. *Kikubwa sina. Kidogo pokea,* "I do not have a big gift. Receive this small one"

20. *Kikulacho ki nguoni mwako,* "What is eating you is in your cloths"

21. *Kuelekeza zi kufuma,* "Aiming is not hitting"

22. *Kumcha Mungu ni mwanzo wa hekima,* "Fear of God is the beginning of wisdom"

23. *Kupendana Amani na Umoja ni uamuzi,* "Love, Peace, and Unity is a decision"

24. *Kuuliza si ujinga,* "Asking is not ignorance"

25. *Kwenda mbio si kufika,* "Running is not arriving"

26. *Mapenzi ni nusu ya wazimu,* "Love is being half-mad"

27. *Maziwa ya mama ni bora,* "Mother's milk is best"

28. *Mimi na wewe,* "You and I"

29. *Mkono mmoja haupigi kofi*, "One hand does not clap"

30. *Mlezi hakosi shida*, "The foster parent never fails to have problems"

31. *Mpaji ni Mungu*, "The giver is God"

32. *Mpanda ovyo hula ovyo*, "Careless sowing leads to careless harvesting"

33. *Mpende akupendae*, "Love the one who loves you"

34. *Mwenye dini hakosi imani*, "He who has religion has faith"

35. *Mwenye nguvu mpishe*, "Let the strong pass"

36. *Palipo na pendo Mungu yupo*, "Wherever there is love God is there"

37. *Pesa fitina ya binadamu*, "Money is man's affliction"

38. *Sichagui sibagui anizikaye simjui*, "I don't choose, I don't discriminate; I do not know who will bury me"

39. *Sifa ya mume ni kupamba mke*, "A man's reputation lies in the way he adorns his wife"

40. *Simba mwenda kimya ndiye mla nyama*, "A quiet lion is the one that eats the meat"

41. *Subira ni njema*, "Patience is good"

42. *Tua kwanza*, "First, calm down"

43. *Tusisahau kwetu*, "Let us not forget our homeland"

44. *Twalipenda azimio la Arusha*, "We like the Arusha Declaration"

45. *Udongo uwahi ulimaji*, "Mold the clay while it is still damp"

46. *Ufukara si kilema*, "Poverty is not disability"

47. *Uleleko jana na leo kalale*, "Wherever you slept yesterday, even today go and sleep there"

48. *Urembo si sura*, "Beauty is not the looks"

49. *Utu ni kitendo chema*, "Humanity is doing a good deed"

50. *Wazazi nawaenzi nipate radhi*, "I respect my parents in order to get blessings"

CHAPTER 7

The Swahili Literary Tradition

Kulla maata samboye hwenda ali mwanamaji.

"Everyone who abandons his own vessel goes as a common sailor (on another's)."

—Swahili saying

THE SWAHILI literary tradition transcribes the experiences of a people at a crossroads of civilizations. This chapter presents that tradition through the words of Swahili proverbs; the verses of the epic of Fumo Liyongo, who occupies an important place in Swahili history and imagination; the prodigious memory of one Muhamadi Kijumwa, a polymath of Swahili in his day, who wrote in the Arabic script; and the writing of the august Shaaban Robert, the doyen of Swahili literature and master of its twentieth-century prose tradition, who wrote in the roman script. These poetic works are but a small sampling of a vast literary tradition the Swahili call *bahari,* a word with multiple meanings, one of which is "vast and extensive" (like the "ocean," another of its meanings). The works mentioned in this chapter show the intricate interweavings of the oral and written eras in the aesthetics of Swahili language composition. What has been written recently is built on oral stylings dating back more than a millennium (Prins 1958, 26). The chapter poses the question of whether an aesthetic canon of expression in a language can exist without writing. The record of Swahili shows that it can and did.

The mix of diverse peoples, cultures, and languages that is the Swahili people is reflected in their primarily oral literary tradition. At face value, an *oral literary tradition* is a contradiction in terms, since *literature* refers to letters and thus to the very distinct prose stylings of written works. But Swahili oral expressions, like many others around the world, take the form of *ngano/hadithi*, "stories"; *vitendawili*, "riddles"; *methali*, "proverbs"; *misemo*, "sayings"; *nyimbo*, "songs"; and *mashairi*, "poetry." These oral genres, or stylized forms of expression, establish a recognized canon within which composers or performers engage listeners and onlookers. The genres have multiple sources reflecting the long history of Swahili contacts with Africans living in oral environments and with literate people from overseas. Thus, the scholars of Swahili expressive culture refer loosely to all sorts of verbal aesthetic as literature, as do Mazrui and Shariff:

> Until a few decades ago, Swahili prose remained essentially oral. Some of these narratives had local origins, both Swahili and non-Swahili (e.g., Somali, Boni, Pokomo, Mijikenda, and Zaramo), while some others were local adaptations of otherwise nonlocal (especially Arabian and Persian extraction). In addition to its local allegoric tales, and animal fables, myths, and legends, the Swahili literary tradition came to be enriched with localized prose from Arab-Persian sources. In addition narratives with Islamic themes, especially those revolving around the lives of the prophets and apostles, came to be featured quite significantly in the Swahili oral prose tradition.[1]

As we shall see, the predominant form of Swahili creative writing has been poetry, which has deep roots in orality, with beginnings in song. Islamic religious poetry has traditionally had a greater chance of being preserved than secular poetry.[2]

I have chosen the proverb as the core of the Swahili tradition of verbal artistry because of its function as art in everyday conversation. Poetry, song, dance, and even prose elaborate pithy insights into living situations. Proverbs are a window through which we can view the literary world of the Swahili as a relic of conversations from yesteryear. The proverb invites attention to language and content. Why do people gather to recite poetry, narrate stories, or tell jokes but hardly ever to recite proverbs, one after the other? The reason is that the uses and meanings of proverbs depend entirely on context. Lacking a moment of engagement, one with others, the proverb floats around without an anchor. Proverbs enable people to focus on and reflect about the issues implicit in a conversation, implications of what is being said that have not yet been articulated. They are distilled nuggets of intuitive understanding, and that expansive, even explosive potential makes them a good place to start to understand the oral artistic corpus of the Swahili.

In the preface to *African Aphorisms* by William Taylor (1891, a3), W. Salter Price says that proverbs are "much matter decocted into few words." That summary, itself aphoristic, is not an understatement with regard to proverbs as gateways to Swahili history through its literary tradition. Jan Knappert (1979) notes that the Swahili proverb is "the perfect tool for poetry," and the Swahili proverb is also a good point of access to riddles, stories, prose, and songs, well beyond poetry—all important reservoirs of memory and sources of knowledge about the story of Swahili.

Proverbs as Records of History

Even though the situations or historical moments to which proverbs may apply are limited only by the knowledge and imagination of the people present in them, some proverbs are phrased in terms that memorialize encounters or events characteristic of historically specific moments. The proverb *Baniani mbaya kiatu chake dawa*, "Evil though the Asian [Indian] may be, his shoe (that he sells) is medicine," suggests that doing business with Asian shopkeepers is worthwhile even if the shopkeepers themselves may be untrustworthy. These merchants were often the owners of the *duka* (small stores) that came to eastern Africa in the first decade of the twentieth century along with British rule and the colonial cash economy, and they were reputed to be particularly untrustworthy traders—recall the story of kanga sales to the women of Swahili in chapter 6. *Duka* comes from the Hindi word *dukawalla,* or "shopkeeper." In chapter 2, we saw that Indians have never referred to themselves nor been included as "Swahili," and that may indicate ambivalence on their part about the local culture and traditions, perhaps reflecting the separation of Hindu and Muslim communities in their backgrounds in western India. Proverbs record the thinking that guided people in dealing with others who were not Muslims. The proverb *Mtumikie kafiri upate mradi wako*, "Serve the infidel and gain your objective," encourages purposeful but cautious engagement with nonbelievers. It must have gained currency after the Swahili coast had become Muslim, perhaps in the Middle Ages around the time of Ibn Battuta's fourteenth-century visit when religious differences marked the wary relationships with inland communities. Recall the proverb *Mreno hatamsahau Mswahili hadi kesho*, "The Portuguese will not forget the Swahili till tomorrow," discussed in the beginning of chapter 5.

A good number of proverbs provide images of slavery and the slave trade that obviously mark 1700–1850 CE as a memorable, if not traumatic, era for many. For instance, take the proverb *Mtumwa ni hayawana adua 'llahi u rasul,* "A slave is a brute beast, an enemy of God and the Prophet," which provides a strong rationalization for enslaving nonbelievers. The socially significant distinction between individuals who had been captured and sold into slavery versus others born into it is encapsulated in the saying *Mtumwa mwenyi busara ni azawao,* "The slave born in slavery is better suited to slavery than the captured one." The preferred slaves were the *azawao* or *mzalia,* that is, those born in slavery, as they would speak Swahili fluently and would have lost their ties to their homelands in the interior. The implication was that the captured slave was always a potential *mtoro,* "runaway/truant" slave, which was evident in the word itself, as *mtoro* comes from the Swahili verb *toroka,* "run away from." Swahili proverbs are quite mum about runaway slaves, but the slaves that found ways to cope with their situations are represented by proverbs such as *Mtumwa mwelewa hafunzwi adabu,* "A smart slave is not taught manners"—that is, one who caught on quickly about what was expected, perhaps with the encouragement of the owner's discipline. The relationship between slave and master was far from equal, hence we have *Hii yafutika, hii haifutiki,* "That [sin] can be blotted out, this one cannot be blotted out." According to Taylor (1891, 17), women commonly used this expression when scolding their slaves, meaning "It is no venial [minor] sin to disobey my orders." Taylor, a missionary, elsewhere distinguished between venial sins committed against *wana-Adamu,* "children of Adam (human beings)," which can be blotted out in the Final Judgment, and others, not forgiveable, against *Mungu,* "God." Thus, the implied mortal sin of disobeying a master indicates that slave owners perceived themselves as gods over their slaves, and this in turn makes a strong statement about the brutalities of the era of slavery in Swahili history. Another proverb—*Mpe, simnyime, na utukuni asende,* "Give him, stint him not, and don't let him go to the market"—was, according to Taylor (1891, 69–70), used to make a host sound generous to a guest while at the same time secretly signaling to the servants an opposite message, that the guest was not welcome and therefore that they should restrain from lavishing attention on the visitor.

Some proverbs refer to historical situations characteristic of the times that produced them. The proverb *Kwenda na ulele-ngoma,* "To go with the Dead March" [lit. "You-are-laid-low"] is the basis of the saying *Ilele Siu ilele!,* "Siu is laid low, is laid low!," which laments the time when the descendants of the (ancient) King Mataka, ruler of Siu, one of the oldest Swahili towns in the Lamu archipelago, was finally overcome by the Omani sultan, Sayyid Said (Taylor 1891, 48). The saying *Mvita nda mwenda-pole, mwenda kwa haraka hukwaa dole,* "Mvita is for the man who goes gently, the man who goes hastily hurts his big toe by stumbling," originates from a historically older name for Mombasa, Mvita; the name is said to have come either from the name of Shehe Mvita, claimed by many Mombasans as the warrior-founder of their city, or from Mombasa's reputation as a place of *vita,* "war." Another possibility is that the name came from *mfita,* "one who hides," given that *-t-* in the Mombasa dialect of Swahili is *-ch-* in the dialects farther north in the Lamu archipelago and the Benadir coast.[3] The irony is that *Mvita* may refer to a place of war or battle, but another ancient name for Mombasa, *Kongowea,* meant a place whose people were welcoming to strangers. Mombasa was a haven of exile well known for hosting deposed rulers from other Swahili cities.[4] Ironically, it has yet to lose this kongowea reputation as a place offering colossal pleasures—so much so that it inspires songs whose composers swear off the temptations of the city, saying *Mombasa siendi tena kuna tambo za mitego,* "I will not go to Mombasa again, there is a network of traps," and *Kuna dogo dogo nyingi,* "There are too many young seductive girls."[5] Mombasa's reputation as a vortex of pleasures untold from which there is no return is a common one. Many inlanders are believed to this day to have disappeared into Mombasa, swept up in the swirl of its legendary attractions.

Another proverb pegged to an actual event is found in Taylor (1891, 44): *Kuolesha huko utakwishilia,* "You will end up only sailing toy boats (and not the real thing)," the proverb says, meaning, "You will never get beyond child's play." Taylor explains that east coast Arabs attributed this proverb to events that led to Sayyid Said's ascension to power as ruler of Muscat and Zanzibar. Allegedly, the young Sayyid (heir to the throne) was sailing toy boats when a powerful relative (an uncle) addressed the proverb to him.[6] The youth understood the saying to mean that his uncle was plotting to usurp the throne. Later, his aunt Bibi Mauza bint el Imam orchestrated the events that led to the sixteen-year-old Sayyid slaying that uncle.[7] The alleged circumstances, whether true or not, foretold a memorably long reign, giving it an aura of inevitability and the ruler an imposing aura of omniscience.

The Swahili Proverb as Verbal Art

Swahili proverbs have an artistic side that tells a good deal about how the Swahili have utilized their language to relay important messages, explain events, and outline general principles that are at the foundation of Swahili life. The saying *Haba na haba hujaza kibaba,* "Little by little fills the big tin," is one of the best-known Swahili proverbs. It rhymes and alliterates around the -*h*- and -*b*- sounds, producing a satisfying rhythm and resonance that permits easy recall. The words *haba na haba,* "little by little [gathering of scarce objects]," suggest struggle, persistence, perseverance, and victory—a value written over everything Swahili. The proverb *Haraka haraka haina baraka,* "Hurry hurry has no blessing," is pleasing in metrical terms as well, with -*h*-, -*r*-, and -*k*- unifying the phrasing.

In Swahili, repeated action words (verbs) and adverbs often have the effect of inducing a sense of carelessness, haphazardness, or shoddiness—not intensification, as one might expect. The word *haraka* means "haste," but *haraka haraka* means "to do something fast at the expense of attentiveness, which yields mediocrity." The saying *Mla mla leo mla jana kala nini?* "The real eater is today's eater not yesterday's—having eaten yesterday is meaningless in today's hunger," with its repetition of *mla,* is a sardonic proverb cautioning against talking about the "good old days" as if they make up for a present that is not great. The alliteration of -*l*- is melodious and quite pleasing. And the repetition of nouns intensifies the focus on the topic of discussion. In the proverb *Mzaha mzaha hutumbuka usaha,* "Taking things lightly [as in caring for a wound by applying medicine] discharges pus [worsens the condition of the wound]," the repetitive use of the word *mzaha,* "jesting," rhymes with the word *usaha,* "pus"—the saying cautions that taking things lightly and paying less attention can bring unwanted consequences. Here again, the use of the vowels -*u*- and -*a*- is harmonious, as is the alliteration of the -*h*- and -*z*- (with -*s*-) in the repeated syllables -*ha*- and -*za*-, culminating in an utterance that clearly has a beat. This proverb warns against dismissing or allowing small things—a scratch, an irritation—to go unattended, leading to a gradual and inexorable worsening. It is a proverb somewhat akin to the English saying "A stitch in time saves nine." An even better parallel to the Swahili *Mzaha mzaha hutumbuka usaha* is an English proverb from medieval times about the "want of a nail." The causality chain rhymes as follows:

> For want of a nail the shoe was lost.
> For want of a shoe the horse was lost.
> For want of a horse the rider was lost.
> For want of a rider the battle was lost.

For want of a battle the kingdom was lost.
And all for the want of a horseshoe nail.[8]

The message is clear—great events are made up of the accumulation of little ones. What illustrates the great consequences of neglect of the minutest detail better than Shakespeare's play *Richard III* (ca. 1591), when we hear King Richard shouting with incredulity, "A horse! A horse! My kingdom for a horse!"

Now consider a personal favorite of mine: *Pema usijapo pema; ukipema si pema tena,* and note the bonanza of alliteration with *-p-* and *-m-* (and the not so different nasal consonant *-n-*). The proverb translates roughly as "A place is good only as long as you do not go there (and stay too long); when you do, its appeal wanes." The point is not far removed from the English saying "Familiarity breeds contempt."

The repetition of nouns is also part of the stock-in-trade of Swahili proverbs—*bandu,* "chip," in the proverb *Bandu bandu huishia gogo,* "Chip by chip a log gets depleted"; *mtu,* "person," in *Ibilisi ya mtu ni mtu,* "The evil spirit of man is man"; and *chovya,* "tasting by dipping a finger in something and licking it," in the well-known proverb *Chovya chovya humaliza buyu la asali,* "Tasting and tasting empties a calabash of honey [lit. tasting honey by dipping a finger repeatedly empties a (full) calabash of honey]." It is up to each of us to consider these and other proverbs we encounter in terms of their aesthetics and implications—the meanings far beyond their words.

Swahili proverbs play with words that are near homonyms, distinguished by only a single vowel or consonant or—as with *mla/mla*—even only by intonation. Similar-sounding words within a proverb play on associations formed by rhyming the crucial contrasts. Consider the skill of juxtaposing *urembo,* "beauty," and *urimbo,* "snare," in *Penye urembo ndipo penye urimbo,* "Where there is finery, there lies the snare." The closeness of *urembo* and *urimbo* (where only *-e-* and *-i-* make the difference) highlights the contrast in the emotional overtones of "beauty" and "snare." Ironic as the English translation may be, the exploitation of the sounds of the Swahili words conveys the lesson that the urembo of the methali is no more than skin deep— "The devil is in the details."

In the proverb *Mtaka nyingi nasaba hupata mwingi msiba,* "He who boasts of his ancestry unduly will bring plenty of trouble upon himself," the words *nasaba* and *msiba* (a punning on consonants that is typical of Arabic) are very similar but mean quite different things. The word *nasaba* refers to lineage, a quality of great importance in Swahili claims of social status—recall that we saw Ali bin Fullani in chapter 2 carefully tucking his ancestry away inside a Koran. *Msiba,* however, is a word usually referring to great sorrow, especially the agony of losing a loved one. The proverb warns that the more one craves fame, the greater the agony of loss will be should the fame wane, as it always does—clearly, a lesson worth keeping in mind in Swahili country, where economic downturns were common from city-state to city-state. Another Swahili proverb, *Mla nawe hafi nawe ila mza-liwa nawe,* "Your dining companion does not die [sympathize] with you save the one you were born with [sibling]," underscores the importance of blood ties. In *Masikini akipata matako hulia mbwata,* "When a poor person has a bonanza his buttocks [mannerisms and walk] make noise [call attention to the fact]." If bragging has a sound, *mbwata* is a sound that fits the bill. The point is straightforward—unaccustomed to wealth, a poor person out of joy tells everyone about his or her newfound fortune, but a wealthy person, by contrast, does not make a big deal of it. We have the attention-grabbing alliteration of -*t*- and the contrast of *pata,* "to get," with the onomatopoeic *mbwata.*

Along with plays on the sounds of the consonants, the repetition of the vowel sounds *a, e, i, o,* and *u* is noticeable in Swahili proverbs, clearly contributing to the audible coherence of the phrases. In *Mla mla leo mla jana kala nini,* the vowel -*a*- integrates the words, as does -*u*- in the proverb *Udugu wa nazi kukutania chunguni,* "The kinship of coconuts meets [happens] in the cooking pot." In *Penye wengi pana mengi,* it is -*e*- that takes control, and in *Pole pole ndio mwendo,* "Slowly, slowly the world moves" or "Easy does it," the -*o*- does the job. In the proverb about beauty being a potential trap, *Penye urembo ndipo penye urimbo,* "Where there is beauty, therein lies the trap," the words *urembo* and *urimbo,* though of minimal contrast, have the -*e*- and -*i*- that make for a pleasant alliteration, for which Swahili oratory is famed.

The attractive and subtly meaningful linguistic attributes of proverbs enable artistic performances of them in many styles and formats, from the spontaneous quip to quite formal patterns. The call-and-response rendition of proverbs demonstrates how verbal art is kept alive. In conversation, a speaker may seek to confirm the attention or agreement of the listener by saying one part of a proverb, expecting the partner to complete it. Thus, when someone says *haba na haba,* "little by little," you, the listener, are expected to complete the proverb, saying *hujaza kibaba,* "fills a big tin," to show respect by confirming that you are listening. This call-and-response dialogue works for some of the proverbs mentioned here: *Bandu bandu,* "Chip off chip off [strip off repeatedly]," is completed with *huishia gogo* "depletes the log"; *Chovya chovya,* "Tasting and tasting," demands *humaliza buyu la asali,* "empties a guard of honey"; *Mzaha mzaha,* "Jest, jest [Taking things lightly]," calls on *hutumbuka usaha,* "discharges pus"; and saying *Mla mla leo,* "The eater eats today," is met with *mla jana kala nini?,* "what did yesterday's eater eat? [it is irrelevant what one ate yesterday]." Proverbs are thus dialogues, not just isolated statements, because they provoke conversation. Refusing to complete the proverb can signal unwillingness to continue with the conversation, a verbal snub. In this way, the proverb is part of the well-known call-and-response style of verbal artistry throughout Africa; as words are presumed spoken to and for others, they are parts of an engagement. In contrast, writing words is a solitary business, done for readers who are not present and may not even be known. The oral qualities of Swahili expression, spoken or written, contrast deeply with the inherent qualities of literacy, as writing.

In addition to finishing one another's proverbial openings, the Swahili also invite conversational partners to fill in the blanks by alluding to well-known proverbs without stating them. For example, a proverb *Jogoo la shamba haliwiki mjini,* "The country [rural] rooster does not crow in the city," says that country bumpkins do not flex their muscles in the city, where they are strangers. This proverb resonates acutely with the centuries-old Swahili reality regarding the stark contrast between city-dwellers (ostensibly the Swahili)—represented by the city rooster—and the people of the nyika (primarily farmers) and farther inland—represented by the country rooster. Thus, one may hear a conversation in which someone says *Ah, Yeye si jogoo la shamba bwana?,* "Oh, don't you know that he is a country rooster sir?" Anyone who speaks Swahili is apt to make the connection to the proverb as well as understand the meaning conveyed—an oblique insult suggesting that "he is a country bumpkin."

Proverbs to Poetry to Prose and a Tune to Go Along

By now, you can appreciate the images and concepts from the Swahili experience that hover over Swahili proverbs. The proverb also informs Swahili poetics, in which counting syllables and making internal rhymes are fundamental. The proverb is also ready-made for call and response. A proverb can be uttered as though it has two *vipande,* "parts," each with an equal number of syllables. The proverb *Akili ni mali,* "Intelligence is wealth," has two parts of three syllables each, *a-ki-li* and then *ni-ma-li*. And our old favorite *Pole pole ndio mwendo*, "Slow slow is the way to go," has two parts, each of four syllables, *po-le-po-le* and *ndi-o-mwe-ndo*.

Proverbs provide the theme of many poems. An example of a proverb with a poem dedicated to it is *Ukuukuu wa kamba si upya wa ukambaa* (lit. "The well-worn rope of *kamba*, 'coconut coir,' is not the newness of the *ukambaa*, 'new raffia yarn'), which is to say that coconut coir, old though it may be, is always stronger than raffia yarn. The poem says:

Ukuukuu wa kamba Si uzima wa mkano:	The worn-out state of coconut coir is not the sound state of a strip of bark:
Haubali kuk'arika Mvua ikenda mno.	The latter is sure to part asunder when the rain is excessive
Huno mtuzi wa k'amba Si borohoa la p'ono	Your prawn curry is not (so bad as) a p'ono-fish hotch potch.
Kulla kwenyi kivuno Ndiko p'ishi ipimwako.	Wherever there is harvest, there is the weighing of grain.

(Taylor 1891, 123)

Many proverb songs in Swahili are rhymed in metrically structured ways. Each line in the two songs that follow is a proverb with twelve syllables—and that is not by chance.

Jitihadi haiondoi kudura—"Effort does not remove fate (God's power)"
Hazifidi nyingi za watu busara—"Men's wisdom does not help them much"
Halirudi liandikwalo hata mara—"That which is written (by God) does not go back"

(Knappert 1979, 47)

Kidole na pete, ulimi na mate—"A finger and a ring, the tongue and saliva"
Uta na upote, makaa na tete—"The bow and its bow-string, charcoal and sparks"
Watoto wapate, Mungu awalete—"Have children, may God send them"

(Knappert 1979, 50)

The proverb *Mbiu ya mgambo ikilia kuna jambo*, "The buffalo-horn for the palaver, when it sounds it means there is something important," recalls a time in the days of Swahili towns when heralds alerted residents to the approach of a dignitary. The attention they commanded was emphasized and preserved in the following ode:

Ngo! Ngo! Ngo! Ngo!	[Four beats on the buffalo-horn.]
Mbiyu ya mgambo,	The buffalo-horn for the palaver,
Ikilia ina jambo!	When it beats it means business!
Msi-mwana naereke jiwe!	She that has no child, let her carry a stone on her back
Kesho kuna mak'utano kwa Surutani	Tomorrow there is an assembly at the Sultan's,
Wake kwa waume!	Women as well as men!

(Taylor 1891, 58)

The classical Swahili poem was a composition of Swahili words designed to make them beautiful to the hearer as they conveyed their message and thus memorable. The author of the *Al Inkishafi*, widely considered the best poem in the Swahili language, stated it plainly:

Maqusudi yangu ya kudhamiri	This is my purpose, this my heart's design
nda kutunga koja kilidawiri	To string pearls in a necklace, verse on verse,
mivazi ya duri ikinawiri	The great, pure pearls of wisdom in the midst,
mikinda ya lulu nyuma nitiye	Small pearls of thought a pendant down behind
Tatunga kifungo kwa kukisafi	The clasp I'll make by polishing my words,
nikipange lulu kulla tarafi	Arrange each gem in order where it fits.
na ina nikite Inkishafi	The poem I'll call "Catechism of a Soul"—
kiza cha dhunubu kinepukiye?	So may Sin's shadow be withdrawn from me

(Sayyid Abdalla bin Ali bin Nasir, *Al Inkishafi*, ca. 1800)

Classical Swahili poetry was not a product of happenstance but a matter of careful construction. The attention paid to structure and to the relationships among all the words is why the two stanzas here speak to the deliberateness of authoring verse—wrestling with words; picking them out; pinning meanings and structures down; making sense; and associating them to places, values, and times that people recognize and care about. It is like trying out a pair of shoes before buying, walking about, running, hopping, and so on. Authors must be keen observers of society and inventive experimenters with words, sounds, and meanings. In poem after poem, Swahili poets have, for centuries, begun, as does Sayyid Abdalla, by expressing their wish to produce their very best work. They have likened writing a poem to making a deliberate, careful selection of beads, stringing them together to create something beautiful that will please and appeal to those who chance to hear the result.

For Sayyid Abdalla and others, the devotion to the task was total, with their choices of words seen as collecting the pearls and gems needed to embrace the meaning of the poem in carefully selected and well-deployed words. Indeed, strict rules of Swahili versification held sway for centuries until the writers of *Mashairi guni*, "noncanonical poetry," arose in the independence era of the 1960s—and not without resistance (Mazrui 2007, 45–82). In his 1954 book titled *Sheria za kutunga Mashairi* (The canons of Swahili versification), Kaluta Amri Abedi emphasizes the importance of *mizani*, "syllable count"; *vina*, "rhyme"; *kituo*, "theme/conclusion"; and *kujitosheleza*, "completeness." The example given here from the *Al Inkishafi* poem has eleven syllables per line, the first three lines rhyming in *-ri* endings in the one stanza and *-fi* ending in the other. The last line is the *kituo*, and it either encapsulates the message or (as in *Al Inkishafi*) serves as a conclusion of what the first three lines have elaborated. *Kujitosheleza* refers to the condition that each stanza must complete the idea it contemplates, meaning an idea ought not be started in one stanza and be completed in another or refer back to a previous one. Classical Swahili poets were wordsmiths of exquisite skill.

The Swahili proverb is story laden. Proverbs are at the heart of storytelling. The one that says *Usinifanye "punda wa dobi,"* "Don't make 'a washerman's donkey' of me," makes direct reference to the tale known as *Punda wa dobi* (The washerman's donkey), in which a rabbit entices a donkey back into the lair of the lion from whom the donkey has escaped, with great difficulty. The tale shows that the donkey, despite its huge ears, hears nothing (perception) and has no heart (wisdom), according to Taylor (1891, 127). Another proverb concerns the boss taking credit when all is well but blaming the *fundi*, "skilled artisan" (and, by extension, any expert), when things do not go well. The proverb *Kikiharibika ni cha fundi Mwalimu, kikifaa ni cha Bwana Su'udi*, "If it [the vessel] breaks, it is Fundi Mwalimu's [lit. the expert teacher-artisan's]; if it works it is Mr. Sudi's [the boss's]." According to Taylor (1891, 31), the story behind this proverb is that an artisan was building a dhow on the shore to the northeast of Mombasa, as one approaches

Free-Town, when he was asked, "*Chombo hiki ni cha nani?*," "Whose dhow is this?" He responded with the words that later became a proverb. The meaning is that the rich man takes credit for that which succeeds and leaves the failures to the hirelings.

If anything rivals the proverb in its antiquity, it is the song. Like the word itself, the song is the living lingual fossil bearing ancient words in the context of a story's universe. Whenever a story is told, songs inevitably show up in it, adding to the merriment, memorization, and meaning of the story. The songs are often in archaic form, as they are sung word for word as they have been handed down through the generations. Thus, they preserve an oral aesthetic canon. Though not Swahili, a well-known example is the Igbo song "Eze elina elina" (King do not eat do not eat), in Chinua Achebe's famous 1958 novel *Things Fall Apart*. That is the song that Ikemefuna, the talented boy from outside the community, sang just before he was murdered.

Eze elina elina	King, do not eat, do not eat!
Sala	Sala
Eze ilikwa ya	King, if you eat it
kwaba akwa oligholi	You will weep for the abomination
Ebe Danda nechi eze	Where White Ant installs king
Ebe Uzuzu nete egwu	Where Dust dances to the drums
Sala[9]	Sala[10]

The song, as Achebe evidently had learned it in an Igbo dialect as a child in the mid-twentieth century, had been preserved unaltered from the deep past of the oral tales in what is now southeastern Nigeria. It is taken from a story in which a pigheaded *eze*, "king," is warned not to eat sacred yams, a taboo with dire consequences—dishonorable death, improper burial rites, and leaving the body as food for white ants. That Achebe does not translate the song symbolizes, in a sense, the immutable antiquity of these cores of traditional tales. They are known verbatim across the always numerous dialects of a language. The Igbo of today understand the quite dated language of the song. Ikemefuna's singing the song as he is about to be killed stays with hearers of the tale and illuminates its meaning, gleaned in Okonkwo's (his killer's) fate.

So too is the song embedded in Swahili folklore. In the well-known story "Sultan Majnun," there is a song that goes:

Mama, mama, mama	Mother, mother, mother,
Nilawa ku makoikoi, nimbe	I come from the evil spirits, to sing.
Ku makoikoi, nimbe,	From the evil spirits, to sing,
Mama wee niulaga	Mother, I have killed
Nunda mla watu	The Nunda (monster), eater of people

(Steere 1870, 280)

The underlined words—*Nilawa ku* and *niulaga*—are not current Standard Swahili but lurk in the dialects of Swahili and the languages of the hinterland. *Niulaga,* "I have killed," and *nilawa,* "I come from," were recognized by the recorder of the song, Bishop Edward Steere, as taken from Yao and Nyamwezi languages in what is now northern Mozambique and central Tanzania.[11] The use of *ku* to reference location is pervasive from the hinterland to the coast to central Africa. No matter how many versions of the story tellers of the tale may create, spontaneously in dialogue with their varying listeners, the song remains constant. The many tellings and retellings of oral narratives, adapted to the occasions of their telling, all elaborate a fixed canon of songs.

Orality and Literacy

It is difficult to frame an oral literary tradition in historical terms, for it is a composite of elements—proverbs and songs—accumulated over centuries and elaborated in an infinite variety of ephemeral individual performances. What the Swahili perform and hear today may contain elements from the remote past, even from the origins of the Bantu language family, up to the late nineteenth century when writing Swahili in Arabic script reached its zenith. The history is thus told better in terms of its performers than in terms of the canon on which they build their performances. What we have are the works of the giants of the Swahili literary tradition as it is now written. I will begin with Muhamadi Kijumwa—a master, literally an embodiment, of the Swahili tradition I seek to illustrate. Kijumwa is by no means alone in his mastery, and toward the close of the chapter, I will mention other walking libraries of the Swahili literary tradition, artists steeped in the tradition who are extending it into contemporary written forms.

Muhamadi Kijumwa

Muhamadi Kijumwa was a man of many accomplishments: musician, singer, dancer, composer of song, wood-carver, plaster-molding expert,

calligrapher, painter, designer, poet, scribe, commentator, teacher of foreigners, and an icon of the Swahili literary tradition. He was the child of
a well-reputed family of Arab descent, and his forefathers held important
positions in the town of Lamu.[12] His complete name was Muhamadi bin
Abubakr bin Umar Kijumwa, to which Europeans added Masihii, "the
Messiah." He was born around 1855 in Lamu. He made the pilgrimage to
Mecca at the age of ten and repeated this distinguishing gesture of piety no
less than four times. He had great talent in artistic expression, playing the
kibangala (a lute) and dancing with an accomplished ability to improvise.
His fame grew from 1890 onward in *beni ngoma* (band music) festivities,
which blended older dance and poetry traditions with more recent ones
drawing on colonial and other influences from overseas. His abilities caught
the attention of the sultan of Zanzibar, who in 1901 invited him to become a
musician in the cosmopolitan environment of the palace.

Kijumwa was also a master carver of the kibangala he loved to play.
Other carvings he did are still part of the Lamu landscape today, where
they can be found on the bows and sterns of dhows and on the famous
heavy wooden doors of the houses of the island. His handiwork decorated
the door of the German post office and the entrance to the Lamu Museum
(Kijuma et al. 2010, 43). His distinctive style of carving blended Zanzibari,
Indian, and Omani floral motifs "with his own unusual motifs of a bird, a
pair of compasses, mangrove seeds and a pointing hand" (Athman 1996,
23). He also did plaster molding on tombstones and on walls.

Kijumwa expressed his decorative genius in Arabic calligraphy and in
painting. In the sacred language of Islam, the flowing letters themselves became a major art form. He inscribed *hirizi*, "amulets," and manuscripts for
the devout people of Lamu. Eventually, he copied manuscripts for Christian
missionaries and European scholars, for whom he also drew title pages with
motifs that were popular among Europeans, such as the dhow (Kijuma et al.
2010, 44). Missionaries used his title pages for their texts, such as St. John's
Gospel and Hichen's Azanian Classics series and many others.[13] In 1888, officials from the German Neukirchen (Reformed) Mission employed him to
copy the pamphlets and texts they used for preaching.

Kijumwa was a copyist, translator, and commentator of classical Swahili poetry and a poet himself. In Lamu, he is remembered for his short
songs and poems and also for *utendi* "epic" poetry published by Europeans. If fundi Kijumwa is remembered only as a scribe, then the *wazungu*
scholars under his tutelage were his junior scribes, doing little more than

transliterating Swahili from Arabic script into the roman letters and then translating the texts from Swahili to English. But Kijumwa understood the Swahili poetic tradition so well that he could explain it to foreigners (Kijuma et al. 2010, 48). He explained the meanings and significance of the material in the documents they produced. He was the brain, "tutor[,] and guide of many scholars" (Kijumwa et al. 2010, 57) behind the collection, transliteration, and interpretation of the well-known European Swahili scholarship of Ernst Dammann, William Hichens, Harold Ernest Lambert (district commissioner in the British administration in 1929), and John Williamson (missionary with the Anglican Church Missionary Society [CMS] in 1934).[14] Indeed, Kijumwa was able to teach Lambert how to compose Swahili poetry, "making him the only European to have written and published Swahili poetry acceptable to the Swahili" (Kijuma et al. 2010, 53; Frankl 1999, 49).

Kijumwa had attracted the attention of these European students and admirers by attending Christian church services, and by 1893, missionaries had already expressed their hope that he would convert to Christianity. He refused until 1932, when he was baptized by Missionary May, in the hope that he would not return to Lamu, where missionaries had gained no converts for decades (Kijuma et al. 2010). But he did return to the island, and the Muslims of the town ostracized him, his wife left him, and his relatives expelled him from the family (Kijuma et al. 2010, 57, 66). Kijumwa died in Lamu in 1945 and was buried according to Islamic rites. That he was Muslim is not in much doubt, as he left a will requesting that his body be buried according to Muslim law. His Islamic piety also appeared in his poems. In *Siraji*, for instance, a poem he wrote to his son Helewa, he uses many references from the Koran to admonish his offspring (in stanza 205) to take the Islamic holy book as a guide in life. This was the same Kijumwa who, it is claimed, wished to be addressed as "Bwana Masihii" by European missionaries and scholars, including Alice Werner and Ernst Dammann (Kijuma et al. 2010, 66).

Kijumwa's many abilities are well captured by the honorific *fundi*—the Swahili word that connotes respect for one's ability to excel at doing something admired. *Nakshi*—a Swahili term that refers to "all kinds of ornaments, no matter whether incised in wood, modeled in plaster or drawn on paper" (Kijuma et al. 2010, 44), described as *kutia nakshi,* "to engrave beauty"—captures the Swahili sense for the unity of concept, the canon, in the diversity of Fundi Kijumwa's expressions of it in plasterwork, wood carvings, calligraphy, poetry, translation, and interpretation. Kijumwa's life embodied the story of Swahili. He was a patrician with claims of Arab descent; he and his family were Muslim and in personal contact with the holy lands of Islam; his cultural skills enabled him to make a living; he was able to befriend outsiders; he was resourceful and unabashed about borrowing from overseas and the African hinterland; and he was eager to share the vast repertoire of Swahili knowledge with those who came in peace to the Swahili crossroad of history and cultures.

Fundi Kijumwa's story underscores the cultivated art of experts and connoisseurs in maintaining the Swahili literary tradition. His life testifies to the seamless connectedness between the oral and the written—like a song as interpreted by a singer and the sheet music inscribing the basic melody from which she sings. Oral literature captures the Swahili experience. Just as nakshi involves making decorative incisions on doors, windows, walls, and tombstones, the proverbs, songs, poems, and narratives decorate, embellish, and add contemporary meanings to a distinctly Swahili tradition. Swahili men and women are the *mafundi* (singular *fundi*); they are the libraries, conduits, producers, scholars, and teachers—many of them sophisticated intellectuals and adept practitioners.

Fundi Kijumwa was at the center of the European understanding of Swahili *tenzi*, "epic poetry." This was particularly so in the case of Ernst Dammann,[15] a missionary scholar who in 1935 began work on Old Swahili poetry after completing a two-year attachment to a missionary station in Tanga (Tanzania). On asking around, he was informed by Missionary May that Kijumwa of Lamu was the expert on Swahili verbal arts. While on route to Lamu to meet Kijumwa, Dammann made a stop at Mombasa, where he met the *liwali* (governer nominated to rule by Omani Arabs) Mbarak Ali bin Hinawy, a collector and scholar of Swahili poetry who lent him a copy of *Chuo cha Herkal (Herekali)*. Upon arrival at Lamu, Dammann began studying with Fundi Kijumwa, using that manuscript. Kijumwa read the *Herikali* for Dammann, explicating its meanings and giving detailed explanations of the lexicon, drawn from his vast knowledge of Old Swahili poetry; he easily clarified misapprehensions advanced by such noted European Bantuists as Carl Meinhof (Dammann's professor at the University of Hamburg) and weighed in on speculations and generalizations that Meinhof and others had made. Fundi Kijumwa was conversant with the detailed description of the ideal Islamic lifestyle, which nurtures the sense of community so vividly portrayed in the epics. Yet Kijumwa's own life revealed he had a critical attitude, essential to his analytical mind, toward all that he faced. In one of his poems, *Nasara wa Arabu,* Fundi Kijumwa pointed out that the monotheistic religions known to him were like "ships each one having a different captain, Musa (Moses), Isa (Jesus) and Muhammad, but all of them heading towards the same port, while the passengers of each ship consider themselves to be the chosen ones, sending the others to hell" (Kijuma et al. 2010, 50). Kijumwa was a keen observer of distinctions between the exclusivism and zealotry of the monotheistic faith traditions of his time and the openness and plurality of the Bantu spirit underlying the cosmopolitanism of Swahili culture.

Were it not for the memory, preservation, and interpretation of Muhamadi Kijumwa, we would not know two other icons of the Swahili literary tradition—Fumo Liyongo and Mwana Kupona. I chose the *Utendi wa Liyongo* (The epic of Liyongo) to illustrate the continuity of proverbs in other genres of the Swahili oral tradition. That a whole story is told in poetry, with the prose secondary, makes for a standard version of a story that, though told in multiple dialects of Swahili, preserves the details of the plot virtually intact. Before introducing the epic of Liyongo, let me say a word about Swahili epics in general.

In the two hundred years between 1730 and 1930, at least seventy-two Swahili epic poems were written, and many are still recited in Swahili towns along the East African littoral today. The *Herekali* (from English "Heraclius"), also known as *Utendi wa Tambuka* or *Utenzi wa Tambuka* (The epic of Tambuka), is dated to 1728, making it one of the earliest known written documents in Swahili. Tambuka is the Swahili rendering of Tabuk, a city in northwestern Saudi Arabia. It is also the title of one of the most famous Swahili epics that has been preserved in Arabic script. The author identifies himself in one of the final stanzas (1,146) as Mwengo, son of Athumani or Osman. The epic was written at Yunga, a royal palace that has since been destroyed, in the old city of Pate. The author notes that the sultan of Yunga wanted an epic on the heroic deeds of the first followers of the Holy Prophet as a way of incorporating Islamic history into Swahili culture. The *Tambuka* tells of numerous events of the Byzantine-Arab wars and Byzantine-Ottoman wars from 628, the battle of Mu'tah, to the fall of Constantinople in 1453 (Knappert 1977, 8).

Most Swahili epics deal with Islamic themes—thirty-seven of them address the life of the Prophet Muhammad. Many tenzi are short and didactic or liturgical. Such tenzi include *Utenzi wa Mwana Esha* (150 stanzas), which describes the nuptials of the Prophet and Aisha (who became known as *umm al-mu'minin,* or Mother of the Believers), and *Utenzi wa Shufaka* (300 stanzas), which extols the ideals of extreme generosity, altruism, and charity. Some of the long tenzi, such as those that narrate the lives of the prophets (Job's legendary patience, "the lives of Adam and Eve," Prophet Yusufu [Joseph]), are of substantial length and have individual heroism as their theme. The centrality of Islam in these epics bonds together all the Swahili city-states as a community vis-à-vis their rural non-Muslim neighbors.

Tenzi have stanzas of four lines of eight syllables and are of varying lengths. The *Katirifu,* written in the mid-eighteenth century by Abu Bakari, the son of Mwengo, has 400 stanzas (1,600 lines) replete with the clamor of arms and chivalry as a villain's plans are exposed to the wrath of the Prophet Muhammed (Knappert 1983, 52). There are epics of much greater length—*Rasi l'Ghuli* (written in the third quarter of the nineteenth century) has 4,368 stanzas (17,000 lines), and *Utenzi wa Badiri* (On the battle of Badr, in 624 CE) has 5,000 stanzas (20,000 lines, each of eight syllables). The Swahili epics of the *Herekali,* the *Huseni,* the *Abdu Rahmani,* the *Mikidadi,* the *Wadachi,* and the *Majimaji* are each composed of 1,000 stanzas (4,000 lines), which is the average length of Swahili tenzi (Knappert 1983, 52). The *Herekali* is an epic poem that will satisfy even the most demanding formalist critic, considering its great length and its highly structured organization (Knappert 1977, 55).

Kijumwa's record of the epic of Liyongo (232 stanzas) along with eighteen of Liyongo's songs were published in a 2006 book titled *Nyimbo za Liyongo, Liyongo Songs: Poems Attributed to Fumo Liyongo.*[16] Liyongo's songs are in three styles—*utendi (described above), utumbuizo, and ukawafi.* In Swahili poetry, *utumbuizo* refers to soothing songs such as serenades, odes, or lullabies; the songs exhibit elements of prosody but are more flexible in form. A defining criterion for *ukawafi* is the irregular syllabic measure, or *mizani,* within the balanced *vipande* parts of the lines. In the *ukawafi,* the number of lines varies (usually between two and four), and different stanzas are all marked by a running rhyme at the end of the last lines of verses throughout the poem.[17] I now turn to one of the most foundational epics in classical Swahili literature, the epic of Liyongo.

Fumo Liyongo wa Bauri (ca. 1600)

Fumo Liyongo wa Bauri is the earliest known Swahili poet. He was held in great awe not just by the Swahili but also by their neighbors, the Pokomo and the Oromo.[18] The Pokomo are a Bantu people who are farmers and freshwater fishermen, living along the Tana River—one of the major rivers that drain into Swahili country. The Oromo (referred to in the epic as the Galla) are famed pastoralists and renowned for their sixteenth-century great migration from Ethiopia that reached and probably established the Swahili city of Gedi, a name said to be from the Oromo language (as mentioned in chapter 4). Importantly, the story of Liyongo places the Nyika people both at the center and also at the periphery of life within the Swahili city-state. Also mentioned in the poem are the hunter-gatherer groups found in the Nyika plains adjacent to Swahili country. It is said that all the oldest Swahili songs are attributed to Liyongo, but we should bear in mind that the hinterland is implicated in their formation and historicization.

Fumo Liyongo is the most revered Swahili folk hero of the oral tradition, especially of the *gungu* (wedding dance songs), as the great nineteenth-century Swahili poet Muyaka bin Haji recorded in a poem:

Liyongo nikwambiyao	Liyongo of whom I am telling you
Shaha wa gungu na mwao	Was the Shaha of the gungu and the mwao
Tena ni mkuu wao	He was also their leader
Huwashinda wote piya	Who excelled them all

(Muyaka bin Haji, in Abdulaziz 1979, 60)

Gungu songs have lines of ten syllables each, with a caesura (pause/rest) after the fourth syllable (Knappert 1979, 64–66). Gungu dance songs are accompanied by drums and are performed at weddings and other occasions of importance to families. Liyongo's song art was of such sophistication that his compositions must have been preceded by a long period during which song art gradually evolved (Knappert 1979, 2). Liyongo was part of an ongoing local tradition of conveying the experience, in his case confronting and solving problems. The Swahili identify with that experience.[19]

In the manner of a scholar, Kijumwa pieced together the strands of the Liyongo story scattered in various tumbuizo in oral sources and manuscripts (Knappert 1979, 49). Liyongo is deemed to have been a real person, thought to have lived somewhere between the years 1230 and 1600.[20] According to a very abbreviated version of one of the best-known stories in Swahili history, he was the son of Bauri, a king of Shanga in the region of the Tana River delta; his mother was Mbwasho. Liyongo disputed the Pate throne with his maternal cousin, Daudi Mringwari, the sultan of Pate.

Liyongo was born a prince destined to rule the Tana delta, which, it seems, was taken away from him by Arabs in collusion with Mringwari.[21] Knappett (1983, 155) has suggested that Liyongo may have been heir to the Pate throne by matrilineal Bantu customary law, in which the king's sister's son inherits the throne, whereas in Islamic law, it is the king's son who ascends (in this case, Daudi, the son of Liyongo's mother's brother). If the Bantu rule of matrilineal succession had prevailed at Pate, this classic plot in the Swahili chronicles would allude to the growing influence of Islamic law and succession as Arab and other merchants took control of the commercial towns from the earlier, local owners of the lands. The story is a direct statement of the hybridity of Swahili society, involving the hinterland, kinship, land, and the Indian Ocean commercial world.

Daudi Mringwari, the sultan of Pate, plotted to get rid of Liyongo (who was a constant threat) by several means—offering a beautiful woman from the hinterland, banishing him to exile, and practicing deception, all of which culminated in a death reminiscent of Greek tragedies. Mringwari first arranged a marriage for Liyongo with a beautiful Oromo woman in the hope that his rival would live with his bride in Oromo country, far away from Pate. With that accomplished, Mringwari then offered a reward for the capture of Liyongo to the *watwa*, as the hunter-gatherers roaming the nyika adjoining the Swahili coast from Mombasa northward were known. The decree for Liyongo's arrest is preserved in the following ode (Miehe et al. 2006):

Fumo wa Shanga sikia	King of Shanga, listen,
shamba mitaa na pwani	cultivated fields, built-up areas and coast
Fumo wa Shanga 'kyambia	the King of Shanga is saying,
watwa mumfungiani.	bushmen, bind him.

The watwa mentioned in the epic include the Wasanye, Waboni, and Wadahalo, all of them non-Bantu and thought to be of Khoisan lineage and still following the foraging way of life. Currently, they are more of Afro-Asiatic (Rendile, Somali, and Oromo) stock in matters of language. Also included prominently were the pastoral Wagala (the present-day Oromo), who were referred to as *wakuu wa mwituni,* "masters of the forest," in the Liyongo epic. The plot on Liyongo's life illustrates exactly what this story has been highlighting—how inlanders were connected to the Swahili city-states. In the epic, Sultan Mringwari solicited the help of the inlanders, promising to pay the Nyika foragers handsomely with material goods. With their help, he managed to lure Liyongo back to Pate, where he captured him and threw him into prison. While in jail, Liyongo produced one of the best-known gungu songs of all time, "Wimbo wa dhiki (The song of agony)", also known as the "Jail Song." In the events that followed, we get a picture of the nurturance provided by the matrilineal Bantu side juxtaposed to the isolating qualities of the sultan's commerce.

In the *Wimbo wa Dhiki*, Liyongo prepared a message for his mother that was to be delivered by Sada, a lowly maid (*kijakazi*) who brought his mother's food to him daily at the prison (families provided food on a daily basis because the prison did not feed inmates well enough). The prison guards, whose responsibility it was to take the food Sada delivered to Liyongo, frequently helped themselves to the good loaves of bread and left the less well-formed ones for their prisoner. So Liyongo composed a song in which he asked his mother to bake an ugly loaf of bread and place a file inside, which he could use to cut the prison chains. The song went as follows:

Ewe kijakazi nakutuma	You maid, I sent you
Hujatumika kamwambie mama	You still don't understand
Ni muinga hajalimuka	Tell my mother who still is ignorant
Afanye mkate pale kati	Let her make me a loaf and put a file inside it
Tupa kaweka nikezee pingu	So that I can cut these handcuffs
Na minyoo ikinyemuka	And free myself of these chains
Nitatage kuta na madari	So that I can cross walls and roofs and break them
Yakiyepuka niue rijali	Let me kill men
Nao wakiwana hiteka	And laugh at them as they fight back
Ningie ondoni ninyepee	Let me go into the reeds
Ja mwana nyoka niingie mwituni	And creep like a fierce snake
Ningurume ja simba buka	Let me enter the forest and roar like a fierce lion

(Harries 1962, 52–55)

The song worked: Liyongo's mother understood the message and did as he requested. Liyongo learned that a death sentence had been passed on him, and upon inquiring, he was told of the day of execution. He then begged to make a dying man's last request, that the guards summon his mother, the town leader, and all the townspeople so that he could bid them farewell. His wish was granted. Upon being informed that all the people, including his mother and the slave girl Sada, were gathered outside the prison to witness the execution, Liyongo next had to figure out a way to break the chains that bound him without being heard. He needed to create a noisy distraction, so he decided to call for a party among the townspeople waiting outside. He requested that horns, cymbals, and other musical instruments be brought so that he could sing a final song. The idea of music for a dying man sounded reasonable to the Pate officials, so they granted him his wish. Upon giving instruction on how he wanted the instruments played, Liyongo then started singing, and when the music was booming, he began cutting himself loose from his shackles. Using the file, he sawed in rhythm with the music—when the noise went low, he ceased, and when it went up, he got back to work. He filed away at his chains unbeknown to the crowd outside until he at last broke free and burst out of the prison door, catching the guards totally unaware and surprising a crowd that scattered in wonderment and fear. Liyongo bid his mother farewell and then vanished into the wild, heading away to the hinterland. He had sung to the slave maid that he would "creep like a fierce snake" and "roar like a lion."

Liyongo's story demonstrates the underlying tension between the Bantu culture, with its kinship ties and domestic ethic, and the world of the Arab traders and their successors, with its emphasis on commerce and material acquistion. The "Song of Agony" is a monument in Swahili folklore in content, form, and function. The allegorical aspects of the song and its performed rendition, which is Bantu in character—the coupling of the noise of drums and singing with the filing away at the chains and the anxiety of hope and anticipation all heighten the drama of escape. Importantly, Liyongo's secret message is delivered by a woman and deciphered and executed by women. The symbolism is hard to miss: Kijakazi and Mbwasho (Liyongo's mother) feature prominently in this liberation story, signaling the larger role women played in the Swahili experience, as related in chapter 6. The relish with which Liyongo describes his intended escape and his aspiration for freedom is juxtaposed with the despair of captivity—the hinterland versus the Swahili city. In the song, the city is for Liyongo a place of betrayal where he loses his inheritance to his own kin; it then becomes a place of incarceration and plots against his life. The hinterland for him is a place of refuge and freedom when life in the city grows too hot to handle.

The intrigues of the coast were played out in the larger geographic space of the African and Indian Ocean world. By this account, we see that the

Swahili were no strangers to the hinterland but had developed "a syncretic and specialized culture along side those of other African people" (Nurse and Spear 1985, 136). Liyongo's life and poems indicate that the social and cultural connectedness between the Swahili and the inlanders was inextricable in the history of the region. These linkages, based on trade, kinship, or food production and distribution, assured the spread of Swahili into the surrounding regions, thereby making the Swahili experience a part of the experience of the larger geographic expanse.

The Swahili literary tradition projects the seamless social network between the commercial towns of the coast and the nyika, between Muslim companions and trading partners and their families and friends from the interior. Thus, Liyongo's story has continued to resonate with the historical experience of Swahili-speaking people through the centuries.

The appeal of Liyongo is that his songs entertain, bear morals, and solve the tensions between the worlds of kin and trade that make the Swahili who they are. His story has many features in common with the heroic tales told inland and overseas. One local figure that comes to mind is Luanda Magere, a famous folk hero of the Luo of Kenya and Tanzania. And as for international comparisons, Knappert (1983, 142) offers the following insights:

> Like Siegfried and Achilles, Liongo is vulnerable only in one spot of his body. Like Roland, he is a bugle blower whose bugle calls are heard far and wide; like Robin Hood, he is a great archer whose arrows never miss; like King Solomon he dies with his head back and upright and stays rigid in that position so that nobody dare approach him. Like the Cid, he fights the enemies of the nation, while the king intrigues against him. Like Ilya Muromiets, the Russian folk hero, he is secretly attacked by his own son.

Sultan Mringwari finally succeeded in doing away with Liyongo by persuading Liyongo's own son to stab his sleeping father in the navel with a copper dagger;[22] this was the only kind of attack that could kill him, a well-kept secret that Liyongo had revealed to his son. After being wounded, Liyongo chased his son to a village well, at which point he died, crouched in a kneeling position as he aimed his bow and arrow (Bantu hunting weapons) at his attacker.[23] Thus ended an epic echoing the tragedies of ancient Greece.

Kijumwa's rendition of the *Utendi wa Liyongo* illustrates the Swahili people's way with words—they are artists of orality, fundis in their language. If I had to choose a language to be used by cheerleaders of a team I cared for, it would be Swahili as spoken by Waswahili. If I could pick a language for "trash talk"—the kind of boasting used to intimidate opponents in a game—I would choose Swahili (again as spoken by a Swahili). If I were to pick a salesperson who could sell anything, a Mswahili with something to sell would be the best in the world. And if I were to wage a war of words, I would get a Swahili verbal warrior to take on my enemies—but I would want it done in spoken form, not in writing.

There is a long history of Swahili speakers' overwhelming efficacy with words. Consider, for instance, the description of Liyongo's deportment in the poem that follows, which was tailored to fit his legendary status in the Swahili imagination:

Kimo kawa mtukufu	He was of glorious stature
mpana sana mrefu	Very broad and tall
majimbo yu maarufu	He became famous in the countryside
watu huja kwangaliya	And people came to look at him
Ni mwanamume swahihi	He was a real man
kama simba una zihi	Strong as a lion
usiku na asubuhi	Be it night or day
kutembea ni mamoja	He freely moved about
Ghafla kikutokeya	If he suddenly appeared to you
mkoyo hukupoteya	You would wet yourself with fright
tapo likakuiliya	You would start trembling
ukatapa na kuliya	You would tremble as you cry out
Mato kikukodoleya	If he focused his eyes on you
ghafula utazimiya	You would faint from fear
kufa kutakurubiya	You would stare death in the face
kwa khaufu kukungiya	As fear would grip you

(Kijumwa, in TUKI 2006, 231–32, verses 7 and 13–15; translation from Harries 1962, 52–55)

These stanzas illustrate just how good Swahili is at painting images in words—something that can be found in other oral cultures of Africa too. Perhaps this dexterity is what led to the word *Mswahili* being used, not entirely in jest, to refer to any "fast talker" or "cunning person"—someone who does not lack for words, someone who always has a sales pitch, an exaggerator. Given the language describing Liyongo, I can imagine the drama with which the words are presented to a live audience. Fear and anxiety constitute the narrative arc of the Liyongo epic. Admiration of the folk hero is built around his defiance of a powerful ruler; his ability to evade capture; his mixing with the pastoral Oromo, the hunter-gatherer Wadahalo, Wasanye, and Waboni, and the farming Pokomo; and his endurance of pain, fighting to his last breath.

Shaaban bin Robert, the Doyen of Standard Swahili

Shaaban bin Robert (also called Shaaban Robert) is considered one of the greatest Swahili writers and intellectuals of twentieth-century East Africa. Indeed, his books are widely thought to be the best exemplars of the written canon. He wrote all his works in the roman alphabet and in Standard Swahili (discussed in chapter 9).

Shaaban bin Robert was born in 1909 in a village called Vibambani, near Tanga, and he was later employed by the colonial administration in its Tanganyika offices, where he worked throughout his life as a clerk. He spent his spare time writing in Swahili, excelling in both prose and poetry. He earned the stamp of approval of the Inter-territorial Language Committee early enough to be widely published by the 1940s. His work is considered a milestone in the development of modern Swahili language and literature. Robert also participated in the language reform organizations of his day, chiefly the Tanganyika Languages Board; the East Africa Swahili Committee; and, most significantly, the East Africa Literature Bureau, which for decades was the key publisher in the region.

The profuse publications of Shaaban Robert are testament to his mastery of the radical standardization being imposed on the Swahili language at the time. His utter love of the language is captured in his poem "Kiswahili," which is ardent in its praise of Swahili as his language.[24] This poem is one of his best-known compositions and an uncontested part of the Swahili canon.

Titi la mama litamu, hata likiwa la mbwa	Mother's breast is the sweetest, canine though it be,
Kiswahili naazimu, sifayo iliyofumbwa	And thou, Swahili, my mother-tongue are still the dearest to me.
Kwa wasiokufahamu, niimbe ilivyo kubwa,	My song springs forth from a welling heart, I offer this my plea

Toka kama mlizamu, funika palipozibwa	That those who have not known thee may join in homage to thee,
Titile mama litamu, jingine halishi hamu	One's mother's breast is the sweetest, no other so satisfies.

Lugha yangu ya utoto, hata sasa, nimekua	The speech of my childhood, now I am fully grown
Tangu ulimi mzito, sasa kusema, najua	I realize thy beauty and have made it all on my own
No sawa na manukato, moyoni mwangu na pua,	And thou refreshest my spirit like the scent of roses blown
Pori bahari na mto, napita nikitumia,	Through desert and o'er ocean may I make thy praises known.
Titile mama litamu, jingine mwangu mwangu	One's mother's breast is the sweetest, no other so satisfies.

In the poem, Shaaban praised the Swahili he spoke from childhood to adulthood, and not once did he mention that it was written. It is ironic that he was extolling Swahili in writing even though the ILC imprimatur restricted use of the vast dialectal riches of spoken Swahili. With this poem, Shaaban alluded to the fact that despite the meddling and controversies surrounding Swahili at the time, no other language could substitute for it. The controversies (discussed in chapter 9) included the ILC's choice of the Zanzibari dialect as the basis for Standard Swahili.

In much of his literary work, Shaaban castigated many issues of the day, including color racism, as in the poem "Rangi zetu (Our colors)" in *Masomo yenye adili* (lessons with a moral) (1967). He applauded the accomplishments of Siti binti Saad (introduced in chapter 6) in *Wasifu wa Siti Binti Saad* (The biography of Siti binti Saad) (1967). He provided advice about life to all in *Mapenzi bora* (Fine love) (1991) and to his children in *Adili na Nduguze* (Adili and his siblings) (1952). He exalted simple but industrious rural living and extolled the humanism of agriculture in *Utubora Mkulima* (farming and fine human qualities) (1968). He reflected on his life and what was to follow in *Maisha Yangu na Baada ya Miaka Hamsini* (My life and fifty years hence) (1991). He propounded a sophisticated, imaginative philosophy in *Kusadikika* (1973), a title whose literal meaning is "to be believable" but one that is closer to "The nature of belief" (Masolo 2010, 162), and *Kufikirika* (1983) (lit. "to be thinkable"), a book whose subject matter is "The nature of ideas" (Masolo 2010). He celebrated being African in *Mwafrika Aimba* (The African sings) (1969). He took time to advise young people on how to be articulate in prose writing in *Kielezo cha Insha* (Guidelines of essay writing) (1966) and *Kielezo cha Fasili* (Guidelines on versification facility) (1968). He wrote on the day of reckoning in *Siku ya Watenzi Wote* (The day of all doers) (1968). And he elevated Swahili poetry to heights previously unattained in *Pambo la Lugha* (The adornment of language) (1960). All these works have earned Shaaban bin Robert, quite deservedly, renown as "the Shakespeare of Swahili." The works are required reading for anyone educated in eastern Africa, especially in the lexicon of artistic Swahili. They are must-reads from secondary school to university in Kenya, Tanzania, and Uganda, making Shaaban one of the greatest sources and teachers of Swahili in the postindependence era. In our story, Shaaban bin Robert is a supreme example of how individuals from the hinterland were able to adapt to changes, embracing the literacy opportunities that were accessible to them and propelling their arts to new heights—even without claiming Arab ancestry.

The Lingual Ligaments of the Swahili Literary Genre

The Swahili proverb is exhibit A in support of the idea that a literary canon—or at least a verbal aesthetic canon—can and does exist in the absence of writing. Swahili conversation revolves around sets of proverbs, the lingual ligaments of conversation. From proverbs, Fumo Liyongo composed poetry; Kijumwa's memory and intellectual prowess elaborated them in many forms; and Shaaban Robert's numerous works, making him the most famous author in living memory, brought these canonical elements of the culture into modern written forms. Through them, one grasps the range of artistic riches bequeathed to the world by the Swahili experience. These people, together with Mwana Kupona, Siti binti Saad, and the other women mentioned in chapter 6, have left us a window through which to view the stories and poetry that encircled them, enriched by infusions from elsewhere in the Indian Ocean world. In the Swahili artistic conceptualization, speaking is performing. Music, chants, songs, poetry, proverbs, aphorisms, riddles, allegories, anecdotes, stories (whether imaginative or describing experience), fables, legends, myths, oral biographies and autobiographies, and drama are the genres through which the oral tradition at the base of Swahili literary products has flourished in writing in both Arabic and, recently, roman scripts. In the next chapter, I will discuss Swahili authorship in Arabic letters.

CHAPTER 8

Writing Swahili in Arabic Characters

WHEN USED for writing African languages, the Arabic alphabet is referred to in Africa as Ajami from the Arabic word *ajam*, meaning "strange" or "foreign." Ajami was used for drawing up trade and other legal documents, for private correspondence, for genealogies of the ruling families, for chronicles of towns, for literary works (primarily poems and epics), and for numerous other purposes.[1] Arabic script was also used to write Swahili, although the origins of the practice have been lost. It is alleged that the Portuguese destroyed centuries-old Swahili documents in Ajami in the sixteenth century when they razed Swahili towns, trying to bring them under their control.[2]

The Ajami script is at the base of most, if not all, Swahili poetry. Swahili versification, even when focused on secular topics, has a tone that is decidedly Muslim and thus Arabic in language. The word *Bismillah*—by which poets declare themselves to be Muslims—or a variant of it always prefaces a poem. It is usually, if not always, written in Arabic without modification for Swahili pronunciation. Closely following the Bismillah are incantations of the Prophet Muhammad and his family. These expressions of piety are seldom rushed and may take several verses in a poem or the entire opening paragraph in prose.

Swahili Writings in Ajami, Seventeenth to Twentieth Centuries

One of the most famous and revered writings in the Swahili language is a poem entitled *Al Inkishafi* (mentioned in chapter 7), which was written around 1800 CE by Sayyid Abdalla bin Ali bin Nasir. I will examine stanzas 1, 10, and 11 of this poem. In its entirety, *Al Inkishafi* has been described as a

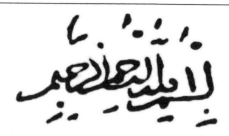

Bi-smillah ar-raḥman ar-raḥim
By the name of God the Merciful the Compassionate

FIGURE 8.1 Bismillah, the preface to most Swahili writings using the Arabic script

"major artistic achievement . . . about the human condition. It is universal, comparing human with human across cultures."[3] As an artistic masterpiece written in the Ajami tradition, *Al Inkishafi* is written in Swahili using Arabic letters to address the Mswahili soul. It is about the destruction of Liyongo's old town, Pate. In its heyday, Pate was an icon of Swahili civilization. It had beautiful architecture, lively streets, and a thriving economy. Its bustling residents were known as *wavaa ng'andu* (wearers of gold), and they were clad in silk and steeped in the material pretensions that pass for opulence and immorality in Muslim cosmology. The poem condemns such materialism by stressing the inevitable culmination of human life in death, mentioning King Solomon as a prime example of human glory "banished and cheated" by death—if it happened to King Solomon, it will happen to all of us.[4]

Bismillahi naikadimu hali ya	I put first "In the Name of God"
kutunga hino nudhumu na	as I compose this poem and I
ar-Rahmani kiirasimu basi	write "The Merciful One" and,
ar Rahemi nyuma ikaye	after that "The Benign One."
Kimakwe kwisa dibaji yangu	My preface is now ended
penda kuonya na moyo wangu	I wish to give counsel to my heart
upitwe na hawa ya ulimwengu	which is overcome by the lusts of the world
hila za rajimi ziughuriye	with the wiles of Satan which deceive.
Moyo wangu nini huzindukani	O my heart, why doest thou not awake?
likughurielo hela ni nini	but what is it that deceives thee?
hunelezi bami kalibani liwapo	thou dost not explain to me for me to discern it
na sura nisikataye	if it have countenance may I not reject it?

There is more than a tinge of the Solomonic lament about the futility of life in the whimper uttered by the glorious king—"meaningless, everything is meaningless, a chasing after the wind." The author offered a life of Muslim piety as the needed preparation for the inevitable. A leading modern Swahili scholar, Ali Mazrui, recommends that one should carry a copy of this poem when visiting the ruins of any Swahili town, reading it aloud on now-deserted sites to remind oneself of the swift passage of monuments to man's vanity.[5] The vivid imagery of *Al Inkishafi* reconstructs human life at its zenith and then its "mysterious collapse and depopulation."[6]

In depicting the ups and downs of Swahili cities in peace followed by the razing of whole cities during war and their rebuilding and recovery, only to go through the cycle again, *Al Inkishafi* has had an impact on the Swahili such that Ali Mazrui recalls his father asking him to read the poem out loud in the time of World War II.[7] In the poem's reflection on divine retribution for hubris and "the cruelty of life upon this planet, in which no man should place his trust,"[8] other Swahili have found *Al Inkishafi*

> a great consolation in all sorts of contexts—one who smuggled a copy into Zanzibar jail when he was incarcerated by the colonial regime; another who believes it saved his sanity only by repeating such sections as he could remember in the same jail after the 1964 Revolution; yet another who had a breakdown after he went bankrupt and [then] partly recovered, often [read] it to himself in a mosque or at night; and many more.[9]

The poem ends with supreme irony, making its point again in that the author himself is "cheated" by death and does not live long enough to finish the work. Engulfed by his own poem, he reminds us that even a builder of a literary monument is seldom in the world long enough to enjoy its success. *Al Inkishafi* is but one example of the range of works written in Ajami, many of which reflect the governance, business, and diplomacy of the coastal towns. Ajami was a medium in which artistic representations of experience were constructed, transmitted, and consumed. A number of adjustments to the Arabic alphabet to support a Bantu language enabled the Swahili literary canon to move from the spoken mode into the written mode. We do not know exactly when this happened, but we do know that Islam reached the eastern African coast around 700 CE, in the seventy-seventh year of the Islamic calendar during the reign of the Umayyad caliph Abdu'l-Malik ibn Marwan (685–705 CE).[10] The earliest known mosques date back to the ninth century CE.[11] Though we can deduce that some people at the coast were literate and may well have been writing, the earliest known manuscripts date only to the sixteenth or seventeenth century. Some specialists think that writing in Ajami goes back only to the eighteenth century and no earlier. But a number of scholars believe that the earliest extant poem written in Ajami is *Swifa ya Mwana Manga* (Ode to Mwana Manga), which they date to 1517 CE or 632 AH ("after the hijra"), the starting date of the Islamic calendar.[12] The leading nineteenth-century European commentator on Swahili literature, Jan Knappert (1979), believed that another poem, *Hamziyya*, dated 1652 CE, was the first, and a specialist named Lyndon Harries (1962) thought the *Tambuka*, dated 1728 CE, was the earliest surviving text. These relatively recent dates for surviving texts could be the consequence of the reported destruction of earlier collections by the Portuguese, in the sixteenth and seventeenth centuries.

The invocation "By God's name! First unto Him I pray as this, my poem's riming, I essay"[13] is the first line of the beloved poem *Al Inkishafi* (see figure 8.2).

Notice how other Arabic words—*qadimu, hali, nudhumu,* and *rasimu*—follow the Bismillah, and see for yourself the framework of Arabic in writing Swahili. In figure 8.2, the Arabic script is the top line, the Latin alphabet transliteration of the Arabic by syllable is the middle line, and the bottom line is Swahili written in the Latin script. The top and middle lines are written and read from right to left, as are all Semitic languages. Writing and reading from left to right came with Latin script when Europeans sought to write and standardize Swahili in the early twentieth century. It is no exaggeration to say that Arabic was in the conscience of the Swahili in a way that no other overseas language was, and the reversal of direction in writing the modern language is an apt metaphor for European attempts to reorient the Swahili from their deep Afrocultural and Islamic consciousness and introduce Christianity in the colonial era.

The foregrounding of every Ajami document with Arabic conventions of phrasing is not limited to Swahili verse but extends also to prose letters,

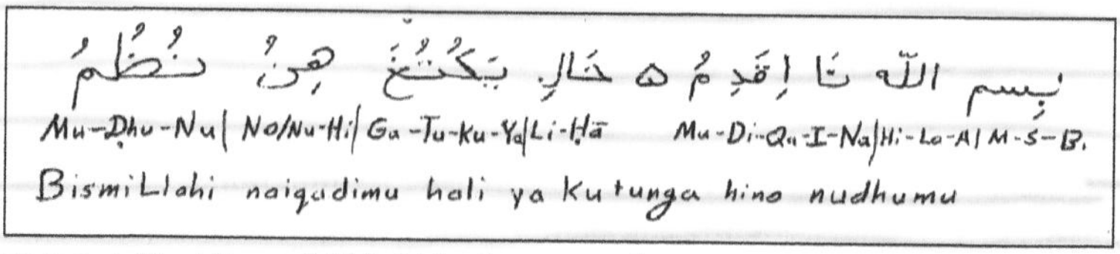

FIGURE 8.2 First line of *Al Inkishafi*, a poem by Sayyid Abdalla bin Ali bin Nasir, ca. 1800

agreements, treaties, and so on. A good portion (sometimes even half) of the texts of some documents is written in Arabic. The other half is written in Swahili using Arabic letters, either unchanged or modified to suit the sounds of the Swahili language. Consider, for instance, the writing in figure 8.3, which is the opening of a personal letter sent by Saʿīd bin ʿIsa to his trading companion in the Congo, Muhammad bin Khalfān bin Khamīs al-Barwāni.[14] This is one of a dozen letters written between 1884 and 1893 from the Stanley Falls district in the Congo (Luffin 2007, 25).

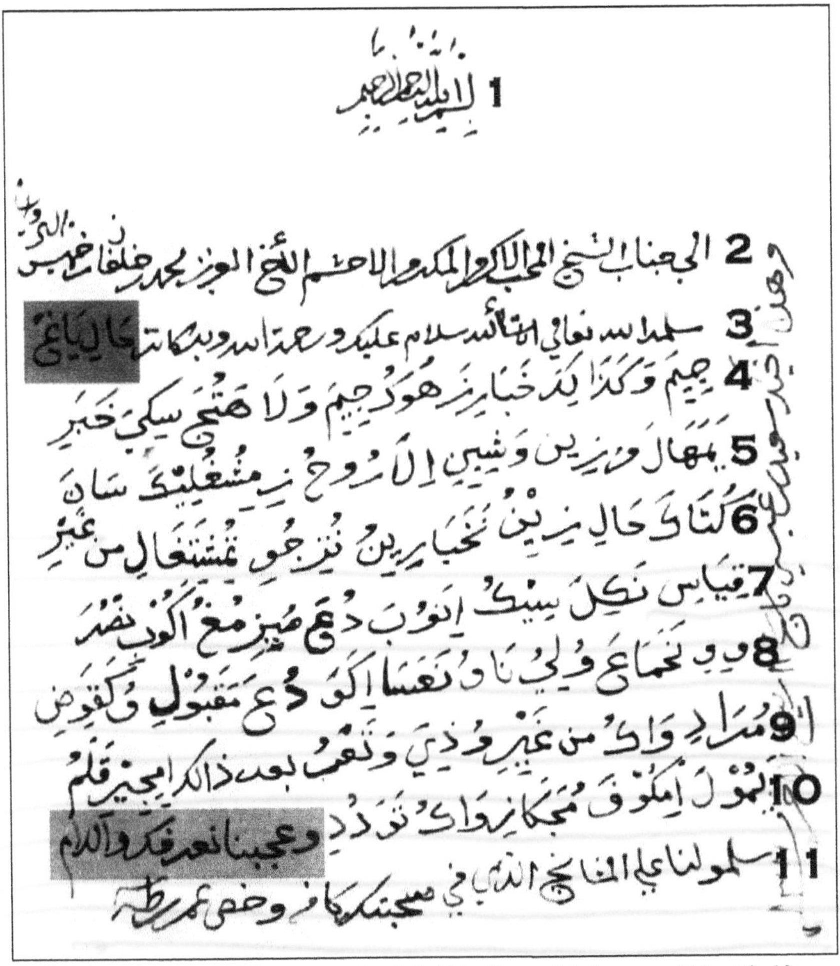

FIGURE 8.3 A personal letter sent by Saʿīd bin ʿIsa to Muhammad bin Khalfān bin Khamīs al-Barwāni, a trading companion in the Congo, one of a dozen letters written in Ajami between 1884 and 1893 from the Stanley Falls district in the Congo (Luffin 2007, 25)

[Lines 1–3 *in Arabic:*] By the name of God the Merciful the Compassionate. To your Honour the dear, generous, venerable, the modest Shaykh Muḥammad bin Khalfān bin Khamīs al-Barwānī, our dear brother, may God the Most High preserve you, with His permission, peace be with you, as well as the compassion and the blessings of God.

[Lines 4–10 *in Swahili:*] I am doing well, everything is in order here. We didn't hear any news from your side, we are worried and we really would like to know how you are. We have been very busy, and everyday I pray God Almighty, so that he gives the victory to you and your companions. If our prayers are accepted, you will obtain what you want without any pain or any trouble. By the way, the will of God has been accomplished, and Tawadudi your slave girl has passed away.

[Line 11 *in Arabic:*] We have been struck [by this event] and we inform you of this. Please greet all the Shaykhs who are with you, especially 'Umar bin Taha. This letter comes from your brother Sa'īd bin 'Īsa, it has been written the 12th of Rabī' al-ākhar 1311 (23 of october 1893).

The Arabic in the excerpt in figure 8.3 might leave the impression that it was taken from a letter written by one Arabic speaker to another, but in fact, this letter was part of a correspondence between two Swahili traders. After the salutations in Arabic, the middle of the letter is all Swahili, written using the Arabic script.

The Swahili portion contains the real reason for writing the letter—to communicate support and good wishes to a business partner and to inform that partner that his slave had died. When the message is completed, there is a concluding switch back to Arabic: "greeting other persons known to him living in the city of the addressee [*sallim la-nā 'alā al-mashāyikh . . .* 'greet the *shaykhs* so and so . . . ']" Then, the text ends with the name of the author, preceded by a formula such as *min akhī-k* ("from your brother so and so") or *kataba-hu al-haqīr* ("written by the humble so and so") and accompanied by the date in the Islamic calendar (Luffin 2007, 18). It is not surprising that many Swahili traders and patricians were quite familiar with Arabic and could conduct entire conversations in that tongue. Reading and writing Swahili in KiArabu—as Ajami becomes in Swahili—was a marker of class distinction, though it did entail certain technical challenges in representing the sounds of one language in a set of phonetic symbols designed to represent another, of a wholly different family of languages.

> All these letters follow the same pattern. They start with an isolated religious formula in Arabic, usually *bi-manni-hi taʿālā* ("by the grace of [God] the very High"), sometimes *bi- smil-lāh ar-rahmān ar-rahīm* ("In the name of God the Merciful the Compassionate"). Then, a sentence in Arabic—usually one or two lines—contains the name of the addressee introduced by re- dundant honorific formulas (like *ilā janāb al-shaykh al-muhabb al-akram al mukarram al-ahs ham al-akh* . . . "to his majesty the dear, generous, respected and pious *shaykh* and brother so and so . . . ") and salutations. (Luffin 2007, 18)

Paying homage to the Arabic language and Islam in writing Swahili in the Arabic script is more than a way to display the piety of the writer. It is showy in the elaborate use of honorifics, and one can expect the pronunciation to be closer to Arabic than to Bantu. Pride in being able to speak Arabic is written all over the note in figure 8.3. As chapter 2 emphasized, speaking Arabic was a marker of social rank among Swahili patricians, an affecta- tion for which the Mombasans were particularly notorious. Arabic interjec- tions, words, and phrases became markers of Swahili spoken and written with social capital. This saliency of Arabic as a marker of prestige, power, and piety is part of the reason why Tippu Tip, the notorious Swahili trader and slaver in central Africa in the later nineteenth century, used an ex- tended name stating his paternal lineage, as is the Arab custom: Hamad bin Muḥammad bin Jumah bin Rajab bin Muḥammad bin Saʿīd al-Murghabī Sheikh.[15] Clearly, the Arabic language was embraced at the personal level, which explains why Ali bin Fulani, whom we met in chapter 2, has a written lineage tucked away in his Koran as one of his most prized possessions. The prestige of Arabic explains why the connectors, *bin,* have prevailed in Ajami Swahili, in place of the Bantu associative, *wa,* as in the name of the famous writer Ngugi wa Thiongʼo (Ngugi son of Thiongʼo) of Kenya.

Arabic Script and Bantu Speech

The adoption of Arabic script presented a problem to Swahili writers in that the phonetic symbols, the letters, made distinctions that were not pres- ent in Bantu languages and did not even approximate other sounds that carried meaning in Swahili. Anyone literate in English who has struggled with spelling in French—or vice versa—recognizes the challenges of using the same Latin letters to represent differing phonetic systems, even in languages that are relatively closely related. The sound systems of Arabic and Bantu languages, including Swahili, are much more remote.

Figure 8.4 lists the letters representing the speech sounds of Arabic.

FIGURE 8.4 Arabic alphabet

The Arabic sounds are far from a perfect match with the Swahili sounds. Arabic sounds, such as 'Ayn, Dhal, Ghayn, and Ha, stand out as foreign. The speech sounds of Swahili marked with an asterisk in figure 8.5 are not found in Arabic—at least twenty-two speech sounds of Swahili have no direct or obvious representation in the Arabic script.

CONSONANTS			VOWELS
b	z	k	a
*bw	*nz	*kw	*e
*mb,	sh	w	i
*mbw	*ch	y	*o
*p	s	*ny	u
*mp	*sw		
*pw	gh		
t	*g,		
t'	*ng,		
*tw	*ng'		
j	f		
*nj	*v		
d	*vy		
*nd	*fy		

FIGURE 8.5 Swahili speech sounds

The differences in the sounds of the two languages make it difficult to represent Swahili words in Arabic letters. How to use the Arabic script to convey meanings in Swahili was as subtle a puzzle as one can devise, but the Swahili met the challenge. Swahili has five vowels similar to those in English—/a, e, i, o, u/—whereas Arabic has only three—/a, i, u/. This dearth of vowels in Arabic compelled the Swahili to be innovative to account for the /e/ and /o/ that are absent in Arabic when writing words such as *lea* ("raise") and *lia* ("cry") or *pinduka* ("overturn") and *pondeka* ("dented"). Consonants were challenging as well, as many of them were not available in Arabic. Left unmodified, the Arabic alphabet could capture only a very limited range of the Swahili vocabulary.

The Swahili devised two ways of capturing the sounds of their spoken language that were missing in the Arabic alphabet. One was to use the script without modification, as in the letter quoted earlier (figure 8.3), in which no change was made on the Arabic alphabet. The meanings captured with this crude technique would have challenged the reader in the way that muffled speech demands the concentration of a listener. In Arabic, vowels are known by context, but this is not the case with Swahili. If readers knew the topic, as in formulaic speech, they could intuit the specifics not represented in writing. With this limited scriptural representation of speech, it would be much harder to convey new information or original thought. We exchange conventional pleasantries without fully articulating them; unfamiliar information requires precise articulation, fuller phrasing, and repetition that is possible in conversation but not in writing.

In figure 8.6, we see that Arabic "*b*" (ب) would have to cover a range of Swahili articulations—*b* plus *mb, p, mp*, and *pw*, none expressed in Arabic letters, and the Arabic "*f*" (ف), for the Swahili *f*, would also have to do for the Swahili *v, vy*, and *fy*, none of which is found in Arabic. Several other Swahili consonants encounter the same gaps in Arabic orthography. As indicated in the figure, the gap between speech and script is big, presenting serious difficulties in expression (Bosha and Nchimbi 1993, 18). Figure 8.6 shows what Arabic letters represent in Swahili without modification (Ajami).[16]

Let us now take a look at the ingenuity of the Swahili in their adaptation of the Arabic script to their own language. Figure 8.3 indicates, for instance, that the scribes of the Congolese documents typically used only the canonical Arabic alphabet, without additional consonants.[17] As in coastal Ajami, Congo Ajami sometimes has one letter corresponding to two different Swahili sounds. In figure 8.3, the Arabic short vowel *damma* is used for both *o*

Arabic			Swahili
ب	(b)	represents	b, bw, mb, mbw, p, mp, pw.
ت	(t)		t, t', ṭ, ṭ', tw
ج	(j)		j, nj
د	(d)		d, ḍ, nd, nḍ
ز	(z)		z, nz
ش	(sh)		sh, ch, ch'
ص	(s)		sw
غ	(gh)		g, ng, ng' (velar nasal)
ف	(f)		f, v, vy, fy
ك	(k)		k, kw, k', kw'
و	(w)		ʋ, (bi-labial fricative)
ى	(y)		y, ny

FIGURE 8.6 Arabic sounds used to represent more than one Swahili sound. (Abdulaziz 1994, 70)

and *u*, and *kasra* is used for both *i* and *e*. The consonants *bā', fā', jīm,* and *ghayn* are read as *b* or *p, f* or *v, j* or *nj,* and *gh* or *ng,* respectively. But some documents use additional dots to distinguish certain pairs of sounds: a *bā'* with three dots spells *p*, a *fā'* with three dots spells *v*, and *'ayn* with three dots spells *ng*. The stress on the syllable is often indicated by a long vowel (as in *sāna, khabāri,* and *yāngu* for *sana, habari,* and *yangu*), but this refinement is not consistent, even within the same text.

Nonetheless, there was a method to the writing and the reading of Ajami adaptations of oral Swahili. The Swahili used what they could of the Arabic script—they did not have the consonant *qaaf* (ق) in their language, so they used it for the "*k*" sound. Thus, the Arabic *waqf* became *wakfu* (sanctification), and *waafaq* (reach agreement) was renderd as *afiki*. In both instances, the Arabic borrowings were also made to conform to Bantu word structure by adding vowels at the ends. In every instance when Swahili speakers did not have a consonant represented in Arabic, they found viable substitutes. The *'ayn* in the Arabic *mu'alim* (leader of the faithful/teacher) is lost in the natural realization of /w/ whenever /u/ and /a/ meet in the Swahili syllable (and elsewhere in Bantu). The result is *mwalimu* (teacher), as Julius Kambarage Nyerere, the first president of independent Tanzania, liked to identify himself.

The inadequacy of the Arabic script presented an opportunity for writers of Swahili to be creative, as their predecessors had been in their oral adaptations of foreign words (see chapter 2). Nothing stayed the same once it got into Swahili hands. The Swahili used the script for what it could provide and then proceeded to make adjustments to the Arabic base as needed to produce an effective Swahili Ajami. Writers of Swahili Ajami pursued no standardized script to which every writer adhered. They employed whatever conventions their particular readers understood. Some authors followed the Arabic script and relied on the reader to be able to navigate through words with the multiple associations of one Arabic letter for several Swahili ones. Such implicit understanding applied in the letters from the Congo shown in figure 8.3. Other authors altered the Arabic script in their own ways.

Among those who did tinker with the Arabic script was Muyaka bin Haji (1776–1840), one of the most prolific and outstanding composers of Swahili verse. His poetry—and that of many others—shows the ingenuity of the Swahili in writing Swahili sounds that were missing in the Arabic script. They made the desired distinctions between sounds while maintaining the method of Arabic writing. A few examples are in order.

The Arabic "*d*" (*daal*) (د) is "dental," meaning a sound produced by placing the tongue on the inside of the upper front teeth and popping air out, but the Swahili "*d*" is "alveolar," produced with the tongue placed on the hard palate, the roof of the mouth immediately above the teeth. To represent this distinction, rather than merely using the Arabic symbol (د) the Swahili added four dots above that symbol. Why use four dots where fewer might have sufficed? The Swahili had done a similar thing for the sound "*t*," which is alveolar in Swahili but dental in Arabic and written as *tā* (ت) but alveolar in Swahili, which is absent in Arabic. Because the Arabic alveolar "*t*" already had two dots, the Swahili added two more and wrote it as indicated in figure 8.7.

Swahili/Arabic Script

t (dental)	ت
t (alveolar)	ت
d (alveolar)	د
d (dental)	د
g	غ
p (labial)	پ
ch	چ
v	ڤ

FIGURE 8.7 Muyaka bin Haji (1776–1840) adaptation of Swahili to the Arabic script. (Abdulaziz 1994, 74)

Simply adding a third dot to the Arabic version to write Swahili could not suffice because the symbol with three dots is already taken to represent the sound "*theh*" the "*th*" sound. To make the writing consistent, the Swahili wrote their alveolar sounds "*t*" and "*d*" with four dots. A simple addition of two extra dots, as seen in figure 8.7, provides the needed distinction. Figure 8.8 is an example of "t" in actual use from *Al Inkishafi*.

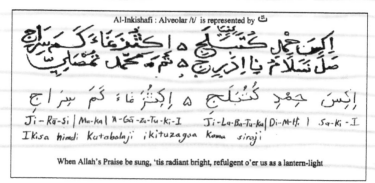

FIGURE 8.8 First and second lines of the third stanza of *Al Inkishafi*, a poem by Sayyid Abdalla bin Ali bin Nasir, ca. 1800

The addition of dots did not stop there. The Swahili sound "*g*" is represented as a *ghain* (غ) modified by adding one or two more dots to make it as indicated in figure 8.7. The Swahili sound "*ch*" is also represented in three forms, as shown in figure 8.7, and "*v*" is represented as *faa'* (ڤ) with two dots added as shown in figure 8.7. Arabic has "*b*" (ب) but lacks the Swahili sound "*p*," so the Swahili added three dots as indicated in figure 8.7 and illustrated again in the *Al Inkishafi* line in figure 8.9.

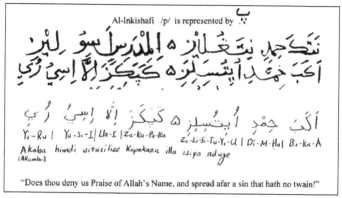

FIGURE 8.9 Third and fourth lines of the second stanza of *Al Inkishafi*, a poem by Sayyid Abdalla bin Ali bin Nasir, ca. 1800

Stacking up symbols was also a common technique. Aspiration, the puff of air that accompanies the pronunciation of Swahili "*p*," "*t*," and "*k*" consonants, is represented by an innovated symbol placed on top of the letter (as seen in figure 8.10), parallel to the rendering of "*t*" and "*k*" that I have just described.

t'	(alv. asp.)	ٿُ	FIGURE 8.10 Muyaka bin Haji (1776–1840) representation of Swahili aspirates using Arabic script. (Abdulaziz 1994, 74)
t'	(dental asp.)	ٿِ	
p'	(asp.)	پُ	
k'	(asp.)	کُ	

The beauty of the altered script is that it stayed very close to the symbols already present in Arabic, which meant that they could be learned with ease; this minimized the risk of confusion about meanings, as well. Representation of aspiration in Swahili Ajami is as shown in figure 8.10.[18] What about *ny, ng, nz, ng', nd, nj, and mb,* which are all foreign to Arabic but the staple of Bantu languages? The idea was to represent the sounds with symbols piled one on top of the other, ordered according to their combinations. Figure 8.11 shows that the Swahili combined the two relevant Arabic symbols into one representation—for "*ny*" the Arabic symbol "*nun*" shown in figure 8.11, which is combined with "*y*" to compose a single symbol written in at least the four different ways depicted in this figure; this was Muyaka's representation of nasals in Swahili Ajami.[19]

ny		کٔ	but also کٔ کٔ کٔ
ng		غٔ	
nz		ڗٔ	
ng'		عٔ	
nd	(alv. nasal)	کٔ	
nd	(dental)	دٔ	
nj		جٔ	
mb		ڮ	

FIGURE 8.11 Muyaka bin Haji (1776–1840) representation of Swahili nasals using Arabic script. (Abdulaziz 1994, 75)

Now let us look at how writers of Ajami put these modified letters together to compose words. Consider Muyaka's writing of the word *nyumba* (house) in figure 8.12, using the modified Arabic alphabet.

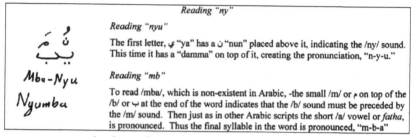

	Reading "ny"
	Reading "nyu"
	The first letter, ﻱ "ya" has a ن "nun" placed above it, indicating the /ny/ sound. This time it has a "damma" on top of it, creating the pronunciation, "n-y-u."
Mba-Nyu	Reading "mb"
Nyumba	To read /mba/, which is non-existent in Arabic, -the small /m/ or ﻡ on top of the /b/ or ﺏ at the end of the word indicates that the /b/ sound must be preceded by the /m/ sound. Then just as in other Arabic scripts the short /a/ vowel or *fatha*, is pronounced. Thus the final syllable in the word is pronounced, "m-b-a"

FIGURE 8.12 Stacking of symbols to represent consonant clusters

The Swahili use of Arabic script parallels the use of Arabic scripts in other parts of Africa that integrated Islamic literacy. Writing about the Pulaar, Wolof, and Mandinka of West Africa, Fallou Ngom (2009) discusses the prevalence of Ajami script. He notes innovations that echo the modifications of Arabic by the Swahili—three dots (known as *ñetti tomb* in Wolof) that are added to some Arabic letters in order to write Wolof consonants and vowels that do not exist in Arabic. Since Arabic's three vowels (*i, a, u*) do not suffice for Wolof, writers employing Wolofal (a version of Wolof that uses Ajami) often use the Arabic kasra (the short, straight line under the letter) to write all the Wolof front vowels (*i, e, ɛ*),[20] and they place the damma sign on top of letters to refer to Wolof back vowels (*u, o, ɔ*). In some Wolofal texts, the vowels ɔ and *o* are also sometimes written using the damma sign with a dot placed inside it.[21]

In addition to adapting the Arabic script by incorporating diacritics, piling up symbols to represent the compound consonants *mb, nd, nz, ng, ng*, and making provisions for the vowels *o* and *e*, the Swahili also took in some of the finer distinctions of Arabic sounds. The varying pronunciations of sounds represented in Latin letters by placing a dot and a line under "*h*"—h, *h*, and *ḥ*—are a case in point. An example comes from *The Jurisdiction of the Sultan of Zanzibar and the Subjects of Foreign Nations* (henceforth *The Jurisdiction*), which is a description of Zanzibar from the perspective of the inhabitants of that island between 1880 and 1890.[22] The author, Sulaiman b. Said Essorami, describes the various jurisdictions that the residents lived under, depending on categories assigned to them by race, religion, employer, residence, and so on. The author's written Swahili uses *h* and *ḥ* for words of Arabic origin and *h* for Swahili Bantu words and Arabic words pronounced in Swahili. The *ḥ* is used in such words as *ṣaḥiḥi* (correct/signature), *ḥakim* (judge), *ḥukumu* (judgment), *baḥarini* (in the ocean), *ḥata* (even), *ḥabari* (news), and *ḥimaya* (jurisdiction); and the *ḫ* is used in words such as *ḫabari, muḫtaṣari,* and *ruḫuṣa.*[23] The *h* is left for non-Arabic words—*hawana* (they don't have), *hana* (she/he doesn't have), or *hupakia* (they load). The word *habari* also turns up spelled both ways. Arabic words using the Swahili *h* remain unchanged—*jahazi* (ship), *fahamu* (know). We saw in chapter 2 that speaking Swahili with the Arabic pronunciation was a marker of pedigree. It was for the pious, the patricians, and the powerful among the Swahili, not for slaves. It is therefore not surprising that Arabisms (Arabic sounds and mannerisms) are plentiful in written documents. In *The Jurisdiction,* we find a flourish of Arabisms in many Swahili words—*'ayn,* for instance, appears to be a favorite; other examples include *ba'adi* for Swahili *baadhi* (some), *ya'ani* for *yaani* (that is), *ma'ana* for *maana* (meaning), and *qo'di* for *kodi* (lease). The use of doubled consonants, typical of Arabic and unwarranted for Bantu, is maintained according to Arabic, the source language—*fedda* for *fedha* (money), *killa* for *kila* (each), and *ḥatta* for *hata* (even).

Writing, a Hallmark of Swahili Civilization

Alongside a thriving oral tradition, there was a writing tradition in Arabic letters by which people (with rulers and elites topping the list) corresponded, drew up trade agreements, wrote their family genealogies such as the *Akbar Pate* (The Pate chronicles), and preserved other Arab records of the rulers of Swahili towns. There was also a literature on both Islamic and secular topics that developed into the Swahili canon, of which we have mentioned *Al Inkishafi* as a great exemplar. And we cannot, of course, forget the songs of Mwana Kupona and Liyongo, which were all authored in Ajami before the Europeans arrived on the scene, as will be discussed in the ensuing chapter. Swahili has been a written language for at least five hundred years (Mazrui and Mazrui 1998, 170). The Swahili's adaptation of the Arabic script was an important milestone for their civilization, as it gave rise to a written literature—a canon—which was something quite common in Africa's Islamic regions. Combining writing with the reading and public performance of poems by the *waimbaji* (singer-dancers), the Swahilized script became one of the true hallmarks of Swahili civilization.

Swahili documents written in Ajami have been almost totally ignored in Swahili scholarship. For decades, students have taken courses in Swahili language and literature and even earned college degrees in these subjects without ever hearing a mention of (let alone encountering) a single Swahili document written in Ajami. In studies of other languages, such an omission would be nothing short of intellectual malpractice. The neglect in various African languages of documents written in Arabic script, as well as other nonroman scripts (especially Amharic, in Ethiopia), was brought to the fore by the celebration of the Nigerian writer Chinua Achebe as "the father of modern African literature."[24] Yet there was no mention of just who should be celebrated for the "premodern" African literature—with quotation marks used here to suggest how the term belittles the literary tradition that has thrived for centuries in all matters historical, always being renewed and revitalized by successive generations through performance, oratory, and writing in different scripts.

It is assumed that many Ajami documents were lost between 1500 and 1700 CE during the numerous Portuguese lootings of Swahili towns (Zhukov 2004, 1), as the documents appearing in the aftermath were of such high quality that they must have represented a literary tradition developed over many years. Though Ajami is still in limited use on the east coast of Africa in places such as Zanzibar and Pemba, much of what is available in Swahili Ajami literature involves scripts collected by Europeans for reasons having more to do with hostility to Islam (as we shall see in the next chapter) and therefore to anything written in Arabic characters rather than with respect for the literary skills that Ajami represented. During the colonial era from the late 1800s to the 1960s, the Germans and the English derailed the use of Ajami in Swahili by introducing and enforcing the use of the roman script. Ironically, the Europeans became the greatest preservers of the tradition that they had truncated. Today, Ajami documents are accessible only in collections named for these colonial missionaries and scholars: the Taylor Papers, Hichens Collection, Werner Collection, Knappert Collection, Whiteley Collection, and Allen Collection, all preserved at the University of Dar es Salaam with copies at the University of London's School of Oriental and African Studies (SOAS). Most Swahili studies have followed the colonial practice of transliterating the documents into Latin script and translating them into European languages, entirely obscuring the Ajami documents behind them.[25] It is easy to fault the translations available in print, and many of the comments and annotations are alarmingly naive.[26] Rather than viewing these published materials as authoritative, we should keep in mind the observation made by Yahya Ali Omar and AnnMarie Drury that the existing publications "represent a single, if well-informed, scholarly and editorial understanding of certain manuscript material."[27] They are not the entire story of the literary creativity of the Swahili people in integrating writing in Arabic characters into their literary canon. There is no short cut to understanding the story of Swahili without careful consideration of Ajami manuscripts.

CHAPTER 9

Colonialism and Standardization of Swahili, 1850s to the 1960s and Beyond

Gũtirĩ mũthũngũ na mũbĩa.
There is no distinction between the colonialist and the padre.

— Gĩkũyũ aphorism

To force Swahili to conform to the grammar of English is like cooking ripe bananas . . . the result is *bokoboko* (a semisolid gelatinous mess) not *mchanyato* (a delicious dish).

— Hamisi Akida

I am not willing to take part in the spoiling of Swahili.

— Sir Mbarak Ali Hinawy

SLAVERY DID not disappear quickly along the Swahili coast. The Europeans arrived in the middle of the nineteenth century with a seemingly urgent antislavery and anti–slave trade rhetoric and agenda, but once they gained nominal control, they moved very slowly. In Zanzibar, the Europeans kept the Omani sultan in place with his plantations and slaves, simply declaring that slavery had been abolished and designating the slaves as servants. French authorities in the islands of the western Indian Ocean devised the term *engagé*—meaning "engaged person"—in place of the legal category of "slave." The French purchased East African engagés to work on the island of

Réunion for five years, claiming that they were teaching them how to labor "in order that they may become wise and clever" (FO 1867, 948) before returning to their country. These obfuscations constituted a bizarre transformation of slavery into a training program that would allegedly benefit uncivilized Africans. The engagé system spurred a voracious demand for African labor, so that by 1861, according to Lord John Russell of the British Foreign Office, "the number of slaves exported from the dominions of the Sultan of Zanzibar and from the neighboring Portuguese territories [is] at upwards of 30,000 annually, . . . whole districts have been depopulated, and town and villages destroyed in the wars that have been carried on for the purpose of procuring slaves for exportation."[1] A slave by any other name was clearly still a slave.

By the late nineteenth century, the Omani Zanzibar leaders faced growing pressures from Europeans, especially the British. The waning fortunes of Bargash bin Said, Zanzibar's last sultan, exemplified the transition from Arab to European political authority. Sultan Said, who ruled Zanzibar between 1870 and 1888, is credited with building the infrastructure of Stone Town, Zanzibar, which included piped water, public baths, roads, parks, hospitals, large administrative buildings, and a police force. He was reputed to be an astute diplomat, concluding treaties with Britain, the United States, Germany, France, and Portugal that were designed to maintain his primacy in the African–Indian Ocean emporium.

However, these diplomatic arrangements compelled him to abolish the slave trade in Zanzibar, even though slaving constituted the main economic artery of his rule. With abolition came disintegration of the control of the northern Swahili towns that his father, Seyyid Said, had built. As the Europeans were undermining the Omani regime, they were also busy signing treaties with inland African societies that accepted nominal German or British protection. Sultan Said soon found himself without subjects, as many cities along the coast signed such treaties with the Germans. A case in point developed when the sultan of Witu (the former ruler of Pate), on the Kenyan coast near Lamu, signed a treaty agreeing to German protection. Said, who viewed Witu as subject to his sultanate, sent troops against the Witu ruler, only to find a German fleet in waiting. He was forced to accept German authority in town after town. As consolation, the British-German agreement of October 29, 1886, permitted Said to rule a 10-mile-wide strip along the coast from Portuguese Mozambique in the south to the Tana River, including some northern towns on the Somali coast. However, this agreement quickly disintegrated.

Swahili resilience and adaptability continued beyond the era of slavery and slave trade into the time of colonialism. But with colonialism, the challenges grew more acute than before. Europeans arriving on the east coast of Africa perceived themselves to be culturally and racially superior to everyone in Africa's hinterland, on the East African coast, and in the world of the Indian Ocean. As they saw it, Europeans needed to intervene in East Africa in order to "civilize" the people there. And Europeans encountered little in Africa that they did not wish to "improve." Their Bible gave them a sense of cultural superiority, and their guns brought fear and lethal force.

The Swahili viewed the European imposition of Christianity as an attempt to overthrow a Muslim way of life that they had cultivated for centuries. Much like the Portuguese four hundred years before, British and German missionaries eventually came to realize that Islam was not limited to the immigrant Omani Arabs and Afro-Arabs who formed the political elite on the East African littoral; rather, they increasingly understood that the faith was an integral aspect of popular Swahili identity. European missionaries nonetheless fervently intruded on the racially and culturally diverse emporium with a mission to supplant Islam. For the Europeans, successful conversion meant that Africans should abandon all their belief systems in order to turn over a proverbial new leaf. And what the Bible could not accomplish, the gun enforced. In this way, the Europeans' weapons enabled a few men to terrorize, control, and humiliate entire communities. However, the Swahili did not hand over their culture, religion, and selfhood to the Europeans without a fight. Recall the case of the Muslim Yusuf Chingulia (discussed in chapter 5), who transformed himself into Dom Hieronimo Chingulia, the Portuguese-educated Christian heir to the Mombasa throne, and then reverted back to Islam once in power, turning on the Portuguese and their converts. When the Portuguese invaded the Africans' city-states, the people responded pragmatically by moving to the hinterlands; similarly, when the Portuguese imposed their Christianity on the region, Chingulia found a pragmatic religious option. Through such resilient attitudes and actions, the Swahili were able to stay resolute, not allowing the Europeans—whether colonial authorities, missionaries, or scholars—to hijack or otherwise shape their language.

From the middle of the nineteenth century until the end of World War I, the lines of the linguistic struggle were drawn by missionaries, who staked out religious territorial claims that would eventually become proxies for colonial political authority. This religious claiming of East African lands was followed by the claims of merchants and politicians, and the government military forces followed close behind. The missionaries and European government officers were united in purpose and often in method. Many older East Africans, in their sixties and seventies in the early twenty-first century, recalled that they were thrashed for being late to church, in the same way that they were given strokes of the cane whenever they were found in default of the colonial poll tax. A Gĩkũyũ aphorism sums up the sentiments of East African people regarding the collaboration of church and colonial forces: when you came right down to it, *gũtirĩ mũthũngũ na mũbĩa* (there is no distinction between the colonialist and the padre). Many Africans considered the missionaries just as detrimental as the government forces.

Claiming the Swahili coast was a necessary prelude to the European takeover of the *bara* (inland). Indirect rule was established, and Swahili, which was spoken wherever interethnic communication was necessary, became the language of choice for the colonial establishment, and Swahili-speaking people became the primary agents. But there was a glitch: the Swahili were Muslim, and their language was full of borrowings from Arabic. From the European perspective, then, the Swahili people had to be de-Islamicized and their language de-Arabized so that they could better serve the interests of Christian missions and colonial governing authorities.

Swahili's Rise in Stature

Swahili's rise in stature inland happened in heavy traffic, linguistically speaking.[2] At play were the hundreds of languages covering the distance between the ocean and the Great Lakes. From the mid-nineteenth century onward, all resistance wars and rebellions against the growing European presence possessed some element of the Swahili language. In central Africa—the Democratic Republic of the Congo (formerly Zaire), Rwanda, Burundi, and Zambia and extending into Malawi—several dialects of Swahili grew between 1870 and 1960. These dialects, often spoken initially by only a few hundred people, would eventually include speakers numbering in the millions. Five of the DRC's eleven provinces were wholly Swahili speaking: the Orientale Province in the north, North and South Kivu in the east, Maniema in the central-east, and Katanga in the south. These populations were concentrated in the urban areas of southeastern DRC. The Katangese spoke a dialect called Shaba Swahili, a name that replaced earlier labels including Katanga Swahili, Congo Swahili, and Kingwana Swahili. Historically for the Congolese, the term *Swahili* has referred to different things. First, it is used as the name of a language distinct from other Congo languages such as Lingala, Tshiluba, and Kikongo. Second, it is a synonym for both *lugha* (language) and *kinywa* (mouth), as in the expression *mu biswahili bwao* (in their Swahili), meaning "in their way of speaking" (Fabian 1986, 4). Accordingly, Kiswahili ya Monpere is "missionary Swahili," or Swahili as spoken by missionaries; Kiswahili ya Union Minière refers to the variety of Swahili developed in the laborers' quarters of the Union Minière mining conglomerate; Kiswahili ya Kalemie is the Swahili of the people of Kalemie, a town in the Katanga Province of the DRC formerly called Albertville; Kiswahili ya Kongolo is Swahili as spoken at Kongolo (also a town in the Katanga Province of the DRC); and Kiswahili ya Kisangani is the Swahili spoken by residents of Kisangani, a town in the Orientale Province formerly called Stanleyville.[3] The *ya* form in *Kiswahili ya* (the Swahili of) is a signature feature of the Swahili of the Congo, in contrast to coastal and Standard Swahili, which uses *cha,* as in Kiswahili cha Zanzibar. Those inland varieties of Swahili were distinguished from *Kiswahili bora*—fine Swahili or coastal Swahili, such as Kiswahili ya Dar, the Swahili of Dar es Salaam.

In present-day Zambia and Malawi in the area between the Luangwa River and Lake Malawi, the Swahili interacted with indigenous Chewa, Tumbuka, Tonga, and Senga peoples. Their encounters were sometimes collaborative, sometimes hostile (Langworthy 1971, 575). The firearms of the Swahili and their employment of mercenary soldiers known as *Ruga-ruga* gave them an overwhelming military dominance (Fotheringham 1891). In the Nyamwezi language, the term *Ruga-ruga* (or *valuga-luga*) refers to young, unmarried, professional soldiers (Shorter 1968, 240) from what is now central Tanzania who employed Nyamwezi terror tactics.[4] Through military might, the Swahili sought to preserve their role as intermediaries of inland trade from the coast to the far reaches of the Congo. By way of example, David Livingstone wrote of a notable Swahili trader, Hamis Wadi Mtao, who restored peace in Tabwa country after violence broke out between chief Chipili Chipioka of the Tabwa kingdom of Nsama and Tippu Tip (Reefe 1981, 147; Wright and Lary 1971, 552), ostensibly using trade Swahili resembling Zanzibari Swahili.

Swahili traders settled in eastern Congo and formed a group called the Bangwana (free men). The Bangwana spoke a variety of Swahili known as Kingwana (the language of free men). In addition, King Leopold recruited Zanzibar auxiliaries to train company troops in the Zanzibar version of Swahili in the Katanga region until 1914. More speakers of Swahili also were brought in as laborers to work in the Katanga mines (Whiteley 1969, 72). Together, these groups formed a sizable Swahili-speaking urban population.

Despite the fact that the king of the Baganda in Uganda, Kabaka Mutesa, had converted to Islam during the initial arrival of the faith in the region, observing the Muslim fast of Ramadan every year from 1867 to 1877, Swahili never really took hold as a language of mass communication in Uganda. Kabaka's court strongly opposed the adoption of Swahili as the administrative language in the Uganda protectorate (Whiteley 1969, 70–71), preferring Luganda. However, the Baganda promotion of Luganda gave impetus for the reactionary use of Swahili among the non-Baganda groups in Uganda, such as the Acholi and the Lango, who had been adversely affected by Baganda rule. The spread of Swahili among non-Baganda people provides the backdrop against which Idi Amin Dada emerged as a speaker of Swahili, using the language to administer his 1971–79 reign of terror in Uganda. Deep-seated tensions in Uganda cycled through Swahili language politics for many decades.

After the abolition of slavery and the gradual decline of the Arab domination of trade from the coast to the interior, the next big thing was the appearance of two European trading companies: the Deutsch-Ostafrikanische Gesellschaft (DOAG), or German East Africa Company, which was founded in 1885, and the Imperial British East African Company (IBEAC), also formed in 1885 and later issued the royal charter of Queen Victoria. These companies regarded any African lands not yet under treaty with a European power as free for the taking. The DOAG and IBEAC set the tone for a profit-driven, "free market" European interest in and engagement with the continent. The companies quickly laid claim to all of Africa's Swahili-speaking regions. The DOAG took over modern Tanzania, then known as German East Africa, and IBEAC took the area to the north, now Kenya, the Swahili coast to the northwestern shore of Lake Victoria. This area was initially called British East Africa and then became the East African Protectorate; later, it was dubbed the colony of Kenya. The German government took over the administration of Tanganyika in 1891, and the IBEAC turned over the administrations of modern Kenya and Uganda to the British Foreign Office in 1895 and 1896, respectively.

The missionaries used Swahili to establish Christianity inland, starting with the publication of a Swahili Bible, Swahili grammar books, and Swahili dictionaries. The colonial administrators also employed the Swahili people and their language to govern the vast territories they occupied in the interior. One of the consequences of the fact that most of the caravan routes went through German East Africa was that modern Tanzania had a greater Swahili presence than did Kenya or Somalia. Indirect German rule was established with Swahili-speaking agents governing on behalf of the undermanned Europeans. The German East Africa Company shifted the use of Swahili in Tanganyika from a language of commerce and diplomacy to a language for imposing and maintaining its forced-labor practices and alienation of lands. Suddenly, Swahili became a language with which to oppress its speakers, tax them, and bring them to obeisance. In this way, some Swahili speakers began to play an intermediary role between the Germans and their colonial subjects. Swahili speakers throughout eastern and central Africa found themselves not only being marginalized along the coast but also being recruited into the forces of conquest and administration inland. As a result, the relationship between the coastal Swahili and the inland communities deteriorated in colonial times.

In the German governing structure, German officers controlled twenty-one districts, with subdistricts mostly controlled by Arab or Swahili *akida* (headmen or messengers) as representative headmen of villages in the German colonial administration. These akida were often alien to the people they governed and ruled in a wanton manner. The centuries-old, trade-driven contact had been replaced by a colonial program that sought to break down local communities through the use of Swahili, a language well known in the interior but belonging exclusively to no one. Accordingly, German indirect rule made Swahili the language of colonial administration in Tanganyika. While Germany was pursuing these colonial ventures, the Germans lost World War I and, with it, their overseas territories. Nonetheless, the linguistic foundation for subsequent British rule had been laid.

Swahili was present when the German East Africa Company met with intense opposition, which lasted until the imperial government took over in 1891 and brought in its military to punish the unruly. Even with military dominance, however, German rule continued to be riddled with unrest, and the Swahili language was central to rebel communication and organization. It is in the fights of resistance during colonialism that we see Swahili at its best—spoken across cultures, languages, and divides. It was used by Muslims and non-Muslims; by those who spoke it as a first language and others who spoke it as a second language; by individuals who employed it as a trade language; and by those who could communicate with only its bare essentials. Some of the largest rebellious movements—including the Abushiri (Arab) rebellion (1888–89), the Hehe rebellion (1891) in the south, the Gogo and Nyamwezi uprisings in the center (1892–94), the Chagga rebellion in the north (1892–93), and the Maji Maji rebellion of 1905–7 (Ogot 1968, 299–300)—had to draw from a mix of indigenous languages, words, phrasings, and pronunciations in their speaking of Swahili. Here, I will use the example of the Abushiri rebellion, which was commanded by a Swahili person and signified an important turning point for the Swahili people.[5]

The Abushiri rebellion took place between 1888 and 1889. It was directed against the German East Africa Company, which had gained control over a number of cities and trading posts along the Indian Ocean coast. But the British and German abolition of slavery and the slave trade, interference in the ivory and rubber trades, and irreverent conduct in mosques had not gone over well, and fighting ensued. The main crisis occurred at Pangani, where a German officer, Emil von Zelewski, secured the cooperation of the *liwali* (the African indirect ruler) by calling in 110 marines from a German warship. Zelewski created a German-style administration and prohibited imports of guns and ammunition, ordered property owners to prove their titles, and imposed taxes. The townspeople accused the Germans of disrupting a service at a mosque, freed prisoners they had taken, and felled the German flagstaff (Iliffe 1979, 92). The Swahili and their Nyika neighbors, along with the Arab traders, revolted. The rebellion was led by Abu Bashir Ibn Salim al-Harthi, a wealthy Swahili of Arab (paternal) and Oromo (maternal) parentage. Abu Bashir's forces were able to capture most of the towns under German control in a series of attacks in September 1888, except for the cities of Dar es Salaam and Bagamoyo and two trading posts, Kilwa and Kivinje, that the Germans had placed under siege. The rebellion received support from the *diwani* (mayors) of cities such as Kilwa and Tanga, who had lost power during the nineteenth century. The Abushiri then took the lead in attacking the German company's agents in its headquarters at Bagamoyo, at Kilwa, and perhaps elsewhere, as they were now committed to restoring the coast's independence. Since the Swahili were part of the hinterland polities, warriors from the interior flocked to southern Swahili towns and issued a two-day ultimatum to the Germans to leave. One can imagine the clamor of hinterland peoples spewing words from their languages or speaking whatever Swahili they could in a variety of accents. The Zaramo who helped attack Bagamoyo, for instance, are a Bantu people who live in the coastal plains and low hills surrounding Dar es Salaam and are closely related to the nearby Luguru people, with whom they share a common language.

The escaped slaves of Kikogwe (a place near Tanga) rallied to Abushiri at Pangani and received communications in Swahili. The most radical elements at Kilwa and Mikindani were Yao (speaking Kiyao) from the remote southern interior. The Germans in Lindi and Mikindani escaped, but two officials in Kilwa barricaded themselves on the roofs of their houses for two days until they were killed. On September 22, 1888, Abushiri rebels proceeded to attack Bagamoyo with an army of 8,000 men, nearly destroying it before 266 German marines from a nearby warship were dispatched to relieve the city. Abushiri resistance spread inland to the Usambara Mountains and then on to Lake Victoria. The German trading company, unable to control the situation, appealed to the German government for aid. Within a few months, the Swahili resistance forces became embroiled in a full-scale war with the powerful German government. Resistance fighters relied on the loyalties of the past, on personal ties between notables and followers, on a long-standing symbiosis between towns and coastal villages, and on the authority of the diwani in each town. The role of Swahili, how it was used, and its importance in rallying the hinterland peoples to the cause was not trivial.

Although the Germans called these rebellions "Arab" uprisings, Abu Bashir's followers were Swahili and included armed slaves and the heterogeneous personnel of the caravan trade. Unlike the Portuguese invaders and Arab occupiers of previous centuries who were met with independent and varied responses from the Swahili city-states, the Germans encountered pan-Swahili opposition—and a Swahili imbued with colloquialisms and innovations from participant cultures and languages of inner Africa. At no time previously had it been necessary to unite the hinterland with the coast to fight a common enemy—until the colonial era. As we will see, in the process of supplying the means to communicate needed in that difficult era, the Swahili language grew and entrenched itself among the noncoastal peoples. Thereafter, it was a resource to tap into for regional communication.

Between 1900 and 1908, Sir Charles Eliot, commissioner and consul-general of the East Africa Protectorate, organized a series of military expeditions to bring stubborn Africans under firmer colonial control. He sent military expeditions against various communities in the region, in particular targeting the Nandi, the Embu, the Gusii, the Kipsigis, the Bakusu, and the Kabras. The language used during these expeditions was Swahili. The colonial defeat of uprisings led to the appointment and imposition of new puppet leaders from the coast to the hinterland who disregarded traditions of governance and did the bidding of the colonial powers. Most were selected primarily because of their ability to speak Swahili (Iliffe 1979, 253). But Swahili became a double-edged sword for the colonizers. They found it to be a suitable medium to establish authority, but so did later Africans both in their efforts to challenge colonial authority during the independence movement that culminated in the 1950s and in eventually overthrowing colonial power altogether. The role of Swahili as a lingua franca enabling people to articulate their shared grievances with the colonial regime remains one of the most significant modern uses of the language. Swahili became the language of the freedom fighter in Africa's Swahili-speaking regions.

The Kenya-Uganda Railway had reached Uganda by 1901, opening up the vast Kenyan highlands to European settlement and creating a Swahili corridor along the railway line, whose prodigious center was a new colonial capital, Nairobi. Then as now, at the various stops along the railway line Swahili could be heard as hawkers sold various items to travelers through the open windows of the trains. There was also a more regularly sustained infusion of Swahili to Uganda as the language of interethnic and interracial communication (Kawoya 1984, 36), in contrast to the earlier situation (before the arrival of Europeans) when the language was spread through trade involving Swahili's ruling elite.

European writers, blinded by notions of language homogeneity and evolutionary stages, approached the history of Congo Swahili as a question of origins. Thus, they sought to establish the exact time, place, and circumstances of the arrival of the Swahili language in central Africa (Polome 1967, 7–8; Schicho and Ndala 1980, 3–10). One such story was advanced by the Frenchman Charles Sacleux (1939, 387) and later by William Whiteley (1962, 72), both of whom credited the trader and slaver Tippu Tip for the introduction of Swahili to Congo. According to Sacleux and Whiteley, Swahili became a trade language in eastern Congo, Rwanda, and Burundi largely due to trading expeditions from 1870 to 1884 led by Swahili-speaking Arabs. Tippu Tip (so named because of the sounds of his guns) may have increased the desire of inlanders to speak and understand Swahili if for no other reason than to warn their families and flee whenever they heard it being spoken. As the language of transacting slavery, Swahili was a language of terror for many.

Edgar Polomé, the noted scholar of Swahili who wrote the influential *Swahili Language Handbook* (1967), was guided by the "Great Man" theory in locating the source of Congo Swahili. The theory was promulgated by Thomas Carlyle, a nineteenth-century Scottish writer and historian who viewed history as the collective biography of divinely inspired Great Men (Hirsch 2002). With this theory in mind, Polomé attributed the spread of Swahili to an influential African trader known as Msiri. He argued that

Msiri's Yeke kingdom in Katanga had served as the diffusion point of Swahili to the larger region in central Africa. Katanga was a highly trafficked region, from which Swahili could spread to the upper Congo. In fact, "a language never spreads like a liquid, nor even a disease or a rumor" (Fabian 1986, 8)—it moves with cultural contact and interaction or engagement between peoples as life goes on. As such, Swahili's spread required sustained, mean-ingful interaction among people who found mutual advantage in speaking the language. The Europeans' misguided "evolutionary" approach, however, ensured that they saw Congo Swahili as similar to coastal Swahili, regardless of the many differences between them. As Johannes Fabian (1986) notes, the Europeans saw central African Swahili as a new kind of dialect that began in a pidgin or argotlike form used in trade and progressed through several intermediate stages before developing into a full-fledged Swahili dialect.

The Europeans erased this dynamic history and the plethora of Swahili variants being spoken in the midst of other indigenous languages. They first took on the agenda of de-Arabizing Swahili.

The De-Arabization of Swahili

European administrators consistently denied the creativity of East African cultures and strove to stem or reduce Islam's central position in Swahili life. The Europeans believed that by using Swahili, they could civilize Africans from the shores of the Indian Ocean to the Great Lakes region and beyond. However, Europeans worked first to "civilize" the Swahili language itself, most significantly by attempting to de-Arabize it—that is, to extricate its Is-lamic elements simply by changing the script from Arabic to Latin. But they were sorely disappointed. An equally futile exercise would be to attempt to remove Latin or French components of the English language or to try to write English in Arabic script in order to remove the influence of Spanish. The Europeans simply declared that everyone was to begin using Lati-nate script immediately, yet they made no attempt to assist people in transi-tioning from the Arabic script to the roman one. Thus, in one swift action, all writers in the Arabic script were retired or forced to operate under-ground. Removing the Arabic script meant that a completely new literacy was needed, which was to be provided and supervised by the Europeans. According to a 1969 Zanzibar government report, more than three decades after the script change 60 percent of the residents of Zanzibar and 35 per-cent of the residents of Pemba were still literate in Swahili in Arabic script. By contrast, only 2 percent of Zanzibaris were literate in the Latin script.[6]

Bishops Edward Steere and William Tozer arrived in Zanzibar in 1864 and established a station without any knowledge of the Swahili language. By 1870, they had produced a handbook of Swahili. As we saw in chapter 8, their handbook ignored the innovative adaptations that the Swahili had employed to accommodate the inadequacies of Arabic script. Changing the script also meant that Bishops Steere and Tozer, and other missionary scholars of Swahili, such as Ludwig Krapf and Arthur Madan (author of Swahili-English and English-Swahili dictionaries, vocabularies, and oral narratives), could borrow from literature written in Arabic script without acknowledgment. In effect, the change of script made it possible for Europeans to claim what had been written by Africans as their own material, without fear of exposure.

Another move that aided the de-Arabization/de-Islamization of Swahili was the shift of the colonial capital of the East African Protectorate from Mombasa to Nairobi after 1907. Nairobi had been created as a transport depot for the Kenya-Uganda Railway in 1896, and by July 1899, it had replaced Mombasa as the headquarters of the rail line. The shift was designed, in part, to reduce Islamic influence over the new colony. Prior to 1907, the government headquarters, as well as the headquarters of the Kenya-Uganda Railway, were based in Mombasa, a city long established as the center of Swahili culture, with a lengthy history of resistance to foreign domination. According to Bethwell Ogot (1968, 256–58): "It would have been contradictory for the protectorate government, which was bent on creating a new society based on British values, to have used Mombasa, with its oriental background as a base. . . . The founding of Nairobi in effect meant the rejection of Swahili culture and its replacement by a European culture."

Actually, the founding of Nairobi meant the dissociation of the Swahili language from Swahili culture, giving it a new domain in the hinterland. The emergence of Nairobi as a center of trade to which all roads led also meant that Swahili, the language of trade, became the language of the new city. Away from the coast and its native speakers, the Swahili language was destined to be heavily influenced by inland people in everyday transactions.

The Geopolitics of Language

Once missionaries agreed that they would teach and preach in Swahili, the choice of a dialect became hotly contested. Swahili has over eighteen recognized dialects, which were arbitrarily grouped into two categories, "northern" and "southern." The dialects are as follows:

Northern Dialects of Swahili

Chimwiini—spoken by 2,000 to 3,000 people

Bajuni (or Gunya or Kitikuu)—spoken by 15,000 to 20,000 from Kismayu to just north of the Tana River along the mainland and adjacent islands, including the Lamu archipelago

Kisiu—spoken by 6,000 to 7,000 people on Pate Island

Kipate—spoken by 2,000 to 3,000 people on Pate Island

Kiamu—spoken by 15,000 to 20,000 people on Lamu Island and the adjacent mainland to the south

Kimombasa—a series of subdialects spoken from Kilifi to Gazi, including Mvita, Jomvu, Kilindini, etc.

Chifunzi—spoken by 1,000 to 2,000 people from Gazi to Wasin in southern Kenya

Southern Dialects of Swahili

Chivumba—spoken astride the Kenya-Tanzania border

Kimtang'ata—spoken along a 20-kilometer stretch south of Dar es Salaam

Kipemba—a number of subdialects spoken on Pemba Island

Tumbatu—spoken on Tumbatu Island and northern Zanzibar Island

Kihadimu—spoken on southeastern Zanzibar Island

Kimakunduchi—spoken on southeastern Zanzibar Island

Kiunguja—formerly spoken only at Zanzibar Town; expanded in the nineteenth century into Zanzibar, Pemba, Mafia, northern Madagascar, and the mainland opposite, including Kilwa

Kimafia—spoken in northern Mafia Island today; formerly spoken in the southern part of the island as well

Kimgao—spoken from south of Kilwa into northern Mozambique

Kimwani—a cluster of subdialects spoken on the northern coast and the islands of Mozambique by 60,000 to 70,000 people

The locations of the dialects are shown in map 2.3 in chapter 2 (Nurse and Spear 1985, 57–63).

No native speakers or local political institutions were consulted regarding which dialect to privilege, nor were the differences among the various dialects considered in terms of suitability for the speakers. A realistic approach to choosing the dialect to standardize would have taken into account its intelligibility to speakers of other dialects and the weight of the literature it bore. If such considerations had been factored in, the Lamu dialect (Kiamu) likely would have been a front-runner because of its centuries-old literary tradition. A central dialect was more likely to be understood than a peripheral one. Swahili literature is also known to have arisen on the islands of Lamu, Pate, and Manda, from whence it spread northward and southward. This origin has led to the assertion that "the geographical center of gravity of the true Swahili language lies between Mombasa and Amu, and nearer to the latter due to the concentration of Swahilis in the north, especially the Bajun. Kiamu is probably understood more easily by more true Swahilis than Kimvita, but Kimvita has spread among more non-Swahili Africans more widely than Kiamu" (Khalid 1977, 164) In terms of both location and literary tradition, then, Kiamu was the most qualified to serve as the standard dialect, with Kimvita (Kimombasa), the dialect of Mombasa, as the runner-up. Kiunguja (the Zanzibari dialect) should not even have been on the list of possible contenders. However, European interference changed events to the advantage of Kiunguja, the language of the superseded Omani sultans. The Europeans favored the language of political control.

The missionaries and colonial authorities thus considered the serious competitors as Kiunguja and Kimombasa. They did not consider Kiamu. Kiunguja, the dialect formerly spoken at Zanzibar Town, had expanded in the nineteenth century into the rest of Zanzibar Island, Pemba, and Mafia. The missionaries, even more than the colonial authorities, did not view all Swahili dialects as equal in importance. Indeed, from the 1880s to 1929, the missionaries became embroiled in a controversy over which dialect to select for use in their proselytizing. Missionaries tended to study and use the dialect of the region in which they were based, and their local preferences led to the legendary period of grammar and dictionary writing wars. In Europe, whoever succeeded in authoring a grammar book and a dictionary set the pathway for the development of a particular language.

Publication was a matter of life and death for the dialects that people actually spoke: there was no consolation prize. The Church Missionary Society in Mombasa studied the dialects spoken in Mombasa and in the neighboring coastal areas, known as Kimombasa. Bishops Steere and Tozer, based in Zanzibar, speedily developed and promoted the Kiunguja dialect. All published dictionaries, grammar books, and translations done for missionary work suddenly became the basis for pleading that the dialect on which these works were based should be adopted as the foundation for the standardization language.

Missionaries claimed that they had the unique authority to determine the "real and authentic" Swahili people, in order to further their own interests. In addition, they believed that they should be the sole arbiters for choosing the "practical and strategic" dialect of Swahili, and they left Africans out of the discussion. Both the CMS and the UMCA fought vigorously to have their preferred dialects selected as the basis for standardization. In the preface of his 1882 dictionary, Krapf wrote, in the accustomed evolutionary style of the time, that "the authentically original Swahili is that of the people of Pate, Lamu, Malindi, Mombasa and Tanga" (Krapf 1882, xi) His claim was based on the theory that Swahili originated in the north, from whence it had spread south along the 2,000-mile coastline to Sofala in Mozambique. On that basis, Krapf argued that Kimombasa, as a northern dialect, was more authentic than Kiunguja, a southern dialect. By selecting a Mombasa dialect, an associated long-standing literary tradition would enrich the lexical component of the language to be standardized.

These early language police were entirely Europeans. The missionaries touted a vertical classification system of Swahili dialects. In 1915, W. E. Taylor (1856–1927), a deacon who was later ordained a priest of the Church Missionary Society in East Africa, alleged that Kimvita, the Mombasa dialect of Swahili, was superior to all others. He stated: "While the genius of the Mombasa dialect eschews the blemishes and excrescences which are to be found in the others—the too patent crudities, ambiguities, and corruptions of the careless South, and the ironbound archaisms of the too conservative Islanders of the North—the Mombasa speech, in its purity, displays and cultivates to the full all their respective excellences" (Taylor, introduction to Stigand 1915, ix). Referred to as England's greatest Swahili scholar of his time, Taylor was the harbinger of the European-based biases favoring the northern towns over those of the south. Descriptions of the south and its people as crude, lazy, indolent, corrupt, and careless abounded in European conceptions of the Southern Hemisphere. The higher-latitude English had, for centuries, described Mediterraneans as lazy, and the deficiencies seemed to increase as one approached the equator, the "deep" south or the "heart of darkness" as Joseph Conrad described it. What is curious about Taylor's remark is that, to him, the central dialect of Mombasa, Kimvita, was somehow purer because it avoided the excesses of being too conservative, as in the north, or too laid back, as in the south. Naturally, Taylor found his rationale in the geography of Mombasa:

[Mombasa] signifies, then, The Curtained Headland, thus depicting with a single touch the outstanding geographical feature of this "hidden isle." . . . How easy then is it to see that while on the one hand the advantages of its "sunken" position would give it a speech which is both insular for purity and continental for catholicity, and while its geographical situation, lying in the midst between the South and the North sections of the Swahili coasts, would secure a balance between the respective branches of the Languages—the sterner stuff of the Mombasians of old, born and bred as it were amid the clang of arms, must have reacted favorably to produce the virile, "puritanic," genius of the Dialect. And it is a fact remarked by the Natives themselves that while the Dialect of Lamu and its congeners, which are discussed in this Book [*Dialect in Swahili* by C. H. Stigand], are affected by the Swahilis at large as affording a mine and a mould for the forms and expressions of most Swahili *Poetry*, and while the Zanzibar group to the South has furnished a lingua franca and a terminology for *Trade*, the Mombasian or Kimvita is the Dialect considered of all others the best fitted for accurate statement and grave discussion—the Swahili for *Prose*, par excellence. (Taylor, Introduction to Stigand 1915, ix)

The idea that geographic location can serve as a proxy for linguistic purity is, of course, profoundly misguided, but it was characteristic of the romanticized racialism of Taylor's time. His "hidden isle" analogy gives the false impression that Mombasa had been safely shielded from outside interferences and corruptions—that it was a pocket of continuity and purity. Taylor can at best be faulted for reproducing the false notion that Europeans of influence, be they clergy, traders, or politicians, had the power to rank Swahili dialects from the purest to the most corrupt. His ill-informed arrogance was inextricable from other presumptuous aspects of colonialism.

The missionaries laid the foundation for subsequent waves of colonial language policing. In valorizing the Mombasa dialect, Taylor argued the superiority of prose over poetry for the purposes of making an "accurate statement" and holding "grave discussions," and he linked this distinction with an insistence that Lamu was the dialect of "Poetry," complementing Kimvita as the dialect of "Prose, par excellence." Taylor's reference to the "sterner stuff of the Mombasians of old" articulated a popular linguistic fallacy of his era—that originally pure languages deteriorate with time. To Taylor, the language used for prose was superior and masculine (that is, virile) in contrast to the softer tones of poetry. His comments were intended to reduce varieties of Swahili toward a standardization that undermined Swahili speakers' centuries-old linguistic adaptations to their varying circumstances. Whereas Swahili people themselves perceived dialect variation to be part and parcel of the character of Swahili as a flexible and facile language, European missionaries immediately introduced a vertical ranking of dialects. It was strategic. Their intolerance of dialectical diversity was a sign of things to come. The missionaries were part of a larger European aim that went far beyond controlling African writing and speech to de-Islamize Swahili; it was a goal that entailed larger modes of thought control. By valorizing a single dialect, the Europeans gained a standard lingual mode through which to govern, collect taxes, and create an arbitrary—dependent and therefore more vulnerable and controllable—elite class in the region.

The Zanzibar dialect, touted by yet another group of missionaries, had the advantage of being spoken in the main market center of the lucrative trade between the hinterland and the Arabian Peninsula and Asia. Zanzibar had remained the undisputed commercial and trade center of eastern and central Africa throughout the nineteenth and early twentieth centuries. The controversy between the missionaries based in Mombasa and those based in Zanzibar intensified in the 1880s with the division of colonial control in eastern Africa between the British in Mombasa and the Germans in Zanzibar. The Germans were forced to relinquish all overseas territories upon their defeat in World War I, thereby leaving the British in control of all of East Africa, including Kenya, Uganda, and Zanzibar, plus mainland Tanganyika; the Belgians were left in charge of Rwanda, Burundi, and the Congo. The plan was to make the entire Swahili coast (except the Mozambican coast to the south) and its principal hinterland a unified, single polity.

The wazungu arrived in eastern Africa with a nineteenth-century European mind-set that a single language and a uniform way of speaking and writing that language were necessary conditions for the formation of a nation-state in the "civilized" European fashion. Multiple dialects were discouraged in favor of single, uniform national languages. In the wake of Germany's nationwide spelling unification mandate in 1910, the authorities imported Europe's nationalizing program to create a common African vernacular. The missionaries in Africa's Swahili-speaking region were therefore very much in step with European history, where the control of writing and speech by educated elites was tied to early twentieth-century European distinctions of class; educated urban elites took up the cause of bringing provincial rural populations "up" to proclaimed national standards. In linguistic terms, these nationalistic crusades proclaimed the utter necessity of having one language and one orthography that all people should speak and all grammar schools should teach.

The colonial need for a single administrative language in eastern Africa, reduced to a stable form that Europeans could learn, was also urgently practical. The lingual complexity of the region was staggering. With over 200 languages in the Democratic Republic of the Congo alone, 120 in Tanganyika, over 50 in Kenya, and over 40 in Uganda, this part of Africa's Bantu-speaking region was the quintessential Tower of Babel.[7]

The nineteenth-century trading expeditions in search of ivory, animal skins, and slaves deep into the heart of Africa had spread the Kiunguja dialect of Zanzibar, the largest market on the coast of of the continent. The colonialists observed that Africans in the interior were more familiar with Kiunguja than with the other dialects and hastily concluded that Kiunguja was the lingua franca throughout vast regions of eastern and central Africa. Such a universal dialect, as they imagined it to be, was exactly what the missionaries needed in order to proselytize, and it would facilitate administrators' creation of a unified tax collection system.

At about the same time, European linguists were identifying the close relationships among the five hundred Bantu languages of central, eastern, and southern Africa (see map 9.1). They determined that Swahili was the key to understanding all the others. The many loanwords in its vocabulary made it also seem uniquely capable of adapting and representing new ideas among the welter of African cultures seen as primitive and unchanging. In the European view, Swahili thus possessed a "semicivilized" culture amid the "savagery" and "Babel" of the rest of Africa. Also important to the Europeans was that it was written and that it claimed centuries of prose and poetry. A single African language of colonial administration would, furthermore, provide the advantage of having indigenous officials throughout the vast colonial hierarchy who would serve the Crown more uniformly. By the nineteenth century, newspapers were being published in East Africa in Swahili; these included *Msimulizi* (The narrator [news-bearer]), the first Swahili paper that was published in 1888 in German East Africa, and *Habari za Mwezi* (News of the month), a monthly news journal that was published at Magila (near Tanga) around 1894 (Whiteley 1969, 60).

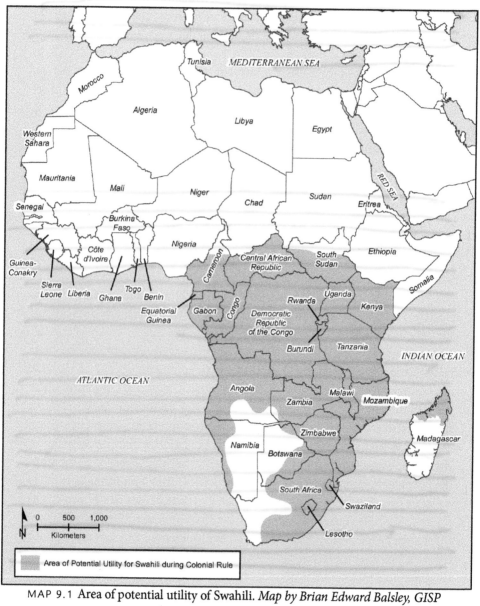

MAP 9.1 Area of potential utility of Swahili. *Map by Brian Edward Balsley, GISP*

The call for a common vernacular came from the highest level: the European governors of Kenya, Uganda, Tanganyika (now under British control), and Zanzibar all publicly supported the establishment of a standard language. An initial meeting was convened in 1925 with the express purpose of selecting a language that "would serve as a lingua franca for use in as large a number of schools as possible" (Whiteley 1969, 79) in the British colony. In the same year, a central publishing committee was set up to supervise the publication of Swahili-language textbooks for government and missionary schools. The adaptation of the largely oral language, with a history of literacy only in Arabic script, to the written medium of colonial administration and education required a number of decisions regarding conventions of spelling and word division in Swahili. The preamble of the 1952 report on African education hints at the pervasive condescension inherent in the European civilizing mission: "All African territories need African statesmen, administrators and technicians of all kinds if self-government is to be a reality. The problem of the educator is to design and provide a system of education which will enable emergent peoples of Africa to take their full place in the modern world" (Mkude 1985, 30). The standardization of Swahili transformed the diversity that was emblematic of the Swahili ethos into an intense contestation over whose dialect would be deemed the single "authentic" bearer of a colonial "Swahili" identity. The diversity of Swahili peoples, cultures, and dialects was to be reduced to a presumed singular Swahili language and identity.

Once the British government committed to its own version of Swahili, the struggle over dialect ascendancy became definitive, and the Kiunguja of Zanzibar won overwhelmingly. Kiunguja had the widest geographic reach throughout eastern and central Africa, making it a tool convenient for the colonial enterprise. Bishop Steere of UMCA further observed, with racialized overtones characteristic of the time, that

there is no way by which those inner lands are so ordinarily or can be easily reached as from Zanzibar and the coast dependent on it, so neither is there any way by which we can make ourselves so readily intelligible, or by which the Gospel can be preached so soon or so well as by means of the language of Zanzibar . . . a language which, through its Arabic relations, has a hold on revealed religion, and even on European thought while, through its negro structure, it is exactly fitted to serve as an interpreter of that religion and those thoughts to men who have not yet even heard of their existence." (Steere and Madan 1884, iv)

The fact that many native speakers of Swahili were appalled at the crudeness and alien vocabulary of Zanzibar market Swahili, which they referred to as a "simpleton language," or *kijingajinga* (Khalid 1977, 121), had no effect on British language policy or on the colonial language police. Strong feelings about the purity of modern colonial Swahili haunt the language to the present day, as the next chapter will elaborate.

Even though the Mombasa and Lamu contenders had, for centuries, been the bearers of a strong and ancient literary tradition, it is not surprising that the big-city dialect of commerce and sultanate headquarters won out. Throughout world history, the winners have selected the languages spoken in capital cities as the standard. During the Phoenicians' commercial expansion around 1100 BCE, their language could be heard in contiguous bands of lands from the northeastern corner of Iberia (modern Spain) to modern Patna in India, a distance of 8,000 kilometers (almost a quarter of the circumference of the globe) (Ostler 2005, 229). Their alphabet is also the basis for all subsequent European alphabets. Much later, around the fourth century BCE, as Greeks became the dominant merchants in the Mediterranean region, the *koine dialektos* (the common talk, or Attic Greek) that was the dialect particular to the leading commercial center of Athens was being used all over the eastern Mediterranean; gradually, it replaced the twenty other dialects of the language that had flourished until that time (Ostler 2005, 229). The linguistic triumph of Athens and Attic Greek provoked resentments among speakers of other Greek dialects similar to the reservations that Swahili-speaking communities all along the coast expressed about Zanzibar and colonial Swahili. A political pamphlet of the fifth century claimed that although Greeks in general spoke their own respective dialects, Athenians spoke a babble of all of them and "barbarian" languages, too (Ostler 2005, 230).

In England, the move toward printed vernacular and standardized English in the late fifteenth century provoked similar objections. Gravitation toward big-city dialects was promoted by William Caxton, the first English printer and publisher, who adopted the dialect of the government capital, London. Though Caxton claimed to follow a policy of reasonable compromise in reducing the spoken language and translating Latin texts into the English of his day, his publications actually converted them into the English of the streets of London (Ostler 2005, 471). Caxton did not have an easy time of it, as several competitors were making claims on behalf of other standards. In this way, he and other printers "fixed the language on the page before its writers and teachers had reached a consensus" (McCrum, Mac-Neil, and Cran 1986, 87). The introduction of the printing press brought "a torrent of Latin words" into English, regarded by some as "half-chewed Latin," and prompted calls for the purification of English—"Latinate borrowings." Bishop Reginald Peacock, an English prelate and a purist of note said that the English language "should be purged . . . instead of *impenetrable*, he proposed *ungothroughsome*; instead of *inconceivable*, he suggested *not-to-be-thought-upon-able* (McCrum, MacNeil, and Cran 1986, 87). The simplification of language can clearly become an absurdity. In this way, the development of standard English paralleled the process of standardizing Swahili, which also saw an infusion of non-Swahili words and grammatical structures.

Standardizing and Policing Swahili

The British and Belgian colonial authorities remained confident in the interwar period that followed, up until 1940, that they could control the future of all of eastern and central Africa. In this high colonial period, the British were busy trying to reduce the local diversity of the towns and other communities along the coast and inland by establishing a single uniform government, a similarly comprehensive legal system, and a matching school system, all conducted through the medium of a superior, standardized Swahili dialect that would trump all other inherited spoken dialects of Swahili. But dressing the diverse ranks of the language in a neat uniform did little to dissuade the speakers of home dialects on the Swahili coast, let alone in the hinterland where Swahili was spoken in its many variants. However, naively confident that they knew best, the Europeans created a standard form after which everyone was to model their Swahili.

The bulk of the work of standardizing Swahili was done during the first nine years (1930–39) of an organization called the ILC for East African dependencies, that is, Kenya, Uganda, Tanganyika, and Zanzibar. The groundbreaking work of standardizing Swahili involved no Africans; no native speakers were included in the decision-making processes. One European expert, Canon G. W. Broomfield, UMCA secretary, offered three reasons for the solely European involvement, all reflecting the imperial arrogance of the time. First, Broomfield argued, Africans were not linguists and therefore were not knowledgeable in the composition of dictionaries and grammars. Second, reflecting a mind-set typical of the white person of his day, Broomfield added explicitly racist reasoning: Africans, he explained, were lazy and could not come up with the vocabulary needed to confront the unfamiliar marvels of European modernity in a timely fashion. Third, evidently aware of the diversity of the dialects that the committee was charged to suppress, he worried that African speakers of them would introduce competition and discord into their deliberations. Broomfield was not alone in his justifications of African exclusion. Europeans assumed that elimination of the diversity of spoken Swahili would "help towards the gradual assimilation of one dialect with another and if left to itself, would develop in different ways in different localities" (Whiteley 1969, 86). In spite of these justifications, the bulk of the committee's information about the Swahili language had been provided by Africans; indeed, without their Swahili informants, the Europeans were helpless when it came to the actual details of the workings and vocabulary of the language. Their primary obsession was de-Arabization and imposing their own kind of order on people they perceived to be unruly.

The impact of the ILC was felt immediately in the form of the rapid publication of grammar books and dictionaries. Broomfield produced *Sarufi ya Kiswahili* (Swahili grammar) in 1931, and Frederick Johnson's *Kamusi ya Kiswahili* (Dictionary of Swahili), based on Standard Swahili, was released in 1935. Bilingual dictionaries (Swahili-English and English-Swahili) followed soon after, in 1939. The Swahili dictionaries that were speedily published by Krapf, Steere, Sacleux, and Madan upon arrival at the east coast of Africa were not simply precursors of standardization; they were in fact products of the aggressive competition in the Europeans' scramble for African territories and the linguistic standardization that would enable them to consolidate their control.

Throughout Swahili history, as we have seen, outsiders who tried to control the East African coast by decree, treaty, fines, martial law, or outright attack found themselves frustrated by a resilient Swahili people and their numerous partners in the hinterland: for every attempted assault, there was a response equal to the challenge. As the British—and, in the interior, the Belgians—sought to reduce the rich diversity of the region to a single people and language subject to their flag and national anthem, the people of Africa's Swahili-speaking regions vehemently opposed and quietly subverted every step they tried to take.[8] These people carried on their linguistic creativity in spite of the colonial authorities' and missionaries' attempts to reduce the rich diversity of their language to a written standard promoted and enforced through schools, print media, and government record keeping.

One may assume that the residents of the Swahili coast had heard their share of "broken" Swahili as diverse communities there and in the interior worked out trade and social networks with one another. Swahili must often have sounded very much like the pidgin variations on the language that are discussed in chapter 10. In the influential metropolis of Zanzibar, most merchants used Swahili for specific, limited purposes with strangers—for example, in making deals, establishing contractual engagements, and haggling and bargaining in markets. It is hard to imagine any more adaptive state of language development. If language is what language does, then speaking or writing Swahili in an externally enforced, impersonally uniform way was as alien a concept as could be imagined, not just at the coast but also in the hinterland. Swahili was a trade language, spoken as a second tongue by people of many other backgrounds—African, Arab, and Indian and eventually also European.

The colonial authorities' purpose in imposing a standard Swahili was not lost to the speakers of Swahili: they became the arbiters of a standard that they bequeathed to speakers of Swahili as a second language. The British strategy was to decouple Swahili from its Islamic coastal culture and religion and to nurture a new, schooled Swahili-speaking elite from the hinterland. For the first time, native speakers of Swahili no longer needed to have been born and raised along the coast. This uprooting of the language from its heritage led to an absurdity, in which the best speakers of the invented "standard Swahili" were its colonial creators and their African pupils, rather than the native speakers of Swahili in its inherently dialectical forms. As was the design, the people of the hinterland started outperforming native speakers of Swahili at the coast in national school exams. Here, we see the fundamental difference between the Swahili nature that sought and embraced diversity and multiplicity and the mzungus' enforced and rigid singularity.

Spelling Swahili

Orthography, or the rules defining the sounds that letters represent in written reductions of speech, never captures all the nuances of sound and inflection and intonation in any language. European criticisms of the unsuitability of the Arabic script for writing Swahili had been hypocritical, especially as writing Swahili in the roman letters of English was equally challenging, albeit in a different way. Spelling Swahili in Arabic script had been carried out by the Swahili as they sought ways to transcribe their language, but the Europeans took it upon themselves to write what they understood of Swahili in the roman orthography for Swahili speakers and other colonial subjects to read. Early missionary attempts to transcribe the language reflected the orthographies of the transcribers' mother tongues. In effect, German missionaries prior to World War I wrote Swahili sounds in German. The current Swahili spellings reflect subsequent revisions by the British according to the ways in which sounds are spelled in English. These examples highlight at least three difficulties: two ways of spelling the sound /ny/, geminate (doubled) consonants (as in *shidda* or *niusso*) that represent German ears more than Swahili voices, and the substitution of the English /v/ sound for the German /w/. This orthography appears to be a result of inadequate understanding and mishearings of Swahili sounds. Germans were spelling Swahili under the influence of German spelling conventions, and the English showed no less favoritism toward their own spellings.

The distortions of the spoken language that Europeans imposed in the writing and spelling of Swahili—and other African languages—went deeper than the written representations of individual sounds. Just as the German orthography of Swahili disregarded Swahili sounds, the French and the English began writing Swahili in their own phonetic images. The English, too, experienced difficulties spelling Swahili, especially with the sound /ni/ in words such as *companion* and *onion,* as well as with the sound /ng'/ in words such as *longing.*

Madan, a missionary bishop for central Africa, described the common initial /ng'/—as in *ngombe* (cow/cattle)—as "a peculiar African sound," though he somewhat contradictorily added "much resembling the –ng which occurs at the end of many English words."[9] Despite the dedication of Ludwig Krapf and his fellow German missionaries, particularly in regard to the favored Kiunguja dialect, it was the English spellings of Swahili that became standard under British rule, after the German loss of influence in the region. Thus, Swahili spelling was reformed from Arabic orthography to roman script, with considerable influence from the spelling conventions of English.

Both British and American readers of written English will appreciate the sensitivity of spelling in their familiar divisions over the orthography of the language they allegedly share. Noah Webster, sometimes called "the father of American scholarship," reformed the spelling of the formerly colonial language in the United States in his 1821 *Dictionary of American English,* with an eye to standardizing the phonetic system and condensing spellings to aid printers setting type. Examples included *cheque,* condensed to *check; colour* to *color;* and *favour* to *favor. Musick* became *music* (although the former spelling is no longer in use today even in Britain); *phantasy* became *fantasy; plough* became *plow;* and *publick* became *public* (the original is no longer in use). Spellings became further simplified in the twentieth century, with *analogue* shortened to *analog; cancelled* to *canceled; catalogue* to *catalog; gramme* to *gram; interne* to *intern; mediaeval* (or *mediæval*) to *medieval; programme* to *program* (in the field of software); *sulphur* to *sulfur; tyre* to *tire* (*tire* is used in the United States and Canada, *tyre* in many other English-speaking areas); and *hiccough* to *hiccup* (though *hiccough* is still sometimes used). (Interestingly, *hiccup* is, in fact, the older form; *hiccough* was inspired by a false analogy with *cough.*) The *Chicago Tribune* adopted many of these simplified spellings in 1934.

Swahili Criticism of Standard Swahili

Colonial European linguistic authorities blended national chauvinism with personal fanaticism in their intense approaches to standardization. They made no apologies about the fact that "some of those who appeared to manipulate the language so arrogantly knew that if they stopped to consider alternatives they would make no decision at all" (Whiteley 1969, 92). It was alleged that the process of selecting words and expressions for inclusion into Standard Swahili was a delicate balance between "over-standardization and freedom of expression" (ibid.).

Swahili critics of the standardization process emerged quite quickly. One memo from a member of Kenya's Education Department appeared in the committee's bulletin of 1934, indicating that the Standard Swahili was an absurdity characterized by "a very exaggerated application of grammatical rules that has led us away from the real Swahili language and made us substitute something which is at its best lifeless though intelligible, at its worst both lifeless and unintelligible" (Whiteley 1969, 87). This critic also observed that the Europeans, by standardizing Swahili, had created a new language in the process, which left them "in the ludicrous position of teaching Swahilis their own language through the medium of books, many of which are not Swahili in form or content, and whose language has but little resemblance to the spoken tongue" (Whiteley 1969, 85). The absurdity stemming from creating a "new language" was captured in a little poem by G. A. R. Savage, a soldier stationed at Jinja in Uganda who was proficient in the Luo, Acholi, and Swahili languages and a member of the ILC Swahili committee:

> The chaps who speak Swahili here
> Have never heard of Bishop Steere
> Sometimes a really zealous learner
> Some concords may pick up from Werner
> But "safi" stuff is heard alone
> When Ratcliffe talks to Elphinstone.[10]

Though meant to celebrate the standard by blaming the Swahili for their ignorance of Bishop Steere's work on the language, Savage captured the supreme paradox of the creation of Standard Swahili. Safi Swahili was, in Europeans' view, a "clean," "pure," and "unadulterated" Swahili that Savage claimed was heard only when B. J. Ratcliffe met H. Elphinstone and jointly authored *Modern Swahili,* a revealingly titled 1932 grammar that fellow Europeans regarded as a model for correct Swahili. Beyond presuming to determine that the Zanzibar Swahili dialect and its speakers would epitomize Swahili identity, Europeans also established themselves as the experts who were qualified to formulate the grammar, vocabulary, manuals, and other teaching instruments of the official language. In this way, Bishop Steere and the rest were deemed by Europeans to be the true possessors and bearers of clean, *safi* Swahili.

Using their agile Bantu prefix to designate the linguistic peculiarities of the people they knew, *ki-*, the Swahili dubbed this absurdity Kizungu, "the language of the Europeans/whites," or Kiserikali, "the governmental language." By their reckoning, Standard Swahili was a new language and not theirs. The displeasure shown by Africans was hardly subtle. When asked to assist the ILC in its work on standardizing Swahili, Sir Mbarak Ali Hinawy, the headman appointed in the 1930s by the Kenya government to handle relations within the Muslim community of the coastal regions, remarked, "*Mimi sikubali kushirikiana katika kukiharibu Kiswahili,*" meaning "I am not willing to take part in the spoiling of Swahili" (Khalid 1977, 218). Standardization could succeed only through a coerced imposition of its use generously promoted as getting everyone to communicate effectively. A torrent of works that conformed to the explicitly sanctioned standard, duly approved in the form of the imprimatur of the Inter-territorial Language (Swahili) Committee, followed.[11] This imprimatur was printed on the first few pages of every book published in the colonial era. It read: "The Swahili in which this book is written has been approved by the Inter-Territorial Language (Swahili) committee for the East African Dependencies. (signed by the Secretary of the I.L.C.)." By those words, writing in any one of the more than a dozen nonstandard dialects was forbidden and profoundly devalued. Literate people were to be taught how to write again, as unschooled Swahili had become ostracized. All the writings, personal and public, done in the native dialects of Swahili were rendered classical virtually overnight.

Standard Swahili as a Double-Edged Sword

The same standardized Swahili that the colonial authorities used to rule eastern Africans in the 1930s and 1940s became one of the primary instruments for their own expulsion in the 1950s and 1960s. Africans of the Swahili-speaking regions appropriated the written language to make demands for self-rule, and their voices were thus heard far and wide in homes and villages otherwise divided by their local dialects. During the high point of the independence struggle of the 1950s, standardized Swahili revealed itself to be a double-edged sword, used by Africans to express demands for freedom and self-rule even though colonial authorities had intended it to give Europeans the linguistic wherewithal to control the populace. Swahili therefore proved to be a lethal weapon in anyone's hands. No one could control, save, or own Swahili for his or her own exclusive purpose or interest. Colonial authorities in the early 1950s, realizing that the political tide was not flowing their way, began an intense scrutiny of the works published by the ILC in pursuit of the strategy of standardizing the language. The colonial administrations criticized and condemned the ILC in a 1952 report on African education: "The existence of Swahili in Kenya and Tanganyika and its place in school teaching is unfortunate, for it seems to have affected adversely the teaching of both the vernacular and of English . . . this is too easy a policy and greatly oversimplifies the utilitarian function of the primary school course (Whiteley 1969, 88)." Forgetting that it had been the governors of the colonial states who had encouraged the formation of the ILC in the 1930s, their successors suddenly became champions of the vernacular languages, which were obviously more beneficial to the strategy of running colonies by the "divide and rule" strategy. The report recommended elimination of Swahili from all schools, government or missionary. It also sought to curtail its use as the language of communication across linguistic boundaries in Kenya. The colonial government in Kenya, facing the crisis of the Mau Mau war in the thirties and realizing the prevalence of Swahili in the movement, forbade its teaching or use in many schools. Nonetheless, the cat was out of the bag. Swahili continued to be used informally in the marketplace and in urban centers, where it could not be controlled, throughout Tanganyika, Kenya, and Uganda, developing a distinct tenor from the coast and the off-shore islands, its native land. Not even the Zanzibari dialect that formed the basis of the standard remained the same once it left the vicinity of the island and its adjacent shores.

By the time of independence in the early 1960s—Tanganyika in 1961, Uganda in 1962, Kenya and Zanzibar in 1963—the varieties of Swahili along the coast used in broadcasting programs competed with up-country Swahili pidgins. Thus, the ILC's initial fear that Swahili would develop differently in different places without absolute enforcement of Standard Swahili was realized. The Swahili that Europeans had attempted to construct, with all its grammar books, dictionaries, and hastily written attempts at literature, ultimately did not reign over the spontaneous dynamism of the languages as spoken in the living communities of the new nations. Even Shaaban Robert, the Tanzanian author who wrote in the new Standard Swahili and has been hailed as the Shakespeare of Swahili literature, produced nothing written that approached the Ajami literature of old. The strange new kind of Swahili desired by the colonial authorities, people who knew the language primarily as a means of control, had acquired a life of its own in the mouths of the citizens of the new nations.

Swahili after Independence

With the singular exception of Tanzania, the newly formed independent states chose English or French as their official language. Kenya chose English, as did Uganda, Malawi, and Zambia, whereas Rwanda, Burundi, and Zaire (the present-day Democratic Republic of the Congo) chose French. The choice was based on the belief that English and French were politically neutral, unlike indigenous languages that, if chosen, were likely to cause social and political unrest among those whose languages were not chosen. Swahili was enlisted in Tanzania as the country's official language, the language of record keeping and transacting government business. The choice was based on the need for national integration under *ujamaa* (African socialism), which would have been unworkable in a European tongue. In Kenya, Swahili was the de facto national language. In 1974, Mzee Jomo Kenyatta, the first president of independent Kenya, made an instant order that Swahili be used in the *bunge* (parliament) in 1974, having worked since 1964 to Swahilize the parliament with little success (Mazrui and Mazrui 1995, 16–17). Zaire chose French as its official language and recognized four other national languages—Kikongo, Lingala, Swahili, and Tshiluba. In Rwanda-Urundi (as Rwanda and Burundi were called in the colonial era), Swahili has served as a vehicular language (that is, as a bridge or working language) alongside Kinyarwanda and Kirundi. The mainland of Tanzania, which resulted from the 1964 union of what was formerly British Tanganyika with Zanzibar, has adopted Standard Swahili to a greater extent than Kenya, Uganda, Congo, Somali, and the others have. One reason for this was the decision made by Tanzania's president, Julius Nyerere, to adopt Swahili as the national language to replace colonial era English in the practice of unity, or *ujamaa* (African socialism). Further, in Tanzania, a new pedagogy, textbooks in a variety of subjects, and especially the work of the Taasisi ya Uchunguzi wa Kiswahili (Coordinating Body for the Development of Kiswahili, or Institute of Swahili Research, a national successor to the ILC) strengthened the presence of Standard Swahili in the country. Ambitious as the goal of adopting Swahili as the national language was, the project has had unprecedented success and contributed to Tanzania's singular distinction as the current stronghold of Standard Swahili. Swahili's place as an African national language was a significant recovery from the serious problems of shifting from German and then English, despite the strong appeal of English in our technological age.

Since independence in the early 1960s, Swahili has developed in very different ways in the countries where it is spoken. Many words for colonial era concepts recommended at the outset of standardization had short life spans. Today, some claim that Tanzanian Swahili is different from Kenyan Swahili and that both differ from Congolese Swahili (the Swahili of the Democratic Republic of the Congo, formerly Zaire), which in turn differs from Ugandan Swahili and no doubt many others, including Somali Swahili. Swahili is valued in Tanzania as a point of national pride, but this is not so much the case in Kenya, where it is still seen by the elite as the language of the *mfanyi* (domestic workers or servants). In Uganda, it has often been referred to contemptuously as "*ulimi wa kipakasi*" (the language of the unskilled worker), to quote Shullenberger and Shullenberger (1998, 63). It has not helped Swahili's reputation in Uganda that it was used by the army and the secret police during the brutal rule of Idi Amin, making it the language of terrorism to the average Ugandan citizen. Acceptance of Swahili has therefore lagged in Uganda.

The "national" varieties of contemporary Swahili, often spoken by nonnative speakers, have incorporated elements of other African languages. Thus, Swahili's strongholds since independence have not been along the coasts of Kenya and Tanzania but rather in the hinterlands. As a result, there is no longer a coherent language community whose members are the authentic bearers of Swahili identity; rather, there are several national groupings of speakers of Swahili. Standard Swahili remains primarily used in the domain of government institutions in the region, as well as in scholarly writings, in formal record keeping, and in national print and broadcast media. Standard Swahili is also the version taught in the academic institutions around the world.

What distinguishes the postindependence era Standard Swahili from the high colonial period Swahili is the critical evaluation of the language by its speakers. Many Africans have been appalled at the continuing infiltration of Swahili by English. Hamisi Akida, a researcher at the Taasisi ya Uchunguzi wa Kiswahili at the University of Dar es Salaam, wrote in the *Taifa Weekly* of January 12, 1974:

> Na kuilazimisha [lugha ya Kiswahili] katika sarufi ya Kiingereza ni kama kupika mchanyato wa ndizi mbivu . . . matokeo yake itakuwa si mchanyato bali bokoboko la ndizi, kwa sababu sarufi ya Kizungu ni kitu mbali na sarufi ambayo ingefaa katika Kiswahili kwa namna nyingi. Ni wazi kwamba maneno ya Kiswahili hayapatani na maneno ya Kiingereza na kwa hivyo ni vigumu kukubali kufuata taratibu na tabia za sarufi ya Kiingereza. Hapa ndipo tunapopata uharibifu wa lugha. (Quoted in Chiraghdin and Mnyampala 1977, 61)

> And to force Swahili to conform to the grammar of English is like cooking ripe bananas . . . the result is *bokoboko* (some semisolid gelatinous mess) not *mchanyato* (a delicious dish of banana), because the grammar of English is something very far removed from the grammar that would be suitable for many reasons. It is obvious that Swahili words do not resemble English ones and it is difficult to make them conform to English structures. This is where we find Swahili being violated. (My translation)

This reference to cooking ripe bananas instead of eating them is the metaphorical equivalent of the absurdity of trying to fix something that is not broken. Abedi Shephardson (Khalid 1977, 218–22) observed that European "fidgeting" with Swahili rendered the language unnatural and de-Africanized. There were forced spellings, invented singulars and plurals of nouns, words that were deemed faulty for not conforming with stereotypes and "repaired," and verb tenses hammered into shapes conforming to English ones. On the whole, the invented and constrained standard became a language with grammar rules that allowed no exceptions, requiring a consistency previously unknown in any human language.

Unfortunately, in reaction to standardization, some advocates of the language have fallen into the trap of believing that such a thing as a pure safi Swahili might have once existed, a kind of reversal of the faith of the colonial language police in a stabilized modernization of the language. They have taken on the task of removing the corruptions of English grammar in Swahili in order to restore it to some imagined state of primordial authenticity. However, it is impossible to undo the anglicization of the ILC. Moreover, there has been no unanimity among the critics of the standard. In fact, all manner of critics—whom we can categorize as purifiers, Afrocentrists, and renegades—have been strongly and sometimes bitterly divided about how authentic Swahili should be spoken. The result has been the creation of many local and international organizations, all aspiring to promote their own vision of the "true" standard.

Swahili Purists ad Afrocentric Purifiers

Swahili purists and Afrocentrics purifiers are both prescriptivists. The premise of Swahili purism is that the best way to introduce new words into Swahili is to base them on the roots of the past and present vocabularies of Swahili. The most prominent camp among the back-to-the source prescriptivists who hold as true the Swahili proverb *jungu kuu halikosi ukoko,* which translates as "The big cooking pot never lacks some crust." The meaning of the proverb is that Swahili the *jungu kuu* (the big pot) has a store of resources (*ukoko,* "crust") that can be tapped into before resorting to borrowing words from elsewhere. The underlying assumption of the *jungu kuu* prescriptivists is that Swahili does not need to take on loanwords from outside to meet the need for new vocabulary to describe a fast-changing modern world, since there are many words already in the main pot of Swahili capable of communicating fresh notions. Even in situations where such words do not exist, the prescriptivists believes that there are plenty of mechanisms within Swahili itself for coining new words. Ahmed Sheikh Nabhany has been the Swahili lexicographer who, perhaps more than anyone else, has plumbed the language in search of resources to curb Arabic and other external influences in Swahili. The rationale behind the Jungu Kuu objective of ridding contemporary Swahili of borrowed vocabulary is that the "Swahili experience" was something of a contradiction, historically speaking, in that the Swahili tongue was itself parented by a variety of peoples and their languages (Chimera, 2000). Put another way, the language was formed by infusions from everywhere. However, this attempt at purification is just as impossible to accomplish as were missionary attempts in the 1920s and 1930s to de-Arabize Swahili.

The purifiers' objective has been to build upon Standard Swahili to restore the beauty and richness of a language that was grossly compromised by the European standardization regime. The purifiers have been caught between the colonial legacy clearly present in the contemporary language and the considerable influence on the development of the language of those who speak Standard Swahili as a second language in mainland Tanzania, Kenya, Uganda, and the Democratic Republic of the Congo. Currently, they have infused the standard language with many words of Bantu origin, but if the purifiers have their way, these may also become candidates for elimination.

By contrast, the Afrocentric reformers of Swahili are semipurists who, although not opposed in principle to the *jungu kuu* idea of Swahili-centrism, have constructed a lingual hierarchy to tolerate borrowing according to a prescribed order. When a new word is needed, according to them, one should first look to Swahili itself; only thereafter should one borrow from local Bantu languages. If that fails, one might then turn to nonlocal Bantu languages and, if the need is still unmet, to non-Bantu African languages. Non-African languages are held in reserve as a last resort. According to the Afrocentric reformers, "Bantu, Arabic, and English are being used in the development of the Swahili lexicon. It would be better that the lexicon of standard Swahili be developed using the Kiswahili language itself, that is, its various languages; then following that words from Bantu and other African languages followed by Arabic and English (Chiraghdin and Mnyampala 1999:64)" (my translation). To semi-purists, Arabic is not an African language and should come as a last resort. To be sure, the relationship between Arabs and the Africans on the east coast of Africa was not one of equality, particulary not after the arrival of the Omani in the eighteenth century. The historical dominance that Arabs enjoyed in the commercial exploitation of Africa and Africans—not least in slave trading and in the trade in ivory and animal hides and skins—informs the attitude of the Afrocentric Swahili enthusiasts.

Afrocentricism in the development of Swahili traces back to the international search among leading African intellectuals for a Pan-African language in the early 1970s. Several, including Wole Soyinka and Ngugi wa Thiongo, have advocated that Swahili should be elevated to serve in that capacity. True to their mission, scholars at the Tanzanian Taasisi ya Uchunguzi wa Kiswahili have added words from languages of Tanzania's mainland into Swahili. The word *shiganga* (boulder) in Swahili is borrowed from the Sukuma word *lishiganga*, with the same meaning;[12] *lweya* (plain land) is taken from the Haya word *olweya*;[13] *tepo* (clone) is from the Mwera language;[14] and *giligili* (synovial fluid, or the bodily fluid that lubricates joints) is from the Nyakyusa word *ulugiligili*.[15] All of these languages are Tanzanian.

To the afrocentrists, there is no denying the complicity of Arabs in the slave trade or in the difficulties of writing Swahili in Arabic script. Yet Islamophobia is not a condition that can be attributed to the Taasisi ya Uchunguzi wa Kiswahili, which, as noted earlier, is the leading institute of Swahili research, based at the University of Dar es Salaam. Indeed, champions of purification such as Shihabdin Chiraghdin and Ahmed Sheikh Nabhany cannot be blamed for the tension between Swahili purifiers and Islam, as they are themselves both Muslim and Swahili. But in emphasizing Swahili's ability to respond to demands for new expressions, they reject the use of Arabic. As for their reasons for this rejection, the purists emphasize the Bantu origin of Swahili and the richness of its numerous dialects in and of themselves. The Afrocentric purifiers see Arabic as removed from the contemporary daily experience of many of the eastern and central African countries whose people speak Swahili and give it life in the region.

The Quest for the "Authentic" Bearers of Swahili

The Swahili purists and Afrocentrists have joined the European standardizers as language police, the term that I use to designate those who attempt— though always unsuccessfully—to control how people speak and write their language. Controversy and conflict over what is authentically Swahili have characterized the flourishing of the language over the last century and a half. As Whiteley (1969, 9) notes, since the 1860s to the present Swahili "has provoked lifelong devotion as well as bitter hostility, from men and women of great sincerity. It has produced its crop of cranks, its irrational antagonists and sentimental devotees, as well as its notable scholars." This chapter has shown that struggles over reducing the spontaneous diversity of Swahili identity to a single standard have their roots in the European attempts to bring colonial order to eastern and central Africa. European missionaries' and colonial governments' efforts to create a "standard" Swahili initiated a process of converting linguistic diversity to a contestation over who, what, and where the "authentic" bearers of a single, potentially homogeneous Swahili identity would be. Zanzibar Swahili was promoted, over strong opposition, and it was subsequently imposed on writers, schools, and government during the colonial era, leaving it as the framework within which simultaneous processes of ongoing diversification and struggles to standardize have continued.

These contests over Swahili identity have paralleled disputes raging around other national languages from the mid-nineteenth century to the present. The colonial ILC did for Swahili what the Academie Française did for French, what the Arabic language academy in Cairo has striven to do for Arabic since 1934, and what President Kemal Atatürk of Turkey did with Turkish in the 1920s and 1930s. However, for Swahili, unlike the other languages of the world, it was European foreigners who created the standard through their publishing of dictionaries and grammar books, as well by imposing themselves as the arbiters of what could be published. In response to this colonial anxiety over Swahili identity, African purists and Arabophobic Afrocentrists have endeavored to recover and direct the integrity in the development of Swahili, even as Swahili has become a language of a great variety of speakers in several modern nations. Joan Temple Dennett's assertion that "English may be the language of the global village but the villagers are far from agreement on what is good use of the language" (Dennett 1992, 379) holds true for Swahili too. Nonetheless, all the purists and Arabophobic lexicographers, as well as other so-called language police including the many organizations established to promote Standard Swahili, have had little success in controlling how people actually speak the language. Swahili pidgins and slangs have blossomed and even taken the lead above and beyond the standard despite the massive efforts of the purists to the contrary, as will become clear in chapter 10.

CHAPTER 10

Modern Swahili

Moving On

Yakhe, lakini si kitu sisi naelewana? Ni kuelewana tu.
Friend, isn't the point for us to understand each other? It is to understand each other.
  —Somali female character in *Vioja Mahakamani*

THERE IS a saying that "Swahili was born at the coast, grew up and prospered in Tanzania, grew sick in Kenya, and died in Uganda and the Congo." The saying quite accurately depicts the increasing use of nonstandard Swahili as one moves away from the East African coast and into the interior regions of eastern and central Africa. The saying distinguishes Swahili speakers who are from *pwani*, "the coast," and those who are from *bara*, "the land's interior," by calling attention to what can be described as "disturbed" Swahili—that is, Swahili that has been influenced heavily by the first languages of people for whom Swahili is a second language. This chapter addresses the ecology of Swahili in what I have called Africa's Swahili-speaking region, in which 100 million people who speak it as a second language have created a diverse array of vibrant, vernacularized Swahili pidgins.

The relative importance of Swahili in the region is evidenced by the fact that it is second to none in Tanzania, whereas in Kenya—which now insists that Swahili is a co-official language—it is eclipsed by English, and in

Congo, it is merely one of the four national languages, along with Kikongo, Lingala, and Tsiluba, and not the dominant one among them. People place value judgments on the Swahili spoken around them according to how much it deviates from the standard and coastal varieties. The undisputed "good" Swahili is that of the coast, the elite Swahili standard in Tanzania and Kenya's institutions and mass media. Though Kenya runs a distant second to Tanzania in the use of Standard Swahili by the populace, it commands a large repertoire of Swahili pidgins, if not leadership in this proliferation of linguistic creativity. In the hierarchy of languages in Kenya, English, the inaugural elite tongue, is at the top, followed by Standard Swahili, then various Swahili pidgins, and finally vernacular versions of Swahili that pay little to moderate respect to either coastal dialects or the standard. In central Africa, the standard hardly makes a dent in terms of popular use. Instead, Swahili in the Congo is a lingua franca spoken with heavy influences from the languages on the ground, both Bantu and French. We saw in chapters 2 and 9 how the Swahili spoken by native speakers along the coast flows along a continuum of dialects from the north (Mogadishu) to the south (Sofala), with further variants on the offshore islands along the way.

As mentioned in chapter 1, speakers of Swahili as a second language today outnumber those who speak it as a first language by a ratio of close to 100:1. With that many "outsiders" speaking Swahili, the native speakers of the language on the coast likely will be no more able to control what happens to their tongue than the missionary and government language "experts" of the colonial era were. The days when coastal Swahili dialects were reference points in the pronunciation, grammar, and semantics of Swahili are long gone. In this chapter, I conclude that despite the efforts of more than a dozen scholarly and cultural societies to promote the use of Standard Swahili, the language will be continually shaped and reshaped by the millions who use it in their daily lives. What that will mean to the venerable Institute of Swahili Research based at the University of Dar es Salaam and to the departments of Swahili at universities in the region is not clear. The numerous lexicographers busy debating what new words to add to the official language and what ones to get rid of may be swimming against the raging tide of spontaneous invention in the streets. The reality is that the stipulations in Standard Swahili about what is grammatical and what is not comprise just an abstract opinion in a context where social usages in the midst of other tongues are continually replenishing a living language. The growing diversity is the price of popularity and politics. Controversies over the correct usage of Standard Swahili and disputes over the demonization of Swahili pidgins are to a large extent sociopolitical.

A pidgin is a simplified language that is formed on an impromptu basis when people who do not share a common language are forced by circumstances (especially trade) to communicate. Pidgins are learned as second languages and are seldom, if ever, the native languages of any communities. They rely on sounds, words, and body language, and their focus is to pass around information practically, without the finesse of a fully developed language.

Swahili pidgins, despite their widespread use, have never been seen as the best hope for Swahili's future as an international language. But they actually are the best hope if the entertainment industry, pop culture, and demographics are anything to go by. In fact, pidgins are the stock in trade in the story of Swahili, the backbone of communication in much of eastern and central Africa, and the driving forces of Swahili's long history of openness and development. Despite the work of colonial and postcolonial governments and more than a dozen local and international professional Swahili organizations to promote Kiswahili Sanifu—the standard variety—as the medium of instruction in school and for governance,[1] the pidgins of Swahili have continued to thrive, particularly the ones in the new sociolinguistic settings of the cities. As in the past, vernacular languages are still major ingredients of the Swahili linguistic potpourri. It is through vernacularization that Swahili remains as relevant today as ever before—or, to put it another way, the ongoing vernacularization of Swahili is how the people make the language their own.

I will begin with the reality on the ground today, discussing how vernacular slangs and pidgins are the air that Swahili breathes to remain alive and relevant. Then, I will describe the ways in which the documented Swahili pidgins of the past reveal a much longer story of how so many have embraced Swahili by vernacularizing it. Because children and youth will continue to flaunt the rules on how best to speak Swahili, they will continue to overshadow the standard, keeping the lingua franca of eastern and central Africa proof positive of the reality on the ground.

Vernacular Swahili

The joys of Swahili are to be found in the differing ways that people speak the language. Whiteley (1969) observed that in areas where people learn Swahili in addition to the other regional languages they speak, many kinds of Swahili have gone unnoticed and unstudied: "There are a number of up-country dialects acquired as a second, third, or even fourth language and used as means of communication between African and Asian or European, or between African and African particularly in the towns where speakers of dozens of Bantu and Nilotic languages all seek a common means of communication. We cannot say with certainty which dialects existed at any particular historical period, nor, as a matter of fact, do we have adequate documentation on the present day situation" (Whiteley 1969, 7). A vernacular Swahili affirms one's ethnicity and origin to informed compatriots. An ethnic Swahili indicates one's upbringing in rural environments, whereas Sheng (the Swahili-English slang spoken in Nairobi) points to an urban upbringing. Individuals who spend the bulk of their lives—particularly from childhood on—in urban areas commonly lose or are able to rein in their vernacular accents and phraseologies and become absorbed into the urban Swahili. Kenya's urbanites know and can imitate a variety of accents and sounds of Swahili's numerous hybrids. They can thus distinguish one variety from the numerous other vernacular forms of Swahili found in other parts of the country, such as Luo-Swahili from the west, Somali-Swahili from the north, and Maasai-Swahili from the pastoralists of the Rift Valley, all from non-Bantu-speaking backgrounds, as well as Kalenjin-Swahili and Kamba-Swahili from Bantu-speaking areas. The more a language group is heard on the city's streets, the more audiences appreciate the lingual-cultural nuances expressed and the better the imitations of it they pride themselves on performing. A number of popular comedians have made a living out of performing these Swahili vernaculars, and masters of ceremonies at weddings, fund-raisers, and civic gatherings switch from one vernacular Swahili to another as an easy way to entertain the assembled guests, particularly when they come from the backgrounds performed.

Vernacular versions of Swahili are usually objects of humor and jest. But there are times when vernaculars can put one in harm's way, even endangering lives, as when they are used to discriminate. Linguistically speaking, every ethnolinguistic community has its "true North"—distinctive sounds that are very taxing for others to pronounce. For instance, speakers of some Swahili vernaculars cannot enunciate the word *kuku* (chicken, in Standard Swahili), and instead, they say *gugu,* which also means a weed (tare or vetch) and "garbage heap."

The phenomenon of hearing and pronouncing the sounds of the language in varying ways may seem straightforward, but it is in fact complex. A case in point is Gĩkũyũ, the Bantu language of the Gĩkũyũ (Kikuyu) of

Kenya; these people comprise the country's most numerous group, numbering about 6 million (or 22 percent of the population).[2] For many Gĩkũyũ speakers (those primarily raised in farmlands and towns where people scarcely speak anything but Gĩkũyũ), the language appears to operate on the principle of sabotaging the sounds of other languages. Certain sounds in English are mispronounced not because of misspelling on the part of Gĩkũyũ speakers (which a literacy campaign could take care of) but because some sound contrasts do not exist in Gĩkũyũ.

In the same way many speakers of Arabic as a first language have problems pronouncing *paul* and *ball* simply because /p/ does not exist in Arabic, the sounds that English speakers contrast as /r/ and /l/, /sh/ and /ch/, /b/ and /mb/, /d/ and /nd/, /g/ and /gh/, and /g/ and /ng/ are the Achilles' heel for the Gĩkũyũ in terms of pronunciation. This weakness is because Gĩkũyũ has only the sounds on the left of each pair (*r, sh, b, d,* and *g*) and not the ones on the right (*l, ch, mb, nd, gh,* and *ng*). The default is to substitute *l, ch, b, d,* and *g* with *r, sh, mb, nd, gh,* and *ng* with *g* for *gh* and *ng,* respectively, because they are the closest equivalents in Gĩkũyũ. To illustrate, if you listen to a large number of Gĩkũyũ native speakers pronounce the English word *boy,* you will hear *mboy,* and for *good,* they will say *ngood;* similarly, the Swahili word *nguvu* (power) will be rendered *guvu.* Then, there is the /r/ and /l/ debacle in which the two sounds are swapped every time, making words such as *rally* come out as *larry*—a tongue twister by all means. In speaking Swahili, Gĩkũyũ speakers will likely say *kula* instead of *kura* (vote), and conversely, they render *kula* (eat) as *kura.* Their pronunciation of sounds also swaps /sh/ and /ch/ from time to time. If you give them a *cheti* (certificate), they will thank you for giving them a *sheti,* which, mercifully, is not a word in Swahili, so no confusion arises.

The song "Mi Mmaasai" ("I am Maasai"), by Abel Loshilaa (aka Mr. Ebbo), caricatures the interaction between the Maasai language and Swahili that produces a Swahili vernacular marked by variations in intonation, shifts in sounds, and pronunciation approximations that alter meanings.[3] One of the features of vernacular Maasai-Swahili is the reversal of order of consonantal sounds in a word—*faraja* (comfort) becomes *fajara* with the *-j-* and *-r-* switched around, and *kinondoni,* the name of a neighborhood in Dar es Salaam (which is itself pronounced *Da si lasama*), transposes *-nd-* and *-n-* to become *kindononi.* The spirited tussle that ensues when Swahili and Maasai play on accents and combine sound forms yields a Maasai-flavored Swahili—a pidgin. The embrace of Swahili by the Maasai is a creative engagement, including calculated transgressions—an important step for a linguistic community that owns Swahili collectively.

Maasai-Swahili also introduces the Maasai language to other countrymen and countrywomen who understand Swahili, thus making the Maasai people feel recognized and not the exotic spectacle the world has made them out to be. Indeed, one of the central devices of humor behind Kenya's popular soap operas *Vitimbi* and *Vioja mahakamani, Redikulas* is the mimicking of Swahili as the various ethnolinguistic communities of the nation speak it. Without poking fun at the distinctive ways in which each group speaks Swahili, pronunciation difficulties can and do become shibboleths—tools for discriminatory profiling in jobs and housing and for targeting certain populations in times of high ethnic tension. As Swahili has long been a means through which its speakers have integrated others, modern Kenyans are taking advantage of their inevitable vernacularizations of the standardized national language to get on with forming a single people out of the many linguistic heritages that the colonialists had used to divide them.

The Pidgins of Swahili

Swahili has never been on a leash despite numerous efforts made by learned societies to influence and lead its development. Davies Mukuria (2001), a scholar of Kiswahili at Moi University in Kenya, disparaging the underlying linguistic diversity of Kenya, makes the purist's comment that "many of those who claim to know Kiswahili can hardly communicate coherently in it through their varied pidginized forms. In other words, such people communicate in their mother tongues using Kiswahili or in Kiswahili using their mother tongues."[4] But this assumption that ungrammatical language does not communicate fails to acknowledge how far the spoken language is from strict adherence to formal rules. Mukuria acknowledges that "errors made in Kiswahili are ignored or they are not noticed,"[5] which confirms that messages keep getting through, even without adherence to rules. Why, one wonders, would Kenyans continue to speak their Swahili pidgins to one another if these vernaculars do not serve their needs effectively? It is unlikely that there was ever a time in Swahili's history when numerous pidgins did not exist. In fact, by its very nature, Swahili must itself have originally been an ungrammatical breaking of several languages. Maasai-Swahili is not new but must have existed ever since the Maasai people made goodwill attempts to speak Swahili well before the colonial era, when they found themselves needing to use it as the language of trade.

Similar spontaneous contexts have led to a variety of other Swahili variants, as newcomers on the coast, Africans from the hinterland, Hindi-speaking immigrants from India, and the English all adapted the language. Thus, we can bring the English effort to standardize Swahili's many dialects into the broader processes of linguistic change as a particular example of vernacularization by non-Swahli speakers. The forms of these Swahili pidgins followed their functions.[6] The hinterland Maasai, Kalenjin, Luo, and Somali adapted Swahili from their languages spoken inland. Indian Swahili, called Kihindi, was the Swahili that immigrant Indians and their descendants spoke to their Swahili-speaking domestic servants and casual labor employees. KiSetla was the Swahili spoken by English settlers in similar contexts of employment, and KiKAR was the pidgin Swahili that African and British soldiers in the battalions of the King's African Rifles (KAR) used to communicate among themselves. More recently, there are the urban pidgins collectively known as Sheng, ostensibly from Nairobi's Eastland inner-city neighborhoods. Thus, KiHindi, KiSetla, KiKAR, and Sheng all emerged from the conversations and socialization and command structures that developed when people of diverse linguistic background needed to communicate. Swahili pidgins are Swahili in ad hoc forms that reflect the long history of the malleability of eastern Africa's principal linguistic framework.

KiHindi Swahili

The word *KiHindi* breaks into two pieces, *Ki-*, which denotes "in the manner/style of," and *Hindi*, "India," referring to the language, mannerisms, and attributes of Indians. Ki-Hindi therefore stands for two languages—Hindi and Swahili spoken "in the accents and mannerisms of Indians." Though the link between India and Swahili country stretches back to ancient times, modern immigrations of Indians to East Africa began in earnest in the 1860s with contract workers brought in by the British to enhance the establishment of the colonial regime. Since then, Indians from Gujarat have been emigrating into East Africa and founding trades and businesses (many are *dukawallas*, "shopkeepers," in Hindi) that have employed large numbers of African workers in Kenya, Tanzania, Mozambique, and Uganda.[7]

In an essay entitled "How the Different Races in Zanzibar Speak Swahili,"[8] Juma Aiey recorded a tongue-in-cheek example of Swahili as spoken by Indians that involved an Indian (*Mhindi*) from Goa complaining about his supper to his African cook, presumably a domestic servant. The Mhindi was expressing displeasure that his dinner was not spicy enough for his stereotypical Indian taste. Here is the transcript of the exchange:

Mhindi: *Pilipili ngapi wewe tia?* "How many peppers did you put?"

African: *Nimetia kumi bwana,* "I put ten sir."

Mhindi: *Sababu kidogo hii namna?* "Why so little?" / *Nani mambia?* "Who told you (to do that)?"

African: *Kanambia bibi,* "Your wife told me."

[The servant answers that it is his (the Mhindi's) wife that gave the order. The Mhindi gets agitated by the implied authority of his wife and says in what appears to be an outburst]

Mhindi: *Nani bibi bele yangu?* "Who is she before me?" / *Bibi kupa mshahara wewe?* "Does she pay you?"

(For the next day the servant is told—)

Mhindi: *Tia ishrini zaidi,* "Put twenty more." [And a warning ensues:] *Mara ya pili mimi fukuza wewe.* "Next time I'll fire you."[9]

The language used in this exchange provides a classic example of master-servant Swahili, in which the master talks down to the domestic servant in a monologue designed to keep the servant in his or her place. (And, of course, the exchange quoted here also indulges the conventional assumption in East Africa that Indians cannot have enough hot pepper in their food.) To establish the facts, the Mhindi asks of the servant, *Pilipili ngapi wewe tia,* "How many peppers did you put?" There is no mistaking what language he is speaking, since *pilipili* (pepper), *ngapi* (how many), *wewe* (you), and *tia* (put) are all basic Swahili. But the nonsyntactical ordering of the words chosen and the lack of a verb tense—compared to the expected rendition in Standard Swahili, *Wewe ulitia pilipili ngapi,* showing both the proper word order and a properly inflected verb, *u-li-tia* (You [past] put)—create a one-sided presumptive use of the language rather then opening a conversation between the two parties. The issue is not when it was done in an effort to understand, which might have followed from the use of a verb tense or time markers such as "earlier today," "this morning," "right now," or the like.

All the other words are used similarly to negate the presence of the servant. The question *Nani mambia?* (Who told him?) indicates the dismissiveness of the boss toward his servant. In using the word *m-ambia* (he/she-tells), the Mhindi employs the third-person pronoambiaun *him/her* to talk to the servant. The stark effect underlines the disregard of a person speaking as though the addressee is not in the room. To address the servant directly, *alikuambia* (*a-li-ku-ambia,* which includes the tense indicator in the verb, *she/he [past] you tell*), or "she/he told you," would have been used. When the poor servant tells the Mhindi it was the Mhindi's own wife who gave the order, the Mhindi gets agitated by the implication of his wife's authority and says in what appears to be an outburst, *Nani bibi bele yangu* (*nani,* "who," *bibi,* "wife," *bele,* "before," and *yangu,* "mine"), or "Who is she before me?"; in Standard Swahili, that would be *Yeye ni nani mbele yangu.* The husband-as-head-of-household motif is projected by the question *Nani bibi bele yangu?* (Who is bibi [wife] before me?).

KiHindi is a pidgin that is encountered in the social world only in uttering it and hearing it uttered. I am therefore at a loss in trying to write it. It has to be heard. In the example just given, the Indian part is not in the vocabulary but rather in the intonations and in pronunciation enriched with Gujarati, Konkaniy, Hindi, and Urdu—the languages typically spoken by Indian emigrants into eastern Africa. Consider, for instance, its notorious substitution of /w/ for /v/, so that the English *words* is pronounced *vards,* as caricatured in the 2012 comedy-drama *English Vinglish.*[10] Indians pronounce the Swahili *wewe* (you) as *veve,* and they also drop *w* within words in Swahili,[11] so that the word *kwenda* (go [away]) (where the /w/ is next to a consonant) becomes *konda* in KiHindi. Swahili words beginning with the consonants *ng, mb,* and *nd* are not part of the sound systems of the Indian languages in question, so they are rendered *g, b,* and *d,* without the *n* and the *m.* As Gujarati, Hindi, and Urdu accents have fueled the rise of the KiHindi pidgin, their particular rendition of Swahili words has culminated into actual borrowings into their own languages. That same domestic vocabulary useful in talking to their employees is properly KiHindi in its ambiguous sense. The following words are not just Swahili as it is spoken by Indians but also words borrowed into Hindi/Urdu and Gujarati: *bakuli* (bowl), pronounced *bakudi*; *kapu* (basket), pronounced *khapu*; *makaa* (charcoal) is *makara* (in Gujarati); *mboga* (vegetable) is *boga*; *mchafu* (dirty) is *chafudo*; *mjinga* (fool) *is jinga*; *mtoto* (child) is *toto*; *muhogo* (cassava) is *mogo*; and *ufagio* (broom) becomes *fagio.*[12]

The KiHindi example indicates that the pidgins communicate much more than the literal messages spoken in them. Speaking in them imposes the strongly hierarchical attitudes of colonial era Indians toward their

servants (and Africans in general) in households, neighborhoods, and
towns. Pidgins, as in this nondialogue of the *tajiri* (boss) talking to the *ki-
jakazi/mjakazi* (female/male worker)—or formerly *mtumwa* (slave)—facil-
itates the voice modulations and pitches of social hierarchy. With political
independence, the tones of Kihindi are becoming more muted.

KiKAR

KiKAR refers to a pidgin Swahili that emerged among African soldiers and
British officers serving together in the East African battalions of the British
colonial army, the King's African Rifles (KAR), in World War I and through
the 1920s and 1930s. African troops recruited from the rural Kenyan highlands did not have a common local language that could be used, and English was out of the question. But Swahili had been utilized for generations
as an informal interethnic language of trade in these densely multilingual
eastern African regions. The KAR took advantage of Swahili's relative familiarity to make it the language of command in its Kenyan barracks. Non-
commissioned officers (NCOs) used this army Swahili to train recruits, and
they taught it to training British officers who served short tours in the KAR.
Recruits underwent four months of basic training in which they were im-
mersed fully in KiKAR pidgin.[13]

KiKAR Swahili pidgin employed a simplified grammatical structure and
borrowed words from the diverse ethnolinguistic communities of the recruits, such as the Luo and Kalenjin from western Kenya and the Kamba and
others from the central regions. It also borrowed technical military vocabulary from the English. According to Mungai Mutonya and Timothy Parsons
(2004, 123), KiKAR was used in the King's African Rifles until the 1930s.

KiKAR slang included a generous borrowing of English
terms, particularly in reference to concepts and items relating to military life. These included: all words of command, all
numbers, parts of a rifle, equipment (bren gun, sling, scabbard);
terms used in a scoring range (marksman, first class, inner, bull,
miss, butts, load, fire); clothing (tie, socks, puttees, shirt, collar,
braces); and ranks (sergeant major, sweeper, sergeant, corporal).
The wholesale borrowing of English terms seems to have been
restricted to concepts most commonly used in commands, pa-
rades and drills. As adapted to Swahili pronunciation, these lexical borrowings from English became *bayoneti* (bayonet), *bastola*

(pistol), *tageti* (target), *skauti* (scout), *kupiga bull* (hit bullseye), and *kupiga miss* (miss a shot or, literally, hit a miss).

KiSetla

KiSetla according to Whiteley (1969) was "found in its purest form where coffee and wheat flourish in preference to coconuts, sweet potatoes and wimbe. . . . Verbs are found in infinitive, imperative and first person singular only."[14] KiSetla was the Swahili-based pidgin that European settlers in colonial eastern and central African farmlands used to communicate, however rudimentarily, with their African workers and servants. In eastern Africa at the end of the nineteenth century, the highland spine of Kenya became one of the centers of large British and other European farms, estates of thousands of acres with grazing cattle and grains. They were staffed by substantial numbers of Africans, whom the settler-farmers regarded with all the disdain of their own aristocratic pretensions and the racism of the era. With luxurious homes also in Nairobi, this "Happy Valley" crowd made Kenya one of the tropical playgrounds of the international aristocratic set, and several of its members became famous—Isak Dinesen, author of *Out of Africa,* was among the best known—or quite notorious for their grandiose follies. Meanwhile, the Europeans displaced numerous former African residents from the lands they farmed, and over time, the resentments sparked by these and other actions on the part of the paragons of colonial arrogance and greed in the 1950s led to the armed rebellion known as Mau Mau, which would be brutally suppressed by the British government..

It is not surprising that, like KiHindi, the KiSetla Swahili pidgin reflected master-servant relationships in terms such as *bwana-boi,* with *bwana* referring to the British and *boi* being the African houseboys. The word *bwana* in Swahili has many meanings, including "Lord" (as in *Bwana Mungu,* or "Lord God"), "lord," "master," "sir," "boss," and even "husband" (in Kenya's hinterland). The word was ideal for the mzungu male, for he considered himself thoroughly superior to the locals in thought and deed and accordingly in absolute control. *Boi* (from English "boy") was the European designation for the African domestic servant, who in settler pidgin was also called *shenzi* (savage). The maturity of the servant did not matter: in fact, most servants were grown men with families, but they were all called boy nonetheless, fitting the image in settler circles of the African as the perpetual child—rustic, uncivilized, undependable, and unpolished.

Commands constituted the main grammatical form of Swahili that Britons used with Africans because much of their communication constituted ordering them around. Using uninflected verb stems of the sort listed in a bilingual dictionary, such as *tia* (put) or *lete* (bring) was the norm, as the following example illustrates.[15] A cook being addressed by the English-speaking settler had a very similar experience to the one serving the Indian in the Kihindi encounter described earlier. Beyond the direct commands, KiSetla simply incorporated the relevant English nouns—for example, "*Tia scones ndani* oven" (literally, "Put scones inside oven") and "*Lete chai pot*" ("Bring teapot"), using the Swahili word *chai* (from Arabic) for the English national drink. No doubt KiSetla pronounced the Swahili verbs in a manner riddled with English accents.

Apart from giving and taking orders, communication in KiSetla was not easy because of the lack of Swahili vocabulary beyond verbs of command. The limits of the pidgin are apparent in an approximation of an intelligible command that the bwana issued to his cook: "*Lete kitu kama ndizi* only round," that is, "Bring something like a banana only round." From this, the poor cook was expected to deduce that the bwana wanted an apple but knew only the Swahili noun for banana, *ndizi*. A predictable lack of comprehension was interpreted by the bwana as insolence or a refusal to understand, and it was reprimanded.

A (presumably) tongue-in-cheek article appearing in the *Kenya Weekly News* on December 23, 1955, offered Britons new to the scene in Kenya advice on what to do when KiSetla yielded no breakthrough to comprehension: "If you are not at first understood, shout. If the native addressed still refuses to comprehend, it is mere contumacy." Speaking louder was thought to make up for incomprehensibility. The Briton was advised always to appear in charge and not to pause to search for appropriate words—"Never hesitate," the white settler was informed. "You are the Big Noise. It is wonderful how the missing word will spring to your lips." It does not require much imagination to realize that such self-importance and miscommunication soon degenerated into cursing and insults. It was richly ironic that the would-be bwana was the one who fell into the savagery that colonial attitudes attributed to Africans. The shouting and arrogance substituted for proficiency, owing to most of the settlers' utter unconcern with mastering the language.

The impossibility of meaningful communication in KiSetla Swahili is memorialized in a joke about a colonial-era mzungu who went to an interview at a government office for a civil service job. He knew only the phrase *njoo hapa* (come here), no doubt because he was so accustomed to calling his servants. Sitting a few yards away from the interviewer (a fellow mzungu), he was asked, in the Swahili part of the interview exam, to say "come here" in Swahili to demonstrate that he could summon his African subordinates. He correctly responded, "*Njoo hapa.*" The interview had started well. The next command to translate was "go there," this time to show he could send subordinates on errands. This phrase the mzungu was unable to translate, so he thought for a moment and then stood up, walked to where the interviewer was sitting, and said "*Njoo hapa,*" or "Come here." The mzungu, it is claimed, passed the exam by demonstrating that he could think on his feet.

Like KiHindi, KiSetla pidgin abstains from inflecting Swahili words—*mimi kupiga wewe* (I-hit-you), using the (dictionary) infinitive form of the verb, instead of *nitakupiga*[16] (I will hit you), or *yeye hapana oa* (he-no-marry) instead of *hajaoa* (he is not married). KiSetla is a minimalist simplification of Swahili, and Anthony Vitale (1980) notes that the heedless spontaneity with which this was done makes it very difficult to find patterns remotely approaching linguistic structure. "Any attempt at categorization or description of the lexical structure of [KiSetla] would be a complex undertaking. The lexical base of S is a continuum. Individual words used are determined by geographical area, social group, general emotional attitude, personal specialization, and the extent of the speaker's command of the standard language as well as KiSetla, and perhaps even mood at the time of speaking." Although a tiny minority of wazungu eventually learned Swahili more proficiently, settlers generally appropriated elements of Swahili for the needs at hand as they saw fit.

These Swahili pidgins—KiKAR, KiSetla, and KiHindi—arose from combining resources of an ethnolinguistic community under the influence of non-African languages, yet there is no modern Arab Swahili pidgin. Perhaps the fact that Arabs never made any real attempt to colonize the hinterland and have always been a small minority among the Swahili meant that Africans did not speak Arabic beyond the sprinkling of Arabic words that appear in Swahili to indicate social status. The difference between pidgins utilizing languages from overseas and mother tongue–influenced pidgins, such as Maasai-Swahili, is that the former do not characterize the way of speaking Swahili of an African ethnic group. KiKAR, KiSetla, and KiHindi are more egalitarian and are open for all to inject input. English and Hindi were the languages of very small minorities, but those minorities wielded a great deal of economic and political power over the speakers of Swahili.

These pidgins of the dominant are the linguistic spaces of class and racial arbitration. Without Swahili's middleman role, communication between foreigners and local populations would have been a problem of even greater magnitude than it was, as it would have required dealing with each linguistic community in a variant of its local language. As things stood, Gīkūyū-speaking house servants spoke KiSetla Swahili with their employers.

Swahili Soap Operas

The Swahili-language soap operas *Vitimbi* and *Vioja Mahakamani* are some of the most successful television shows in Kenya, on air since independence and now running for close to three decades. *Vioja Mahakamani*, a comedy series, is by far the country's most popular program.[17] It is set in a courtroom and focuses on moments in the daily *vioja* (drama) of life that illustrate the interpretations of Kenyan civil and criminal law that apply to everyone's existence.[18] The offenders, who are usually ignorant of the law, are brought before the court to answer charges or to serve as witnesses. They include Kenyans from different language backgrounds around the country. The cases are as varied as human experiences and include carjacking, extortion, witchcraft (as in the selling of human body parts of albinos), unfair business practices (such as relationships between landlords and tenants), employment-related issues (as when an educated couple employs underage children as household help), the arrogance of rich people, the reality of poverty, and spousal abuse (especially as it relates to male dominance).

The proceedings are captivating and even riveting for a linguist in the ways that they portray how diverse ethnicities in Nairobi and Kenya communicate in Swahili, as landlords and tenants or neighbors in conflict show how to talk across and through their linguistic divides. *Vioja Mahakamani* depicts reality to lessen the frustrations of communication—and miscommunication—in these calculatedly fraught confrontations. Beyond the language itself, gestures (a tilt of the head, holding the head with both hands, pointing, arm throwing, pacing, and so forth) as well as yells, cries, and laughter all complement the words or convey important information. Swahili appears in soap operas as an opportunity, a national linguistic resource in the making. The judge and the prosecutor speak Standard Swahili, but the defendants and the witnesses often speak Swahili accented with Luo, Gīkūyū, Luhya, Kamba, Somali, Maasai, or another of Kenya's no fewer than forty-two vernaculars.

Soap operas are popular forms of entertainment that require and impart cultural and linguistic literacy to everyone—from the rural villages to the popular quarters of the cities to the government offices in the vaulted halls of justice. The situations depicted captivate because of their familiarity. There is a man who wants to marry as many wives as possible but is not disturbed by the fact that his first marriage was a Christian one conducted in a church. There is an episode about a Maasai man who thinks he has a right to graze his cattle anywhere, including the city center in downtown Nairobi; viewers think this assumption is not so far-fetched in a city where herds of goats, sheep, and cattle have been seen grazing leisurely within city limits. That the Maasai will do anything to feed their animals needs little explanation in Kenya, and if that is so, why not in Uhuru Park and the various gardens of the City in the Sun, as Nairobi is called.

Episode 11B of *Vioja Mahakamani* provides an excellent example of heavily accented Somali Swahili in which *haa* (yes) and *yakhe* (friend) are used instead of the Swahili *ndiyo* and *rafiki,* respectively.[19] In the episode, the prosecutor interrogates the witness in Standard Swahili. What is striking are the numerous discrepancies between the rough phrasings of the "Somali lady" and the prosecutor's determined translations into the grammatical statements of Standard Swahili. Calling people *yakhe,* as the Swahili lady does, is a common aspect of Somali conversation, and just as in Maasai-Swahili, sounds that do not exist in the Somali language are replaced by others—for example, *baloti* (plot) in Somali Swahili is properly *ploti* in Standard Swahili. Something of the attitudes of speakers of Swahili vernaculars is reflected in the final response the Somali lady gives when the prosecutor has tried to correct her pronunciation of the word *ploti*—she replies, "*Yakhe, lakini si kitu sisi naelewana? Ni kuelewana tu,*" "Friend, isn't the point for us to understand each other? It is to understand each other." Her statement speaks directly to the function of spontaneous communication, as contrasted with adherence to the rules of Standard Swahili that institutions of authority, such as the court (the judge and the prosecutor), seek to impose on the vulnerable people brought before them. Beyond the elite institutions, speakers in the streets communicate effectively enough in fast-moving situations without paying keen attention to the prescribed grammatical rules or formal vocabulary, as the Somali lady in *Vioja Mahakamani* corrected points out to the prosecutor.

Sheng

The vernacular rural Swahili tongues that abound in the hinterland have their urban cousins, the best-known being Nairobi's Sheng. The spontaneous irregularities of KiSetla, KiKAR, and KiHindi are child's play compared to the vibrant complexity of Sheng. This vernacular has grown from the confluence of Swahili and the multiple other languages that urban immigrants have brought to the cities from every part of the country, all enriched with borrowings from English; it has flourished in the streets and in the digital ambiance in which its youthful speakers communicate.

It is important to distinguish between the ad hoc Sheng codings of English phrases, on the one hand, and standardized borrowings from English, on the other, as illustrated in the following inventory of items relating to automobiles, all of which are English words made Swahili in form: *betri* (battery), *boneti* (bonnet, or hood in US English), *breki* (brake), *feni* (fan), *gia* (gear), *haigia* (high gear), and *hudi* (hood). The list continues with *indiketa* (indicator), *injini* (engine), *kabureta* (carburetor), *klachi* (clutch), *madigadi* (mudguard), *mira* (mirror), and *mota* (motor). And there are more still: *pampu* (pump), *rialaiti* (rear light), *redieta* (radiator), *reguleta* (regulator), *taya* (tire), and *waya* (wire).

These technical terms entered Swahili as local mechanics in eastern Africa assimilated English vocabulary into Swahili to be able to talk about their work in repairing cars.[20] All these words can be recognized readily as English terms indigenized to conform to the intonations of spoken Swahili. Indigenized phonetics places the stress on the penultimate (second to last) syllable; vowels are inserted between all double consonants (as with *madigadi* for "mudguard"); and a vowel is added to any English word that ends in a consonant. These modulations of pronunciation arise in much the same way as Americans say *Eye-rack* for the country Iraq instead of *E-rahq*, as Arabic speakers pronounce it. A more apt example is the variant English pronunciations of *Kenya*, which is often rendered as *Key-knee-a*. To get it right in Swahili, the Spanish *-gna-* sound comes in handy, in that the proper rendition is *Keh-gna*.

Swahili has taken in ample supplies of English loanwords, usually following these conventions of Swahili pronunciation (especially the penultimate stress). The following poem uses the words *biya* (beer), *wisiki* (whiskey), *champeni* (champagne), *sipiriti* (spirits), and *sitimu* (steam), probably to advertise foreign alcohols, as opposed to *pombe ya mnazi* (coconut beer) and other local brews.

Wa wapi wanywao *biya*	Where are the drinkers of beer,
wisiki, na champeni	whiskey and champagne?

sipiriti inangiya	Spirits are going in [the throats]
kwa rahisi madukani	more cheaply in the shops' bars;
sitimu ni mara moya	Drunkenness is instantaneous;
mara hamutambuwani	Suddenly you no longer recognize each other.

(Knappert 1979, 34)

Sheng is another matter altogether; it obeys no rules, phonetic or other-wise. It is the ultimate renegade Swahili.[21] It defies definition as an argot,[22] a slang,[23] or a pidgin. The initial *Sh-* in the name refers to *Swahili* and the final *-eng* to *English,* but Sheng is both those languages and many others—it uses words from the entire variety of languages that have come its way. The expanding urban populace has embraced English through Swahili, but when it comes to Sheng, the Swahili is complicated by the interbreeding of grammars, vocabularies, and sounds in addition to hybridizing accents and pronunciation. The words *gudi bai yanisiki mai dali* found in the early nineteenth-century poem by Sheikh Swadi bin Ali of Lamu translate to *"good-bye makes me sick my darling"* in the following verse:

Haifai kutoyuwa yangu hali	It is not good (for you) not to know my state,
nili hai kwako siweki badali	As long as I live I have no substitute for you
gudi bai yanisiki mai dali	Good-bye makes me sick my darling

(Jan Knappert 1979, 34) (my translation)

The word *yanisiki* (*ya-ni-siki—it-me-sick—*"it makes me sick") takes the English adjective *sick* and converts it to a verb. And that simple process—innocent as it seems—opens up an entire universe of ways in which Sheng can incorporate words from any language, not just English. Verbs from English are particularly targeted in Sheng, producing such terms as *nitakue-mailia* (I will e-mail you), compiled by wrapping the English word *e-mail* in Swahili verb parts—*ni-* (I) and *ta-* (future tense), the *-ku-* object marker (for "you" singular in Swahili), the prepositional affix *-i-* (indicating to/for), and a final vowel, *-a,* that is called a verbalizer and always completes the verb. Virtually any English verb can be Swahilized in Sheng. In the 2012 film *Nairobi Halflife,*[24] a character looking for a job says *"nioganaizie kawaks,"* combining *oganaizi* (organize) and *wak* (work) to convey the message "hire me, give me a job" (literally organize a small job for me); all in all, there is much English and little Swahili here. The word *nioganaizie* parses as *ni-* (me) *oganaiz-* (organize) *-ie* (for), thus meaning "organize for me (hook me up)," and *kawaks* is *ka-* (diminutive) *-waks* (a little work, or a small job), which is more often phrased as *kajob* (casual employment). Further examples of the Swahilization of English that is rampant in Kenya include *tutago* (*tu-ta-go*—we-[Swahili future tense]-go, or "we will go"), *mcheki* (*m-*check-*i*—he-/she-check), and *chali ya* mine (buddy of mine), in which English is used within Swahili grammar, or whole words are used in Swahili, as in *moti ya mine* (motorcar of mine [my car]).

Sheng brings together features from other pidgins to make a unique urban blend that we can best refer to as slang. It is the vibrant hip language spoken by *jamaa wa mtaa* (neighborhood guys, or buddies), the de facto owners of Nairobi's Eastlands neighborhoods, as distinguished from *maagush* (the country bumpkins), seen as more rustic and identified by their ethnically infected Swahili. Urban hip crowd friends are *mabeshte* (pronounced *mah-behshtay*), who *bonga* (talk) as opposed to *kutweng* (twanging)—that is, speaking English "through the nose," the way that white people from Britain and the United States are perceived to speak. Kenyans are not alone in hearing twangs when whites speak English.[25] When I was growing up, buddies were *mamen* (my men—a rehabilitating colloquial play on the demeaning colonial use of the word *boys*) or *chali* (which doubled for *boy* and *boyfriend*). These terms were likely taken from war films in the 1970s (the genre most available in movie theaters of the time), which were laden with NATO lingo and military jargon for the enemy in Vietnam—for example, the letter *C* stood for "Charlie" and *VC* stood for "Viet Cong" or, in the radioman's idiom, "Victor Charlie."

Sheng bears pidgin characteristics in that it simplifies the vocabulary that it borrows. A typical reduction is to borrow a syllable or two of an English word and add *-o* at the end of the shortened English form, thus making many words that rhyme. In the word *negotiate*, for instance, only the first syllable, *neg*, is taken, and an *-o* is added to it to produce the Sheng word *nego*. Other examples include *president* shortened to *prezo*, *physics* shortened to *fizo*, *Saturday* to *sato*, *United States* to *steeto*, and *thirty* to *thaato*. It is also common to put *o-* at the start as well as the end of words. Thus, for example, from the word *Nakuru*, the name for one of Kenya's cities, the middle fragment *-kur-* is taken and the vowel *o* is added on both ends to form the Sheng name for the city, *Okuro*. Other examples include *oruaro* from the Swahili *suruali* (pants), *oruro* from *ndururu* (five cents), and *oshago* from *gishagi* (village). Also not to be overlooked is the strategy of English "pig Latin," which involves moving the first syllable of a word to the end and adding the long vowel -*ay*, as in *igpay* for "pig." In Sheng, similarly, the word *moja* (one) may be pronounced *jamo, tumbo* (stomach) would be rendered *mbotu*, and *nyumba* (house) would be pronounced *mbanyu*.

Sheng Goes Literate, in Its Way

If texting is any guide, Sheng appears to be taking the lead with regard to where Swahili is headed. Texting is growing rapidly in Kenya and Tanzania. In 2008, there were 16.3 million mobile phone subscribers in Kenya, a country whose population of approximately 38 million then included about 22.5 million people over the age of fifteen. In the first quarter of 2010, Kenya's mobile phone density (teledensity) was above 51 percent, with mobile subscriptions increasing from 19.4 million to 19.9 million in the fourth quarter of 2009, the additional half million representing a rise of 2.7 percent. During the same period, mobile phone subscriptions increased by 33 percent to a nationwide total of 2.7 million users, thanks to social networking done largely through mobile phones. According to the Communications Commission of Kenya (CCK), a whopping 99 percent of Internet subscriptions between January and March 2010 pertained to mobile phones (Karanja 2010).

Tanzanians have also taken to mobile phones in a dramatic way. According to the *Citizen* (March 19, 2010), there were over 17 million mobile phone users in Tanzania compared to fewer than 300,000 a decade earlier, an increase (albeit from a low base) of 5,000 percent. According to the Tanzania Communications Regulatory Authority (TCRA), the number of mobile subscribers increased from about 16.2 million to nearly 17.5 million just in the three months between September and December 2009. Teledensity in Tanzania stood at 43 percent in 2010—that is almost one telephone for every two people, compared to one telephone for every hundred people in 2000 and 2001, when the country's teledensity was at 1 percent.

Today's young people have been dubbed "generation text" (Thurlow 2003). The pervasiveness of texting is hard to overstate. Everyone is texting: teenagers, young adults, and even parents, and text lingo is creeping into speech. Texting is in fact a new form of literacy that has bypassed the written Standard Swahili of the schools. It is manufactured in the full range of associations in the social sphere—family, friends, business, news flashes, and so on. If ever there was a necessary literacy campaign, it would be to impart the ability to decipher text communications: this new kind of literacy might well revive interest in the synching of education to utilitarianism—adaptability, immediacy, simplicity, playfulness, and elegance, all hinged on relevance.

Swahili text messaging in Kenya and Tanzania is often done in a mixed code of elements from Swahili and English. To appreciate the challenge of texting in Kenya and Tanzania, it is important to remember the linguistic diversity of the potential networks of any individual's "followers." Kenya has at least 42 languages and Tanzania about 120, three times as many. Texting in such multilingual situations has meant that people are becoming extraordinarily resourceful and innovative in finding ways to write across the linguistic and social barriers just the way Swahili enabled multiethnic people to communicate for centuries in interpersonal situations.

In addition, it is important to note that most of the languages spoken widely in the region are seldom written, save for Swahili. Local languages are written only cursorily and with no established conventions to make them intelligible among strangers. The rapid and heavy adoption of writing through texting by people of predominantly nonliterate backgrounds merits attention in the ongoing story of modern Swahili, even though the circles of formal education devoted to Standard Swahili are on silent mode with regard to the digital real-world lives of the students in their classrooms. Although proficiencies in Kenya and Tanzania vary in both English and Standard Swahili, with most people having little to no command of the written languages, texting is in most instances drawn directly from speech. The spontaneous language of texting in a linguistic landscape of spoken diversity is not only of theoretical interest to scholars studying the interface between speech and writing but also a vibrant new chapter in the story of Swahili.

To understand texting and the kinds of linguistic acrobatics that go into it, one has to recognize both the challenges of writing to communicate across multiple cultures and languages, including the numerous Swahili pidgins, and the distinctive accessibility of texting. Everyone in Kenya and Tanzania with a cell phone is either already texting or an aspiring texter. Yet no one has had to conduct a literacy campaign to teach people how to write the messages they send. Rather, texting lingo is being established in a kind of free market of orthographic creativity: whatever communicates—whatever spellings, abbreviations, and diction catch on—is what becomes convention.

Texting is popularizing literacy in a spontaneous derivative of Swahili and English, wresting language out of the hands of authorities who prohibit writing anything but their own formal conventions to the dynamic world of real-time, real-life social interactions, where the linguistic rubber hits the road to genuine communication.

Texting rejects the distinction between business and pleasure, mixing the two with abandon. The only constraint is that the texts bear meanings in their moments—that is, texting is not writing for writing's sake or for readers unknown, at some indefinite time. Individuals, groups, and communities are using the texting feature of the mobile phone on what matters to them in the moments of their daily lives. Such concerns include, among many others, improving the quality of health care that patients get from their physicians, circulating money (most notably among the unbanked, i.e., people without bank accounts), paying bills, passing immediately useful information, and most of all accessing the Internet. Texting saves time, eliminates or greatly reduces uncertainty in the moment, gives raw information as events are taking place, and above all enhances wealth-generating ventures by improving security in processing orders and circulating cash. Texting may even become an income generator if such enterprises as Txteagle, an artificial intelligence system, succeed in enabling several billion subscribers of mobile phones living in developing countries to earn money by completing routine processing tasks online for remote employers.

What language enables communication by texting, given the multiplicity of languages in Kenya and Tanzania? Unless otherwise specified, the examples I cite here are taken from Twitter, from Facebook, and from individual communications. There are some excellent studies of the language of texting, Sandra Nekesa Barasa's 2010 work being among the most thorough. She captures many features of texting in a variety of texting environments, and she even attempts to distinguish the language of texting in Kenya from that used in Tanzania. In just a handful of examples from her work, it is easy to see that English is prevalent in texting done by some Kenyans. I have distinguished the flow of different languages through the following mixed statement, using "Sw" for Swahili, "Eng" for English, and "Sh" for Sheng.

> They changa-d some becks for him to use in lipa-r-ing the loan before he uza-s the ha-o
>
> Eng Sw+Eng Eng Sh Eng Sw + Eng Eng Sw+Eng Sh
>
> They contributed some money to help him service the loan before he sells the house.[26]

Here is another actual example of texting from a Kenyan who is probably more fluent in English than Swahili.

kuactivate free drinks lazima uchape kidrink cha guamsa during
the dei! Au sio?

Sw+Eng Eng Sw Sh Sw+Eng Sw Sh Eng Sw

activation of the free drinks voucher should be preceded by a
huge drink during the day, or not?[27]

These two concoctions of Swahili, English, and Sheng are good examples of
modern Swahili. Anyone who knows both Swahili and English will understand them, but someone who knows only English or only Swahili will not
comprehend much.

The upright defenders of Standard Swahili use such examples as evidence of the impending demise of a thousand-year-old language. But far
from being a death knell, they actually show that Swahili is as alive as ever,
not as the standard language of the colonial occupiers but as a language that
people are constantly stirring, shaking, and tinkering with, indigenizing it
to meet their needs. These are the natural dynamics of development for a
language spoken by a cosmopolitan people.

Swahili Dynamism in Pidgins and Texting

Just as the Africans of the hinterland who arrived at the coast in the nineteenth century shifted to Swahili, people who do not speak another common language in contemporary eastern Africa have taken in and adapted
Swahili to bridge the resulting communication gap. But the classical Swahili
spoken as a native language at the coast is a bridge too far for the peoples
of the hinterland, who do not share or feel any loyalty to its deep cultural
heritage. They need language only for immediate communication, pragmatically and without conventions of region or class. Hence, the pidgins
emerge as a rough-and-ready consequence of the truly democratic process
of linguistic and cultural interaction. Pidgins are wonderfully useful in
spontaneous encounters, in that they include or co-opt without excluding
or alienating. They are open.

In case you are wondering why other languages do not just incorporate
Swahili vocabulary into their own grammars, it is because Swahili is the
lingua franca and shared nurturing base of the pidgins. There are, of course,
other pidgins besides Swahili in the marketplace of mixing throughout modern Africa. These pidgins and creoles are the untold story of contemporary

Africa's linguistic landscape. In West Africa, Fallou Ngom (2003 and 2004), Fiona McLaughlin (1995 and 2001), and others have written about the use of multiple languages in the city of Dakar and the country of Senegal, which parallels the Swahili story. Just as Sheng has been Swahilizing English, Wolof in Senegal has been Wolofizing French. Similarly, in South Africa, Tsotsitaal, a mixed language based on Afrikaans (*taal* means "language") associated with *tsotsis* (Sesotho for "thugs"), and Isicamtho, a pidgin that can be built over the grammar of any of the South African Bantu languages (including Xhosa, Tsonga, Tswana, and Venda) but most often used in Zulu and Sotho, are of the same spirit as Sheng. Pidgins are trendy, as a look at Cameroon reveals:

> Of the over 200 indigenous languages spoken by Cameroonians, only Pidgin enjoys the privilege of being spoken by people from all walks of life and social strata. Pidgin is no longer restricted to small talk; it is no longer the language of the uneducated. Although for a long time, Pidgin has been perceived as a language used mostly by illiterate and semi-literate persons, this mixed language has now gained currency among the educated in Cameroon as well. It has attained the status of language of literature, business and music. Cameroonian writers and other artists employ Pidgin in order to ensure group solidarity and to reinforce a sense of belonging. Francis Njamnjoh, Peter Vakunta, Patrice Nganang, Mongo Beti and Ferdinand Oyono to name but a few frequently resort to pidginization as a mode of linguistic and cultural appropriation.[28]

Swahili is spoken in a continuum in a manner very similar to Jamaican, in that "not every Jamaican makes such a clear-cut distinction between Standard and Creole English" but rather swings back and forth along a continuum between the two.[29] Swahili pidgins come in numerous varieties, and one must live in certain locales to fully understand them and be understood in them. Conversely, most people come into contact with Standard Swahili only in schools. They operate somewhere in the middle. Pidgins express local experience, are highly pragmatic in nature, and are for the most part inviting in that, for instance, it does not take much time for a speaker of one kind of Sheng to understand another. This is also the case with regard to Africa's other pidgins: "There are a number of English-related pidgins and creolized languages all the way down the west coast of Africa, the

Caribbean, in parts of North America, which are, with a certain amount of adjustment, mutually intelligible, because they were developed by speakers who originally spoke African languages."[30] Swahili pidgins share some interesting parallels with Krio (spoken as a lingua franca in Sierra Leone and Gambia, especially in Freetown, the capital of Sierra Leone). Swahili pidgins are not primitive, quaint, or inefficient versions of the mother tongue. They are languages in their own right at various points along the continuum conventionally dubbed Swahili. Their grammatical structure is partly non-coastal and non–Standard Swahili, but what else in this flexibility is new?

Most Krio words have obvious English roots. A word like *man* transfers unchanged. But then, under the processes of creolization, it begins to work overtime: *man klos* (man's dress), *man pawa* (man power = strength), *manpus* (tomcat). Equally, there are words that have African roots. *Manafiki* (deceitful, untrustworthy—Yoruba: *mana fiki*), *manyamanya* (to pulp something—Twi: *manyamanta*), *mao* (to be initiated into rituals—Yoruba: *mavo*), *mara* (to behave foolishly—Mende *malama*), *manti-manti* (very large—Temne). The "spirit" of Krio, for all its English borrowing, is African. The majority of Sierra Leone is speaking a kind of English that is, to the average British or American eye and ear, virtually a foreign language.[31]

The same story of linguistic fluidity is told with local variations throughout Southeast Asia and the Pacific basin,[32] not just in the pidgins of the black world. The process is unrelenting and is emblematic of what has always taken place with Swahili and also of how completely new languages may emerge under conditions of rapid globalization. Though pidgins are denigrated, belittled, and often dismissed as wayward lingo to be suppressed by strict adherence to standard forms, they are nascent languages. There are pidgins wherever people who do not speak a common language have to live with each other. They indicate that language formation is a spontaneous development as diverse people seek to exploit the situations they encounter to make a living.

Digital communication has enabled the youth to become literate in their own social environment, thus illustrating the dictum that language is what language does (Mugane 2010). The appeal of texting is the freedom with which people are able to communicate multilingually using whatever words they share, regardless of their language sources, and abandoning the formal conventions of language use. People using Swahili adopt or create a set of meaning-making symbols, signs, and acronyms, drawing from the languages of their surroundings but used most often in conversational register characterized by immediacy, simplicity, playfulness, relevance, and even elegance—just as Swahili grows.

CHAPTER 11

Swahili in African American Life

AFRICAN AMERICANS sometimes refer to Africa as "the motherland," and if there is any language symbolizing the motherland for them, it is Swahili. But of the hundreds of languages in Africa, Zulu and others of them familiar by name, why has Swahili become this important source of symbols and cultural concepts for African Americans?

Unlike Hollywood and Western media that promote negative stereotypes of Africa and Africans, African Americans have embraced the continent's most positive attributes. For them, potential cultural inspirations in the homeland are not restricted to one particular place or people; rather, they have drawn their Africanisms from diverse regions all over the continent. African Americans adorn themselves with West African attire, including kente cloth from Ghana, *dashiki* (a Yoruba word meaning "shirt"), *buba* (Yoruba women's wrap), and *gele* (Yoruba women's head scarf). Some even pour libations to their ancestors in the manner of many West African communities. However, the Swahili language and culture have come to play a special role in African Americans' cultural inspirations. In the same way that many ethnic groups throughout eastern and central Africa have established social networks mediated by Swahili, African Americans also have constructed aspects of their cultural symbolism from the Swahili world. They have taken names, symbols, idioms, and vocabulary from its Bantu components as well as words from the transoceanic world of the Indian Ocean (as discussed in chapter 2). What better language to adopt than the language of a resilient and resourceful people in Africa?

African American interests in the attire, names, symbols, and ceremonies of western Africa would seem more direct than their choice of Swahili. Most of those who were sold in the transatlantic slave trade were taken from West Africa, and African Americans are more likely to be of West African heritage rather than descended from the other side of the African continent, where there is no such strong historical link through the Middle Passage. The prevalence of Swahili among African Americans begs further explanation.

Beyond Swahili's wide geographic reach in Africa, its prominence in Hollywood movies and its status as the most commonly taught African language in the United States are due in part to its accessibility to English speakers. This accessibility can be attributed to the absence of the tones common in African languages and to the colonial version of the language created by English speakers. To these factors we can add the inspiration of one person: Mwalimu Julius Kambarage Nyerere, the first president of the United Republic of Tanzania. President Nyerere's actions and policies regarding Swahili in the 1960s catapulted its esteem and significance considerably, not least among the African Americans who were then seeking sources in Africa for the pride they felt and prominently declared in being black. Nyerere was the vanguard of a new kind of education similarly dedicated to pride in being African, and one aspect of this reform was developing a pedagogy in Swahili. Nowhere else did an African country or society go so boldly against or beyond the language of the colonialists, and his indigenous lingual advocacy inspired many in the United States. Part of Tanzania's national anthem goes as follows:

Mungu ibariki Afrika	God bless Africa
Wabariki Viongozi wake	Bless its leaders
Hekima Umoja na Amani	Wisdom, unity, and peace
Hizi ni ngao zetu	These are our shields
Afrika na watu wake.	Africa and its people
Chorus:	*Chorus:*
Ibariki Afrika, Ibariki Afrika	Bless Africa, Bless Africa
Tubariki watoto wa Afrika.	Bless us, the children of Africa

Nyerere's reform invoked the philosophy of African socialism—or ujamaa—as a way to free Africans from the humiliations of colonialism and neocolonialism. His pride in being African had a profound appeal for the architects of Kwanzaa, the weeklong African American celebration of the community building and independence at the heart of Ujamaa. Recognizing the importance of this cultural and political engagement, Nyerere actively welcomed African Americans to Tanzania. And for their part, African

Americans engaging with the homeland learned about Swahili's history as a language of resistance against colonial oppression, in Tanzania as well as in Kenya, Uganda, and parts of what is now the Democratic Republic of the Congo. Swahili's history of dignified resilience inspired its adoption by African Americans in the black freedom movement of the 1960s.

During that decade, young black political activists in the United States were searching for an identity that went beyond the "anarchist impulse of leather jacketed young men armed to the teeth, rising out of the urban ghetto," as described in the 1968 poem "Black Dada Nihilismus" by LeRoi Jones (later known as Amiri Baraka). The incorporation of Swahili connected the movement to positive aspects of the homeland, including its history of resistance against colonial power that blacks viewed as analogous to their own exclusion from equal rights and full integration in US society. Swahili words enriched African American discourse and rhetoric regarding black resistance against white racism. In the pages that follow, I will outline inspirations drawn from Swahili by four African American political activists: Maulana Karenga, Amiri Baraka, Pete O'Neal, and Stanley "Tookie" Williams. Although many of their political beliefs and methods of resistance—including the advocacy of violence—remain controversial to this day, my purpose here is neither to endorse nor critique their views but rather to illuminate the vital presence of Swahili in this important era of US political history.

African American Swahili

In September 1965, Maulana Karenga (also known as Ron Karenga and born Ronald McKinley Everett on July 14, 1941) founded the "US" Organization. The word US referred to "us," that is, African American blacks, as opposed to "them," the whites. The organization was founded on a political doctrine that Karenga developed and referred to as *Kawaida* (a Swahili word meaning "tradition and reason"). Karenga's contribution to the Black Power discourse was his introduction of the notion of black cultural nationalism as a form of revolutionary praxis (Kawaida publications 1977, 101). He used Swahili words and concepts to articulate his vision of the ideal black community, and his use of the language contributed to its enduring popularity in the United States.

Karenga created the holiday Kwanzaa in 1966. The word *Kwanzaa* is taken from the Swahili *kwanza* (first), inspired by the custom in a good number of African communities of gathering together to celebrate the first fruits of the harvest.¹ The extra *-a* at the end makes it something of a neologism. Kwanzaa is based on the concept of *nguzo saba* (seven pillars, in Swahili). These pillars all bear Swahili names: *umoja* (unity), *kujichagulia* (self-determination), *ujima* (collective work and responsibility), *ujamaa* (economic cooperation), *nia* (purpose), *kuumba* (creativity), and *imani* (faith). The seven principles are an adaptation of President Nyerere's philosophy of Ujamaa. In a 1977 publication, *Kwanzaa: Origin, Concepts, Practice*, Karenga wrote: "Kwanzaa is not an imitation, but an alternative, in fact, an oppositional alternative to the spookism, mysticism and non-earth based practices which plague us as a people and encourage our withdrawal from social life rather than our bold confrontation with it." The Kwanzaa holiday, celebrated during the traditional Christmas season from December 26 to January 1, was deliberately designed to be oppositional, creating an alternate focus for African Americans living in a white-dominated and commercialized society (turning toward socialism and anticapitalism). Karenga explained that the holiday "was chosen to give a Black alternative to the existing holiday and give Blacks an opportunity to celebrate themselves and history rather than simply imitate the practice of the dominant society." Kwanzaa has since evolved to become popular among African Americans as well as among some nonblack Americans.

Karenga's creation of Kwanzaa actively linked the political and cultural struggles of African Americans to those of Africans through Swahili language and culture. Karenga's inspiration by Nyerere gave Swahili a prominence among African Americans over Yoruba, Ewe, Twi, and other West African languages that the Africans who were taken in the transatlantic slave trade had spoken but whose descendants in America had not inherited them. Karenga found Swahili to be a medium capable of expressing the ideals of the holiday. He compared the importance of Swahili to black people around the world to that of Hebrew to Jews worldwide (Karenga 1993, 15). Through Kwanzaa, Swahili, as the source of symbols revitalizing black culture in the diaspora, has gained considerable visibility.

Although the Swahili used by African Americans draws its inspiration from Africa, it has a character unto itself. The words are easily recognizable as taken from what is considered to be Standard Swahili. The reason for Karenga's choice of Zanzibari Swahili (the trade dialect) is very likely due to his admiration for Julius Nyerere's Ujamaa philosophy of black political action. Nyerere was an inland Tanzanian, who like other inlanders was influenced by the official written version of Swahili blessed by the colonial government (actually the Zanzibari dialect). However, African Americans did not just sprinkle Swahili words into their speeches for solidarity with the homeland: rather, they adapted the language, much like the inland communities of eastern and central Africa who had made Swahili their own.

African Americans freed their usage of Swahili from the standard spoken on the continent in several interesting ways, five of which I will mention here. First, the initial method by which African Americans connected with Swahili was by changing their American names to Swahili ones. They carefully constructed the names they adopted to convey a revolutionary message or highlight the endeavors of African Americans in the struggle for justice. For instance, Don Luther Lee, a renowned African American author and poet, took the name Haki Madhubuti, which means "real/concrete justice." His choice constituted a mission statement for the movement and in this way paralleled Africans' choices of names that have concrete meanings relevant to the times and lives of their bearers. Parents in Africa's Swahili-speaking region and elsewhere have a tendency to name their children in ways that reflect their hopes and aspirations for their offspring.

Second, African Americans took on Swahili titles to indicate the dignity of holding leadership roles. Amiri Baraka, the name that activist LeRoi Jones took for himself, is an interesting example of a proper name that doubles as a title. *Amiri* comes from *amuru,* which (borrowing from Arabic) is Swahili for "command." The term is commonly used by army generals, who in Swahili are called *Amiri Jeshi* (army) in Arabic. *Baraka,* another term from Arabic, denotes "blessing/blessedness." Hence, the name Amiri Baraka symbolizes "commander/master of blessings," capturing the change in LeRoi Jones's philosophy from wanton destruction (as in his poem "Black Dada Nihilismus") to black community building. Commenting on Karenga's use of Swahili, which greatly influenced him, Amiri Baraka noted:

> Swahili was used by Karenga, as he explained in his doctrine, ostensibly because it was a non-tribal language, a kind of lingua franca for all the continent. . . . There was also a pamphlet, *The Quotable Karenga,* which some of "the advocates," as members of the US organization were called, had put together, which consisted of quotes from Karenga. Karenga also had a formal *Doctrine,* some of it published in bits and pieces in the *Quotable,* some other parts in the *Kitabu,* the book of the Kawaida

doctrine. The advocates I saw looked well disciplined and dedicated. All had Swahili names. Karenga's practice was to give out
a Swahili name as a last name, the way it existed in many East
African countries, such as Tanzania, Kenya, Uganda. So that a
person could be James Tayari or Ken Msemaji. Karenga gave out
the names, naming each advocate according to his attributes.
So that Tayari meant "ready," implying that that advocate was
ready to make revolution. Msemaji meant "orator," it was given
because Ken Msemaji could heavy rap! (Baraka 1984, 251–52)

The titles that leaders of the Black Power movement took for themselves
also reflected an adaptation of Swahili that did not emphasize its Islamic
component. LeRoi Jones abandoned the Arabic-derived Amiri Baraka and
took the title Imamu. It is noteworthy that this word, also Arabic-derived
(from *imam*), is rendered in as *Imamu* in Swahili (where all words must end
in one of five vowels, /a/, /e/, /i/, /o/, or /u/) and not in the final consonant of
the Arabic form. The two words resemble each other so closely that including the /u/ in *Imamu* indicates the Black Power movement's attention to
Swahili as an African language rather than to its Arabic aspect. Jones stated
the following:

> Under Karenga's influence, I changed my name to Amiri, Bantu-
> izing or Swahilizing the first name and the pronunciation of the
> last name as well. Barakat in Arabic is pronounced "Body-cot,"
> the Swahili drops the "t" and accents the next-to-last syllable,
> hence Baráka. Amiri with the rolled "r" is pronounced "Amidi."
> The name change seemed fitting to me . . . not just the meaning
> of the name Blessed Prince, but the idea that I was now literally
> being changed into a blacker being. I was discarding my "slave
> name" and embracing blackness. It is Chancellor Williams, the
> historian, who points out, however, that the many new Yusefs
> and Omars should remember that those Arabic names for black
> people are as much slave names as Joseph and Homer. One from
> Anglo-American slavery, the other from Arab slavery. (Baraka
> 1984, 267)

Note that none of the definitions given for *Imam/Imamu* fit Amiri
Baraka's work without some embellishment. The term is understood to be a
concept of the Islamic world with at least one of a number of meanings:

1. In law and theology, the caliph who is successor to Muhammad as the lawful temporal leader of the Islamic community.

2. The male prayer leader in a mosque.

3. The Muslim worshiper who leads the recitation of prayer when two or more worshipers are present.

4. A male spiritual and temporal leader regarded by Shiites as a descendant of Muhammad divinely appointed to guide humans.

5. An earthly representative of the 12 such leaders recognized by the majority form of Shiism.

6. A ruler claiming descent from Muhammad and exercising authority in an Islamic state.

7. Any one of the founders of the four schools of law and theology.

8. An authoritative scholar who founds a school of law or theology.

(based on *American Heritage Dictionary* 2014)

At weddings where Amiri Baraka officiated as Imamu, the groom was given the title of Saidi, the Swahili/Bantu pronounciation of *Sayyid,* which means "master," "lord," "chief," or "mister" in Arabic. *Said* denotes direct descent from the Prophet Muhammad through his two grandsons, Hasan and Husayn. The title conveys respect in Islamic codes of conduct and is found all over the Islamic world. In the Maghrebi Arabic of northwestern Africa, it is *Sayyid, Sayyidi, Sayyed, Sayid,* or *Sidi*; in Turkish, it is *Seyed, Seyit, Seyyid,* or *Seyyed*; in India (Urdu, Punjabi, Sindhi, Bengali, and Gujarat), it is *Syed, Saiyad, Saiyed,* or *Sayyid*; in Persia, it is *Sayyed* or *Sayed*; in Malay, it is *Syed*; and in Pashto (Afghanistan), it is *Sayed*.[2] The name and title that Ron Karenga chose is Maulana, a Swahilized version of the Arabic *Mawlana,* which is a form of respectful address to a sovereign as "our Lord" or "our Master." In Swahili, it is a title for revered members of a community. In eastern Africa, one would be hard-pressed to find Imamus, Saidis, and Maulanas who were not Muslims. African Americans converted these religious titles to secular ones.

In a third adaptation, the African American Swahili of the Black Power movement extended the meanings of the words borrowed into it. *Dada* is used commonly in Swahili to mean "sister," the oldest female sibling, or the feminine equivalent of "brethren." Dada in Black Power lexicon meant a sisterhood of black women (not women of other races). Surprisingly, the black brotherhood did not adapt the Swahili *ndugu,* "brethren." Other

Swahili words, such as *kawaida,* which Maulana Karenga used for "tradition and reason," are not the most commonly used words for these concepts in Africa. To explain the extent to which kawaida promoted Swahili in the African American discourse, Karenga wrote: "Kawaida is not eclecticism because it borrows from the sociohistorical context to which it owes its existence. Kawaida critically examines various contributions to Black and human history, and makes a selective analysis of what is real and relevant, extracts it, integrates it into its system and then, puts it in the service of Black liberation" (Karenga 1977, 139).

A fourth feature of African American Swahili is its anglicized words and word order. For "birthday party," African American usage combines the words *kuziliwa,* "to be born," and *karamu,* "feast," in the English order, as *kuziliwa karamu.* However, in eastern Africa, "birthday feast" would be *karamu ya kuzaliwa.* In Swahili, noun phrases are "head-initial," that is, the first word is the noun and the second one its modifier; English, by contrast, is "head-final," with modifiers preceding the noun. The Black Power movement thus anglicized its Swahili. More obvious examples of Swahili English in the diaspora are provided in the following examples, which use the English pluralization marker /s/ to pluralize Swahili nouns: *hekalus* (temples), *malaikas* (good spirits), *mumininas* (believers), *karamus* (feasts), *mwanafunzi* (apprentice teachers).

A fifth characteristic of African American Swahili is the extension of meanings of Swahili words that were essential in defining black cultural nationalism. In the preceding examples, *malaika* means "angel" in African Swahili but "good spirits" for African Americans. Similarly, *mwanafunzi,* "disciple or child of a master," extended the meaning of the term for "student" in eastern African Swahili to mean "apprentice-teacher." Extending meanings of Swahili words enables African Americans to adapt their association with African life and struggles to concepts, symbols, and images that reflect the black liberation struggle unique to the United States.

Swahili, Black Arts, Pan-Africanism, and the Black Power Movement

The Black Arts Repertory Theater/School (BARTS), which had an auditorium seating 120 on West 130th Street in New York City, was founded in 1965 and directed by LeRoi Jones, the principal architect of the black arts movement. The movement spread to every US city. Although the original theater did not survive for long, it became associated with many famous personalities in black arts, including poets Larry Neal and Sonia Sanchez as well as the musician Sun Ra. LeRoi Jones was thoroughly impressed when he met Maulana Karenga in 1966. Jones took to using Swahili as the source of the metaphors and concepts of his poetry and also utilized some of Karenga's Swahili vocabulary.

The founders of the Karamu House theater in Cleveland, for instance, used Swahili naming to claim their multiracial establishment as a black creation:

> Karamu House in Cleveland, Ohio is the oldest African-American theater in the United States. Many of Langston Hughes's plays were developed and premiered at the theater. In 1915, Oberlin graduates Russell and Rowena Woodham Jelliffe opened what was then called Settlement House . . . where people of different races, creeds and religions could find a common ground. The Jelliffes discovered in the early years, that the arts provided the perfect common ground, and the work of the Playhouse Settlement began. The early twenties saw a large number of African Americans move into an area from the south. Resisting some pressure to exclude their new neighbors, the Jelliffes insisted that all races were welcome. What was then called the Playhouse Settlement quickly became a magnet for some of the best African American artists of the day. Dancers, print makers, actors, writers all found a place where they could practice their crafts. Reflecting the strength of the Black influence on its development, the Playhouse Settlement was officially renamed Karamu House in 1941.[3]

Commenting on the futility of black machoism, LeRoi Jones/Amiri Baraka remarked:

> The worst thing a person could be, as far as Karenga was concerned, was *ovyo,* a Swahili word meaning "random," a person acting at random, disorganized and unpredictable. This was the problem with the "basic blood," as Karenga called blacks. (Baraka 1984, 253)

The antithesis of ovyo was to turn young black males into responsible men through practicing a form of martial arts called *yangumi* (Swahili for something associated with a punch), *tabura* (African drills), and firearms training, all of which were designed to produce bodily discipline in the black youth. Confirmation that Swahili was the most valorized African language in black America in the 1960s is found in LeRoi Jones's autobiography, where he mentioned that "the most way-out dude" in his flying squadron when he was in the air force (which he joined in 1954, reaching the rank of sergeant) was Yodo (Yodofus T. Syllieabla), a man who referred to himself as "the high priest of Swahili, the czar of yap" (Matlin 2006, 101).

The presence of Swahili in the cultural wars of the United States can be gleaned as well from Baraka's work in a confederation called the Committee for Unified Newark (CFUN, pronounced *see-fun*). Founded in 1968, CFUN comprised three groups, two of which followed the kawaida doctrine, demonstrating the committee's broad agenda.

> The first was the Spirit House Movers, Baraka's theater troupe, which practiced *Kawaida*. The second was Black Community Defense and Development, another *Kawaida* affiliate originating in East Orange, New Jersey, which specialized in martial arts. The third component was the United Brothers, a predominantly middle-class and almost exclusively male group of Newark citizens, for whom black power entailed wresting control of municipal governance and public employment from Newark's Italian American, Irish American, and Jewish minorities and instituting leadership from within the city's black majority. The culmination of their endeavors, in 1970, was the election of Kenneth Gibson in Newark as the first black mayor of a major northeastern city. (Matlin 2006, 105)

CFUN drew on Swahili for some of its fundamental symbols and concepts. A CFUN nationalist bookstore was named Nyumba ya Ujamaa (House of Brotherhood), and temples were called by the Swahili name *hekalu*. The Congress of African People that Baraka inaugurated in 1970, which gained affiliates from New York to California, was conceived using Swahili names and idioms:

> At CFUN's peak in the early 1970s, most of its full-time membership of approximately three hundred lived in communal housing and applied *Kawaida* to every aspect of life-style and occupation. Around two-thirds were employed in CFUN enterprises, including a publishing house (Jihad), nationalist bookstore (*Nyumba ya Ujamaa*), and the African Free School. Activity centered on three *hekalus*, or temples, on Stirling Street, High Street, and Belmont

Avenue. Over a thousand part-time members made up CFUN's Community Council. No organization rivaled CFUN's visibility or influence within Newark's black community. In 1970, Baraka promoted national black power coalition politics by inaugurating the Congress of African People (CAP), an umbrella organization including CFUN and soon claiming twenty-five affiliate branches from Brooklyn to San Diego. Existing studies of Baraka's nationalist activism have focused on his instrumental role in Kenneth Gibson's election and on CAP's central involvement in the annual black power conferences. (Matlin 2006, 105–6)

Black NewArk, a monthly CFUN newspaper, also published a Swahili lesson to popularize Swahili in the African American urban community:

Former advocate Saidi Nguvu remembers his "respect" for "Elder Counselor" Baba Mshauri, born in 1898, a "wise man who really gave us a lot of guidance." One "Kiswahili Lesson" printed in CFUN's monthly newspaper, *Black NewArk,* imparted: "Mazazi (parent) Wazazi (parents) Mzee (elder) Wazee (elders)." The newspaper, sold by advocates in the community at large, was thus a means of conveying cultural nationalist values to blacks outside the organization. In this ideological context, however, the adoption of Kiswahili as a pan-African language was one aspect of Kawaida's problematic assumption of a unitary "African personality" and "traditional" social structure. (Matlin 2006, 108)

CFUN's organization included an elaborate hierarchy designed on what was claimed to be African models of generational authority and a quasi-military code of rank and discipline to accommodate unemployed black youth within a new urban community social order:

In CFUN, by contrast, the potentially wayward energies of youthful masculinity, *Ovyo,* were contained and controlled within a structure that privileged seniority and maturity. The young boys of the Super Simbas, or Little Lions, grew into *Simba Wachanga* (Young Lions), which status they retained from the ages of 16 to 25. On reaching maturity, the *Simba* were "promoted" to be *Mwanafunzi* (Apprentice Teachers) and subsequently *Saidi* (Lords). Higher authority lay with the *Wazee* (Circle of Elders). (Matlin 2006, 102)

All the words italicized in the passage—*Simba, simba wachanga, mwana-funzi, saidi,* and *wazee*—are Swahili: *simba,* meaning "lion"; *changa,* meaning "toddler"; *mwanafunzi,* which combines *mwana* and *funzi* to denote "student"; and *saidi,* from *Sayyid,* an honorific title usually identifying male descendants of the Prophet Muhammad. CFUN's *Simba,* or "lion," aimed at nurturing responsible young men who would be able to develop and defend the black community.

According to Mazrui and Mazrui (1998, 35), in Nyerere's Tanzania Swahili acquired the dignity of being an idiom countering class oppression, the bearer of the message of African socialism (Ujamaa). The Sixth Pan-African Congress, held in Dar es Salaam in 1974, put Tanzania in the limelight as the location of the resurgence of transcontinental Pan-Africanism. The organizers of the congress wanted to establish connections between African liberation movements and African Americans. It is estimated that on the eve of the congress, close to eight hundred African Americans were living in Tanzania. They included Pan-Africanists, followers of Marcus Garvey, members of the Black Panther Party, and others. Even Malcolm X had visited East Africa, in 1964, where he met a number of African heads of state, including Julius Nyerere of Tanzania and Jomo Kenyatta of Kenya.

Nyerere gave asylum to Pete O'Neal, the famous fugitive Black Panther, in Tanzania, where he remains to this day. Several other Black Panthers also visited or resided in Tanzania. O'Neal's presence there, along with that of Bill Sutherland, a Pan-Africanist advocate of Mahatma Gandhi's nonviolence, made Tanzania well known and longed for by many African Americans. O'Neal has been instrumental in facilitating exchanges for short educational courses among young African American and Tanzanian students. In 1990, he and his wife (also a former Black Panther) founded the United African-American Community Center (UACC) in Dar es Salaam, which offers free art, language, and computing courses.

Julius Kambarage Nyerere, the first president of the United Republic of Tanzania, gave Swahili the cosmopolitan definition that made it so suitable for the African Americans as well. Nyerere extended the meaning of *Waswahili* from a term that originally referred only to people of the East African littoral to a label that distinguishes ordinary Tanzanians and, by extension, ordinary Africans who fought off colonialism, both from Europeans and from other Africans of quickly amassed wealth. The ethnicized term *Swahili* ultimately came to carry sociopolitical connotations of class, including all marginalized people of African descent, especially the poor.

For Julius Nyerere, being Swahili was not merely prestigious; it also helped to construct an intercontinental Pan-African identity. Internationally, Nyerere's use of the word *ujamaa* has had such an impact that it has been used among Australian Aborigines and across the globe from London to Papua, New Guinea (Mazrui and Mazrui 1995, 133). The number of US colleges and universities with Ujamaa cultural centers is in the hundreds.

Swahili and Black Inner-City Gangs in the United States

Many African American gang members also use Swahili, not only as a source of names but also as a code for communications among themselves. *Kumi* was created in the mid-1980s by inmate Leonard Fulgham, also known as "Mousy Brown" (deceased in 2012 at Folsom Prison), along with a few others while they were housed at San Quentin State Prison. Prior to the creation of KUMI, also called KANO (Kumi African Nation Organization), Fulgham and other members of the Black Guerrilla Family (BGF) became unsatisfied with the way BGF was being run and formed a group known as the 415, which is the area code for parts of California's Bay Area. Sometime later, they began utilizing the Swahili word *Kumi* (Koo-me), meaning "10," which is 4 + 1 + 5.[4] The name BGF is rendered in African American Swahili as *Weusi Gaidi Jamaa* (*Weusi* meaning "black," *Gaidi* meaning "guerrilla," and *jamaa* meaning "family"), for Black Guerrilla Family.[5]

Stanley "Tookie" Williams (1953–2005), the founder of the Crips gang in Los Angeles, explained in his book *Blue Rage, Black Redemption* that learning Swahili was a regular undertaking among gang members in the San Quentin prison:

> Recapturing a more accurate picture of black history inspired all of us on the yard to teach ourselves to speak Swahili. We had to be autodidactic—self taught—and continue learning from one another as well. Outside the yard after each exhaustive workout of burpies and "Kenya laps" (very fast laps), we'd walk around in small groups and practice Swahili. When Young Kerm moved into the cell between Ghetto and me, our study regimen included him in an hour each weekday practicing Swahili. (Williams 2004, 280)

Williams ended his speeches saying, "*Bumani*—that's Swahili for 'peace.'" Invoking Swahili articulated a certain identity with Africa in radicalized African American consciousness. It is in this context that Williams talked about how he came to change his name to Ajamu Niamke Kamara with the aid of his fellow inmates Treach and Evil:

> I decided to embrace Swahili names. Treach and Evil chose several Swahili names that best depict the type of person I have become. Treach chose Ajamu meaning, "He that fights for what he wants." Evil chose Niamke, "God's gift." The third name all of us adopted was Kamara, "He who teaches from experience." In choosing names for one another Evil became Ajani, "He who fights for possession," and Treach became Adisa, "One who makes himself clear." As part of my transition and redemption I'm extremely proud to have as my Swahili name Ajamu Niamke Kamara, which resonates with who I am. (Williams 2004, 303–4)

The words *Ajamu* and *Kamara* in Swahili are probably adaptations from other languages. Only the word *niamke* is originally Swahili. It means "God's gift" in African American (Tookie's) Swahili, but in African Swahili, it translates as "that I may awake." The connection between the two is a mysterious one; it might be a good subject of conversation between Africans and African Americans who speak Swahili, should the occasion arise.

The idea of Swahili as the language of black history has sometimes been opposed on the grounds that African Americans came from areas along Africa's Atlantic coast, not from the Indian Ocean region where Swahili originated. Such views hold that this history is represented better by favoring languages such as Akan (Ghana), Igbo (Nigeria), Wolof (Senegal), Fulani (Senegal), and Yoruba (Nigeria) as more accurate ethnolinguistic identifications for African Americans. Mazrui and Mazrui's book *The Tower of Babel* posits that argument applies a kind of "Global Africa" strategy that Europeans have used to divide and conquer people along ethnolinguistic lines (Mazrui and Mazrui 1998, 35–36). Yet as these authors point out:

> It is not completely true that East Africa did not feature in the European slave trade across the Atlantic Ocean. There were Portuguese, Spanish, and French connections in eastern Africa that contributed in no small measure to the translocation of Africans. The Portuguese are known to have procured Africans to be enslaved from the East African coast from the very beginning of their encounter with the region in the fifteenth century. At first the Portuguese also supplied enslaved Africans to the French.

But as a result of recurrent Swahili struggle against the Portuguese, the French turned their attention to the East African port of Kilwa and made their own arrangements for procuring slaves. The Spanish are known to have taken thousands of enslaved Africans from the Swahili coast around the Cape to South America (Nicholls, 1971, 200). Furthermore, slave raids in western Africa sometimes went deep into the Congo, where Bantu languages akin to Swahili were spoken . . . close to sixty percent of enslaved Africans imported in ships known to the British Foreign Office between 1817 and 1843 came from Bantu-speaking areas of the continent . . . over a third of the linguistic Africanisms in the Gullah language of South Carolina are, in fact, of Bantu origin. (Mazrui and Mazrui 1998, 36)

Recently, the "discovery" of Palenquero, a Spanish-based Creole that is heavily influenced by the Kikongo language from the Congo and Angola,[6] in San Basilio de Palenque in Colombia supports Mazrui and Mazrui's point. The *International Herald Tribune* of October 18, 2007, reported the following:

Palenquero is thought to be the only Spanish-based Creole language in Latin America. But its grammar is so different that Spanish speakers can understand almost nothing of it. Its closest relative may be Papiamento, spoken on the Caribbean islands of Aruba, Bonaire and Curaçao, which draws largely from Portuguese, Spanish and Dutch, linguists say. It is spoken only in this village and a handful of neighborhoods in cities where workers have migrated. . . . The survival of Palenquero points to the extraordinary resilience of San Basilio de Palenque, part of whose very name—Palenque—is the Spanish word for a fortified village of runaway slaves. Different from dozens of other palenques that were vanquished, this community has successfully fended off threats to its existence to this day. . . . Palenquero was strongly influenced by the Kikongo language of Congo and Angola, and by Portuguese, the language of traders who brought African slaves to Cartagena in the 17th century. Kikongo-derived words like ngombe (cattle) and ngubá (peanut) remain in use here today.

Although it is very difficult to identify the single source language of a given word, the term *ng'ombe,* for "cattle," is widespread in Bantu languages, including Swahili. Both *ng'ombe* and *nguba* are from Kikongo, a Bantu language. African Americans have been inspired by other Bantu languages as their histories have become better known, including Zulu. Oprah Winfrey was reported in the *Chicago Tribune* of June 15, 2005, as claiming to be of Zulu ancestry. Tookie Williams, in *Blue Rage, Black Redemption,* likened his approach to expanding the West Side Crips gang to Shaka Zulu's conquest and assimilation of non-Zulu tribes:

> In a bastardized version of Shaka Zulu's brilliance in absorbing other tribes to make them Zulus, I did the same with the West Side Crips, though I did not know that my strategy paralleled Shaka Zulu's until many years later. I pushed the West Side Crips so far west that only the Pacific Ocean could thwart further expansion. (Williams 2004, 165)

Within the black underworld, Swahili has functioned as a metaphor with nuances that are difficult to capture in their entirety, as with any variant of language worked out among intimate, even secretive companions.

Swahili as the African American Language of Choice

The symbolic power of Swahili is the core of its appeal to African Americans. The black liberation struggle in the United States during the 1960s appropriated Swahili, the language of independence struggles in Africa. African Americans took Swahili terminology and political inspiration—most notably, solidarity and cooperation from Julius Nyerere's notions of Ujamaa—and made them their own. They stretched the meanings of the original Swahili words, added nuances, and spelled and pronounced them differently to establish a paradigm of their own that placed slavery and racism in the same category as colonialism and neocolonialism. This conceptual and linguistic linkage proclaimed the parallels between the struggles of African Americans and those of Africans in Africa, thereby capturing what many see as the reality that binds African communities globally.

The black underworld in the United States has adopted Swahili—but not because it merits a greater affinity with the diasporic African than other languages of Africa. Rather, Swahili has been adopted because when it is combined with Kente cloth from Ghana, Yoruba religion from Nigeria, and other western African traditions and cultural practices observed by a number of African Americans, it builds a composite that is free of the divisions that arise among African ethnolinguistic groups in their competition for places in modern nation-states. Pan-Africanism gained momentum in the diaspora before it developed deep roots on the African continent. Swahili later crossed the ocean and provided the appropriate grounding from which diasporic blacks could observe Africa at a distance; they found it attractive and then proceeded to prune it for its better qualities. Thus, despite the many fragilities and fissures within and across African countries and regions, Kariamu Welsh-Asante's observation still rings true:[7]

> It is the diasporan African who can conceptualize and contextualize different traditions under one rubric. It is the diasporan African's privilege and position that allows her to see Africa as a concept as well as a diverse and multicultural component. (Welsh-Asante 1993, 1)

Movers and shaker in the US motion picture industry saw Swahili as a niche language through which they could draw African Americans to their films. Though most Americans watching a movie with dialogue in African tongues seldom know the specific language being used, an analysis of the languages in movies (including the ones listed at the end of this chapter) indicates that Swahili was employed in numerous films. It served as a reservoir of black dignity and solidarity, undermining racial stereotyping by depicting characters such as Uhura in *Star Trek,* the pioneering black woman on this major television series turned movie franchise. Her name reminds knowledgeable viewers of Jomo Kenyatta's ringing slogan of Kenya's struggle for national independence—*Uhuru* (Freedom). Use of such names gave Swahili a boost over other African languages in the same way as Kwanzaa had.

Swahili has been an inexhaustible resource for symbols of identity that never quite mean the same thing for everyone concerned. We have seen a wide range of symbolic appropriations of Swahili by Pete O'Neal, the Black Panther fugitive living in exile in Tanzania; Amiri Baraka of the Harlem Renaissance; Maulana Karenga, the founder of Kwanzaa; Nichelle Nichols, Uhura of *Star Trek* fame; and the late Tookie Williams, founder of the Crips and Nobel Peace Prize nominee.

CHAPTER 12

Swahili Is for the Living

UNLIKE MANY languages that have to look back to better times, past glories, and a reign that is threatened or no more, Swahili has steadily gained momentum, and its future looks most promising. In these closing remarks, I want to briefly comment on why Swahili has been on the right path and, in the process, mention what Swahili is in a position to tells us (as other languages are not) about what propels a language to reach global status.

I have said that Swahili is a language alive because its history is one of multiplying and expanding horizons. The more people, languages, cultures, ethnicities, and races Swahili has encountered, the smoother its path toward expansion has been. The accolades Swahili bears today are not a culmination but a platform—the ground on which it stands poised to take advantage of the times in furtherance of its development. Yes, Swahili is the language of communication and the major lingua franca in over eleven African countries. Yes, Swahili is the first African language to become an official language of the African Union. Yes, Swahili is the most widely taught African language in academic institutions in Africa, the United States, Europe, and Asia. Yes, Swahili is the most widely broadcast sub-Saharan African language on the globe. And yes, Swahili is the language of the African American holiday Kwanzaa. Swahili returns a "no" verdict concerning the claims made about other global languages. No, Swahili has not risen up as a result of empire building and conquest; rather, that has happened through co-optation and adaptation of surrounding peoples and languages. No, Swahili is not a language of economic, political, and cultural dominance; it is merely a lingua franca spoken in a great variety of ways. No, Swahili's success is not a result of some intrinsic genius of the language as opposed to other languages; it is a second language to most. No, Swahili is not one uniform language; it never was and never will be. Rather, it is a language whose spoken form is raw and is constantly being refurbished as it is put to use. And no, the effort to promote the standard dialect or any other variety of Swahili as the correct form has never been and never will be successful. The standard form is itself in regular and sustained surrender to the vernacular forms of Swahili, in that forms deemed ungrammatical yesterday are today's correct variants. The yays and nays just listed tell us something that is world historical about the characteristics and diagnostics of how languages become global—and not just Swahili. The resounding message Swahili conveys about global languages is that they establish their relevance in the daily lives of ordinary people and sustain that vibrancy by a well-cultivated cosmopolitan ethos. The might of Swahili is not maintained by those in power from their palaces and ivory towers but by ordinary people in the highways and byways of everyday life.

Few words can rival *Harambee* in describing why Swahili is for the living. That simple word captures the ways in which, in ordinary interactions, Swahili is constituted, acquired, and used. *Harambee* means "all pull together." It is an old cry that one Swahili fisherman would holler out to fellow fishermen, urging them to apply themselves to the task of pulling in unison as they hauled their nets to the shore. In Kenya, the term is a watchword that has historically meant communal voluntary work to accomplish a task individuals are unable to handle alone. Nowadays, it more commonly refers to the gathering of multitudes to contribute money for someone in need to further his or her education; to cover medical costs; or to build schools, churches, hospitals, and the like deemed to be for the public good. The word *Harambee* is the national motto of independent Kenya and is inscribed on Kenya's coat of arms to signal the importance of working together selflessly to build the nation. The word is a superb metaphor for the growth and development of Swahili. It captures the phenomenon that is at the very core of Swahili experience and existence—the whole is an ever emerging product of the interaction, cooperation, and collaboration of many. The Swahili have always been a harambee people, "pulled together" in genes, culture, and language. The Swahili are not one people out of many like the famous dictum *E Pluribus Unum* but rather from many a new kind of many, or *E Pluribus a novus Pluribus*—a hybrid whose diversity in constitution is its appeal and traction. Just think of the many pidginized Swahili verbal and written forms used on the ground by none other than the young people (who are by far the largest demographic majority) and you will know in whose hands the future of Swahili is vested. If you compare that with how the institutionally supported standard form of Swahili is faring, you will see the writing on the wall. Standard Swahili may well become like classical Arabic, a language much known in reading but seldom used in the real world. If Standard Swahili is to become a viable living language, it will have to take a leaf from vernacular Swahili and allow itself to be fed by many tributaries of accents and languages—exactly what has brought Swahili thus far. It is in its brokenness that Swahili is whole. Broken Swahili, covering the entire expanse of the Swahili-speaking region, is the yardstick with which to measure the chances the language has for maintaining relevance in the future in the spheres that matter the most. A language that is alive cannot be fixated on speaking in accordance with the dictates and concerns of learned societies, clubs, and organizations. Any dialect that is adjunct or nonoverlapping with communication in its raw form will lose the crucial life-giving properties needed for its survival and fall by the wayside.

By a language that is alive, I mean a language that cuts across horizontal and vertical human relationships. Swahili was (and still is) the great equalizer that operated horizontally among traders, sailors, dockworkers, farmers, fishermen, masons, carpenters, leatherworkers, boatbuilders, clerics, musicians, everyone from the sultans to the freeborn to the slaves. What people spoke was a language designed to get a message across to others in the pursuit of accomplishing their tasks. They were doing communication that coalesced into the tongue that was finally dubbed Swahili. Indeed, Swahili came to be used to describe coastal dwellers in the fourteenth century, after the language had been in existence for more than half a millennium. In the process of expanding, Swahili has served as a conduit of borrowings, tapping overseas languages as well as the indigenous languages of the hinterland, which no doubt has made Swahili familiar to those who do not speak it. Swahili is a living language, for through it Siti binti Saad broke the glass ceiling with her voice introducing Swahili songs to millions, thereby making Swahili an internationally known language. A language that is alive counts on new infusions into its linguistics. The Swahili adage *Mgeni njoo mwenyeji apone,* "Visitor come so that the native may be well," states a fundamental principle in the language's evolution—that Swahili is a language that is vested, crucially and perennially, in the influx of new ideas and things through the mouths of people.

The story of Swahili raises doubts about the hypothesis that the conquest of neighbors, empire building, and domination of the world's resources are necessary conditions for languages to become what Nicholas Ostler (2005) cals "empires of the word." The explanation given for the rise of French to a global language between the seventeenth century and the middle of the twentieth century is instructive. At the height of French dominance (as the language of diplomacy spoken across European royal courts and into Russia by the Russian nobility), the Berlin Academy in 1782 decided to find out why French was the leading international language. The academy announced an essay-writing competition on the topic "How has French become the world's universal language?"[1] The participants were asked to go beyond stating the obvious to explain why French had reached and maintained that status and to speculate on where it was headed. Of the twenty-two essays received, two prizes were awarded. One went to a Frenchman, Antoine de Rivarol—one of Voltaire's protégés—and the other went to Jean-Christ Schwab, a German professor at the Academy of Stuttgart. Rivarol's winning essay emphasized the genius of the French language, stating that it was a clearer, simpler, and more concise language than all others and, indeed, the most refined language in the world. Schwab wrote that it was not so much the genius in the language but the political superiority and spirit of conquest that made French so appealing to the world.

From this historical record, we can identify the two theories that circulate to explain how a language becomes global. One is the conquest/dominance theory, and the other is the genius/elegance theory. Judging by the winning essays, the learned members at the Berlin Academy voted not for one or the other but for both. There is evidence to suggest that were another survey conducted today by the French Academy (L'Académie française), the same two theories might carry the day, with the genius theory ahead of the dominance one. Some assert that "in the back of any francophone's mind is the idea that an ideal, pure French exists somewhere."[2] Its eloquent use is deemed a marker of high social status. Due to the human effort that has gone toward guiding its development, French is considered a "monument" or "a work of art" that, unlike all others, is a "finished" language.[3] France's power and dominion (in the so-called Francophone countries) are therefore conflated with the genius and elegance of French. Jared Diamond's idea that *The Fates of Human Societies* (to use his book title) are determined by *Guns, Germs, and Steel* does not explain the fates of human languages. For a language to be alive, it is not necessary for it to conquer its neighbors, build an empire, and dominate the world's resources. Swahili is one of the top ten international languages without being one of the class of languages that Ostler (2005) calls "empires of the word." Rather, it is its egalitarian aspect, its tending of horizontal relations, and its vibrancy in real life that make it "a language alive."

Important as it is to remember a language's laurels from the past, one cannot assess the significance of the language and its chances of rising again based on past glories. A memory is just that. When the importance of languages is evaluated in terms of conquest, it should not surprise anyone to see that languages wane and fizzle as kingdoms fall. Even for French, the story suggesting that conquest and genius are behind the rise of the language is a counterfeit tale. Examined through the vitality of its vernacular forms (other than just Parisian French), especially in its pidgin forms as spoken in Francophone countries, French is actually thriving in much the same way that Swahili is. It is in this vein that reading Achille Mbembe (2011) one gleans that the time for French departments to consider teaching pidgin French is here.[4] The French language is far from a "finished" language or a "monument." Instead, it is a language that is evolving in an interesting world where it is being Wolofized in Senegal and manipulated (Bantuized) in multiple ways in the plethora of Congo's languages. And so far as there is conquest, it is the vernacular languages people speak that have the upper hand in shaping and maintaining the liveliness of the standard dialect. Though often judged ungrammatical, these vernaculars are the key to its continuing currency and vitality.

English is particularly instructive in the way it has come to attain the spectacular role it plays in our world today, whereas before 1600 CE the language was, as Shakespeare put it, "of small reatch, it stretcheth no further than this iland of ours, naie not there over all." After 1600 CE and on to the present, through "armies, navies, companies, and expeditions, the speakers of English including Scots, Irish, Welsh, American, and many more"[5] have carried the language to all corners of the world. Today, it is spoken by more than a billion people, and it is a primary language of the Internet as well as the language of business and of air traffic control, transcending borders, cultures, and divides.[6] But beyond that, it is the language of scholarship, with over half a million words recorded in the *Oxford English Dictionary* and an almost equal number of technical and scientific words that are not listed in dictionaries. The success of the language is seen as an act of genius, such that "there must be something inherently beautiful or logical about the structure of English to explain why it is now so widely used."[7]

Looking at Swahili in the context of the languages of the global north and how each one has had to rule people over sea and land to gain prominence, it becomes obvious that Swahili is exceptional, indeed idiosyncratic, in its membership in the top ten international languages. And given that it has no holy book of its own, that it has a literary canon that is largely oral, and that it is at its best in rogue ways, we can see that the genius or elegance of Swahili lies elsewhere, apart from what is written in it and separate from the people it has conquered. If we reverse the gaze as I have done in this book and look at other languages from the vantage point of Swahili, we begin to see how some languages gain ascendancy in the global arena and others do not. In this regard, English is what it is today because of its many versions (or Englishes) and, yes, its pidginized vernaculars that cover the planet, not because everyone is interested in speaking English like the British or the Americans (who themselves speak it in a great variety of ways). Put concisely, English is the Swahili of the world.

Ngugi wa Thiong'o, the famous Kenyan novelist, claimed that in contrast to the major languages of the world whose rise was based on its speakers' conquest and imperialism over the poor and weak, Swahili did not grow "on the graveyards of other languages." Yet Swahili and other significant lingua francas are said to be the big destroyers of Africa's indigenous languages, much more so than English, French, or Portuguese. The story of Swahili shows, however, that even as it replaces indigenous languages, it is undergoing a metamorphosis itself, incorporating many features of the languages it is replacing. What emerges are Swahilis that include identifiable elements of local languages.

The encounter with the pidgins of Swahili does not lead us to cower in fear that Swahili is taking over; instead, it invites us to view Swahili as something made, by and large, in the image of Africa's indigenous languages. The story in this book places a premium on the study and description of area languages and cultures as necessary steps in understanding how Swahili is modernizing itself as it grows and rises to the needs and challenges of the present. The indigenous languages have a lot to tell us about the old and new emerging blends of languages enfolded in Swahili. Future narratives in the story of the language will need to include in-depth analyses of the creative syncretism and adaptations of Swahili.

Further Reading

FULL BIBLIOGRAPHICAL details for all sources are provided in Works Cited.

Chapter 2: Swahili, the Complex Language of a Cosmopolitan People

If there is a must-read concerning the Swahili language in ancient times as well as everything said in this chapter, it is Derek Nurse and Thomas Spear, *The Swahili: Reconstructing the History and Language of an African Society* (1985). The book shows how linguistic information has a greater reach back in history than written documents, and it underlines the futility of seeking to locate a specific origin of Swahili people and language. Also see Felix Chami, "A Review of Swahili Archeology," *African Archeological Review* 15, no. 3 (1998); Chapuruka Kusimba and Sibel B. Kusimba, *East African Archeology: Foragers, Potters, Smiths, and Traders* (2003); Chapurukha Kusimba, *The Rise and Fall of Swahili States* (1999); and Mark Horton, *Shanga: The Archaeology of a Muslim Trading Community on the Coast of East Africa* (1996) for current work in the archaeology of the Swahili coast.

For a good discussion of who is Swahili and how the Swahili people drew from overseas lands thanks to the seafaring vessel, see Abdul Sheriff, *Dhow Cultures of the Indian Ocean* (2010). Also see Mark Horton and John Middleton, *The Swahili: The Social Landscape of a Mercantile Society* (2000). There is a good deal there on the complexity of the Swahili, with a focus on how Arabs and Indians factored into the equation.

The vignette with which I opened this chapter comes from C. H. Stigand, *The Land of the Zinj: Being an Account of British East Africa, Its Ancient History and Present Inhabitants* (1913). Stigand's book exemplifies the misrepresentations and pontification that Europeans brought to the story of Swahili.

For European sources on the history of the East African coast relevant to this chapter, see G. S. P. Freeman-Grenville, *The East African Coast: Select Documents from the First to the Earlier Nineteenth Century* (1962). It contains all the written documents by geographers and travelers, as well as Swahili chronicles written locally in Arabic script. These records underscore that the east coast of Africa was one of the world's busiest crossroads.

For an early general discussion of the Swahili chronicles, see A. H. J. Prins, "On Swahili Historiography," *Swahili, Journal of the East African Swahili Committee* 28, no. 2 (1958), and H. Neville Chittick and Robert I. Rotberg, eds., *East Africa and the Orient: Cultural Syntheses in Pre-colonial Times* (1975). This latter volume contains the essays "Peopling of the East African Coast" by Neville Chittick and "Arab Geographers and the East African Coast" by J. Spencer Trimingham, which are relevant to the discussion in this chapter.

For a look at the physical evidence of Kenya's past at the Indian Ocean coast, with suggestions about how the Swahili emerged, see James Kirkman, "Some Conclusions from the Archaeological Excavations on the Coast of Kenya" (1975) in the same volume.

On local claims about Swahili origins, see James de Vere Allen, *Swahili Origins: Swahili Culture and the Shungwaya Phenomenon* (1993). It is an excellent source for Swahili traditions about Shungwaya as the original homeland of the Swahili.

For linguistic genealogy, Ethnologue.com gives the Niger-Congo, Atlantic-Congo, Volta-Congo, Benue-Congo, and Bantoid as the path of branches to which Swahili belongs. For details within the Bantu family, see Malcolm Guthrie, *Comparative Bantu: An Introduction to the Comparative Linguistics and Prehistory of the Bantu Languages* (1967–71).

For earlier and more primary sources on the history of East Africa with relevance to the Swahili culture and history, see Richard Burton, *Zanzibar: City, Island, and Coast* (1967); Frederick Johnson, *Madan's English Swahili Dictionary*, published by The Interterritorial Language Committee of the East African Dependencies in 1939; and G. S. P. Freeman-Grenville, *The Swahili Coast, 2nd to 19th Centuries: Islam, Christianity, and Commerce in Eastern Africa* (1988), as well as his *East African Coast*, cited earlier in this section. Also see W. H. Whiteley, *Swahili: The Rise of a National Language* (1969), especially chapter 2.

For books written on the Swahili people that have informed this chapter, see A. H. J. Prins, *Swahili-Speaking Peoples of Zanzibar and the East African Coast (Arabs, Shirazi and Swahili)* (1961); J. S. Kirkman, *Men and Monuments on the East African Coast* (1964); Ireri Mbaabu, *New Horizons in Kiswahili: A Synthesis in Developments, Research, and Literature* (1985); and Randall Lee Pouwels, *Horn and Crescent: Cultural Change and Traditional Islam on the East African Coast, 800–1900* (1987).

For the Swahili diaspora in Asia, see Joseph E. Harris, *The African Presence in Asia: Consequences of the East African Slave Trade* (1971), and William Wilson Hunter, *The Imperial Gazetteer of India*, vol. 6 (1886). On the history of East Africa, see Roland Oliver and G. Mathew, eds., *The History of East Africa*, vol. 1 (1963); John Sutton, *A Thousand Years of East Africa* (1990); and L. W. Hollingsworth, *A Short History of the East Coast of Africa* (1951). There are also several good chapters on the east coast of Africa in Bethwell Ogot and J. A. Kieran, eds., *Zamani: A Survey of East African History* (1968).

For Swahili history written in Swahili, two good sources to begin with are David P. B. Massamba, *Historia ya Kiswahili: 50 BK hadi 1500 BK* (2002), and Shihabdin Chiraghdin and Mathias Mnyampala, *Historia ya Kiswahili* (1977).

For general discussion on linguistics and language relationships, see Merrit Ruhlen, *The Origin of Language: Tracing the Evolution of the Mother Tongue* (1994).

To sample contemporary stories of European languages from which I have drawn parallels, see David Crystal, *The Stories of English* (2004); Robert McCrum, Robert MacNeil, and William Cran, *The Story of English* (1986); Nicholas Oestler, *Empires of the Word: A Language History of the World* (2005); and Jean-Benoît Nadeau and Julie Barlow, *The Story of French* (2006).

Chapter 3: A Grand Smorgasbord of Borrowings and Adaptation

For more on Swahili dialects and their varied borrowings from their historical neighbors, see Derek Nurse and Thomas J. Hinnebusch, *Swahili and Sabaki: A Linguistic History* (1993); Nurse and Thomas Spear, *The Swahili: Reconstructing the History and Language of an African Society, 800–1500* (1985); and Spear, "Early Swahili History Reconsidered," *International Journal of African Historical Studies* 33, no. 2 (2000).

Numerous examples of borrowings into Swahili from other languages can be found in Shihabdin Chiraghdin and Mathias E. Mnyampala, *Historia ya Kiswahili* (1977), and Ireri Mbaabu, *New Horizons in Kiswahili: A Synthesis in Developments, Research, and Literature* (1985). Mbaabu also includes a discussion of how Swahili has been an important reservoir of vocabulary for the Kikuyu, Luhya, Kalenjin, and Dholuo languages of Kenya.

For information about the strong influence of Arabic in the Swahili lexicon, see Ibrahim Bosha and A. S. Nchimbi, *Taathira za kiarabu katika kiswahili pamoja na kamusi thulathiya (Kiswahili-Kiarabu-Kiingereza)* [The influence of Arabic language on Kiswahili with a trilingual dictionary (Swahili-Arabic-English)] (1993).

For extensive information on the infusion of Indic words into Swahili, see Abdulaziz Lodhi, *Oriental Influences in Swahili: A Study in Language and Culture Contacts* (2000).

There are numerous sources of information regarding borrowings in Africa's colonial languages—French, English, German, and Portuguese—as any search will reveal. The following titles make for a good start: David Crystal, *The Stories of English* (2004); Robert McCrum, Robert MacNeil, and William Cran, *The Story of English* (1986); Nicholas Ostler, *Empires of the Word: A Language History of the World* (2005); and Jean-Benoît Nadeau and Julie Barlow, *The Story of French* (2006).

Chapter 4: A Classical Era: The Peak of Swahili Prosperity, 1000–1500 CE

One book that stands out with regard to the representation of Swahili maritime culture is Abdul Sheriff, *Dhow Cultures of the Indian Ocean: Cosmopolitanism, Commerce and Islam* (2010); it is an excellent explication of Swahili life, culture, and language as part of the world of the Indian Ocean connected by the seafaring vessel. A. H. J. Prins, *Sailing from Lamu: A Study of Maritime Culture in Islamic East Africa* (1965), provides a wealth of information on Swahili maritime culture and an in-depth study of Swahili boat architecture in terms of design and function. For a greater study of the seafaring vessels of the Indian Ocean, Clifford Hawkins, *The Dhow: An Illustrated History of the Dhow and Its World* (1977), is a fine read with many photographs and sketches, as is David Howarth and Robin Constable, *Dhows* (1977).

For readings regarding the early city-states of the Swahili civilization and their histories, see G. S. P. Freeman-Grenville, *The East African Coast: Select Documents from the First to the Earlier Nineteenth Century* (1962). On the archaeology of the East African coast, see Chapuruka Makokha Kusimba and Sibel B. Kusimba, eds., *East African Archeology: Foragers, Potters, Smiths, and Traders* (2003); Kusimba, *The Rise and Fall of Swahili States* (1999); Christopher Ehret and Merrick Posnansky, *The Archeological and Linguistic Reconstruction of African History* (1982); and J. de V. Allen and Thomas H. Wilson, *Swahili Houses and Tombs of the Coast of Kenya* (1979). On Swahili archaeological excavations, see Felix Chami's many publications on the subject, beginning with "A Review of Swahili Archeology," *African Archeological Review* 15, no. 3 (1998).

On ancient Swahili cities, see J. S. Kirkman, *Gedi: The Palace* (1963), and Mark Horton, *Shanga: The Archaeology of a Muslim Trading Community on the Coast of East Africa* (1996).

For more on the Swahili civilization, see J. Middleton, *The World of the Swahili: An African Mercantile Civilization* (1992); Neville Chittick, "The Shirazi Colonisation of East Africa," *Journal of African History* 6 (1965); Horton, "Early Muslim Trading Settlements on the East African Coast: New Evidence from Shanga," *Antiquaries Journal* 67 (1987); Roland Oliver and G. Mathew, eds., *The History of East Africa*, vol. 1 (1963); and Basil Davidson, *African Civilization Revisited: From Antiquity to Modern Times* (1991).

Chapter 5: Consolidation of a Popular Language, 1500–1850s

On the Portuguese invasion of East Africa, see J. Strandes, *The Portuguese Period in East Africa* (1968); F. J. Berg, "The Coast from the Portuguese Invasion," in B. A. Ogot and J. A. Kieran, eds., *Zamani: A Survey of East African History,* rev. ed. (1968); and Malyn Newitt, *Portuguese Encounters with the World in the Age of the Discoveries* (2002).

On the work of Portuguese missionaries, see G. S. P. Freeman-Grenville, *The Mombasa Rising against the Portuguese, 1631: From Sworn Evidence* (1980), and Sir John Milner Gray, *Early Portuguese Missionaries in East Africa* (1958).

For a more general history of eastern Africa surrounding the Portuguese reign, see Gideon S. Were and Derek Wilson, *East Africa through a Thousand Years: A History of the Years A.D. 1000 to the Present Day* (1968); Bethwell Ogot and J. A. Kieran, eds., *Zamani: A Survey of East African History* (1968); Basil Davidson, *African Civilization Revisited: From Antiquity to Modern Times* (1991); and Roland Oliver and G. Mathew, eds., *History of East Africa*, vol. 1 (1963).

For Portuguese travelogues concerning the Swahili city-states, see G. S. P. Freeman-Grenville, *The East African Coast: Select Documents from the First to the Earlier Nineteenth Century* (1962).

Also see Jan Knappert, *Four Centuries of Swahili Verse: A Literary History and Anthology* (1979). And take a look at James S. Kirkman, *Fort Jesus: A Portuguese Fortress on the East African Coast* (1974); Kirkman, *Fort Jesus, Mombasa,* 4th ed. (1981); and C. R. Boxer and Carlos de Azevedo, *Fort Jesus and the Portuguese in Mombasa, 1593–1729* (1960).

On some of the atrocities of Swahili slavery, see Frederick Cooper, *Plantation Slavery on the East Coast of Africa* (1977), and David Livingstone and

Horace Waller, *The Last Journals of David Livingstone, in Central Africa, from Eighteen Hundred and Sixty Five to His Death; Continued by a Narrative of His Last Moments and Sufferings, Obtained by His Faithful Servants, Chuma and Susi* (1875). With regard to local and transoceanic Swahili slave trade, see Joseph E. Harris, *The African Presence in Asia: Consequences of the East African Slave Trade* (1971); Leda Farrant, *Tippu Tip and the East African Slave Trade* (1975); Sir John Gray, *History of Zanzibar, from the Middle Ages to 1856* (1962); and I. N. Kimambo and A. J. Temu, *A History of Tanzania* (1969).

On Arab relations before the arrival of the Portuguese, see A. H. J. Prins, *The Swahili-Speaking Peoples of Zanzibar and the East African Coast (Arabs, Shirazi, and Swahili)* (1961), and James S. Kirkman, "Omani Relations with East Africa before the Arrival of the Portuguese," *Proceedings of the Seminar for Arabian Studies* 12 (1982).

Chapter 6: The Women of Swahili

For documentation of Swahili women of historical import, see G. S. P. Freeman-Grenville, *The East African Coast: Select Documents from the First to the Earlier Nineteenth Century* (1962). Reports of influential women of the region appear in the earliest records about the east coast of Africa compiled by Chinese travelers, by Marco Polo, by the Portuguese, and by Swahili chroniclers. Women are also plentifully mentioned in slavery records and in colonial and postcolonial literature.

For information about the women of Swahili as the "advance guard" of Swahili commerce and its spread inland, see Johannes Fabian, *Language and Colonial Power: The Appropriation of Swahili in the Former Belgian Congo, 1880–1938* (1986), and Mark Horton and John Middleton, *The Swahili: The Social Landscape of a Mercantile Society* (2000).

For a list of Swahili women kings and information about Swahili women's lives, songs, dance, and cultural practice, see Kelly Askew, *Performing the Nation: Swahili Music and Cultural Politics in Tanzania* (2002), and Askew, "Female Circles and Male Lines: Gender Dynamics along the Swahili Coast," *Africa Today* 46, nos. 3–4 (1999).

For examples of inland women's connections with and influence on Swahili material culture, see Linda W. Donley-Reid, "The Power of Swahili Porcelain, Beads and Pottery," *Archeological Papers of the American Anthropological Association* 2, no. 1 (1990). For more on the origin, design, styles, names, meaning, and significance of the kanga/leso cloth, see Sharifa

Zawari, *Kanga: The Cloth That Speaks* (2005); Rose Marie Beck, "Aesthetics of Communication: Texts on Textiles (Leso) from the East African Coast (Swahili)," *Research in African Literatures* 31 (2000); and Jean Allman, ed., *Fashioning Africa: Power and the Politics of Dress* (2004).

For illustrations of ways to wear the kanga, see Jeannette Hanby and David Bygott, *Kanga: 101 Uses* (1984).

For the use of the kanga as a communicative tool between women, see Rose Marie Beck, *Ambiguous Signs: The Role of the Kanga as a Medium of Communication* (2001).

For the use of the kanga cloth as attire symbolizing freedom among former slaves on the east coast of Africa, see Laura Fair, "Dressing Up: Clothing, Class and Gender in Post-abolition Zanzibar," *Journal of African History* 39, no. 1 (1998).

Chapter 7: The Swahili Literary Tradition

For a more current discussion of Swahili literature and of Liyongo, see Alamin Mazrui, *Swahili beyond the Boundaries: Literature, Language, and Identity* (2007), including the references therein.

For a look at the general Swahili literary canon, see these works by Jan Knappert: *Four Centuries of Swahili Verse: A Literary History and Anthology* (1979); *Epic Poetry in Swahili and Other African Languages* (1983); *Four Swahili Epics* (1964); *A Survey of Swahili Songs with English Translations* (2004); *A Survey of Swahili Islamic Epic Sagas* (1999); and *The A–Z of African Love Songs* (2003). Also see Lyndon Harries, *Swahili Poetry* (1962).

For a study of modern Swahili poetry, see Abdillatif Abdalla, *Sauti ya Dhiki* [Voice of agony] (1973), and for a discussion of the influence of Islam on Swahili poetry, see Knappert, *Four Centuries*, xix and xvii.

On the secularization of Swahili poetry, Muyaka bin Haji (1776–1856) is credited with bringing poetry "out of the mosque and into the marketplace." See Mohamed H. Abdulaziz, *Muyaka: 19th Century Swahili Popular Poetry* (1979). Also see Harries, *Swahili Poetry* (1962), and William Hichens, *Diwani ya Muyaka bin Haji Al-Ghassainy* (1948).

For Swahili prose, fiction, and drama, see Elena Zubkova Bertoncini, *Outline of Swahili Literature: Prose, Fiction, and Drama* (1989). On Swahili prose (early literary products, memoirs, autobiographies, the Swahili Chronicles, and more), see Jack D. Rollins, *A History of Swahili Prose, pt. 1, From Earliest Times to the End of the Nineteenth Century* (1983).

Chapter 8: Writing Swahili in Arabic Characters

For representative examples of Swahili documents written in Arabic script, the go-to place is G. Miehe et al., eds., *"Nyimbo za Liyongo"—Liyongo Songs: Poems Attributed to Fumo Liyongo Collected and Edited by the Liyongo Working Group* (2006). See also see chapter 2 of Helmi Sharawy, ed., *Heritage of the African Languages Manuscripts: Ajami* (2005). The book provides samples of Ajami documents from among the Hausa, Fulani, Wolof, Mandinka, Songhai, and Tamasheq languages.

Anyone interested in Swahili Ajami (and other languages) may turn to the Africa's Sources of Knowledge Digital Library at Harvard University, http://www.ask-dl.fas.harvard.edu/collection, and the Swahili Manuscripts Database at SOAS, http://www.swahilimanuscripts.soas.ac.uk/; also see A. Zhukov, "Old Swahili-Arabic Script and the Development of Swahili Literary Language" (2004) Those interested in Sudanic Africa should read Marina Tolmacheva, "The Pate Chronicle: Edited and Translated from MSS 177, 321, 344, and 358 of the Library of the University of Dar es Salaam," *Sudanic Africa* 5 (1994).

For information about Ajami literature in West Africa, see Fallou, "Ahmadu Bamba's Pedagogy and the Development of Ajam Literature," *African Studies Review* 52, no. 1 (April 2009), and Ngom, "Ajami Scripts in the Senegalese Speech Community," *Journal of Arabic and Islamic Studies* 10 (2010).

Works referring to Ajami include Ann Biersteker and Ibrahim Noor Shariff, eds., *Mashairi ya Vita vya Kuduhu: War Poetry in Kiswahili Exchanged at the Time of the Battle of Kuduhi* (1995). Also see L. Harries, *Swahili Poetry* (1962); J. Knappert, *A Survey of Swahili Islamic Epic Sagas* (1999); Adria LaViolette, "Swahili Cosmopolitanism in Africa and the Indian Ocean World, A.D. 600–1500," *Archaeologies: Journal of the World Archaeological Congress* 4, no. 1 (2008); Yahya Ali Omar and AnnMarie Drury, "The Swahili Manuscript Project at SOAS," *Swahili Forum* 9 (2002) AAP (Afrikanistische Arbeitspapiere) 72; Marguerite Ylvisaker, *Lamu in the Nineteenth Century: Land, Trade, and Politics* (1979); Kitula King'ei, "Historical and Folkloric Elements in Fumo Liyongo's Epic," *Folklore* 16 (2001); and Y. A. Omar and P. J. L. Frankl, "A 12/18th Century Swahili Letter from Kilwa Kisiwani (Being a Study of One Folio from the Goa Archives)," *Afrika und Übersee* 77 (1994).

Chapter 9: Colonialism and Standardization of Swahili, 1850s to the 1960s and Beyond

On issues pertaining to Swahili in central Africa—expeditions and campaigns, religious and secular colonization, colonization and language, labor and language, and the illusions of colonial power—see Johannes Fabian, *Language and Colonial Power: The Appropriation of Swahili in the Former Belgian Congo, 1880–1938* (1986), and Harry W. Langworthy, "Swahili Influence in the Area between Lake Malawi and Luangwa River," *African Historical Studies* 4, no. 3 (1971).

For more on missionary and Swahili language issues during the midnineteenth century along the east coast of Africa and inland, see Bethwell Ogot and J. A. Kieran, eds., *Zamani: A Survey of East African History* (1973); Chauncy Hugh Stigand, *The Land of Zinj: Being an Account of British East Africa, Its Ancient History and Present Inhabitants [with illustrations]* (1913); Edgar Polome, *Swahili Language Handbook* (1967); W. H. Whiteley, *Swahili, the Rise of a National Language* (1969); E. S. Odhiambo Atieno, T. I. Ouso, and Williams Ouso, *A History of East Africa* (1977); and Gideon S. Were and Derek A. Wilson, *East Africa through a Thousand Years: A History of the Years A.D. 1000 to the Present* (1968).

For the earliest Swahili dictionaries and grammars, see Edward Steere, *A Handbook of the Swahili Language: As Spoken at Zanzibar* (1870); Ludwig Krapf, *A Dictionary of the Suahili Language . . . with Introduction Containing an Outline of a Suahili Grammar* (1882); A. C. Madan, *English-Swahili Dictionary* (1930); and Madan, *English-Swahili Vocabulary* (1911). The earliest dictionaries—the *Standard English Swahili Dictionary* and *Standard Swahili English Dictionary*—were published in 1939 by the ILC. These were founded on Madan's Swahili-English and English-Swahili dictionaries. For one of the earliest monolingual Swahili dictionaries, see Frederick Johnson, *Kamusi ya Kiswahili yaani kitabu cha maneno Kiswahili* (1935).

For the first Swahili dictionary in French, see Charles Sacleux, *Dictionnaire swahili-français* (1939). For a Swahili-German dictionary, see Hildegard Hoftmann, *Suaheli-deutsches Worterbuch* (1963).

For Arabic dominance in the Swahili lexicon, see Ibrahim Bosha, *Taathira za kiarabu katika kiswahili pamoja na kamusi thulathiya (Kiswahili-Kiarabu-Kiingereza)* [The influence of Arabic language on Kiswahili with a trilingual dictionary (Swahili-Arabic-English)], ed. A. S. Nchimbi (1993).

For a description of the Rugaruga, see L. Monteith Fotheringham, *Adventures in Nyasaland: A Two Years' Struggle with Arab Slave-Dealers in Central Africa* (1891).

For Swahili settlements in east-central Africa and the protracted tensions between the Swahili/Arab ruling elite and the Europeans before World War I, see Marcia Wright and P. Lary, "Swahili Settlements in Northern Zambia and Malawi," *International Journal of African Historical Studies* 4 (1971); Norman R. Bennett, *Arab versus European: Diplomacy and War in Nineteenth-Century East Central Africa* (1986); and of course Fabian, *Language and Colonial Power*.

For a strong and bitter critique of Standard Swahili, see Abdallah Khalid, *The Liberation of Swahili from European Appropriation* (1977).

For a study of how the Swahili linguistic and cultural experience compares to some major international languages, see David Crystal, *The Stories of English* (2004); Robert McCrum, Robert MacNeil, and William Cran, *The Story of English* (1986)); Nicholas Ostler, *Empires of the Word: A Language History of the World* (2005); and Jean-Benoît Nadeau and Julie Barlow, *The Story of French* (2006).

Specialized Swahili dictionaries are fast becoming numerous thanks to the Taasisi ya Uchunguzi wa Kiswahili (Institute of Swahili Research) based at the University of Dar es Salaam. For a Swahili dictionary of social science, see James Lewton Brain, *Kamusi ya maneno ya utaalamu wa mambo ya kibinadamu* [A short dictionary of social science terms for Swahili speakers] (1969), and its translation by the author, *A Social Science Vocabulary of Swahili* (1968).

For language and linguistic terminology, see David P. B. Massamba, *Kamusi ya isimu na falsafa ya lugha* (2004). For business and economics terminology in Swahili, see Zubeida Zuberi Masabo and A. R. Chuwa, *Kamusi ya biashara na uchumi: Kiingereza-Kiswahili* (1999).

For Swahili terminology pertaining to science and technology, see *Kamusi Awali ya Sayansi na Tekinologia* (1995) by TUKI.

For a standard dictionary of biology, physics, and chemistry terms in Swahili, see, the Swahili dictionary of biology, physics, and chemistry terminology titled *Kamusi sanifu ya biolojia, fizika na kemia: Taasisi ya Uchunguzi wa Kiswahili* (1990), and the dictionary of linguistics and languages titled *Kamusi sanifu ya isimu na lugha* (1990).

For ornithology in Swahili, see Musa Maimu, *Kamusi ya ndege wa Tanzania* [A glossary of birds of Tanzania] (1982).

For legal terminology in Swahili, see Rashidi Kawawa, *Swahili Legal Terms* (1968); Ivan Sertima, *Swahili Dictionary of Legal Terms* (1970); and A. B. Weston and Dar Es Salaam College, *Swahili Legal Terms* (1968). For a compendium of Swahili names, see Sharifa Zawawi, *What's in a Name? Unaitwaje? A Swahili Book of Names* (1993).

Chapter 10: Modern Swahili: Moving On

On Sheng vocabulary, see Ireri Mbaabu and Kipande Nzunga, *Sheng-English Dictionary: Deciphering East Africa's Underworld Language* (2003). For Sheng studies, see David Arthur Samper, "Talking Sheng: The Role of a Hybrid Language in the Construction of Identity and Youth Culture in Nairobi, Kenya" (PhD diss., 2002); Chege Githioria, "Sheng: Peer Language, Swahili Dialect or Emerging Creole?," *Journal of African Cultural Studies* 15, no. 2 (2002); and John Mugane, "Necrolinguistics: Linguistic Death-in-Life," *Du Bois Review* 2, no. 2 (2005). For a sample linguistic study of 1970s Sheng in East Africa, see Carol Myers-Scotton, "The Context Is the Message: Morphological, Syntactic and Semantic Reduction and Deletion in Nairobi and Kampala Varieties of Swahili," in I. F. Hancock, ed., *Readings in Creole Studies* (1979).

For more about Swahili and other pidgins and Creoles in Africa and the world, see John A. Holm, *Pidgins and Creoles* (1988).

For the KiSetla pidgin Swahili spoken by white settlers in the Kenya highlands and elsewhere, see Holm, *Pidgins and Creoles*; A. J. Vitale, "KiSetla: Linguistic and Sociolinguistic Aspects of a Pidgin Swahili of Kenya," *Anthropological Linguistics* 22, no. 2 (1980); and W. H. Whiteley, *Swahili, the Rise of a National Language* (1969).

For information about military Swahili in the colonial period, see Mungai Mutonya and Timothy H. Parsons, "KiKAR: A Swahili Variety Spoken in Kenya's Colonial Army," *Journal of African Languages and Linguistics* 25, no. 2 (2004).

For the accomplishments of Standard Swahili and also an attack on Sheng as viewed by some on the ground, see *Kiswahili: A Tool for Development—The Multidisciplinary Approach*, Department of Kiswahili and Other African Languages, Moi University and Chakita, editors, Naomi Shitemi and Mwanakombo M. Noordin; assistant editors, Allan I. Opijah and Davies M. Mukuria (2001). The essays by Clara Momanyi and Davies M. Mukuria are particularly telling in regard to some prevailing attitudes about renegade Swahili.

For an extensive discussion of the use of language in computer mediated communication (CMC) in Kenya, see Sandra Nekesa Barasa, "Language, Mobile Phones and Internet: A Study of MS Texting, Email, IM and SNS Chats in computer mediated communication (CMC) in Kenya" (PhD diss., University of Leiden, 2010), which examines CMC genres including Short Messaging Service (SMS), E-mail, Instant Messages (IM), and Social Network Sites (SNS); see https://openaccess.leidenuniv.nl/bitstream /handle/1887/16136/Language;jsessionid=AA4AA9F11B00C43344648743471 8CC20?sequence=1.

Chapter 11: Swahili in African American Life

For a personal history of Stanley "Tookie" Williams, see his *Blue Rage, Black Redemption: A Memoir* (2004).

For a discussion of Karenga's philosophy, see Alamin Mazrui, *English in Africa after the Cold War* (2004), especially chapter 4.

For the story of LeRoy Jones's transformation using Swahili, see Imamu Amiri Baraka, *The Autobiography of LeRoi Jones/Amiri Baraka* (2000). For a discussion of LeRoi Jones, see Daniel Matlin, "'Lift Up Yr Self!' Reinterpreting Amiri Baraka (LeRoi Jones), Black Power, and the Uplift Tradition," *Journal of American History* 93, no. 1 (2006).

For more on Swahili in African American history, see Kariamu Welsh-Asante, *The African Aesthetic: Keeper of Tradition* (1993), and Ali A. Mazrui and Alamin M. Mazrui, *The Power of Babel: Language and Governance in the African Experience* (1998).

For information about Kwanzaa holidays, see Maulana Karenga, *Kwanzaa: A Celebration of Unity, Community and Culture* (2008).

For examples of the use of Swahili by African Americans listed by the police, see http://www.policemag.com/blog/gangs/story/2011/01/a-swahili-dictionary.aspx. For Cleveland history in which Swahili is invoked, see http://ech.cwru.edu/ech-cgi/article.pl?id=KH. And finally, for samples of *Star Trek* episodes relevant to this chapter, see http://www.startrek.com /startrek/view/series/TOS/character/1112511.html.

NOTES

Chapter 1: Swahili, a Language Alive

1. The World Bank estimates that 120 to 150 million people speak Swahili as a second language; William J. Frawley (2003, 181) puts the number at a minimum of 75 million, and *Ethnologue* has it as 40 million. This book takes the higher number as closer to the reality, given that Swahili is well known as a lingua franca in countries whose populations far exceed 150 million.

2. Soyinka has on many occasions suggested Swahili as the lingua franca for the entire continent of Africa—most recently at an April 20, 2005, talk at Harvard University's Du Bois Institute Colloquium, entitled "Vectors of Language."

3. John Ndembwike (2006, 72) says that when traveling to Namibia, South Africa, Angola, Lesotho, Botswana, Swaziland, or Mozambique, it is not uncommon to run into people who speak Swahili. According to him, "Many of the echelons of the Southern African liberation movements speak Swahili."

4. Problems abound with counting languages, not just in terms of the technical dilemma of distinguishing what is a language and what is a dialect or variant but also in terms of the European obsession with naming and classifying Africans. See Makoni and Pennycook (2007, 1–41), and Fabian (1986).

5. Bogonko (1992, 243).

6. Notable in this regard is the International People's Democratic Uhuru Movement (InPDUM), which organizes around the question of democratic rights for African people, as well as the understanding that self-determination is the highest expression of democracy.

7. Maulana Karenga, professor of black studies at California State University–Long Beach, created the African American holiday known as Kwanzaa (the Swahili word for "first"), which runs from December 26 to January 1.

8. Mazrui and Mazrui (1995, 133).

9. Whiteley (1969, 60).

10. Mazrui (2007, 95).

11. According to Paul M. Lewis, Gary F. Simons, and Charles D. Fennig (2014), the current estimates list the following as the most widely spoken languages: Chinese (1.197 billion) spoken in 33 countries, Spanish (406 million) in 31 countries, English (322 million) in 101 countries, Arabic (223 million) in 59 countries, Hindi (260 million) in 4 countries, Bengali (193 million) in 4 countries, Portuguese (202 million) in 11 countries, Russian (162 million) in 16 countries, and Japanese (122 million) in 3 countries.

12. According to *Hispanic News,* only 17 percent of Hispanics speak Spanish fluently by the third generation, and by the fourth generation, that figure drops to 5 percent. See http://banderasnews.com/0610/edat-losespanish.htm (accessed January 13, 2015).

Chapter 2: Swahili, the Complex Language of a Cosmopolitan People

1. By itself, the term *Swahili* is an adjective, not a proper noun. This is why, in English, we speak of Swahili land, Swahili cities, Swahili culture, Swahili history, and so on. In reference to the language, *Swahili* is a root to which prefixes *Ki-, u-, m-,* and *wa-* are added to make nouns—*Kiswahili* (Swahili language or style), *Uswahilini* (Swahili country), *Uswahili* (Swahiliness), *Mswahili* (Swahili person), and *Waswahili* (Swahili people). Speaking in Swahili, the prefixes are unavoidable, but the nouns that the English adjective modified make it possible for me to omit them, except when I need them to draw attention to the Bantu features of the language.

2. Horton and Middleton (2000, 5).

3. Pouwels (1987, 8).

4. *Periplus of the Erythrean Sea,* written by an Alexandrine Greek at about 100 CE.

5. Chami (1998, 199).

6. Many have assumed that the navigators were the Indians, Chinese, and others but not the Swahili; Africans, according to this view, were the dockworkers and provided the muscles that lifted, pushed, filled, and emptied the vessels in the seafaring enterprise, not expert sailors. The story of Swahili, however, urges us to stay clear of definitive categories pertaining to race and ethnicity, since one person's view of an African is another's view of a Persian or an Arab. Mwamaka Sharifu's story such as the one at http://www.chinadaily.com.cn/english/doc/2005-07/11/content_459090.htm (accessed January 13, 2015) suggests that this observation should extend to the Chinese.

7. According to Marina Tomalcheva, "The word 'Zanj' (sometimes 'Zinj') is a collective noun which frequently occurs in mediaeval Arabic texts with reference to Africans. Occasionally, it is used as a toponym, more frequently as an ethnonym. In the Caliphate, the word Zanj usually referred to slaves. In West Africa, too, the word denoted a category of serf population. In the East African context, however, the reference was usually to free inhabitants of the area, implicitly recognized as a majority, if not the sole population group." Tomalcheva examines the use of the word *Zanj* in this respect, i.e. in relation to black people of East Africa in their domicile. She discusses the criteria used by Arab authors to distinguish the Zanj from the other, non-Zanj peoples, the internal composition of the Zanj, the changing affective content of the term, and its etymology." See http://www.africabib.org/rec .php?RID=119520915&DB=p.

8. Harris (1971, 5); Hunter (1886, 287).

9. Ibn Battuta, quoted in Freeman-Grenville (1975, 29–31).

10. Gibb (1962, 379–80), *The Travels of Ibn Battuta, A.D. 1352–1354.*

11. Horton and Middleton (2000, 16).

12. Freeman-Grenville (1962, 27–31); Watson (1983, 54).

13. Prins (1961, 17).

14. Swahili is ranked easiest of all languages indigenous to Africa for Americans to learn. See http://www.effectivelanguagelearning.com/language-guide/language-difficulty (accessed January 14, 2015).

15. The remark is often attributed to George Bernard Shaw but also to Oscar Wilde and to Winston Churchill; it appears to have no definitive origin.

16. I discuss the spread of Swahili inland in chapter 5 and the rise of Swahili pidgins in chapter 10.

17. Nurse and Spear (1985, 22).

18. Horton and Middleton (2000, 209).

19. Werner (1916, 358). The words available from the Hadimu dialect recorded by Alice Werner sounded very much like the Bantu languages of the hinterland.

20. Horton and Middleton (2000, 17).

21. Ibid., 19–23.

22. Ibid., 21–22.

23. Ibid., 17.

24. Ibid., 19–23.

25. Of the 61 languages listed in *Ethnologue* for Kenya, 13 are Afro-Asiatic, 27 are Niger-Congo, and 13 are Nilo-Saharan. Two—Dahalo and Ndorobo (El Molo and Yaaku) spoken in Kenya (and dying)—have lost their former Khoisan roots, but Dahalo still has clicks in it, though it is now classified as Cushitic.

26. Sutton (1968, 79) in *Zamani*; Ambrose (1982, 106).

27. The Mazruis need no introduction, as they are the most widely known Mombasa family. The Akhbar Pate gives a chronological description of thirty-two reigns of Nabhani kings of Pate, beginning with Sulayman bin Sulayman bin Muzaffar al Nabahani, who arrived in Pate in 1203–4 CE (Tolmacheva 1993, 527–48).

28. Collins and Burns (2007, 102).

29. Knappert (1967, 9).

30. Knappert (1979, 110).

Chapter 3: A Grand Smorgasbord of Borrowings and Adaptation

1. The asterisk indicates a linguist's hypothesized form of an ancestor word or root of a word.

2. The formal linguistic expression of hypothesized, or reconstructed, ancient roots of modern words is distinguished by the forward slashes. In this case, /gwand/ represents the shared basic phonemic components, or sounds—an initial consonant g-, a vowel, and a nasalized -d- that express an idea, in this case, "sheep." Modern languages, depending on the phonetic tendencies (accent, pronunciation) that distinguish them, manifest this ancient consonant-vowel-consonant cluster in varying (but internally very regular) ways. In Lamu, the initial g- in the root has been nasalized (ng-), the vowel has closed from -a- to -o-, and the final consonant is supplemented by that dialect's reliance on concluding words with vowels, in this case -i. Thus, we have /gw/ = ng- + /a/ = -o- + /d/ = -nd- + I, or the hypothetical root /gwand/ => ng'ondi (Kiamu for "sheep").

I will not spell out other examples of how modern words derive through the sound changes that define languages from ancient roots (and in turn enable linguistics to reconstruct their origins), but one is often able to see the general patterns of matches between hypothetical ancient roots and modern specific articulations.

3. Here is one more example: the *ma-* in *maziwa* is a grammatical prefix in modern Swahili, not part of the root. The derivation therefore starts with the /il/ = z-, the /-i-/ remains -i-, the bilabial /-b-/ softens to -w-, and the concluding /-a/ matches the vowel at the end of the core word.

4. According to Nurse and Spear (1985, 46), "The major sound innovations within Sabaki indicate that in the homeland of the ancestors, the Elwana and the Swahili were adjacent, while the homelands of Comorians, Pokomo, and Mijikenda were also adjacent." The following table indicates the sound changes involving /t/ in the adaptation process.

SWAHILI AND AREA LANGUAGES	SOUTHERN CUSHITIC ETYMOLOGY	CURRENT WORD	CHANGE
Kitikuu, KiPate, KiSiu, Lower Pokomo, Mijikenda	*-tama 'sorghum/millet' *-tama	/-chama/ /-hama/	/t/ to /ch/ /t/ to /h/
Comorian	*-tama	/-rama/	/t/ to /r/

5. The following table indicates the sound changes involving /-gwand/ "sheep" in the adaptation process.

SWAHILI AND AREA LANGUAGES	SOUTHERN CUSHITIC ETYMOLOGY	CURRENT WORD	CHANGE
Lower Pokomo	*-gwand- 'sheep'	/-ngozi/	/nd/ to /zi/
Kiunguja, Chivumba	*-gwand	/-ng'onzi/	/g/ to /ng'/, /d/ to /zi/
Kingazija	*-gwand	/-gondzi/	/d/ to /zi/
KiAmu	*-gwand	/-ng'ondi/	/g/ to /ng'/, /d/ to /di/

6. Note that the sound represented notionally by "ʔ," which is common in Cushitic but challenging for Bantu speakers to pronounce, was dropped by speakers of all dialects of Swahili. The sounds produced by both upper and lower lip action to make the sound "b" was replaced with "w," a softer sound also produced on the lips.

8. English speakers also have borrowed this as "Satan," directly from Hebrew (opponent, obstructer), a Semitic language like Arabic.

9. According to dicitionary.com, *tobacco* is a 1580s word from the Spanish *tabaco*, in part from an Arawakan (probably Taino) language of the Caribbean, said to mean "a roll of tobacco leaves" (according to Las Casas 1552) or "a kind of pipe for smoking tobacco" (according to Oviedo 1535). Scholars of Caribbean languages lean toward Las Casas's explanation. But Spanish *tabaco* (also It. *tabacco*) was a name for medicinal herbs from the early fifteenth century, from the Arabic *tabbaq*, which was attested since the ninth century as the name of various herbs. So the word may be a European one transferred to an American plant.

10. Nurse and Hinnebusch (1993, 286).

11. Middleton (1992, 22).

12. Ibid.

13. The word *nana* is from Tupi-Guarani, a Native American language in the Caribbean area; from there, Columbus and then the Portuguese distributed the plant and its fruit throughout the Indian Ocean and the Pacific. The word means "excellent fruit" (Okihiro 2009, 74).

14. True or not, this is an appropriate satire that recalls the arbitrary way nations were carved up in the "scramble for Africa" of the 1880s.

15. Alan Mcrae, in "A Famous Trade Coin," *Australian Coin Review* 356 (February 1994): 30, says that the Maria Theresa Thaler (MTT) "came to be used as currency in large parts of Africa until after World War II. It was common from North Africa to Somalia, Ethiopia, Kenya, and down the coast of Tanzania to Mozambique. Its popularity in the Red Sea region was such that merchants would not accept any other type of currency."

16. Arabic borrowings from Swahili are rare or unrecoverable. The word *dhow* is reputed to be of eastern African origin, ostensibly borrowed by Arabic through the Swahili word *dau.* Gibb (1929, 235), for example, claims that the *dhow* derives from the Swahili language of Africa's east coast; they say dhow plied the Indian Ocean and the Arabian and Red Seas, enabled by their triangular (lateen) sails. The planks of their hulls were sewn rather than nailed together, making them more flexible in high seas than ships fastened togther with nails. By the thirteenth century, the pilot steered the dhow with a rudder situated at the stern of the ship. See http://castinet.castilleja .org/users/pmckee/africaweb/swahilistates.html (accessed January 14, 2015).

Chapter 4: A Classical Era: The Peak of Swahili Prosperity, 1000–1500 CE

1. See http://www.usnews.com/science/articles/2011/06/28/coconuts-may-hold-clues-to-ancient-civilization?PageNr=2 (accessed January 14, 2015).

2. Sheriff (2010, 79), quoting Carr Laughton in Prins (1965, 77).

3. Report by Diana Lutz in the Science section of the *US News & World Report* of June 28, 2011: "Coconuts May Hold Clues to Ancient Civilization: Written in Coconut DNA Are Historical Clues"; see http://www.usnews.com/science/ articles/2011/06/28/coconuts-may-hold-clues-to-ancient-civilization?PageNr=2 (accessed January 14, 2015). See also B. F. Gunn, L. Baudouin, and K. M. Olsen, "Independent Origins of Cultivated Coconut (*Cocos nucifera* L.) in the Old World Tropics," *PLoS ONE* 6, no. 6 (2011): e21143, doi:10.1371/journal.pone.0021143, http:// www.plosone.org/article/info%3Adoi%2F10.1371%2Fjournal.pone.0021143.

4. "The big surprise was that there was so much genetic differentiation clearly correlated with geography, even though humans have been moving coconut around for so long" (Washington University, St. Louis, 2011).

5. See Gunn, Baudouin, and Olsen, "Independent Origins."

6. Miehe et al. (2006).

7. Ibid., 5. Mulokozi and Sengo (1995), of the Institute of Swahili Research, claim that many Swahili respondents believe Fumo Liyongo lived before the thirteenth century.

8. Sheriff and Ed Ferguson (1991, 37–38); Harrow (1991).

9. The song and translation is in Miehe et al. (2006, 70–71). Mulokozi and Sengo (1995), of the Institute of Swahili Research, claim that many Swahili respondents place Fumo Liyongo's existence before the thirteenth century.

10. Ken Albala, *Food Cultures of the World Encyclopedia* (Santa Barbara, CA: Greenwood Press, 2011), 192.

11. Nyimbo za Liyongo (2006, 66–67). Mulokozi and Sengo (1995) of the Institute of Swahili Research claim that many Swahili respondents place Fumo Liyongo's existence before the thirteenth century.

12. Miehe et al. (2006, 66) and Mulokozi and Sengo (1995).

13. Pigafetta and Skelton (1969, 63–64).

14. The etymology of the Swahili word *nazi*, for "coconut," is mysterious. The word that closely resembles *nazi* is *nathi* in Kikuyu, which denotes "gooseberry." It may be that *nazi* is derived from an old Bantu word for a kind of fruit.

15. Nabhany (1979, 8–9).

16. The information about ships is obtained from the Beit Al Ajaib Museum (the House of Wonders Museum), located in Zanzibar.

17. TUKI (2001), *Kamusi ya Kiswahili-Kiingereza*.

18. Maxwell (1885, 99).

19. Sheriff (2010).

20. The information about the *waungwana* is from Nurse and Spear (1985, 22–24).

21. Knappert (1971, 1).

22. Ibid.

23. Gibb (1929, 123–24).

24. According to Berg (1968, 40), "The functions of a sheikh were mostly political, and sheikhships were not regarded as being hereditary within a single clan, though in practice they sometimes were. As a rule, actual kinship, as defined by patrilineal descent, extended no further than the clans or mbari. Linking several clans together in a single taifa seems historically to have been a matter of political convenience."

25. Laitin and Samatar (1987, 12).

26. Oliver and Fage (1966, 30), and Lewis (1988, 20).

27. Trimingham (1964, 5–6n).

28. Gibb (1929, 123–24).

29. Freeman-Grenville (1975, 57).

30. Duarte and Dames (1989, 22), *The Book of Barbosa*.

31. Duarte Barbosa, writing in 1517–18. Duarte and Dames (1989, 189).

32. Ibn Battuta, in Freeman-Grenville (1962, 29–31).

33. Barbosa, in Freeman-Grenville (1962, 131).

34. J. S. Kirkman, "Gedi or Gede," *Encyclopaedia of Islam*, 2nd ed., ed. P. Bearman, Th. Bianquis, C. E. Bosworth, E. van Donzel, and W. P. Heinrichs, Brill Online, 2014, *Reference*, Harvard University. January 9, 2014. See http://referenceworks.brillonline.com/entries/encyclopaedia-of-islam-2/gedi-or-gede-SIM_2429.

35. Freeman-Grenville (1962, 256).

36. Ibid., 63.

37. Miehe et al. (2006, 40–43).

38. As mentioned by Miehe et al. (2006).

39. Newitt (2002, 12–13), quoting Oliver and Mathew (1963).

40. Freeman-Grenville (1962, 19–20).

41. Archaeological information in this section is from Nurse and Spear (1985, 17–20).

42. Brill and Houtsma (1993, 1216).

43. The information about Shanga is taken from Nurse and Spear (1985, 17–20).

44. Horton (1996).

45. Nurse and Spear (1985, 6).

Chapter 5: Consolidation of a Popular Language, 1500–1850s

1. Other accounts attribute the name to Diaz himself. See "Cape of Good Hope," *Encyclopædia Britannica Online Academic Edition*, http://www.britannica.com/EB-checked/topic/238708/Cape-of-Good-Hope (accessed January 14, 2015).

2. Halliday (1992, 66).

3. Checkers is a board game played by two people, each using twelve pieces known as checkers. The object is to jump over the opponent's pieces and remove them from the board.

4. In Brazil, java plum fruit is variously *jambuláo, jaláo, jameláo,* or *jambol* (Morton 1987, 375–78). See http://www.hort.purdue.edu/newcrop/morton/jambolan .html (accessed January 14, 2015).

5. Freeman-Grenville (1980, xxvii).

6. Kavey (2010, 157–58).

7. Lagneau-Kesteloot (1972, 86).

8. Newitt (2002, 13).

9. Strandes (1968, 129–30).

10. According to Knappert (1979).

11. Taylor (1891, 95). The translation is mine.

12. This refers to whitish or yellowish matter running from closed eyes, usually during sleep.

13. So the story goes according to Taylor (1891, 95–96).

14. Examples are from Stigand (1915, 27).

15. Ibid., 27–28.

16. Ibid., 26.

17. Freeman-Grenville (1962, 140–41).

18. Examples are from Stigand (1915, 27).

19. When Ahmad bin Sa'id founded the al-Busa'idi dynasty of Oman in 1744, the Mazrui leader Muhammad bin Uthman refused to recognize the change of ownership of Mombasa and proclaimed himself governor of Mombasa. Soon, Pate, Malindi, Pemba, Zanzibar, and Mafia became independent also. In 1746, Omani agents murdered Muhammad bin Uthman and imprisoned his Mazrui brother Ali ibn

Athman, who escaped, rallied the people, overthrew the new governor, and executed the assassins. Ali ibn Athman (r. 1746–55) proclaimed himself sultan at Mombasa and seized Pemba, but a family quarrel prevented him from taking over Zanzibar. His successor, Mas'ud ibn Nasir (r. 1756–73), cooperated with Pate and developed Mombasa's relationship with the inland nyika, extending Mazrui influence from Pangani to Malindi. Sanderson Beck, "East Africans, Arabs, and Europeans 1700–1856," http://www.san.beck.org/16-12-EastAfrica.html (accessed January 14, 2015).

20. Chris and Susan McIntyre, *Zanzibar, Pemba, Mafia* (2013, 10).

21. A full description of slave types is provided in Campbell et al. (2008, 131–36).

Chapter 6: The Women of Swahili

1. *Periplus of the Erythrean Sea* was written by an Alexandrine Greek around 100 CE.

2. Mirza and Strobel (1989).

3. Stigand (1913, 115–16).

4. Taylor (1891, 95).

5. Mirza and Strobel (1989).

6. Ibid.

7. Jerome Becker was a lieutenant in the Belgian army in the 1880s Belgian Congo and was a member and later commander of the Third Expedition, organized by the Brussels Committee of the Association Internationale Africaine (AIA).

8. Becker (1887, 147), translated in Fabian (1986, 27).

9. Alpers (1984, 678).

10. Rizk (2007, 92).

11. Allen (1971, 8).

12. Ibid., 9; Mbele (1996).

13. Jahadhmy (1975, 28); also Mazrui (2007, 18).

14. Allen (1971, 9).

15. See Mbele (1996, 80–81).

16. Tomalcheva (1993, 131, 201).

17. Ibid., 101–2.

18. Stigand (1913, 38–44).

19. Ibid., 43.

20. Ibid., 38.

21. Taylor (1891, 95). The translation is mine.

22. Translation is interpretive. The literal translation of the successive lines is as follows:

> Miguel the white man, you are a involved in a lie (being deceived)
> Your eyes have produced discharge (causing you not to see properly)
> Why leave the parade
> To go to a hut in the courtyard?

23. More examples include *mtawi*, "a wizard," which is *mchawi* in Kiunguja; *mtele*, "rice," which is *mchele*; *Nt'i*, "country," which is *nchi*; and *tui*, "leopard," which is *chui* (Stigand 1915, 26–27).

24. Mbele (1996, 74).

25. Ibid., 80–81.

26. The Swahili believe *mtesi* is a branch/leaf that should never be brought into the house lest conflicts arise.

27. Angus Stevenson, ed., *Oxford Dictionary of English* (Oxford University Press, 2010), Oxford Reference Online, accessed October 18, 2013.

28. See http://adventuresrevisited.blogspot.com/2008/02/wimbo-wa-miti-song -of-trees.html.

29. Picture taken from http://photography.nationalgeographic.com/photography /enlarge/rainbow-baobab-tree-joubert.html (accessed January 15, 2015).

30. The baobab tree has multiple uses, and in this it rivals the coconut tree, described in chapter 4. Its wood is too fibrous for structural construction, but the bark is shredded into strands of fiber for use as rope, baskets, nets, snares, and cloth. Tonics and cosmetics are derived from the roots, and a kind of soup is made from the large palmate leaves. The seeds may be ground into a coffee substitute or eaten fresh, and the white pulp is used as cream of tartar for baking. The hollow trunks of living trees have served as homes, storage barns, places of refuge or worship, and even prisons or tombs. See http://goafrica.about.com/od/krugernationalpark/a /baobab.htm (accessed January 15, 2015).

31. The other half of the poem is addressed to Muslims and includes many spiritual references to the hereafter.

32. *Mwana Kupona*, verse 11.

33. Ibid., verse 12.

34. Ibid., verse 13.

35. Ibid., verses 15–19.

36. Ibid., verses 22 and 23.

37. Ibid., verses 27–36.

38. Shariff (1991, 46), in Harrow (1991).

39. Mazrui (2007, 17).

40. The epic of *Mwana Kupona* did inspire Mohamadi Kijumwa (the prolific brain-house or knowledge trove of Swahili discussed in chapter 7) to write a poem entitled *Siraji* (The lantern) to his son, giving him *wasia* (advice) on life. His poem is a study of Swahili as spoken in Lamu. Insofar as Kijumwa communicates to his son how to conduct himself as a Mswahili of dignity, his poem balances with Mwana Kupona's, and we might pair the two to discern the ideal Swahili husband and Swahili wife. Having the benefit of Mwana Kupona's poem, Kijumwa tells his son in verses 171 and 172 that

Mke wako mpumbaze	Comfort [literally dazzle] your wife;
Kwa uwezalo mweneze	what you can give, pass it on to her;
na wewe simteleze	do not make her upset
nde ukalimatia	by delaying when you are out.
Na siku ya kukwambia	And the day she tells you:
niwata nawe *ridhia*	"Leave me," you should consent;
ni *kheri* kuitokea	it is better to leave her,
ama ukaiyutia	otherwise you will regret it.

The italicized words in the original are from Arabic. Kijumwa also tells his son (in verse 180) that returning to a former wife may lead to regret because (in verse 187) *afuatao moyo faida huiyutia*, "the one who follows his heart, the only return he gets is regret." Unlike Mwana Kupona, who did not address the son-in-law to whom her daughter should devote her life, Kijumwa, in verses 174 and 176, includes advice to his future daughter-in-law, in the manner in which one might advise one's own daughter, pleading with her not to stay where she is not wanted:

Wethu *binti* sikia	Listen, our daughter,
mwana mume kikwambia	when your husband tells you
thakuwata buraia	"I will divorce you and free you of all obligations,"
akitinda nena haya	when he has completed the words, just say "alright."
Sikia sana *binti*	Listen carefully, my daughter
na siketi usiketi	you should never ever stay;
utadumu na *laiti*	you would go on lamenting
ukitoandamana haya	if you do not follow these [words]

In Kijumwa's *Siraji,* we see Arabic words (the italicized Swahili words) strewn just as in Mwana Kupona's poem and the sound changes one experiences when speaking Kiamu.

41. Fair (2001, 248).

42. Ibid., 247.

43. See ibid. and the references quoted there.

44. Rizk (2007, 94).

45. *Wasifu wa Siti binti Saad* by Shaaban Robert (1967, 40).

46. Fair (2001, 248).

47. This is cotton cloth from India worn by slaves.

48. *Wasifu wa binti Saad* by Shaaban Robert (1967, 40).

49. Askew (2002, 110).

50. Mmari (2011), unpublished paper ibid.

51. Al- Amni bin Aly Uwongozi (1955, 1)

52. Willis (1993). Also Mmari 2011, unpublished paper ibid.

53. There were small colonies of Gujarati-speaking Indian merchants with well-established businesses in this area. These Indians had their stores at the coast and were important financiers of the slave trade—though few of them actually ventured into the hinterland. From 1896, they extended their activities to the interior as the Kenya-Uganda Railway was being built, supplying goods, services, and transport for the builders. From the 1890s, there was an influx of Gujarati Indians into East Africa, and they took advantage of the trade and craftsmanship as the Europeans established their colonial administration (Morris 1956, 194–95).

54. Mirza and Strobel (1989, 77).

55. Khadi courts (or Khadis' courts) comprise a court system in Kenya that enforces limited rights of inheritance, family, and succession for Muslims.

56. Freeman-Grenville (1975, 133–34).

57. Zawawi (2005, 26–27).

58. This is a piece of cotton cloth with colored bands, worn wrapped around the body.

59. Iddi is a religious holiday that marks the end of Ramadan, celebrated by all Muslims.

60. Beck (2000, 114–15).

61. The literal translation of the expression *mchele moja mpishi mwingi* is "one rice many cookings."

62. Known as *Azimio la Arusha*, the Arusha Declaration is Tanzania's policy of African socialism, *Ujamaa*, and self-reliance, passed in 1967.

63. Zawawi (2005, 3) continues, "Descendants of the Arab-African speakers plus Omani rule of Mombasa, Zanzibar, Pemba and Dar es Salaam from the 19th century brought about long term residence of over 300 years of coming and going of family members between Gulf States and East Africa coastal regions not simply trade contacts. Throughout the Gulf States—Oman, the United Arab Emirates, Kuwait and Qatar—the movements of people contributed to an amalgam and fusion of the region's many socio-cultural compositions. Arabic is the language of the region but many immigrants from East and Central Africa speak Swahili as their first or second language and have spoken it for centuries. *Kangas* are among the leading artistic and cultural links between East Africa an Oman, as well as the other countries of the Gulf States."

64. He also says that "along with Swahili language, cuisine and music, *Kangas* are agents of continuity across a vast diaspora. A twelfth-century item of fashion remains as popular today in Swahili communities as far apart as China, Indonesia, Russia and the United States. *Kanga* names speak to all." See Zawawi (2005, 86).

65. Gunderson and Barz (2000, 167).

66. Donley-Reid (1990, 56).

67. Ibid., 55.

68. Du Bois (1999, 157).

69. Ibid.

70. Willis (1993, 169).

71. Taylor (1891, a3).

Chapter 7: The Swahili Literary Tradition

1. Mazrui and Shariff (1994, 93).

2. Ibid.

3. Stigand (1913, 103).

4. Berg (1968, 37).

5. *Mombasa siendi tena* was composed and sung by Fundi Konde (1924–2000), a very popular guitarist from the Giriama who lived in the immediate hinterland of the Swahili on the Kenya coast and therefore knew of Mombasa's attractions as a place of no return.

6. Taylor (1891, 44).

7. Burton (1872, 290).

8. See http://www.mainlesson.com/display.php?author=baldwin&book=people &story=nails. (Accessed 01/15/2015).

9. Achebe (1994, 42).

10. Ibid.

11. Steere (1870, vii).

12. The points mentioned here about Kijumwa's life are taken from Kijuma et al. (2010), and also Knappert (1983).

13. Kijuma et al. (2010, 44n59).

14. The so-called (by collectors rather than by the artistic creator) Dammann Collection, Hichens Collection, and Werner Collection are now at the School of Oriental and African Studies and can also be viewed? online at http://www.swahilimanuscripts .soas.ac.uk/perl/Project/listSwahiliCollections.pl (accessed January 15, 2015).

15. Ernst Dammann (later Dr. Ernst Dammann) was a graduate student from the University of Hamburg under the tutelage of Dr. Carl Meinhof. He had gone to the Swahili coast in 1933 to serve in a mission and church at Tanga; see Kijuma et al. (2010, 65).

16. Miehe et al. (2006).

17. The distinction between the *utumbuizo*, the *ukawafi*, and the *utendi* is ambiguous, as they could be classified as quite logical subtypes of one another. For that discussion, Miehe et al. (2006).

18. Knappert (1999, 96–97).

19. See King'ei (2001).

20. Freeman-Grenville, in *Chronology of African History* (1973), places Liyongo at about 1580. James Kirkman believes that Liongo may have lived around 1600 CE. Mulokozi and Sengo (1995) of the Institute of Swahili Research claim that many Swahili respondents place Fumo Liyongo's existence before the thirteenth century. Kijumwa's epic rendition of his life, though written in the twentieth century, was built from connecting free-floating fragments about the Swahili society centuries before.

21. Knappert (2004, 18).

22. The version of the epic by Edward Steere (in 1870) has it that it was a nephew, not his own son—a moot point in Bantu calculations of kinship, where a brother's son (nephew) and a birth son are both classed as sons, that is, males of the same generation related through brothers.

23. King'ei (2001).

24. Translation by Ali Jahadhmy, Anthology of Swahili Poetry (1975, 3).

Chapter 8: Writing Swahili in Arabic Characters

1. Zhukov 2004, 2.

2. Andrey A. Zhukov, "The Dating of Old Swahili Manuscripts: Towards Swahili Paleography," *Swahili Language and Society*, no. 9 (1992): 60.

3. Ali Mazrui in Sayyid Abdalla bin Ali bin Nasir (1977, 7–8).

4. Ibid., 60.

5. Ali Mazrui in ibid., 8.

6. Ali Mazrui in ibid., 7–8.

7. Ali Mazrui in ibid., 9.

8. James de Vere Allen in Sayyid Abdalla bin Ali bin Nasir (1977, 18.)

9. Ibid., 22.

10. Knappert (1979, 4).

11. Andrey Zhukov (2004, 1–15).

12. Mulokozi and Sengo (1995).

13. *Riming* is an archaic spelling of *rhyming*.

14. This letter is in Luffin (2007, 25–26). He reports that a number of Ajami manuscripts are available in several museums and archives in Belgium—the Royal Museum of Central Africa (MRAC), the Belgian Foreign Ministry, the Library of the University of Liege, and the Army Museum in Brussels.

15. *Bin* in Arabic refers to "son of" (a named father), as *von* does in German, *de* in Romance languages, and *Mac* or *O'* in Scottish and Irish, all with the same connotation of social significance attached to the connection thus affirmed. The concluding *Sheikh* is a title of honor.

16. Abdulaziz (1979, 70).

17. Luffin (2007).

18. Abdulaziz (1979, 74).

19. Ibid., 75.

20. These are technical phonetic symbols used to represent sounds precisely, independent of the languages in which they occur.

21. Ngom (2010, 14).

22. Essorami (2001, 7).

23. Ibid., 16–89.

24. *The Guardian*, July 10, 2007; see http://www.theguardian.com/books/2007/jul/10/chinuaachebe (accessed January 15, 2015).

25. See http://mercury.soas.ac.uk/perl/Project/index.pl?project=swahili (accessed January 15, 2015).

26. See, for instance, Jan Knappert's comments on the poems in his 1979 book *Four Centuries of Swahili Verse*, where most of the interpretations of the Gungu songs leave the reader with the impression that the Swahili are absurdly carnalistic.

27. Omar and Drury (2002, 16).

Chapter 9: Colonialism and Standardization of Swahili, 1850s to the 1960s and Beyond

1. Harris (1971, 10).

2. Here, we are continuing from where we left off in chapter 5.

3. There also have been subdialects, including Kiswahili ya Pierre Placide, which was used in the Jamaa religious movement founded by Placide Tempels, a Belgian missionary in the 1950s.

4. The Ruga-ruga made sure they looked hidious and menacing, and their warlike nicknames were meant to instill fear. Their leader went by the name Nyungu-ya-Mawe, which is Swahili for "pot of stone"—a pot, that is, that cannot break; and had several descriptive names in Nyamwezi including *nzwala mino ga vanhu* "wearer of

300 NOTES TO PAGES 199-229

human teeth," *kafupa mugazi* "spitter of blood," *kania vanhu "defecator on people,"* and *kandele ka nsimba* "lion skin."

5. Iliffe (1979) narrates what happened as follows.

6. According to Bennet (1986) and Lodhi (2000).

7. According to the book of Genesis, chapter 11, there was a time following the Great Flood when humans who spoke one language resolved to build a city and a tower tall enough to reach heaven and were making considerable progress when to stop them God made them unable to understand each other. Their city was called Babel "because God there confounded the language of all the Earth."

8. In the spirit of James C. Scott's (1985) "weapons of the weak" or any "guerrilla" strategy where you turn the strength of the enemy back against them.

9. Madan (1905, xiv).

10. He is referring to Ratcliffe and Elphinstone (1932, xviii and 310). Also quoted in Whiteley (1969, 79).

11. Mulokozi (2005, 26) lists the following individuals as secretaries between 1930 and 1970:

Frederick Johnson	1930–37
B. J. Ratcliffe	1937–49
R. A. Snoxall	1949–52
H. E. Lambert	1952
W. H.Whiteley	1953–58
J. W. T. Allen	1959–61
J. Knappert	1961–64
W. H. Whiteley	1965–67
J. A. Tejani	1968–70

12. Sukuma is a Bantu language spoken in northwestern Tanzania between Lake Victoria and Lake Rukwa, from Shinyanga to the Serengeti plain; see http://www .ethnologue.com/language/suk (accessed January 15, 2015).

13. Haya is a Bantu language spoken in Tanzania in the Kagera region, mainly the Bukoba urban and Bukoba rural districts; see http://www.ethnologue.com /language/hay (accessed January 15, 2015).

14. Mwera is a Bantu language spoken in southeastern Tanzania, mostly in the Lindi region, Nachingwea, Ruangwa, and the Lindi urban and Lindi rural districts, north of Makonde; see http://www.ethnologue.com/language/mwe (accessed January 15, 2015).

15. Nyakyusa is a Bantu language spoken in Tanzania's South Mbeya region, Lake Malawi north end, and in the Iringa region, Makete district. It is also spoken in Malawi; see http://www.ethnologue.com/language/nyy (accessed January 15, 2015).

Chapter 10: Modern Swahili: Moving On

1. Many schools throughout Kenya, Uganda, and Tanzania have departments of Kiswahili and student-led Swahili clubs meant to promote standard Swahili, in addition to the numerous professional organizations dedicated to the cause. I can only mention a handful here:

BAKITA (Baraza la Kiswahili la Taifa, or National Swahili Board)

BAKIZA (Baraza la Kiswahili Zanzibar, or Zanzibar Swahili Board)

CHAKA (Chama cha Kiswahili Afrika, or African Council of Swahili)

CHAKITA (Chama cha Kiswahili cha Taifa, or National Council of Swahili)

CHAUKIDU (Chama cha Ukuzaji wa Kiswahili cha Dunia, or Association for the Promotion of Swahili Worldwide)

TAKILUKI (Taasisi ya Kiswahili na Lugha za Kigeni, or Institute of Swahili and Foreign Languages)

TUKI (Taasisi ya Uchunguzi wa Kiswahili, or Institute of Swahili Research)

UKUTA (Usanifu wa Kiswahili na Ushairi Tanzania, or Standardization of Swahili and Poetry in Tanzania)

2. See New Updated Guthrie List Online by Jouni Filip Maho, 2009, http://goto .glocalnet.net/mahopapers/nuglonline.pdf (accessed January 15, 2015).

3. See http://www.youtube.com/watch?v=ZLtuxYaKkoo Fahari Yako, Royal Productions (accessed January 15, 2015).

4. Mukuria (2001, 91).

5. Ibid.

6. A pidgin is a grammatically simplified form of a language, used for communication between people not sharing a common language. Pidgins have a limited vocabulary, some elements of which are taken from local languages, and they are not native languages but arise out of language contact between speakers of other languages.

7. See Saeed Khan, "Gujarat's Romance with East Africa Many Centuries Old," *Times of India*, September 24, 2013.

8. Cited by Whiteley (1969, 49).

9. Quoted in Vitale (1980, 50).

10. This is a movie whose plot involves an Indian housewife who enrolls in a course to learn English because her daughter and husband, who are proficient in English, are embarrassed by her inability to speak the language whenever their elite family is in the company of educated friends.

11. Vitale (1980, 49).

12. Whiteley (1969, 49).

13. Mutonya and Parsons (2004, 116).

14. Whiteley (1969, 5).

15. Ibid.

16. The sentence word *nitakupiga* parses as follows: *ni* = I, the *-ta-* = future tense marking, the *ku-* = "you singular," and the verb is -piga, meaning "hit."

17. See sample shown at http://www.kenyawebtv.com/index.php/shows/vioja -mahakamani (accessed January 15, 2015).

18. See http://www2.jumptv.com/seo/vioja_mahakamani/vioja_mahakamani.htm (accessed January 15, 2015).

19. From *Vioja Mahakamani, pt. 11B* (my translation); see http://www.youtube .com/watch?v=FgoYB1kT3Bg (accessed January 15, 2015).

20. Knappert (1979, 33–34).

21. The discussion on Sheng follows Mugane 2005, 169–75.

22. This is the slang restricted to a neighborhood or a cohort group of people, mostly youths.

23. This is a form of language thought by some to be a coarse and unrefined hybrid speech.

24. *Nairobi Half Life* is a 2012 Kenyan film directed by David "Tosh" Gitonga.

25. Zimbabweans, in fact, call the whole English-speaking elite in their country the *nose brigades* because they speak an English accented as closely as possible to that of Europeans and Americans. The butt of the joke is just how phony many of them sound.

26. Barasa 2010, 56.

27. Ibid., 18.

28. See http://www.langaa-rpcig.net/+Pidgin-Cameroon-s-Lingua-Franca-or+ .html (accessed January 15, 2015).

29. McCrum, MacNeil, and Cran (1986, 311).

30. Ibid., 315.

31. Ibid., 316.

32. Ibid.

Chapter 11: Swahili in African American Life

1. The Zulu and the Swati kingdoms, for example, hold the first fruit ceremony, in which the king or paramount chief eats (or tastes) the new season's harvest and is the first person in the nation to do so—something observed by David Livingstone, who in writing about the Tswana noted, "The other tribes will not begin to eat the early pumpkins of the new crop until they hear that the Bahurutse have 'bitten' it." See http://africanhistory.about.com/od/southafrica/a/FirstFruit.htm (accessed January 15, 2015).

2. This information can be found in Mattar (2004).

3. From *The Encyclopedia of Cleveland History,* http://www.nationmaster.com /encyclopedia/Karamu-House (accessed January 15, 2015).

4. See the story at http://www.sfgate.com/news/article/5-inmate-gangs-dominate -California-s-prison-system-2696806.php (accessed January 15, 2015).

5. The BGF Swahili is from Gabe Morales, author/trainer/gang specialist, owner of Gang; see http://www.gangpreventionservices.org/BGF.asp (accessed January 15, 2015).

6. Congo is a place well within reach of the Swahili sphere of influence, unlike Angola, the modern nation in the far southwestern part of Africa.

7. The name Kariamu is defined as meaning "one who reflects the almighty"; see http://www.allbabynames.com/BabyName/African/Kariamu.aspx (accessed January 15, 2015).

Chapter 12: Swahili Is for the Living

1. For the story on the competition, see chapter 5 of Nadeau and Barlow (2006).
2. Ibid., 64.
3. Ibid.
4. Mbembe (2011).
5. McCrum, MacNeil, and Cran (1986, 9).
6. See http://www.youtube.com/watch?v=6gxaN-hagTY&feature=endscreen (accessed January 15, 2015).
7. Chrystal (2012, 7).

Works Cited

Abdalla, Abdilatif. 1973. *Sauti ya dhiki.* Nairobi: Oxford University Press.

Abdulaziz, Mohamed H. 1979; repr., 1994. *Muyaka: 19th Century Swahili Popular Poetry.* Nairobi: Kenya Literature Bureau.

Abedi, Kaluta. 1958. *Sheria za Kutunga Mashairi na Diwani ya Amri.* Kampala: Eagle Press, 1954.

Achebe, Chinua. 1958. *Things Fall Apart.* New York: Anchor Books.

Albala, Ken. 2011. *Food Cultures of the World Encyclopedia.* Santa Barbara, CA: Greenwood Press.

Allen, J. de V. 1993. *Swahili Origins: Swahili Culture and the Shungwaya Phenomenon.* London: James Currey.

Allen, J. de V., and Thomas H. Wilson. 1979. *Swahili Houses and Tombs of the Coast of Kenya.* London: AARP.

Allen, J. W. T. 1971. *Tendi: Six Examples of a Swahili Classical Verse Form with Translations and Notes.* New York: Africana Publishing 1971.

Allman, Jean Marie. 2004. *Fashioning Africa: Power and the Politics of Dress.* Bloomington: Indiana University Press.

Alpers, Edward A. 1984. "Ordinary Household Chores: Ritual and Power in a 19th-Century Swahili Women's Spirit Possession Cult." *International Journal of African Historical Studies* 17 (4): 677–702.

———. 2009. *East Africa and the Indian Ocean.* Princeton, NJ: Markus Wiener Publishers.

Aly, Al-Amin bin. 1955. *Uwongozi: Kimekusanya mashauri na mafunzisho ya mambo yenye kuwainua waislamu na kuwaongoza ndia njema katika dini na dunia.* 3rd ed. Mombasa: East African Muslim Welfare Society.

Appiah, Anthony. 2006. *Cosmopolitanism: Ethics in a World of Strangers.* New York: W. W. Norton.

Ashton, E. O. 1947. *Swahili Grammar (Including Intonation).* 2nd ed. London: Longmans, Green.

Askew, Kelly Michelle. 1999. "Female Circles and Male Lines: Gender Dynamics along the Swahili Coast." *Africa Today* 46 (3/4): 67–102.

———. 2002. *Performing the Nation: Swahili Music and Cultural Politics in Tanzania.* Chicago: University of Chicago Press.

Athman, Athman H. 1996. "Styles of Swahili Carving." AAP (Afrikanistische Arbeitspapiere) 47:11–29.

Baraka, Amiri. 1984. *The Autobiography of LeRoi Jones.* New York: Freundlich Books.

Baraka, Imamu Amiri, and William J. Harris. 2000. *The LeRoi Jones/Amiri Baraka Reader*. 2nd ed. New York: Thunder's Mouth Press.

Barasa, Sandra Nekesa. 2010. "Language, Mobile Phones and Internet: A Study of SMS Texting, Email, IM and SNS Chats in Computer Mediated Communication (CMC) in Kenya." PhD dissertation, University of Leiden.

Barbosa, Duarte, and Mansel Longworth Dames. 2010. *The Book of Duarte Barbosa, an Account of the Countries Bordering on the Indian Ocean and Their Inhabitants*. Farnham, UK: Ashgate.

Barbosa, Duarte, and Ferna Es. 1866. *A Description of the Coasts of East Africa and Malabar, in the Beginning of the Sixteenth Century*. London: Printed for the Hakluyt Society.

Beachey, R. W. 1976. *A Collection of Documents on the Slave Trade of Eastern Africa*. London: Collings.

———. 1976. *The Slave Trade of Eastern Africa*. New York: Barnes and Noble Books.

Bearman, Peri J. 2006. *Encyclopaedia of Islam*. 2nd ed. Leiden: Brill.

Beck, Rose Marie. 2000. "Aesthetics of Communication: Texts on Textiles (Leso) from the East African Coast (Swahili)." *Research in African Literatures* 31:104–24.

———. 2001. "Ambiguous Signs: The Role of the Kanga as a Medium of Communication." In *Swahili Forum VIII: In Honour of Gudrun Miehe, December 2001*, AAP (Afrikanistische Arbeitspapiere) 68: 157–69. Cologne, Germany: Institut für Afrikanistik, Universität zu Koln.

Beck, Sanderson. "East Africans, Arabs, and Europeans 1700–1856." At http://www.san.beck.org/16-12-EastAfrica.html (accessed January 14, 2015).

Bennett, Norman R. 1986. *Arab versus European: Diplomacy and War in Nineteenth-Century East Central Africa*. New York: Africana Publishing.

Berg, F. J. 1968. "The Swahili Community of Mombasa, 1500–1900." *Journal of African History* 9 (1): 35–56. http://www.jstor.org/stable/179919 (accessed January 14, 2015).

Bertoncini, Elena. 1989. *Outline of Swahili Literature: Prose, Fiction and Drama*. Leiden: Brill.

Biersteker, Ann Joyce, and Ibrahim Noor Shariff. 1995. *Mashairi ya vita vya Kuduhu* [War poetry in Kiswahili exchanged at the time of the Battle of Kuduhu]. East Lansing: Michigan State University.

Blok, Henry P., ed. 1948. *A Swahili Anthology with Notes and Glossaries*. Leiden: A. W. Sijthoffs.

Bogonko, Sorobea N. 1992. *Reflections on Education in East Africa*. Nairobi: Oxford University Press.

Bose, Sugata. 2006. *A Hundred Horizons: The Indian Ocean in the Age of Global Empire*. Cambridge, MA: Harvard University Press.

Bosha, Ibrahim, and Atwaya S. Nchimbi. 1993. *Taathira za kiarabu katika kiswahili pamoja na kamusi thulathiya (Kiswahili-Kiarabu-Kiingereza)* [The influence of Arabic language on Kiswahili with a trilingual dictionary (Swahili-Arabic-English)]. Dar es Salaam: University Press.

Boxer, C. R., and Carlos de Azevedo. 1960. *Fort Jesus and the Portuguese in Mombasa, 1593–1729*. London: Hollis and Carter.

Brain, James Lewton. 1968. *A Social Science Vocabulary of Swahili.* Syracuse, NY: Program of Eastern African Studies.

———. 1969. *Kamusi ya maneno ya utaalamu wa mambo ya kibinadamu* [A short dictionary of social science terms for Swahili speakers]. Syracuse, NY: Syracuse University, Maxwell Graduate School of Citizenship and Public Affairs.

Brill, E. J., and Martijn Theodoor Houtsma. 1993. *E. J. Brill's First Encyclopaedia of Islam, 1913–1936.* Repr. ed. Leiden: Brill.

Brode, Heinrich. 1969. *Tippoo Tib: The Story of His Career in Central Africa.* Chicago: Afro-Am Press.

Burton, Richard Francis. 1872. *Zanzibar.* London: Tinsley Brothers.

———. 1967. *Zanzibar: City, Island, and Coast.* New York: Johnson Reprint.

Campbell, Gwyn, Suzanne Miers, and Joseph C. Miller, eds. 2008. *Women and Slavery.* Athens: Ohio University Press.

Chami, Felix. 1998. "A Review of Swahili Archeology." *African Archeological Review* 15 (3): 199–218.

Chaudhuri, K. N. 1990. *Asia before Europe: Economy and Civilisation of the Indian Ocean from the Rise of Islam to 1750.* Cambridge: Cambridge University Press.

Childers, Erskine B. 1960. *Common Sense about the Arab World.* New York: Macmillan.

Chimera, Rocha. 1999. *Kiswahili: Past, Present and Future Horizons.* Nairobi: Nairobi University Press.

Chiraghdin, Shihabdin, and Mathias E. Mnyampala. 1977. *Historia ya Kiswahili.* Nairobi: Oxford University Press.

Chittick, Neville. 1965. "The Shirazi Colonisation of East Africa." *Journal of African History* 6:275–94.

———. 1974. *Kilwa: An Islamic Trading City on the East African Coast.* Nairobi: British Institute in Eastern Africa.

Chittick, H. Neville, and Robert I. Rotberg, eds. 1975. *East Africa and the Orient: Cultural Syntheses in Pre-colonial Times.* New York: Africana Publishing.

Collins, Robert O., and James M. Burns. 2007. *A History of Sub-Saharan Africa.* New York: Cambridge University Press.

Cooper, Frederick. 1977. *Plantation Slavery on the East Coast of Africa.* New Haven, CT: Yale University Press.

Crystal, David. 2004. *The Stories of English.* Woodstock: Overlook Press.

———. *English as a Global Language.* Cambridge: Cambridge University Press, 2012.

Davidson, Basil. 1991. *African Civilization Revisited: From Antiquity to Modern Times.* Trenton, NJ: Africa World Press.

Dennett, Joan T. 1992. "World Language Status Does Not Ensure World Class Usage." In *Writing and Speaking in the Technology Professions: A Practical Guide,* edited by David F. Beer. New York: IEEE Press.

Doke, Clement Martyn. 1935. *Bantu Linguistic Terminology.* London: Longmans, Green.

Donley-Reid, Linda W. 1990. "The Power of Swahili Porcelain, Beads and Pottery." *Archeological Papers of the American Anthropological Association* 2 (1): 47–59.

Du Bois, W. E. B. 1999. *The Souls of Black Folk: Authoritative Text, Contexts, Criticism.* New York: Norton.

Ehret, Christopher, and Merrick Posnansky. 1982. *The Archeological and Linguistic Reconstruction of African History.* Berkeley: University of California Press.

Elton, James Frederick, and Henry Bernard Cotterill. 1879. *Travels and Researches among the Lakes and Mountains of Eastern and Central Africa: From the Journal of J. Frederic Elton.* London: F. Cass.

Essorami, Sulaiman bin Said bin Ahmed, Gustav Neuhaus, and Katrin Bromber. 2001. *The Jurisdiction of the Sultan of Zanzibar and the Subjects of Foreign Nations.* Würzburg: Ergon-Verl.

Fabian, Johannes. 1986. *Language and Colonial Power: The Appropriation of Swahili in the Former Belgian Congo, 1880–1938.* New York: Cambridge University Press.

Fair, Laura. 1996. "Identity, Difference, and Dance: Female Initiation in Zanzibar, 1890 to 1930." *Frontiers: A Journal of Women's Studies* 17 (3): 146–72.

———. 1998. "Dressing Up: Clothing, Class and Gender in Post-Abolition Zanzibar." *Journal of African History* 39 (1): 63–94.

———. 2001. *Pastimes and Politics: Culture, Community, and Identity in Post-Abolition Urban Zanzibar, 1890–1945.* Athens: Ohio University Press.

Farrant, Leda. 1975. *Tippu Tip and the East African Slave Trade.* London: Hamilton.

Foreign Office (FO), Great Britain. 1867. *British and Foreign State Papers,* vol. 49: *1858–1859.* London: William Ridgway.

Fotheringham, L. M. 1891. *Adventures in Nyasaland: A Two Years' Struggle with Arab Slave-Dealers in Central Africa.* London: Sampson Low.

Frankl, P. J. L. 1999. "H. E. Lambert (1893–1967): Swahili Scholar of Eminence (Being a Short Biography together with a Bibliography of His Published Work)." *Journal of African Cultural Studies* 12 (1): 47–53.

Frawley, William. 2003. *International Encyclopedia of Linguistics.* 2nd ed. Oxford: Oxford University Press.

Freeman-Grenville, G. S. P. 1962; repr. 1975. *The East African Coast: Select Documents from the First to the Earlier Nineteenth Century.* Oxford: Clarendon Press.

———. 1973. *Chronology of African History.* London: Oxford University Press.

———. 1980. *The Mombasa Rising against the Portuguese, 1631: From Sworn Evidence.* London: Oxford University Press.

———. 1988. *The Swahili Coast, 2nd to 19th Centuries: Islam, Christianity and Commerce in Eastern Africa.* London: Variorum Reprints.

Gibb, H.A.R. 1929. *Ibn Battuta: Travels in Asia and Africa.* London: G. Routledge & Sons.

———. 1962. *The Travels of Ibn Battuta, A.D. 1325–1354.* Cambridge: CUP for the Hakluyt Society.

Gill, S. 1999. "Mahasthangarh: A Riverine Port?" In *Archaeology of Seafaring: The Indian Ocean in the Ancient Period,* edited by H. P. Ray, 235. New Delhi, India: Pragati.

Gilroy, Paul. 1993. *The Black Atlantic: Modernity and Double Consciousness.* Cambridge, MA: Harvard University Press.

Githioria, Chege. 2002. "Sheng: Peer Language, Swahili Dialect or Emerging Creole?" *Journal of African Cultural Studies* 15 (2): 159–81.

Gray, John Milner. 1958. *Early Portuguese Missionaries in East Africa*. London: Macmillan.

———. 1962. *History of Zanzibar, from the Middle Ages to 1856*. London: Oxford University Press.

Gunderson, Frank D., and Gregory F. Barz. 2000. *Mashindano! Competitive Music Performance in East Africa*. Dar es Salaam: Mkuki na Nyota Publishers.

Gunn, B. F., L. Baudouin, and K. M. Olsen. 2011. "Independent Origins of Cultivated Coconut (*Cocus nucifera* L.) in the Old World Tropics." *PLoS ONE* 6 (6): e21143. doi: 10.1371/journal.pone.0021143.

Guthrie, Malcolm. 1948. *The Classification of the Bantu Languages*. London: Oxford University Press for the International African Institute, 32 pp.

———. 1967–71. *Comparative Bantu: An Introduction to the Comparative Linguistics and Prehistory of the Bantu Languages*. 4 vols. London: Gregg International Publishers.

———. 1970. *Comparative Bantu: An Introduction to the Comparative Linguistics and Prehistory of the Bantu Languages*. Farnborough, UK: Gregg Press.

Halliday, Michael A. K. 1992. "New Ways of Meaning: The Challenge to Applied Linguistics." In *Language Contact and Language Conflict*, edited by M. Putz, 61–95. Amsterdam: Benjamins.

Hanby, Jeannette, and Bygott, David. 1984. *Kanga: 101 Uses*. Nairobi: Hanby & Bygott Publishers.

Harries, Lyndon. 1962. *Swahili Poetry*. Oxford: Clarendon Press.

Harris, Joseph E. 1971. *The African Presence in Asia: Consequences of the East African Slave Trade*. Evanston, IL: Northwestern University Press.

Harrow, Kenneth W., ed. 1991. *Faces of Islam in African Literature*. Portsmouth, NH: Heinemann.

Hawkins, Clifford W. 1977. *The Dhow: An Illustrated History of the Dhow and Its World*. Lymington, UK: Nautical Publishing.

Hichens, William. 1948. *Diwani ya Muyaka bin Haji Al-Ghassainy*. Johannesburg: University of Witwatersrand.

Hirsch, E. D. 2002. *The New Dictionary of Cultural Literacy*. 3rd ed. Boston: Houghton Mifflin.

Hoftmann, Hildegard. 1963. *Suaheli-deutsches Worterbuch*. Leipzig, Germany: Verlag Enzyklopadie.

Hollingsworth, L. W. 1951. *A Short History of the East Coast of Africa*. Rev. ed. London: Macmillan.

Holm, John A. 1988. *Pidgins and Creoles*. Cambridge: Cambridge University Press.

Horrocks, Geoffrey C. 1997. *Greek: A History of the Language and Its Speakers*. London: Longman.

Horton, Mark. 1987. "Early Muslim Trading Settlements on the East African Coast: New Evidence from Shanga." *Antiquaries Journal* 67. London: Oxford University Press.

———. 1996. *Shanga: The Archaeology of a Muslim Trading Community on the Coast of East Africa*. London: British Institute in Eastern Africa.

Horton, Mark, and John Middleton. 2000. *The Swahili: The Social Landscape of a Mercantile Society*. Malden, MA: Blackwell.

Howarth, David Armine, and Robin Constable. 1977. *Dhows*. London: Quartet Books.

Hunter, William W. 1886. *The Imperial Gazetteer of India 6*. London: Trubner.

Iliffe, John. 1979. *A Modern History of Tanganyika*. Cambridge: Cambridge University Press.

Jahadhmy, Ali. 1975. *Anthology of Swahili Poetry* [Kusanyiko la mashairi]. Nairobi: Heinemann Educational Books.

Johnson, Frederick. 1935. *Kamusi ya kiswahili yaani kitabu cha maneno ya kiswahili*. London: Sheldon Press.

———. 1939. *A Standard Swahili English Dictionary (Founded on Madan's Swahili-English Dictionary)*. London: Oxford University Press.

Karanja, Michael. 2010. "Mobile Phone subscribers hit 19 m." *Capital Business: Business and Politics in East Africa* (August). http://www.capitalfm.co.ke/business/2010/08/kenya-mobile-phone-subscribers-hit-m/.

Karenga, Maulana. 1977. *Kwanzaa: Origin, Concepts, Practice*. San Diego, CA: Kawaida Publications.

———. 1993. *Introduction to Black Studies*. 2nd ed. Los Angeles: University of Sankore Press.

———. 2008. *Kwanzaa: A Celebration of Unity, Community and Culture*. Los Angeles: University of Sankore Press.

Kavey, Allison. 2010. *World-Building and the Early Modern Imagination*. New York: Palgrave Macmillan.

Kawawa, Rashidi Mfaume. 1968. *Swahili Legal Terms*. Dar Es Salaam: Legal Research Centre and Faculty of Law.

Kawoya, Vincent F. K. 1984. "Investigation in the Patterns of Non-verbal Communication Behaviour Related to Conversational Interaction between Mother Tongue Speakers of Swahili." *Swahili Language and Society: Papers from the Workshop Held at the School of Oriental and African Studies in April 1982*, edited by Joan Maw. Vienna: Afro-Pub.

Khalid, Abdallah. 1977. *The Liberation of Swahili from European Appropriation*. Nairobi: East African Literature Bureau.

Kijuma, Muhamadi, Gudrun Miehe, W. Hichens, Clarissa Vierke, Sauda A. Barwani, Ahmed Sheikh Nabhany, and Ernst Dammann. 2010. *Muhamadi Kijuma: Texts from the Dammann Papers and Other Collections*. Cologne, Germany: Koppe.

Kimambo, Isaria N., and A. J. Temu. 1969. *A History of Tanzania*. Nairobi: East African Publishing House.

King'ei, Kitula. 2001. "Historical and Folkloric Elements in Fumo Liyongo's Epic." *Folklore* 16:78–86, http://haldjas.folklore.ee/folklore (accessed January 14, 2014).

Kirkman, James S. 1963. *Gedi: The Palace*. The Hague: Mouton.

———. 1964. *Men and Monuments on the East African Coast*. London: Lutterworth.

———. 1974. *Fort Jesus: A Portuguese Fortress on the East African Coast.* Oxford: Clarendon Press.

———. 1975. "Some Conclusions from the Archaeological Excavations on the Coast of Kenya." In *East Africa and the Orient: Cultural Syntheses in Pre-colonial Times,* edited by H. Neville Chittick and Robert I. Rotberg, 226–47. New York: Africana Publishing.

———. 1981. *Fort Jesus, Mombasa.* Mombasa: National Museum of Kenya.

———. 1982. "Omani Relations with East Africa before the Arrival of the Portuguese." *Proceedings of the Seminar for Arabian Studies* 12:35–38.

———. 2006. "Gedi or Gede." In *Encyclopedia of Islam,* 200. Leiden: Brill.

Knappert, Jan. 1964. *Four Swahili Epics.* Leiden: Drukkerij "Luctor et Emergo."

———. 1967. *Traditional Swahili Poetry: An Investigation into the Concepts of East African Islam as Reflected in the Utenzi Literature.* Leiden: E. J. Brill.

———, ed. 1971. *Swahili Islamic Poetry: Introduction, The Celebration of Mohammed's Birthday.* Leiden: E. J. Brill.

———. 1977. *Bantu Myths and Other Tales.* Leiden: Brill.

———. 1979. *Four Centuries of Swahili Verse: A Literary History and Anthology.* London: Heinemann Educational.

———. 1983. *Epic Poetry in Swahili and Other African Languages.* Leiden: Brill.

———. 1999. *A Survey of Swahili Islamic Epic Sagas.* Lewiston, NY: Edwin Mellen Press.

———. 2003. *The A–Z of African Love Songs.* London: Karnak House.

———. 2004. *A Survey of Swahili Songs with English Translations.* Lewiston, NY: E. Mellen Press.

Krapf, Johann L. 1882. *A Dictionary of the Suahili Language . . . with Introduction Containing an Outline of a Suahili Grammar.* London: Trubner.

———. 1969. *A Dictionary of the Suahili Language.* New York: Negro Universities Press.

Kusimba, Chapurukha M. 1999. *The Rise and Fall of Swahili States.* Walnut Creek, CA: AltaMira Press.

Kusimba, Chapuruka, and Sibel B. Kusimba. 2003. *East African Archeology: Foragers, Potters, Smiths, and Traders.* Philadelphia: University of Pennsylvania Museum of Archeology and Anthropology.

Laitin, D., and S. Samatar. 1987. *Somalia: Nation in Search of a State.* Boulder, CO: Westview Press.

Lagneau-Kesteloot, Lilyan. 1972. *Intellectual Origins of the African Revolution.* Washington, DC: Black Orpheus Press.

Langworthy, Harry W. 1971. "Swahili Influence in the Area between Lake Malawi and Luangwa River." *African Historical Studies* 4 (3): 575–602.

LaViolette, Adria. 2008. "Swahili Cosmopolitanism in Africa and the Indian Ocean World, A.D. 600–1500." *Archaeologies: Journal of the World Archaeological Congress* 4 (1): 24–49.

Lewis, Geoffrey L. 1999. *The Turkish Language Reform: A Catastrophic Success.* Oxford: Oxford University Press.

Lewis, Myrddin Ioan. 1971. *Ecstatic Religion: An Anthropological Study of Spirit Possession and Shamanism.* Hammondsworth, UK: Penguin Books.

Lewis, M. Paul, Gary F. Simons, and Charles D. Fennig, eds. 2014. *Ethnologue: Languages of the World, Seventeenth edition.* Dallas, Texas: SIL International.

Livingstone, David, and Horace Waller. 1875. *The Last Journals of David Livingstone, in Central Africa from Eighteen Hundred and Sixty-Five to His Death. Continued by a Narrative of His Last Moments and Sufferings, Obtained by His Faithful Servants, Chuma and Susi.* New York: Harper and Bros.

Lodhi, Abdulaziz. 2000. *Oriental Influences in Swahili: A Study in Language and Culture Contacts.* Göteborg, Sweden: Acta Universitatis Gothoburgensis.

Luffin, Xavier. 2007. "On the Swahili Documents in Arabic Script from the Congo (19th Century)." *Swahili Forum* 14:17–26. http://www.qucosa.de/fileadmin/data/qucosa/documents/9108/14_03_Luffin.pdf.

Madan, Arthur C. 1887. *Kiungani; or, Story and History from Central Africa.* London: G. Bell and Sons.

———, ed. 1905. *An Outline Dictionary Intended as an Aid in the Study of the Language of Bantu and Other Uncivilized Races.* London: Henry Frowde.

———. 1911. *English-Swahili Vocabulary.* London: Society for Promoting Christian Knowledge.

———. 1930. *English-Swahili Dictionary.* London: Oxford University Press.

Madan, Arthur C., and Edward Steere. 1941. *English-Swahili Vocabulary.* London: Sheldon Press.

Maimu, Musa. 1982. *Kamusi ya ndege wa Tanzania* [A glossary of birds of Tanzania]. Dar es Salaam: Tanzania Publishing House.

Makoni, Sinfree, and Alastair Pennycook. 2007. *Disinventing and Reconstructing Languages.* Buffalo, NY: Multilingual Matters.

Masabo, Zubeida Zuberi, and A. R. Chuwa. 1999. *Kamusi ya biashara na uchumi: Kiingereza-Kiswahili.* Dar es Salaam: Taasisi ya Uchunguzi wa Kiswahili, Chuo Kikuu cha Dar es Salaam.

Massamba, David Phineas Bhukanda. 2002. *Historia ya Kiswahili: 50 BK hadi 1500 BK.* Nairobi: Jomo Kenyatta Foundation.

———. 2004. *Kamusi ya isimu na falsafa ya lugha.* Dar es Salaam: Taasisi ya Uchunguzi wa Kiswahili, Chuo Kikuu cha Dar es Salaam.

Masolo, Dismas A. 2010. *Self and Community in a Changing World.* Bloomington: Indiana University Press.

Matlin, D. 2006. "'Lift Up Yr Self!' Reinterpreting Amiri Baraka (LeRoi Jones), Black Power, and the Uplift Tradition." *Journal of American History* 93 (1): 91–116.

Mattar, Philip. 2004. *Encyclopedia of the Modern Middle East & North Africa.* 2nd ed. Detroit: Macmillan Reference USA.

Maw, Joan, and David J. Parkin. 1984–85. *Swahili Language and Society: Papers from the Workshop Held at the School of Oriental and African Studies in April 1982.* Vienna: Institut für Afrikanistik.

Maxwell, William E., ed. 1885. *Note and Queries by Royal Asiatic Society of Great Britain and Ireland. Malayan Branch* 99. Singapore: Government Printing Office.

Mazrui, Alamin M. 2004. *English in Africa after the Cold War.* Clevedon, UK: Multilingual Matters.

———. 2007. *Swahili beyond the Boundaries: Literature, Language, and Identity.* Athens: Ohio University Press.

Mazrui, Alamin M., and Ibrahim Noor Shariff. 1994. *The Swahili: Idiom and Identity of an African People.* Trenton, NJ: Africa World Press.

Mazrui, Ali Al. 1986. *The Africans: A Triple Heritage.* Boston: Little, Brown.

Mazrui, Ali Al, and Alamin M. Mazrui. 1995. *Swahili State and Society: The Political Economy of an African Language.* Nairobi: East African Educational Publishers.

———. 1998. *The Power of Babel: Language and Governance in the African Experience.* Oxford: James Currey.

Mbaabu, Ireri. 1985. *New Horizons in Kishwahili: A Synthesis in Developments, Research, and Literature.* Nairobi: Kenya Literature Bureau.

———. 2007. *Historia ya usanifishaji wa Kiswahili.* Dar es Salaam: Taasisi ya Uchunguzi wa Kiswahili, Chuo Kikuu cha Dar es Salaam.

Mbaabu, Ireri, and Kipande Nzunga. 2003. *Sheng-English Dictionary: Deciphering East Africa's Underworld Language.* Dar es Salaam: Chuo Kikuu.

Mbele, Joseph L. 1996. "Wimbo wa Miti: An Example of Swahili Women's Poetry." *African Languages and Cultures* 9 (1): 71–82.

Mbembe, Achille. 2011. "Provincializing France?" *Public Culture* 23 (1): 85–119.

McCrae, Alan. 1994. "A Famous Trade Coin." *Australian Coin Review* 356 (February).

McCrum, Robert, Robert MacNeil, and William Cran. 1986. *The Story of English.* New York: Viking.

McIntyre, Chris, and Susan McIntyre. 2013. *Zanzibar, Pemba, Mafia* 10. Guilford, CT: Globe Pequot Press.

McLaughlin, Fiona. 1995. "Haalpulaar Identity as a Response to Wolofization." *African Languages and Cultures* 8 (2): 153–68.

———. 2001. "Dakar, Wolof and the Configuration of an Urban Identity." *Journal of African Cultural Studies* 14:153–68.

Middleton, John. 1992. *The World of the Swahili: An African Mercantile Civilization.* New Haven, CT: Yale University Press.

Miehe, G., A. Abdalla, Z. M. F. Al-Bakary, A. N. J. Bhalo, A. Nabhany, A. Baschiera, C. Dittemer, F. Topan, M. H. Abdulaziz, S. A. M. Khamis, and Y. A. Omar, eds. 2006. *"Nyimbo za Liyongo"—Liyongo Songs: Poems Attributed to Fumo Liyongo Collected and Edited by the Liyongo Working Group.* Dar es Salaam: Taasisi ya Uchunguzi wa Kiswahili.

Mirza, Sarah M., and Margaret Strobel. 1989. *Wanawake watatu wa kiswahili: Hadithi za maisha kutoka Mombasa, Kenya—Kaje wa Mwenye Matano, Mishi wa Abdala, na shamsa Muhamad Muhashamy.* Bloomington: Indiana University Press.

Mkude, Dan. 1985. "The Fate of Standard Swahili." In *Swahili Language and Society,* edited by Joan Maw and David Parkin. Beiträge zur Afrikanistik 23 (33): 25–34. Vienna: Afro-Pub.

Mmari, Judith. 2011. "Circumstances, Challenges and Responses: The Lives of Mombasa Women 1840–1950." Boston University: Center for African Studies unpublished manuscript.

Momanyi, C. 2001. "Matumizi ya Kiswahili katika Njia Panda: Mtazamo wa Kiisimu-Jamii." In *Kiswahili: A Tool for Development—The Multidisciplinary Approach*, edited by Naomi L. Shitemi and Mwanakombo M. Noordin; associate editors Allan I. Opijah and Davies M. Mukuria. Eldoret, Kenya: Moi University Press.

Morris, H. S. 1956. "Indians in East Africa." *British Journal of Sociology* 7 (3): 194–211.

Morton, Julia Frances. 1987. "Jambolan." In *Fruits of Warm Climates*, edited by Curtis F. Dowling, 375–78. Miami, FL: J. F. Morton.

Mugane, John M. 2010. "Learning How to Learn Languages: The Teaching and Learning of African Languages." *Language and Linguistic Compass* 4 (2): 64–79.

———. 2005. "Necrolinguistics: Linguistic Death-in-Life." *Du Bois Review* 2 (2): 159–86.

———. "Africa's Sources of Knowledge—Digital Library | Project ASK-DL," http://ask-dl.fas.harvard.edu/ (accessed January 15, 2014).

Mukuria, Davies. M. "Making Kiswahili a True National Language of Kenya." In *Kiswahili: A Tool for Development—The Multidisciplinary Approach*, edited by Naomi L. Shitemi and Mwanakombo M. Noordin; associate editors Allan I. Opijah and Davies M. Mukuria. Eldoret, Kenya: Moi University Press, 2001.

Mulokozi, M. M. 2005. "Miaka 75 ya Taasisi ya Uchunguzi wa Kiswahili (1930–2005)." *Kiswahili, Jarida la Taasisi ya Uchunguzi wa Kiswahili (Journal of the Institute of Kiswahili Research)* 68, edited by J. S. Madamulla and Y. M. Kihore. Dar es Salaam: University of Dar es Salaam.

Mulokozi, M. M., and Tigiti S. Y Sengo. 1995. *History of Kiswahili Poetry, A.D. 1000–2000: A Report*. Dar es Salaam: Institute of Kiswahili Research, University of Dar es Salaam.

Mutonya, Mungai, and Timothy Parsons. 2004. "KiKAR: A Swahili Variety in Kenya's Colonial Army." *Journal of African Languages and Linguistics* 25:111–25.

Myers-Scotton, Carol. 1993. *Social Motivations for Codeswitching: Evidence from Africa*. Oxford: Clarendon Press.

———. 1979. "The Context Is the Message: Morphological, Syntactic and Semantic Reduction and Deletion in Nairobi and Kampala Varieties of Swahili." In *Readings in Creole Studies*, edited by I. F. Hancock, 111–28. Ghent, Belgium: E. Story-Scientia.

Nabhany, Ahmed Sheikh. 1979. *Sambo Ya Kiwandeo: The Ship of Lamu-Island*. Edited by Gudrun Miehe and Thilo N. Schadenberg. Leiden: Afrika-Studiecentrum.

Nadeau, Jean-Benoît, and Julie Barlow. 2006. *The Story of French*. New York: St. Martin's Press.

Nasir, Abdallah bin Ali. 1977. *Al-Inkishafi*. [Catechism of a soul]. Nairobi: East African Literature Bureau.

Ndembwike, John. 2006. *Tanzania: The Land and Its People*. 2nd ed. Dar es Salaam: New Africa Press.

Ndembwike, John. 2009. *Tanzania: Profile of a Nation*. Dar es Salaam: New Africa Press.

Newitt, Malyn. 2002. *Portuguese Encounters with the World in the Age of the Discoveries*. Aldershot, UK: Ashgate.

Ngom, Fallou. 2003. *Wolof*. Munich: Lincom Europa.

———. 2004. "Ethnic Identity and Linguistic Hybridization in Senegal." *International Journal of the Sociology of Language* 170:95–111.

———. 2009. "Aḥmadu Bamba's Pedagogy and the Development of Ajamī Literature." *African Studies Review* 52 (1): 99–123.

———. 2010. "Ajami Scripts in the Senegalese Speech Community." *Journal of Arabic and Islamic Studies* 10:1–23.

Nurse, Derek, and Thomas J. Hinnebusch. 1993. *Swahili and Sabaki: A Linguistic History*. Berkeley: University of California Press.

Nurse, Derek, and Thomas Spear. 1985. *The Swahili: Reconstructing the History and Language of an African Society, 800–1500*. Philadelphia: University of Pennsylvania Press.

Odhiambo Atieno, E. S., T. I. Ouso, and Williams Ouso. 1977. *A History of East Africa*. London: Longman Group.

Ogot, Bethwell A., and J. A. Kieran, eds. 1968. *Zamani: A Survey of East African History*. Nairobi: East African Publishing House.

Okihiro, Gary Y. 2009. *Pineapple Culture: A History of the Tropical and Temperate Zones*. Berkeley: University of California Press.

Oliver, Roland, and J. D. Fage. 1966. *Short History of Africa*. Oxford: Clarenden Press.

Oliver, Roland, and Gervaise Mathew, eds. 1963. *The History of East Africa*. Oxford: Clarendon Press.

Omar, Yahya Ali, and AnnMarie Drury. 2002. "The Swahili Manuscript Project at SOAS." *Swahili Forum* 9, AAP (Afrikanistische Arbeitspapiere) 72, 9–17.

Omar, Y. A., and P. J. L. Frankl. 1994. "A 12/18th Century Swahili Letter from Kilwa Kisiwani (Being a study of one folio from the Goa Archives)." *Afrika und Ubersee* 77:263–72.

Ostler, Nicholas. 2005. *Empires of the Word: A Language History of the World*. New York: HarperCollins.

Peek, Philip M., and Kwesi Yankah, eds. 2003. *African Folklore: An Encyclopedia*. New York: Routledge.

Pigafetta, Antonio, and R. A. Skelton. 1969. *Magellan's Voyage: A Narrative Account of the First Circumnavigation*. New Haven, CT: Yale University Press.

Polome, Edgar C. 1967. *Swahili Language Handbook*. Washington, DC: Center for Applied Linguistics.

Pouwels, Randall Lee. 1987. *Horn and Crescent: Cultural Change and Traditional Islam on the East African Coast, 800–1900*. Cambridge: Cambridge University Press.

Prestholdt, Jeremy. 2008. *Domesticating the World: African Consumerism and the Genealogies of Globalization*. Berkeley: University of California Press.

Prins, A. H. J. 1958. "On Swahili Historiography." *Swahili, Journal of the East African Swahili Committee* 28 (2): 26–40.

———. 1961. *The Swahili-Speaking Peoples of Zanzibar and the East African Coast (Arabs, Shirazi and Swahili)*. London: International African Institute.

———. 1965. *Sailing from Lamu: A Study of Maritime Culture in Islamic East Africa.* Assen, the Netherlands: Van Gorcum.

Ratcliffe, B. J., and Howard Elphinstone. 1932. *Modern Swahili.* London: Sheldon Press.

Reefe, Thomas Q. 1981. *The Rainbow and the Kings: A History of the Luba Empire to 1891.* Berkeley: University of California Press.

Rizk, Mohamed El. 2007. *Women in Taarab: The Performing Art in East Africa.* Frankfurt am Main: Lang.

Robert, Shaaban. 1952. *Adili na nduguze.* London: Macmillan Education.

———. 1960. *Pambo la lugha.* Johannesburg: Witwatersrand University Press.

———. 1966. *Kielezo cha insha.* Nairobi: Oxford University Press.

———. 1967. *Masomo yenye adili.* London: Nelson.

———. 1967. *Wasifu wa Siti binti Saad.* 1st ed. Dar es Salaam: Evans Brothers.

———. 1968. *Kielezo cha fasili.* London: Nelson.

———. 1968. *Siku ya watenzi wote.* London: Nelson.

———. 1968. *Utubora mkulima.* Dar es Salaam: Nelson.

———. 1969. *Mwafrika aimba.* Nairobi: Nelson.

———. 1973. *Kusadikika: A Country in the Sky.* Nairobi: East African Literature Bureau.

———. 1983. *Kufikirika.* Repr. ed. with questions added. Nairobi: Oxford University Press.

———. 1991. *Maisha yangu: na Baada ya miaka hamsini.* New ed. Dar es Salaam: Mkuki na Nyota.

———. 1991. *Mapenzi bora.* Dar es Salaam: Mkuki na Nyota.

Rogers, Susan Carol. 1975. "Female Forms of Power and the Myth of Male Dominance." *American Ethnologist* 2 (4): 727–56.

Rollins, Jack D. 1983. *A History of Swahili Prose.* Leiden: Brill.

Ruhlen, Merritt. 1994. *The Origin of Language: Tracing the Evolution of the Mother Tongue.* New York: Wiley.

Sacleux, Charles. 1939. *Dictionnaire swahili-français.* Paris: Institut d'ethnologie.

Said, Edward W. 2003. *Orientalism.* New York: Vintage Books.

Samper, David A. 2001. "Talking Sheng: The Role of a Hybrid Language in the Construction of Identity and Youth Culture in Nairobi, Kenya." PhD dissertation, University of Pennsylvania.

Schicho, Walter, and Mbayabo Ndala. 1980. *Kiswahili von Lumumbashi: Sprachverwendung U. Sprachwertung am Beispiel E. Afrikan. Grossstadt.* Vienna: Afro-Pub C/o Inst. für Afrikanistik.

Scott, James C. 1985. *Weapons of the Weak: Everyday Forms of Peasant Resistance.* New Haven, CT: Yale University Press.

Sertima, Ivan. 1970. *Swahili Dictionary of Legal Terms.* S.l.: S.n.

Sharawi, Helmi. 2005. *Heritage of the African Languages Manuscripts: Ajami.* Bamako, Mali: Afro Arab Cultural Institute.

Shariff, Ibrahim. 1991. "Islam and Secularity in Swahili Literature." In *Faces of Islam in African Literature,* edited by Kenneth W. Harrow, 37–57. Portsmouth, NH: Heinemann.

Sheriff, Abdul. 2010. *Dhow Cultures of the Indian Ocean: Cosmopolitanism, Commerce and Islam.* New York: Columbia University Press.

Sheriff, Abdul, and Ed Ferguson. 1991. *Zanzibar under Colonial Rule.* London: James Currey.

Shitemi, Naomi L., and Mwanakombo M. Noordin, eds. 2001. *Kiswahili: A Tool for Development—The Multidisciplinary Approach.* Allan I. Opijah and Davies M. Mukuria, associate editors. Eldoret, Kenya: Moi University Press.

Shorter, A. 1968. "Nyungu ya Mawe and the Empire of the Ruga-Rugas." *Journal of African History* 9 (2): 240–41.

Shullenberger, Bonnie, and William Shullenberger. 1998. *Africa Time: Two Scholars' Seasons in Uganda.* Lanham, MD: University Press of America.

Spear, Thomas. 2000. "Early Swahili History Reconsidered." *International Journal of African Historical Studies* 33 (2): 257–90.

Steere, Edward. 1870. *Swahili Tales, as Told by Natives of Zanzibar.* London: Bell & Daldy.

Steere, Edward, and A. C. Madan. 1884. *A Handbook of the Swahili Language, as Spoken at Zanzibar.* London: Society for Promoting Christian Knowledge.

Stigand, C. H. 1913. *The Land of Zinj: Being an Account of British East Africa, Its Ancient History and Present Inhabitants [with illustrations].* London: Constable.

———. 1915. *A Grammar of Dialectic Changes in the Kiswahili Language.* Cambridge: Nobel Press.

Strandes, Justus. 1968. *The Portuguese Period in East Africa.* Nairobi: East African Literature Bureau.

Strobel, Margaret. 1979. *Muslim Women in Mombasa, 1890–1975.* New Haven, CT: Yale University Press.

Sutton, John Edward Giles. "The Settlement of East Africa." In *Zamani: A Survey of East African History,* edited by Bethwell A. Ogot and J. A. Kieran, 86–88. Nairobi: East African Publishing House.

———. 1990. *A Thousand Years of East Africa.* Nairobi: British Institute in Eastern Africa.

Taasisi ya Uchunguzi wa Kiswahili (TUKI). 1990. *Kamusi sanifu ya biolojia, fizika na kemia.* Dar es Salaam: UNESCO: SIDA.

———. 1990. *Kamusi sanifu ya isimu na lugha.* Dar es Salaam: TUKI.

———. 1995. *Kamusi awali ya sayansi na tekinolojia.* Dar es Salaam: Ben & Co.

———. 2001. *Kamusi ya Kiswahili-Kiingereza.* Dar es Salaam: TUKI.

———. 2006. *Nyimbo za Liyongo, Liyongo Songs: Poems attributed to Fumo Liyongo Collected and edited by The Liyongo Working Group.* Edited by G. Miehe, A. Abdalla, A. N. J. Bhalo, A. Nabahany, A. Baschiera. C. Dittemer, F. Topan, M. H. Abdulaziz, S. A. M. Khamis, Y. A. Omar,and Z. M. F. Al-Bakary. Dar es Salaam: TUKI.

Taylor, William Ernest. 1891. *African Aphorisms; or, Saws from Swahili-Land.* London: Society for Promoting Christian Knowledge.

———. 1894. *Injili ya Luka.* London: [British and Foreign Bible Society].

Thurlow, Crispin. 2003. "Generation Txt? The Sociolinguistics of Young People's Text-Messaging." *Discourse Analysis Online* 1(1). Retrieved April 25, 2011, from http://extra.shu.ac.uk/daol/articles/v1/n1/a3/thurlow2002003-paper.html.

Tolmacheva, Marina. 1993. *The Pate Chronicle Edited and Translated from MSS 177, 321, 344, and 358 of the Library of the University of Dar Es Salaam.* East Lansing: Michigan State University Press.

Trimingham, J. Spencer. 1964. *Islam in East Africa*. Oxford: Clarendon Press.

Vincent, William. 1800. *The Periplus of the Erythrean Sea . . . Containing, an Account of the Navigation of the Ancients . . . With Dissertations*. London: Printed by A. Strahan.

Vitale, Anthony J. 1980. "Kisetla: Linguistic and Sociolinguistic Aspects of a Pidgin Swahili of Kenya." *Anthropological Linguistics* 22 (2): 47–65.

Washington University in St. Louis. "Deep History of Coconuts Decoded: Origins of Cultivation, Ancient Trade Routes, and Colonization of the Americas." *ScienceDaily*, www.sciencedaily.com/releases/2011/06/110624142037.htm (accessed January 5, 2015).

Welmers, William Everett. 1973. *African Language Structures*. Berkeley: University of California Press.

Welsh-Asante, Kariamu, ed. 1993. *The African Aesthetic: Keeper of the Traditions*. Westport, CT: Greenwood.

Were, Gideon S., and Derek A. Wilson. 1968. *East Africa through a Thousand Years: A History of the Years A.D. 1000 to the Present Day*. New York: Africana.

Werner, Alice. 1916. "The Wahadimu of Zanzibar." *Journal of the African Society* 15:356–60.

Weston, A. B., and Dar es Salaam College. 1968. *Swahili Legal Terms*. Dar es Salaam: Legal Research Centre and Faculty of Law, University College.

White, Luise, Stephan Miescher, and David William Cohen, eds. 2001. *African Words, African Voices: Critical Practices in Oral History*. Bloomington: Indiana University Press.

Whiteley, Wilfred Howell. 1969. *Swahili, the Rise of a National Language*. London: Methuen.

Williams, Stanley Tookie. 2004. *Blue Rage, Black Redemption: A Memoir*. New York: Simon and Schuster.

Willis, Justin. 1993. *Mombasa, the Swahili, and the Making of the Mijikenda*. Oxford: Clarendon Press.

Worger, William H., Nancy L. Clark, and Edward A. Alpers, comps. 2001. "The Impact of Abolition, 1807–99." Chapter 4 in *Africa and the West: A Documentary History*, vol. 1: *From the Slave Trade to Conquest, 1441–1905*, 117–23. Oxford: Oxford University Press.

Wright, M., and P. Lary. 1971. "Swahili Settlements in Northern Zambia and Malawi." *African Historical Studies* 4 (3): 547–73.

Ylvisaker, Marguerite. 1979. *Lamu in the Nineteenth Century: Land, Trade, and Politics*. Boston: African Studies Center, Boston University.

Zawawi, Sharifa. 1993. *What's in a Name? Unaitwaje: A Swahili Book of Names*. Trenton, NJ: Africa World Press.

———. 2005. *Kanga: The Cloth That Speaks*. New York: Azaniya Hills Press.

Zawawi, Sharifa M. 1979. *Loanwords and Their Effect on the Classification of Swahili Nominals*. Leiden: E. J. Brill.

Zhukov, Andrey. 1992. "The Dating of Old Swahili Manuscripts: Towards Swahili Paleography." *Swahili Language and Society*, no. 9.

———. 2004. "Old Swahili-Arabic Script and the Development of Swahili Literary Language." *Sudanic Africa* 15:1–15.

Index